Companion to Property Law and Practice

A Guide to Assessment

Companion to Property Law and Practice

A Guide to Assessment

Robert Abbey

Solicitor, Legal Practice Course Director, University of Westminster, Consultant with Russell Jones and Walker Solicitors, The Law Society's Chief External Examiner in Property Law and Practice

Mark Richards

Solicitor, Senior Lecturer in Law, University of Westminster

OXFORD
UNIVERSITY PRESS

OXFORD

UNIVERSITY PRESS

Great Clarendon Street, Oxford OX2 6DP

Oxford University Press is a department of the University of Oxford.
It furthers the University's objective of excellence in research, scholarship,
and education by publishing worldwide in

Oxford New York

Auckland Bangkok Buenos Aires Cape Town Chennai
Dar es Salaam Delhi Hong Kong Istanbul Karachi Kolkata
Kuala Lumpur Madrid Melbourne Mexico City Mumbai Nairobi
São Paulo Shanghai Taipei Tokyo Toronto

Oxford is a registered trade mark of Oxford University Press
in the UK and in certain other countries

Published in the United States
by Oxford University Press Inc., New York

British Library Cataloguing in Publication Data
Data available

Library of Congress Cataloging in Publication Data
Data available

ISBN 0-19-9270317

Typeset by Newgen Imaging Systems (P) Ltd, Chennai, India
Printed in Great Britain
on acid-free paper by
Ashford Colour Press Ltd, Gosport, Hampshire

For Alison and Lesley

PREFACE

'Very few laws remain the same. Once enacted, they are likely to be studied, modified, amended, then often repealed altogether. This constant tinkering by judges and lawmakers is usually a good thing. Bad laws are weeded out. Weak laws are improved. Good laws are fined tuned.'

The Last Juror
John Grisham

In our experience, students on the Legal Practice Course often have difficulty in translating their knowledge into very good or excellent examination answers. All too often after a subject assessment, we hear a student say, 'I worked hard, I thought I knew my subject but I under-performed in the exam.' This book seeks to address this common problem by identifying, and offering guidance on, ways of transferring the knowledge acquired during the course into commendation or distinction level answers to subject assessments.

We think that part of the problem lies in the fact that Property Law and Practice is an inherently practical subject. As such, a study of it differs in approach to other areas of previously studied substantive law. The technical rules of conveyancing are often complex and intimidating and of course have to be mastered—but that is not enough to succeed. The key to excellence is the ability to apply those rules in a practical and often commercial context. We hope this book will go some way towards achieving this aim.

Mark Richards
Robert Abbey
London
May 2004

ACKNOWLEDGEMENTS

We acknowledge permission to reproduce the following copyright material.

Crown copyright is reproduced with the permission of the Controller of HMSO and HM Land Registry.

The Standard Conditions of Sale (4th Edition) and the Law Society's standard form of contract are reproduced for educational purposes only by kind permission of the Law Society and the Solicitors' Law Stationery Society Limited.

Stat Plus Group plc for permission to reproduce the Epitome of Title form.

Land Registry forms are reproduced with the permission of Laserforms.

OUTLINE CONTENTS

DETAILED CONTENTS

TABLE OF CASES

TABLE OF LEGISLATION AND RULES

STATUTORY INSTRUMENTS

SOLICITORS' PRACTICE RULES 1990

1 INTRODUCTION TO THE BOOK AND ITS FORMAT

1.1 PROPERTY LAW AND PRACTICE, THE SUBJECT, AN OVERVIEW IN THE CONTEXT OF ASSESSMENT

Property Law and Practice covers all aspects of the major subject matter of Conveyancing. It is the transfer of legal title to property but of course by now this will be well known to you. You now need to apply your Property Law and Practice knowledge to questions that you may encounter in your examinations that on the Legal Practice Course (LPC) are usually called subject assessments. This book is here to help you in this endeavour.

1.1.1 THE SOURCES OF PROPERTY LAW AND PRACTICE

It is likely that you will benefit from a reminder of the foundations upon which Property Law and Practice has been built. You should therefore reflect upon how Property Law and Practice rests upon the three stanchions of land law, contract law and equity and trusts. When you are faced with examinations you will have gone through your course and will perhaps be over concerned with detail. It is therefore of benefit to just stand back a moment and consider the broader view, to give you the kind of holistic understanding of the subject that will help with your examination answers. Remember also that Property Law and Practice concerns itself with several other areas of the law such as company and partnership law, succession, planning law and especially several parts of revenue law. It is this diversity that makes Property Law and Practice a difficult subject to grasp. However, a brief look at the three main supports will help you get to grips with the full perspective of this broad subject.

As you might expect a strong understanding of land law is critical for success in Property Law and Practice. If you are still unsure of some fundamentals of land law you will surely have trouble with Property Law and Practice. If you are still in doubt about such matters as easements or restrictive covenants then we firmly suggest that you go back to your land law notes and refresh your memory of the salient points. We also suggest you look again at a suitable textbook and recommend 'A Textbook on Land Law' by Mackenzie and Phillips (Oxford University Press) as a clear and direct guide to the fundamentals of this important buttress to Property Law and Practice.

In the context of assessment a clear understanding of land law is a fundamental prerequisite of Property Law and Practice. Indeed, The Law Society in their written standards specifically state that this is the case for the Legal Practice Course. The precise guidance is that the course is based on the assumption that students will have prior knowledge and understanding of the nature of legal estates and interests, equitable interests, easements, covenants and mortgages, joint ownership and unregistered and registered title (including the registration of charges). It is assumed further that students will have prior knowledge and understanding of formation of contract, formalities of written contracts, misrepresentation and remedies for breach of contract. Accordingly you will appreciate that there will inevitably be questions in examinations that will test not just your knowledge of the conveyancing process but also these foundations of land law on which Property Law and Practice is built.

You will have seen from the Law Society's guidance notes about the LPC written standards that contract law is considered to be just as important for students of Property Law and Practice as land law. When you consider that conveyancing is about the transfer of title and these transfers are in the main made by contract then you will readily appreciate why contract law plays such an important part. Should you end up being a property practitioner you will do well to actively maintain your knowledge of the fundamentals of contract law as you will regularly encounter transactions concerned with it. As you now know each conveyance on sale will involve the actual preparation of a written contract. Indeed your land law will tell you that without a written contract containing all the terms of the agreement there is no deal! (If this information comes as a surprise to you then please look again at the Law of Property (Miscellaneous Provisions) Act 1989 for clarification.)

So, in these circumstances it is not difficult to anticipate questions in Property Law and Practice that will examine your understanding of contract law as well as its application in conveyancing. However, it goes further than just the formation of valid contracts. You will also need to know about misrepresentation and in particular remedies for breach of contract. It is clear that these areas are of particular interest to examiners and a thorough grounding in both topics is advisable if you wish to do well in your subject assessment.

Then there is the potentially opaque support subject of equity and trusts. This important stanchion to Property Law and Practice is not so obviously relevant as land law and contract law, but it is nevertheless a pervasive element in Property Law and Practice and certainly as far as assessment is concerned. Why is this? Frankly, it is because this complex area provides challenging questions that are just ripe for a subject assessment/ examination. For example, the whole topic of third party rights is a fertile and attractive location for your examiner to find questions that will concern equity and trusts in the context of the conveyancing process. Co-ownership however, is the topic for the kind of challenging question beloved of examiners. You will therefore need to be absolutely clear on the law relating to trusts and in particular trusts of land. You will need to understand the differences between tenants in common and joint tenants and their relevance to joint ownership in Property Law and Practice. Finally, you will need to remind yourself about the equitable remedies that are available. It is one thing to understand their availability in theory but it is another to actually apply them to a practical situation. Property Law will in practice be an area that will give rise to the application of those equitable remedies. This being the case they will inevitably end up in subject assessment questions. You have been warned!

So, the key to understanding the nature of Property Law and Practice in the context of assessment is to appreciate how it calls upon these various strands of the law. In doing so it brings together other parts of the law that you should have encountered and which you will now need to apply on a practical basis. You will need to be able to integrate these other areas into your knowledge and understanding of the conveyancing process. It means that you must abandon a discrete approach to learning and applying the law. Property Law and Practice requires you to blend your knowledge and this will need to be displayed in your answers. Moreover, many elements apply to both domestic and commercial properties. As such you need to understand the fundamentals of both items to enable you to be prepared for exams and practice.

1.1.2 THE FORMAT OF THIS BOOK

In this book we adopt the signpost format at the start of each chapter. We list for you the contents so that you can be aware of what you are about to encounter in your reading. Something you could adopt in some of your examination answers! So, at the start of each chapter there will be an introduction followed by an overview of the subject and a look at some problem areas. We will then move on to examine in depth Subject Assessments that relate to the topic covered by the chapter. (The last chapter brings together many of the chapter topics in an examination of subject assessments that cover several concerns in one question.) In each case we look at Subject Assessment Questions, provide a commentary upon the type and content of each subject assessment question and give suggested answers. This is followed by a selection of subject specific Multiple Choice Questions followed by Answers to the Multiple Choice Questions. We then move onto a section of Short Answer Questions with Suggested Answers. We believe that by doing so we will have covered virtually all the forms of assessment you may encounter in your Property Law and Practice subject assessment. Finally, each chapter concludes with a list of references to wider reading including from practitioner texts and by a list of relevant websites for more information.

1.2 SUBJECT ASSESSMENT/EXAMINATION TECHNIQUE GENERALLY

Now that you will have understood what will be expected of you in a Property Law and Practice subject assessment or examination it is appropriate to consider how you should approach the method. We will now consider the method by which you are required to show your abilities in the subject assessment or examination. Therefore, to help we set out below some hints and tips to enhance and improve your examination technique:

1.2.1 FIRST OF ALL REMEMBER THE MNEMONIC P.A.T., PAUSE AND THINK

It is our experience that too often students see a question that triggers off a line of thought and immediately they are away and writing! Always give yourself time to think about the answer required. This is why exams often have dedicated reading time at the beginning, to allow you time to read, inwardly digest and then think through your proposed answer before putting pen to paper. Sometimes examiners will make questions look deceptively simple when in fact they are really quite demanding. Another examiner's trick is to set a question that is apparently about a particular topic when really a good answer requires you to consider more than one area. Therefore, never rush ahead without careful reflection. If it means writing less, then so be it. Students are sometimes misled into thinking that the length of their answer will earn them more marks. This is simply not so and could militate against you when an examiner has to hunt through a lot of superfluous information to find what is actually relevant.

1.2.2 KNOW YOUR TUTOR

Wherever possible, it is always a good move to try to detect the areas of interest shown by the Tutors who will be responsible for your examination paper. Clearly for some of you this will be almost impossible as some professional examinations are of course prepared by other examiners who have not taught you. This predicament will be considered subsequently. For those that can identify their Tutor's areas of interest they would be well advised to reflect upon the likelihood of just those areas appearing as a topic for the exam. If there is an external examiner setting the questions then really all you can do in those circumstances is to try to see the frequency of the appearance of certain topics in your strategic approach to the examination.

1.2.3 WHAT IS TOPICAL?

By this we mean has there been a change in the law during the time of your Property Law and Practice course? If so, this could very well end up as a topic for a question in your subject assessment. Think for a moment that you are your Tutor who is about to write your examination paper. You have had this responsibility for the last six years and have in that time had to write at least twelve such papers, when resits are taken into account. Each time your Tutor must produce something different and yet sufficiently demanding so as to be a satisfactory test of your knowledge and ability to apply it to the question. Accordingly it is hoped that you will appreciate that if the law has changed it is one way your Tutor can come up with a novel question arising from a virgin topic that is going to really test your knowledge. It will also show whether or not you were paying attention in class as of course the change in the law will be declared by your teachers and will be so new as to be missing from all your textbooks. A couple of important recent examples were the changes caused by the Land Registration Act 2002 and the changes brought about by the introduction of Stamp Duty Land Tax in the Finance Act 2003. Questions after the introduction of these reforms looked as if they were asking about the old law whereas of course the examiner wanted to see if students were aware of the conspicuous changes caused by these two statutes.

1.2.4 **MATTERS FOR YOU TO CONSIDER BEFORE THE ACTUAL SUBJECT ASSESSMENT/EXAM**

Be sure you know when and where the subject assessment/examination is to be held. It is awful to see candidates arriving late, all flustered and confused simply because they did not check on the time and place for the examination. Go to revision classes. It is not unknown for 'hints' to be given as to examination or revision topics. Do not miss the opportunity of asking your Tutor to explain again any area that you are really not quite sure about. Remember to claim your entitlements. Many institutions will give extra time to students with special needs. If you are so entitled please note this extra time will only be granted on request, so do ask. Seek help when necessary. Many students experience pre-exam nerves. This is an expected response to the stress of the impending examination but if it becomes so strong that it interferes with your revision seek help. Many institutions have support services that can help and that will get you back to the task in hand. Ignore others! Your other student colleagues will not as a matter of student honour ever admit to actually doing any revision or indeed any work at all! Of course it is all bravado and bluster. Do not be fazed by it as bragging is all that it is. You will have a revision plan and you must stick with it right up to your examination. Finally bear in mind what was last taught on the course. It is the case that the topic that was last taught can often form the basis for a question in the examination. The preparation of the examination paper could coincide with the preparation of the materials for the topic and as a result it could subsequently appear in a question.

1.2.5 **KNOW YOUR SUBJECT ASSESSMENT/EXAMINATION TYPE**

Not all examinations are the same. The current vogue is for open book exams, but what exactly do your Tutors mean by 'open'? Before getting anywhere near the time for the exam make sure that you know exactly what you can and what you cannot take in with you. Also, exercise some discretion about what you choose to accompany you in the examination room. You only have a finite amount of time to write the exam so you do not want to be shuffling through too many textbooks for your own good. A core text plus your own notes should in most circumstances be sufficient; a wheelbarrow full of practitioner texts will only delay and confuse you. If you can take in books please be aware that this does not mean you can give up on acquiring your own memory store of knowledge. You will not have the time to continually look up the answer to the question. Examiners will be aware that the books are available and will adjust the style of the question to take this fact into account. Use your textbook and indeed your notes to confirm your knowledge when you may be a little unsure. The book and notes should serve as a source of confirmation of your knowledge and not as the source of your knowledge. There is a more detailed and specific section containing guidance on open book exams at 1.3.1 below. Finally, be aware that many institutions now use two-part subject assessments. Be prepared for these by making sure you know when and where they are to take place and what the constituent elements of each part will be. For example, will you be completing answers to multiple choice questions in the first part and transactional questions in the second or will the order be reversed? In which part will short answer questions occur? Is one part open book and the other closed? The moral is always to be sure of the nature and format of each part of a two-part subject assessment. They are in two parts for a reason; try to be sure you know what that is.

1.2.6 APPRECIATE THE IMPORTANCE OF GOOD TIMING

All examinations are finite and will contain questions or parts of questions that have to be dealt with separately during the examination. This being the case, if you know the number of questions to be answered, always work out in advance the time you can allow to each. This may sound simple but it is of critical importance. You will be tempted to go on writing on one question when you should really be concluding your effort so that you can devote sufficient time to all the questions. Some exams have extra reading time, some do not. Always allow for reading time if there is none allotted. Use the reading time properly by actually reading the questions and all supporting material as carefully as possible and by thinking about the question. Remember P.A.T.

1.2.7 WHAT TO DO ON SITTING DOWN AT YOUR EXAMINATION DESK

As *The Hitchhiker's Guide to the Galaxy* rightly expounds, Don't Panic! If you have completed your preparation properly you should be quietly confident, but if not now is too late and panicking will not help. Once again remember P.A.T. and when confronted with the examination paper give yourself time to consider all aspects of the several points concerned. Look to see if there are marks shown for the various sections of the paper. If there are, this is a great help to you in deciding which parts require greater effort than others earning fewer marks. The marks apportionment should therefore reflect the time apportionment wherever possible. Read the preliminary instructions on the examination paper twice. This way you should take in some of the most important information all of which is there for a reason. For example, a part or parts of the examination may be compulsory; you should take note and complete your work accordingly. Always read these instructions before launching yourself into the body of the paper. As to the questions, read all of the paper from start to finish, so that you can then decide where your preferences lie. Finally, remember to read all the accompanying documents with the examination paper. Property Law and Practice exams will typically rely upon specimen deeds and documents, all of which must be closely reviewed by you so that you will appreciate how they relate to the question concerned.

1.2.8 ANSWER STYLE

It is probably the case that in most of your previous exams an essay would be an appropriate way of answering almost all the questions encountered. Well, this is where that practice ends. Examiners will in many cases have a marking scheme that will include style marks for your answer. You should therefore understand that if the question is in the style of, say, an office memorandum, that your answer should follow the same format. Similarly if the question asks you for a note of your advice, somehow your answer must be constructed to provide exactly that. Style marks are very easy to pick up if you just use P.A.T. to allow you to prepare your answer in the format sought by the examiner. Do not resort to mere essay answers for all your questions, you will lose easy marks by doing so. So if the question asks you to raise requisitions on title (questions about title problems), and to give reasons for them then do precisely that. First set out the proposed requisition and them set out your reason for posing this question. One last hint in this section, remember this is a practical subject where answers may need to be seen to replicate office procedures. In the office time is money and so if you are recording, say a meeting with the client put in an estimated time record at the end. This will show the examiner you understand how an office functions and the marker should be suitably impressed.

1.2.9 ANSWER STRUCTURE

What is an answer? Answer—something with a beginning, a middle and an end. This may seem trite but if you can noticeably structure your answers in this way the examiner will begin to note and appreciate your approach. The last thing an examiner will want to encounter is a long and indeterminate rambling answer. When a well-structured answer is encountered, it is a refreshing experience for the marker who will respond positively to your effort as a result. Get the marker on your side with this important element in your examination technique. This tripartite structure can be further considered.

- The beginning. This perhaps is the fundamental part of your answer. It is where you should grab the marker's attention by a tight, yet logical introduction to the answer. Try at the very outset to show to your marker that you know what is expected of you and that you will be answering the question in full in the body of your answer. Try to indicate your answer by signposts just like we did at the start of this chapter.

- The middle. This must be where you demonstrate your knowledge and your application of it to the facts of the transactional problem. Elements of this process will be considered subsequently.

- The ending is almost as important as the beginning. Try to leave your marker with a final impression of structure by ending with a paragraph or at least a sentence summing up and concluding the flow of your answer. Do not leave your marker with the impression that you stopped where you did simply because you ran out of time or things to say!

1.2.10 TRANSACTIONAL QUESTIONS

When dealing with Property Law and Practice questions it is clear that in the main problem type questions based on a transaction for a client will be the norm. This being so when using the structure outlined above you could extend that approach in your answer by opening with a clear identification of the area of law involved followed by a more detailed statement of that area. You should then apply the law to the particular circumstances of the question and complete your answer with a conclusion that sums up your advice to the client.

1.2.11 THINGS TO REMEMBER WHEN IN 'THE MIDDLE', SEE 1.2.9 ABOVE

Always cite your authorities. In Property Law and Practice statute plays an increasingly pre-eminent role. Cases will always be relevant but you will need to be aware of the major statutes involved. You should be aware at least of s. 1 of the Law of Property Act 1925 and the core elements of the Land Registration Act 2002! Recent practice changes can arise from recent case decisions. For this reason, always keep an eye on reported cases in the press. However, there is another reason for keeping up to date on recent decisions and that is because they can form the basis of questions in your subject assessment/ examination. As has been noted before, examiners will need to find original scenarios for their questions. This being the case a recent decision is a heaven sent opportunity for your examiner to adopt those facts for your question. Remember if you cannot recall the name of a case do not ignore it, simply refer to it as 'in a reported case' or 'in a recent case' if you know it to be novel. Your time in the exam is limited and you may need to repeat long and awkward statute names in your answer. Try writing the Leasehold Reform and Housing and Urban Development Act 1993 a few times and you will understand the problem! To limit the time wasted in this way, if you know you will have to repeat the title after the first instance, insert a short form thus ('the L.H.U.D.A.') and use it subsequently.

1.2.12 CHECK DATES

In many cases dates are in an examination question for a significant reason. Has a time limit expired, is the application out of time or has a priority period any time remaining? Always consider the chronology of the answer carefully as it may be the key element of the whole question. This is particularly the case for searches and the submission of registration applications to Land Registry. Dates are also of importance in abstracts of title in unregistered land. Is the root of title at least fifteen years old? Similarly in a commercial lease renewal have the strict time limits set out in Part II of the Landlord and Tenant Act 1954 been complied with? Accordingly, never overlook the importance of dates in the question.

1.2.13 DECIPHERABILITY

Write clearly. There is nothing more annoying to a marker than having to spend excessive time on a script trying to read an answer let alone understand it. Leave lines between sections; it highlights the structure in your answer. Underline headings for the same reason. Start each question on a fresh page and remember to number your answers. It all helps to get the marker on your side.

1.2.14 OTHER KINDS OF EXAM QUESTIONS

We set out in the following chapters examples of ten multiple-choice questions that you might encounter in a subject assessment. Thereafter you will find some typical short answer questions that can also feature in a subject assessment and which cover matters that are relevant to the chapter topic(s). Answers to both are also set out in each chapter. Remember one crucial piece of guidance concerning multiple choice questions Never leave multiple-choice answers with a blank multiple-choice. If there are four possibilities and you are not sure of the answer select the one you think might be right, after all you have a one in four chance of getting it right! Also look at the instructions on the paper. If it says select the right answer on the paper by circling the correct choice then do just that. Do not make a tick or underline your selection, as the strict response would be to fail you even though the selection may be correct. Also it is possible that none of the answers given are right. In these circumstances follow the rubric in the question paper and explain in the relevant way why none of the listed answers apply.

1.2.15 THE LPC PERVASIVE AREAS

The LPC is not just about Business Law and Practice, Property Law and Practice and Litigation and Advocacy. It is also concerned with topics or subjects that are so important that they are said to pervade the course. They have become known as the 'pervasives'. They exist in:

(a) the Ethical Context, being an introduction to Professional Conduct and Client Care, including the Solicitors' Accounts Rules and Financial Services and Markets regulation;

(b) the European Context, being EU law and Practice;

(c) the Taxation Context, being both direct and indirect taxation; and finally

(d) the Human Rights Context.

Any Legal Practice Course must ensure that these areas are taught and developed in the context of the other elements of the course, wherever appropriate; these pervasive areas must by their very nature 'pervade' the course.

You therefore need to appreciate that you will be assessed in Professional Conduct and Financial Services and Markets regulation. However, this is no ordinary form of examination. This is because this unusual type of assessment can arise in any LPC subject assessment, without warning (as it does in real life). You will not be told that it is a professional conduct issue but will have to spot this. Several of those conduct questions in assessments will be taken (most probably four in total) and then aggregated to give you a mark for professional conduct. You must score 50% overall to pass professional conduct. You must pass this unusual form of assessment in order to pass the LPC. You will encounter several of this type of assessment in this book. However, just as in the exam setting we will not highlight where, as to do so would defeat the purpose of hidden pervasive assessment. However, you must be alive at all times to the possibility of such a problem occurring within a Property Law and Practice assessment (or for that matter in any other LPC assessment).

1.2.16 LAST BUT NOT LEAST, SPECIAL CIRCUMSTANCES

If there are special circumstances that may have adversely affected your performance make sure the institution has some evidence to explain your difficulties. If you were unwell a doctor's certificate is vital. Indeed if you were aware of the circumstances before the exam make sure the institution knows as well. Always supply reliable evidence to back up your assertions. Simply your statement that you had a head cold will not do, third party support with written evidence is required.

1.3 PROPERTY LAW AND PRACTICE AND SUBJECT ASSESSMENTS/EXAMINATIONS

We have tried to show you good examination practice throughout the above section and where necessary we have highlighted this with reference to certain elements from within Property Law and Practice. In this section we want to reinforce this with one or two further comments relevant specifically to Property Law and Practice and open book assessments.

You will now appreciate from your own course how broad a subject Property Law and Practice is and how widespread the potential is for the content of the likely questions in your examination. Your first problem is therefore to make sure you remain relevant at all times during the writing of your answer. Keep focused on the problem and the requirements of a structured answer. It could be of use, if you can exercise this form of self-discipline, to just look again at the question half way through your answer to make sure that you are keeping to wholly relevant material. Always bear in mind you need to answer the question set by the examiner and not the question you had hoped might come up and for which you may have misguidedly strategically revised. Furthermore, it is worth repeating that markers are not impressed by length, they are impressed by relevance and organisation.

Make sure you adopt a modern approach to the subject. The Law Society's National Conveyancing Protocol has, for good or ill, been around now long enough for it to appear in all your textbooks. Accordingly, be aware of the nature of the scheme and how it differs from the traditional system. Little things can count a lot towards showing your grasp of the material and this is just as true for the Protocol. Use 'buyer' in place of 'purchaser' and 'seller' for 'vendor', even if some of your older Tutors still find it difficult to adopt the modern idiom. (No doubt there will be instances of this in this volume for which we readily apologise!) Adopt the vocabulary of the Protocol wherever possible and use it in your answers. Of course that is not to say you should blandly accept the Protocol as a system without flaws; be ready to criticise the system, with examples and explanations, if you think this is justified.

Remember that many of your Tutors will teach across several subjects and that as a consequence you should expect questions that mix several topics. Co-ownership is a classic example of this where a question will arise in Property Law and Practice but where there will be valid information from family law, land law and indeed equity and trusts. Combine all your knowledge and use it in the context of the Property Law answer. Obviously you will not earn many marks by dwelling too long on the family law aspects or other aspects not seen as directly involved as Property Law and Practice. Therefore your task is to balance the information from other topics to show sufficient understanding of the need sometimes to integrate your knowledge whilst still being able to clearly show to the examiner your proficiency in Property Law and Practice. The point is that in practice your client will not turn up with a simple conveyancing problem all neatly placed in its own compartment. The client is far more likely to present to you a set of facts that could well stretch across several parts of the law all of which could well lead to litigation and advocacy!

Specifically, what kind of question can you expect in a Property Law and Practice subject assessment? Well of course you will know that the subject itself is an intensely practical one. It will therefore come as no surprise that most questions you will encounter are going to be transactional. This means that you must solve theoretical but practical problems for a 'client' by using your own Property Law/Conveyancing knowledge. However, there will also be multiple choice type questions as well as short answer questions. Examples of all three types of assessment questions are contained within all the following chapters.

1.3.1 OPEN BOOK ASSESSMENTS AND PROPERTY LAW AND PRACTICE

LPC providers have adopted the open book format because in practice you would be able to consider several sources of materials and the teaching teams wish to replicate the position in practice for problem solving. However, there are dangers for the unwary LPC student. You should all therefore note the following points for guidance:

- You must learn the material from each course compulsory subject including pervasive areas. You cannot simply rely on books during the exam. You will not have time constantly to refer to the texts. Your books should only be used sparingly, for very technical points or to confirm your memory recall. Over the years the LPC tutors have noted that candidates who refer constantly to their books in the exams seem to perform less well than those who do not.

- Open book exams are more complex than degree examinations and this course is at post-graduate level. You must think and analyse to formulate an answer to the problem at hand, you must be discriminating in your answer. A 'put down everything' or 'copying out of the book' approach regardless of relevance is usually penalised. It is for you to show to the examiners that you understand the difficulties posed by the questions and can provide a solution.

- Do not spend excessive amounts of time trying to find answers in your books. There is a fundamental core of knowledge that all solicitors should have if they practice within a particular area and they do not need to check in books. You should know a substantial part of this core before going into the examination room.

- The LPC contains many forms of assessment. You might be tempted to direct your efforts solely from assessment to assessment. This would be a learning method that your LPC staff would not support. You need to assimilate the detail each week as the course unfolds. Do not wait until the ends of the blocks to learn the materials; do it on a continual basis and you should be able to approach your subject assessments with confidence.

- We recommend that you take into the exams no more than two A4 binders of materials and notes contained within lever-arch files along with one or more textbooks specified by the area leader. The Course or Subject Leader for exams may specifically prohibit some books and this prohibition will be stated in your examination instructions. The information on which to base your answers to the examination questions will be found within the issued materials, handouts, exercises and notes, or the recommended textbooks.

1.4 AND FINALLY; A FEW CONCLUDING WORDS OF WISDOM WHICH, IF NOTHING ELSE, YOU SHOULD COMMIT TO MEMORY

First of all, remember the answers we have provided are not model answers but are our attempts to provide suggestions of what we consider to be commendation or distinction level answers. If you feel you could have presented the material in a more efficient manner for any particular question, have the courage of your convictions and write the answer in your own style.

P.A.T., Pause and Think remains our key piece of advice for all of your time in the examination hall. Remember, a moment or two of careful reflection can be all that is necessary to allow you to integrate all the random thoughts and recollections running around in your mind that will come together as your answer. Give yourself the time to put together a coherent and structured answer; it will make all the difference to your performance generally. Try to emulate our start to this chapter by listing at the start of your answer the bare bones of your structure. It immediately grabs the attention of your marker and, on the assumption that you are on the right lines, the marker will be on your side for the rest of the marking session. The use of these early signposts will be a refreshing change and will help your answer to stand out from all the others in the marker's looming tower of scripts.

Be aware of the importance of time management. If marks are shown on the paper for each section of it, immediately work out the amount of time you need to apportion in the same proportions as the marks are allocated. If marks are mentioned, allocate the time in proportion to the number of questions on the paper. Stick closely to your timetable and try not to over shoot your time limits. Remember the next question you write may turn out to be a rich source of marks for you but if you run out of time for your answer you may be limiting the possibility of further marks.

Finally good luck with all your examinations but, frankly, if you prepare properly luck will not be an important factor in your success.

2 | REGISTERED AND UNREGISTERED CONVEYANCING; TAKING INSTRUCTIONS

2.1   INTRODUCTION

The two land systems, registered and unregistered, will of course be familiar to you from your land law studies. They are, however, of such fundamental importance to an understanding of Property Law and Practice that you will invariably review them again at the start of your LPC. You will reconsider in particular the principles of land registration and you should expect to receive examination questions that test your core knowledge in this area. Pay particular attention to the reforms introduced by the Land Registration Act 2002.

Third party rights and their means of protection feature prominently in this part of the property law and practice syllabus and are popular with examiners. Do not overlook the changes in this area brought about by the 2002 Act. Third party rights crop up time and again in subject assessments and in different contexts at that. Consider, for example, the second part of standard question 4 in this chapter and question 1 in chapter 3 dealing with the draft contract. Overriding interests are a particular favourite when it comes to problems concerning registered land. The possibility of unlawful occupiers and the necessity for vacant possession on completion are of constant concern to the conveyancer, and there is much case law on the subject.

Whereas third party rights appeal to the examiner, the topic 'Taking instructions' is normally well liked by you, the LPC student. This could be because it is your first contact with a 'client', and on a vocational course like the LPC, the initial mock-interview may well be the first time you have actually *felt* like a solicitor advising a client. Most students seem to enjoy the experience ('learning by doing') and usually say they learn a lot from it. If this applies to you, the opportunity of tackling a question on this topic could be just up your street. If you see a question and fancy it, why not answer it first and get some early marks under your belt?

Do remember that taking instructions is not just a fact-gathering exercise. Of course, you should be seeking to obtain as much information as possible to carry out the whole transaction, but your client will also need advice and help with important decisions, whether they be financial or otherwise. For example, the client may want guidance on the types of survey available or the different methods of co-ownership. Some students (and practitioners!) find it beneficial to prepare and learn a checklist of the key points which may be discussed at the initial interview; note the word 'may' though—your advice must always be relevant. Refer to the checklists at 2.2.2 below.

The client's initial instructions may reveal professional conduct matters and you should be ready for them. If the examiner wants to test your knowledge and understanding of the rules about client care or acting for more than one party, then a 'taking instructions' type question is the perfect vehicle. You will note that these issues are discussed in the answers below. Other topics of a pervasive nature will also feature at the 'taking instructions' stage. For example, the Financial Services and Markets Act 2000, money laundering and the possibility of the proceeds of sale attracting capital gains tax (CGT).

2.2 AN OVERVIEW OF THE SUBJECT AND A LOOK AT SOME PROBLEM AREAS

2.2.1 REGISTERED AND UNREGISTERED CONVEYANCING

The traditional system of conveyancing of unregistered land has been in existence for centuries, although it was overhauled by the Law of Property Act 1925. This was accompanied by the Land Registration Act 1925, which fully put in place the new reforming system of land registration. It also signposted the way towards the gradual but inevitable dominance of registered land. The whole unregistered system relies upon the existence of written documents, of deeds, to show to a buyer a period of unchallenged ownership which will substantiate the seller's ownership. At present, statute stipulates a minimum period of unchallenged ownership of fifteen years (Law of Property Act 1969, s. 23). The major problem of the unregistered system is that there is an almost total reliance on the integrity of the title deeds. If they are, either in part or in whole, lost, damaged or forged, severe problems will inevitably arise for the owner seeking to prove title. Furthermore, the mere existence of deeds does not guarantee any title, though buyers may take comfort from the existence of deeds stretching back over time along with the actual occupation of the property by the seller.

For registered land the Land Registration Act 2002, which came into force on 13 October 2002, has fully repealed the Land Registration Act 1925. The 2002 Act paves the way for electronic conveyancing under which it is intended that the register should be a complete and accurate reflection of the title to the land. The intention is that it should be possible to investigate title to land on-line, with the absolute minimum of additional enquiries, searches and inspections. The 2002 Act has also made fundamental changes to the law of adverse possession as it relates to registered land. Life is now much harder for the intending squatter of registered land and, as a result, a clear incentive presents itself to owners of unregistered land to apply voluntarily for their titles to become registered. This will assist the Land Registry's aim of achieving full registration of title in England and Wales by 2012. Despite this, nearly 20% of land in England and Wales is still currently unregistered and it is important that LPC students learn how to deal with an unregistered title when they come across it (see Chapter 5). For those of you who have studied land law before the 2002 Act came into force, it is important that you acquaint yourself with the new law as soon as possible. In particular, study the important areas of overriding interests, protection of third party interests and the changes to the law of easements. Too many law students begin their LPC with at best only a hazy recollection of land law principles!

As far as the differences between registered and unregistered conveyancing are concerned you will be pleased to learn that, for the most part, they are not substantial, the main area of contrast being the searches that should be carried out. Having said that, it is well worth memorising the overall conveyancing procedure for both systems at an early stage of your course. This will stand you in good stead as you progress to study the different aspects of conveyancing in more detail. The main differences between registered and unregistered conveyancing are as follows:

Action	Unregistered Title	Registered Title
Taking instructions	No fundamental difference	No fundamental difference
Draft contract	No fundamental difference	No fundamental difference
Pre-contract searches	Pre-contract enquiries of seller	Same
	Local Search	Same
	Water Search	Same
	Inspection of the property	Same
	Search of Index Map	Not needed
	Central Land Charges Search	Not needed
	Environmental search	Same
	Other searches—depends on property location	Same
Deduce title	By abstract or epitome of title	By official copies, title plan and supporting official copies of filed deeds
Investigate title	By examining abstract or epitome of title and checking against originals	By examining official copies and checking for any overriding interests
Exchange of contracts	No fundamental difference	No fundamental difference
Preparation and approval of purchase deed	Drafted by buyer's solicitor—conveyance or more commonly TR1 transfer deed	Drafted by buyer's solicitor—prescribed form of transfer deed (TR1 for transfer of whole)
Pre-completion search	Central Land Charges Search plus bankruptcy search against buyer if acting for lender	Land Registry Search plus bankruptcy search against buyer if acting for lender
Prepare for completion	No fundamental difference	No fundamental difference
Completion	Title deeds handed to buyer's solicitor. Legal estate passes on completion	Buyer's solicitor receives transfer deed executed by seller. Legal estate does not pass on completion

Post-completion	Buyer registered as proprietor on first registration within two months of completion	Buyer registered as proprietor within priority period of Land Registry Search. Legal estate passes on registration

2.2.2 TAKING INSTRUCTIONS

The first interview will enable you to gather essential facts, but it should also be used, where necessary, to furnish the client with important advice on how to proceed. It gives you the opportunity to instil confidence in the client of your abilities as a conveyancer. To this end always try to see the client in person. Too many firms cut corners by relying solely on the telephone for obtaining instructions (some cut-price conveyancers will say they cannot afford to see clients at all!) but in the long run this may be a false economy, for clients will normally prefer to meet their solicitor at an early stage. It is our view that, ultimately, it is still the high level of service that impresses clients more, not the low level of fees; and a satisfied client is one who will return to you with future instructions. If a personal interview is impossible, at least ensure that the instructions received and advice given over the telephone are clear, and backed up with a letter of confirmation to the client.

In our experience students often make silly mistakes when conducting or explaining a first interview with a client. Always remember to note down basic information such as the client's name, address and contact telephone numbers—this is sometimes overlooked! Other errors include forgetting who pays stamp duty land tax (the buyer), who pays the estate agent's commission account (the seller) and who pays any capital gains tax (the seller). Remember that giving survey advice to a buyer is a rule of thumb and the type of survey you recommend will depend primarily on the age of the property. Regarding mortgage advice, these days, endowment mortgages should generally be avoided at all costs with the usual recommendation being a repayment mortgage, especially for first time buyers who are looking for the cheapest option in terms of monthly outlay.

When giving advice to joint buyers on co-ownership explain the differences between a joint tenancy and a tenancy in common simply, clearly and without using legal jargon. The simplest way is to say that in a joint tenancy they both own all the property, whereas in a tenancy in common they own separate shares. If a joint tenant dies the survivor takes the deceased's 'share' automatically, but if a tenant in common dies, the deceased's share passes under his or her will or intestacy. You can make a recommendation as to which method is suitable but ultimately it is the client's choice, so don't get too fraught over which method they should choose—just explain the options!

There follows some checklists to assist you when considering questions on taking instructions. You may also find these useful when preparing for an interviewing and advising assessment in Property Law and Practice.

Taking instructions generally:

- Obtain client's full names, address and contact telephone numbers.
- Has your firm acted for the client before (relevant to client care advice)?
- Is it necessary to check client's identity (relevant to money laundering and mortgage fraud)?
- Confirm address of property and tenure.
- Is it a residential or commercial property?

- Details of any estate agent's involved. Obtain copy of agent's particulars. Any preliminary deposit paid to agents?
- If it is a commercial transaction, have the parties agreed heads of terms? If so, what are they?
- Details of solicitors acting for other side.
- Price agreed.
- Other terms agreed, e.g. sale of chattels, likely completion date?
- Which fixtures will remain or be removed?
- Does client have a related sale or purchase, which has to be synchronised with this transaction?
- Who occupies the property (relevant to third party rights and vacant possession)?
- If it is a commercial lease are there any sub-leases?
- Is property near river or railway or in unusual location (relevant to searches and enquiries)?
- Advise on costs and prepare brief financial statement. Remind client about other expenses, e.g. removal fees.
- How much deposit will be paid or received on exchange?
- If you are dealing with a lease, is it the grant of a new lease or the assignment of an existing one?
- Is there anything additional you need to know from the client or upon which the client requires your advice, which may be relevant to this particular transaction?
- Advise the client how long it should all take and what the next steps will be.

Additionally when acting for a buyer:

- How will purchase price be financed? If client requires a mortgage, consider mortgage advice.
- How will deposit payable on exchange be financed?
- Advice on survey.
- If more than one buyer, advice on co-ownership.
- Confirm proposed use of property (relevant to planning and any restrictions in the title).
- Advise the client whether stamp duty land tax is payable. Can you apportion the price between land and chattels to reduce or eradicate stamp duty land tax?
- If client presently in rented accommodation, advice on giving landlord notice to end tenancy.

Additionally when acting for a buyer and a lender:

- Do not act for a buyer and a private mortgagee unless the transaction is not at arm's length and no conflict of interest arises. If in doubt, do not act for both parties.
- When acting for a buyer and institutional lender check compliance with r. 6(3) of the Solicitors' Practice Rules 1990.

- Also check the mortgage instructions contained in the CML Lenders' Handbook.

Additionally when acting for a seller:

- Where are the title deeds? If property is mortgaged, obtain full name and address of first mortgagee plus mortgage account number, so you can write to mortgagee requesting deeds on loan.

- Are there any second or subsequent mortgages? Obtain details of *all* outstanding mortgages on property including names and addresses of lenders and amounts outstanding.

- Did you act for the client when the property was bought? If yes, it may be helpful to get the old file from store.

- What are client's instructions regarding sale proceeds?

- If Protocol being used, client to complete Property Information Form.

- Advise client not to stop mortgage repayments or cancel building insurance until completion.

- Will Capital Gains Tax be payable on sale proceeds? Confirm whether principal private dwellinghouse exemption applies.

- On an assignment of a commercial lease has the client approached the lessor for consent to assign (if required)?

2.3 SUBJECT ASSESSMENTS

Here are some examples of subject assessment questions in the area of taking instructions and registered and unregistered land. Commentary and a suggested answer accompany the standard assessment questions. These are then followed by multiple choice questions (with answers) and short answer questions with suggested answers.

2.3.1 STANDARD ASSESSMENT QUESTIONS, COMMENTARY AND SUGGESTED ANSWERS

Question 1

Emily Mayle has recently instructed you to act for her on the sale of Appletree Cottage, a detached property with grounds of just under one hectare. The conveyancing partner in your firm acted for her when she purchased the property two years ago, and remembers that she was quite fortunate at the time to secure such a large mortgage with the Cornshire Building Society.

Emily is a senior travel guide and spends much of the year 'on the road' conducting guided tours of Great Britain and Ireland. She owns another house in London.

Emily has told the conveyancing partner that Appletree Cottage is in fairly poor condition and there are signs of dry rot in the study. She had some woodworm and damp treatment carried out a few years ago and believes there may be some guarantees somewhere.

Emily borrowed about £3,000 from her bank last year to finance the installation of central heating at Appletree Cottage. She thinks the bank may have a second charge.

The purchaser is Lydia Walmsley whose father is an established client of the firm. Lydia would like you to act for her as well as Emily in order to speed things along and also hopefully to save on costs.

Emily has an appointment to see you tomorrow. What further information will you require from Emily and what advice will you give her?

Commentary

There are two distinct parts to this question, the first relates to information the second to advice, and the preferred answering approach would be to deal with each part separately.

The first part of the question is essentially a fact-gathering exercise. It appears on the face of it to be quite straightforward but to gain high marks you will have to pay close attention to the detail of the question. If you request irrelevant information (e.g. a plan) you are likely to be penalised by the marker.

As far as the second part is concerned, relevance again is the key to a successful answer. There are obvious areas of advice which must be covered—such as the professional conduct rule against acting for both parties, but other more practical issues should not be overlooked. For instance, given the recent slowdown in the property market the possibility of Emily finding herself with 'negative equity' should be contemplated, and this is explained in the suggested answer below.

You will notice the reference to 'hectare' in the first paragraph and this should immediately alert you to the probable inclusion of a CGT point—why else would it be mentioned?

Suggested answer

Before advising Emily on her sale we would seek from her as much relevant information as possible. This will prevent us from overlooking important matters and should enable us to give full and proper advice at an early stage.

The following information will be required from Emily:

(a) Full names and address of Emily together with home and work telephone numbers and email address.

(b) The agreed price.

(c) Confirmation of full address of property and whether it is freehold or leasehold. If leasehold, ask Emily for the last receipt for payment of rent and buildings insurance details (if arranged by landlord).

(d) Details of the mortgage with Cornshire Building Society, including address of the branch and mortgage account or roll number. These details may be apparent from the firm's old file relating to Emily's purchase of Appletree Cottage. We shall need to request the deeds on loan from the Society and request a note of the outstanding balance.

(e) Details of the mortgage to the bank (if any). An inspection of the title will establish for certain whether a legal charge has been registered by the bank.

(f) Whether anyone else, apart from Emily is living in the property and, if so, whether that person has made any financial contribution towards its purchase or any subsequent improvement. It may be necessary for us to procure that person's consent to the sale proceeding.

(g) Details of any estate agents who may have arranged the sale and the buyer's solicitors (if known).

(h) Whether the prospective buyer Lydia has paid a preliminary deposit to the estate agents. If so, this must be taken into account by us in our completion statement.

(i) Details of any chattels to be included in the sale and whether Lydia will pay extra for these.

(j) Whether Emily intends to take with her any fixtures. If so, they must be specifically excluded in the contract of sale, otherwise they will be deemed to be included. We could ask Emily to complete the fixtures, fittings and contents form.

(k) Does Emily have a completion date in mind? Has this been discussed with Lydia?

(l) Have any other terms been agreed between Emily and Lydia?

(m) Whether Emily is intending to buy another property and if so, is it dependent on the sale of Appletree Cottage? If there is no related purchase, what are Emily's instructions regarding the net proceeds of sale on completion?

(n) Is there a chain of transactions? If the National Protocol is being used we shall require Emily's authority to disclose information about the chain to Lydia's solicitors.

We would advise Emily generally as follows.

We are told that Emily purchased Appletree cottage two years ago with the aid of a large mortgage. There also appears to be a second charge secured in favour of a bank. Given the recent stabilisation and even fall in house prices she should be alerted to the fact that the price at which the house is now being sold could be less than the total amount owing on the mortgage or mortgages to which the property is subject. This situation is known as 'negative equity'. It may be the case that Emily has agreed a lower price than she would have liked because of the cottage's poor condition. The buyer's solicitors will on completion require an undertaking from our firm that the existing mortgage(s) will be discharged on completion and clearly we would be unable to do this if a negative equity situation has arisen.

We can ascertain from the old purchase file the amount of the loan from Cornshire (or perhaps Emily can tell us), but we shall need an up-to-date redemption figure from the Society itself before we can assess the true position. We should warn Emily that if she has negative equity, the cottage cannot be sold unless funds are available from elsewhere to repay the total indebtedness secured on the property.

Emily has indicated that the buyer would like our firm to act for her as well. Rule 6 of the Solicitors' Practice Rules 1990 prohibits a solicitor from acting for more than one party in a conveyancing transaction at arm's length, subject to certain exceptions. Lydia's father is an established client of the firm (one of the exceptions), but we are not told that Lydia is an established client. Even if she were, we must bear in mind that the exceptions would not apply where there is a conflict of interest. We would therefore advise that Lydia must instruct another firm of solicitors to act for her.

As far as the poor condition of the property is concerned, we would advise Emily that this is a matter for the buyer under the maxim 'caveat emptor'. Emily is under no duty to disclose physical defects but she must be careful not to deliberately conceal a defect (e.g. the dry rot), otherwise this could amount to a fraudulent misrepresentation on her part that the property is not defective (see *Gordon v. Selico Co Ltd* [1986] 1 EGLR 71). We would ask her to try and find the woodworm and damp guarantees because copies should to be sent to Lydia's solicitors with the seller's Property Information Form (or, if the National Protocol is not being used, with replies to preliminary enquiries).

Emily must be advised of the possible liability to capital gains tax (CGT) as a consequence of the sale. The Taxation of Chargeable Gains Act 1992 provides for CGT on any gain made on the disposal of a chargeable asset. The gain however is exempt where the sale is of a person's principal private dwelling house (PPD), including grounds of up to half a hectare. Prima facie, CGT will be payable on Emily's land in excess of half a hectare unless she can show that such land is necessary for the reasonable enjoyment of the dwelling house. Any chargeable gain can be reduced or eradicated entirely by setting against it her personal annual exemption for CGT.

It should be noted that the PPD exemption would only apply if the property has been Emily's only or main residence throughout her period of ownership. However, various periods of absence can be disregarded for this purpose and, from the given facts, Emily's time away on business would not appear to disqualify her from the PPD exemption.

She owns another property in London and we must advise her that the PPD exemption can only apply to one property. Accordingly she must make an election as to which house the exemption will apply. It may of course be the case that Emily is selling the property for less than she paid for it, in which case there is no gain and no possibility of CGT!

The Law Society has issued Written Professional Standards on the question of the information on costs which solicitors should give to their clients. These standards are not mandatory but represent a safe and preferred method of practice. Accordingly we would give Emily the best information possible about the likely costs of the sale, including VAT and all disbursements.

We must also have regard to Rule 15 of the Solicitor's Practice Rules 1990 which deals with client care. Emily should be told who is to have the day-to-day conduct of the file, the name of the partner responsible for overall supervision and the name of the person in the firm whom she can contact if she has a problem with the service provided.

Other aspects of client care of which Emily should be advised are the future action to be taken to progress the matter, the likely timescale of the transaction and when we will next contact Emily. We should offer her a brief explanation of the conveyancing procedures and estimate how long before exchange of contracts and completion. It is a requirement that the costs and client care information should be confirmed to the client in writing.

Question 2

Your principal has asked you to prepare a briefing paper for one of the firm's clients, Mr Shoab Akram, who is considering going into the property investment business and would like to know a little more about the workings of the registered land system. Mr Akram has a degree in law and is familiar with legal concepts. The briefing paper should deal specifically with the following matters:

(a) An outline of the main differences between the registered and unregistered land systems (8 marks)

(b) An explanation of the nature and effect of registration of title (15 marks)

(c) A brief description of the form of a registered title (5 marks)

Commentary

Those of you who have acquired a sound and thorough knowledge of the land registration system and how it operates should relish this question and see it as an opportunity for good marks. Those of you whose feel for the subject is unsure should try to avoid it (although you may be in crisis if all questions are compulsory!). If you attempt it, you must remember to answer the questions as written, not the question you wished had been written. Resist the temptation to write everything you know about registered land.

The subject matter is fundamental to a proper understanding of conveyancing practice in England and Wales and consequently this type of question could arise quite often. If you learn the relevant material thoroughly and structure your answer carefully, we can assure you it will pay dividends.

The question is in three sections and you will note that more marks are given for part (b) so naturally you should apportion your time to allow longer time for this part. When explaining the present law concerning registration of title remember to refer to the Land Registration Act 2002. The Land Registration Act 1925 was repealed by the 2002 Act and thus is of historic interest only!

Lastly, note that you are asked to prepare a briefing paper to a client so remember to produce your answer in this format.

Suggested answer

<u>Briefing Paper for Mr Shoab Akram</u>

(a) <u>An outline of the main differences between the registered and unregistered land systems</u>

The present system of land registration was introduced by the Land Registration Act 1925 in order to simplify conveyancing. The 1925 Act was repealed on 13 October 2003 by the Land Registration Act 2002 ('the 2002 Act'). The detailed rules of the registered land system are to be found in the Land Registration Rules 2003.

The general aim of the registered land system is to record details of the ownership and enjoyment of land (other than those discoverable on physical inspection of the land) on a central land register. A prospective purchaser of the land is then able to discover from an examination of the register the nature of the existing interests affecting the land to be acquired. The state provides a guarantee as to the accuracy of the registered title and indemnifies those prejudiced by the operation of the system.

The principal objective of the 2002 Act is to facilitate a future system of electronic dealing with land by making the register a complete and accurate reflection of the state of the title of the land at any given time.

The intention is that it should be possible to investigate title to land on-line, with the minimum of additional searches, inspection and enquiry.

By contrast, title to unregistered land is not entered in a central register, but is contained in the title deeds of the land in question. These are held by the owner (or mortgagee if the land is mortgaged). A separate investigation of the title by the buyer's conveyancer is therefore required upon each occasion the land is purchased. The seller must supply the buyer with an abstract or epitome of the title, which shows that the estate has been correctly conveyed during at least the last fifteen years (Law of Property Act 1969 s. 23).

In unregistered conveyancing the legal estate passes to the buyer when the deeds are handed over on completion. In registered conveyancing, the legal estate passes to the buyer upon completion of the post-completion registration of the buyer as registered proprietor.

(b) The nature and effect of registration of title

Strictly speaking it is not the land that is registered but the estate in the land, so there may be more than one title registered in respect of the same piece of land. Thus, for example, a freehold, a headlease and a sublease could all exist in respect of the same land.

The titles capable of substantive registration in their own right are set out in s. 3(1) of the 2002 Act. They are freehold and leasehold estates in land, rentcharges, franchises and profits à prendre in gross.

Unregistered titles are required to be substantively registered ('first registration') within two months of a 'qualifying event' (s. 6(4) of the 2002 Act). This is known as compulsory registration. The events inducing first registration are laid down in s. 4(1) of the 2002 Act. The principal events are:

(i) a transfer of a qualifying estate (a qualifying estate is either a legal freehold estate or a legal leasehold estate which has more than seven years left to run);

(ii) a grant of a lease for a term of more than seven years; and

(iii) a protected first legal mortgage of a qualifying estate.

It should be noted that a reversionary lease of any term granted to take effect in possession more than three months after the date of grant must also be registered (s. 4(1)(d)). A reversionary lease is where the tenant has a right to take possession at a future date.

As well as compulsory registration it is possible for an owner of unregistered land to apply for voluntary first registration. This is often done by developers of unregistered land wishing to sell each plot as registered land, or by owners of particularly complex unregistered titles who wish to simplify the job of proving title when they come to sell.

Upon receiving the application for first registration Land Registry will investigate the unregistered title and allocate one of the following classes of title:

(i) Absolute

This is recognised as being the most reliable and marketable title that exists. Section 9(2) of the 2002 Act provides that a person may be registered with absolute freehold title if the registrar considers that the title is such as a willing buyer could properly be advised by a competent professional adviser to accept. The legal estate is vested in the proprietor together with all the interests subsisting for the benefit of the estate, e.g., easements. As far as burdens are concerned, the proprietor takes subject only to the interests set out in s. 11(4) affecting the estate at the time of first registration. These are:

(a) interests which are the subject of an entry in the register in relation to the estate. (These can only be registered charges, notices and restrictions because cautions and inhibitions are prospectively abolished under the 2002 Act).

(b) unregistered interests which fall within any of the paragraphs of Schedule 1 (i.e. interests which override first registration)

(c) interests acquired under the Limitation Act 1980 of which the proprietor has notice.

(ii) Possessory

This class of title will be registered where the registrar is not satisfied with the documentary proof of ownership and consequently the proprietor will be subject to any adverse interests in existence at the date of first registration. Typically, a possessory title is granted where the title deeds have been lost or the applicant's title is based on adverse possession.

(iii) Qualified

This is very rare. It has the same effect as registration with absolute title save that the state guarantee does not apply to some specified defect.

(iv) Good leasehold

This too has the same effect as absolute title save that the proprietor is subject to any estate right or interest affecting the right of the landlord to grant the lease. Thus unlike absolute leasehold title, the state guarantee does not extend to the freehold and any superior leasehold titles. Typically, this class of title will be granted where the superior title is neither registered nor deduced to the registrar's satisfaction.

There is provision in s. 62 of the 2002 Act for possessory, qualified and good leasehold titles to be upgraded in certain circumstances. Examples of these are the conversion of good leasehold to absolute where the superior titles are deduced to the registrar's satisfaction, and possessory to absolute where the proprietor has been registered with possessory title for twelve years and is still in possession.

(c) The form of a registered title

Each registered title is allocated a unique title number. The register for each title is divided into three parts:

(i) Property Register

This states whether the title is freehold or leasehold and, if the latter, it will give brief lease details. It also gives a short verbal description and refers to the Registry's title plan. This plan is prepared by the Land Registry (based on the Ordnance Survey map) for use with the title in question. The land within the title is edged red and matters peculiar to the title may also be shown, e.g. blue tinting for a right of way.

(ii) Proprietorship Register

This records the class of title (e.g. absolute) and the name and address of the registered proprietor. It may also contain entries protecting third party rights and restricting the power of the owner to deal with the land (e.g. a notice, restriction or pre-13 October 2003 caution).

(iii) Charges Register

This sets out all encumbrances subsisting at the date of first registration (sometimes by reference to a later schedule) together with all subsequent charges or encumbrances. Examples of these would be restrictive covenants, mortgages and leases.

Question 3

RICHARDS ABBEY AND PARTNERS, SOLICITORS
INTERNAL MEMORANDUM

To   The Trainee Solicitor

From   The Conveyancing Partner

I have received instructions from Mr Joshua Dean and Miss Laura Woosey who wish to buy 10 Eldon Place, a victorian terraced cottage, for £62,000. The price includes some furniture and fixtures and fittings, the value of which the clients believe to be about £2,000.

Joshua and Laura are first time buyers and are presently living in rented accommodation.

Laura has £15,000 on deposit at her building society. The balance of the purchase price will have to be borrowed and the clients will want some guidance on this. They have agreed to share the mortgage outgoings and the costs of purchase equally.

Joshua would like to work from home and is thinking of converting part of the property into an office.

My secretary has arranged an appointment for them to see you tomorrow. Please prepare a note of the advice you intend to give Joshua and Laura when you see them.

Commentary

This question is in the form of a memorandum from a partner so the appropriate way to respond would be by reply memorandum in note form. An essay answer would be likely to lose you marks for inappropriate style.

The question is very specific when it asks 'What advice will you give . . . ?'. It does not (as does question 1) ask you to detail the information you will be seeking from the client (e.g. addresses, telephone numbers, etc.) Accordingly, you should follow your principal's instructions and note only your intended *advice*.

There is a fair amount to cover so you cannot afford to go into too much detail in any one area, but allow yourself enough time to cover all the important points. For instance, don't spend too long on the finer distinctions of joint tenancies and tenancies in common at the expense of missing something as crucial as the survey.

Be relevant. Your advice should be tailored to meet the facts and you will lose marks for advice which is beside the point because that will demonstrate an inability to differentiate according to your clients' circumstances. For example, you might decide to advise at length on the different categories of survey, but if you stop and think, there is really little point in going into great detail about a survey you will not be recommending!

Be practical. It is easy to overlook obvious matters like explaining how long the conveyancing process will take. First time buyers will always want to know when they can move in. How often does one hear the complaint, 'Our solicitor never told us it would take this long'? You will also note the practical point concerning the giving of notice of withdrawal to the Building Society.

Two final points. First, notice the three 'pervasive' subjects mentioned in the suggested answer: professional conduct, financial services and taxation. Never overlook the importance of these. Secondly, note the overlap between different parts of the Property Law and Practice syllabus (e.g. inspection of the property is covered under searches) and other areas of legal practice (e.g. suggesting the clients should make wills).

Suggested answer

RICHARDS ABBEY AND PARTNERS, SOLICITORS
INTERNAL MEMORANDUM

To   The Conveyancing Partner

From   The Trainee Solicitor

The clients require guidance as to the type of mortgage they will require, but we cannot be sure that they will even be successful in getting one. Obviously, we must advise the clients not to enter into a binding contract until their financial arrangements are in order, and any mortgage offer must be in writing and approved by the clients and ourselves.

In giving mortgage advice we must have regard to the provisions of the Financial Services and Markets Act 2000 which regulates the conduct of investment business. Generic advice as to the type of mortgage (e.g. repayment mortgage as opposed to endowment mortgage) will not be caught by the Act, but advice that a particular lender should be used may fall within the definition of mainstream investment business if the mortgage is linked to an investment product. To give such advice we must be authorised by the Financial Services Authority (FSA). Only a few hundred specialist firms throughout the country are currently authorised by the FSA and I believe our firm is not one of them. If our clients require mainstream investment advice we should refer them to a duly authorised third party (ATP).

We must advise the clients on appropriate sources of finance such as banks, building societies or insurance companies. If the firm has an arrangement with a lender for the introduction of clients, this must comply with the Solicitors' Introduction and Referral Code 1990.

We must consider how much the clients need to borrow. The purchase price is £62,000. Laura is contributing £15,000 so, assuming the clients have funds available to cover costs and disbursements (which we must check), the amount of the loan will be roughly £47,000. If the property is worth £60,000, the loan would be roughly equivalent to 78% of market value. In this event the clients should be advised that the lender is likely to require the additional security of a mortgage indemnity guarantee. This will cover the mortgagee's potential loss in the event of it failing to recover the full amount of the loan on a re-sale. The indemnity policy will incur a single one-off premium (normally several hundred pounds) which will be borne by the buyers through a reduction in the mortgage advance.

In addition, an institutional lender will often only lend a maximum of three times the main bread-winner's salary plus once the other's salary. We must check that our clients' earnings meet this criteria because if they do not, the purchase probably cannot proceed without a further injection of capital on their part.

What type of mortgage should the clients have? We would discuss those currently available and explain how they work, in particular the three most popular ones, repayment, endowment and pension, and work out the most suitable for our clients. The factors we would consider are the relative cheapness of the repayment mortgage, the availability of tax relief on a pension mortgage and, on an endowment mortgage, the risk that the policy proceeds may be insufficient to discharge the capital loan. Our clients have no dependants, so a mortgage linked to an endowment life policy is probably not appropriate. If either of them is self-employed or not part of a company pension scheme they should consider a pension mortgage. Otherwise, their best option would appear to be the ordinary repayment method which is generally the least expensive.

Finally, the clients must be advised that their home is at risk if they fail to comply with the terms and conditions of the mortgage. Accordingly it would be sensible to ensure that the anticipated monthly repayments are not unrealistically high in proportion to the clients' income. We must also advise that the conditions of the mortgage offer will almost certainly preclude any business use at the property. This would thwart Joshua's plans to work from home, although this would depend very much on their nature and extent. If in any doubt, the client should be advised to seek an assurance in writing from the proposed mortgagee that his plans would not contravene the mortgage conditions.

There are two further points on the question of Joshua's plans to work from home. He should be advised that any material change of use or alteration to the structure of the house may require planning permission. In addition, if part of the house is used *exclusively* for business purposes, he will lose his principal private dwelling exemption from CGT in respect of the part so used.

We would advise Joshua and Laura of the *caveat emptor* rule ('let the buyer beware') which is particularly important here because the clients are buying a very old property. We would explain to them briefly the nature and effect of the three types of survey generally available: the ordinary valuation, the house buyer's report and valuation and the full structural survey. In this case, given the age of the property, we would recommend, notwithstanding the additional cost, a full structural survey. The clients' mortgagee will want an ordinary valuation, so rather than incur two survey fees, the clients could ask the mortgagee to arrange the structural survey upon which they can then both rely (provided the mortgagee's surveyor is reputable!).

In view of the property's age the surveyor may recommend some remedial work and the clients should be warned that the mortgagee might make a retention from the mortgage advance until the works have been carried out.

A prudent solicitor would always advise a buyer to have a survey but Joshua and Laura should also be advised to undertake their own physical inspection of the property and its neighbourhood. Although we would raise pre-contract enquiries of the seller's solicitors, it does no harm for the buyers themselves to be on the look-out for potential problems like non-owning occupiers or undisclosed rights of way across the land.

The clients should be advised of the two ways in which the beneficial interest in the property can be held, namely either as joint tenants where on the death of one the deceased's interest accrues to the other by survivorship, or as tenants in common where either party's interest is capable of being disposed of during their lifetime, or by will or intestacy.

In this case a presumption of a tenancy in common will arise because the parties are contributing to the purchase price in unequal shares. However we should still advise the clients to expressly record in a separate trust deed (a) that they will hold as tenants in common, and (b) what proportion of the beneficial interest is held by each of them. This should help to prevent any later disputes. You mentioned Laura's capital injection of £15,000 and that both clients will share the costs of the purchase and mortgage outgoings equally so I calculate their respective beneficial entitlements to be Laura: 62.5% and Joshua: 37.5%.

As the clients' shares can be given by will or pass on intestacy, we should strongly advise them to make wills.

They should appreciate that a deposit of 10% (sometimes less) of the purchase price will be payable on exchange of contracts. Presumably this can be provided by Laura from her deposit account but if the money is on long-term deposit she will need to give notice of withdrawal immediately if she is to avoid, or at least save on, interest penalties.

You mentioned that the clients are in rented accommodation. They will have to give notice to their landlord to terminate the tenancy and they should check the terms of their tenancy agreement. We should advise them not to give notice of termination however until they have a binding contract to purchase 10 Eldon Place; otherwise they could find themselves homeless.

A stamp duty saving may be possible if the purchase price is apportioned between the price for the house and the price for the chattels. *Ad valorem* stamp duty land tax of 1% of the purchase price is payable where the price of the land exceeds £60,000, but no duty is payable where the price does not exceed £60,000. Moreover, no stamp duty land tax is payable on the sale of chattels at all. You say the clients believe the value of the chattels to be £2,000. Provided this is a true valuation an apportionment can properly be made to bring the price of the house down to £60,000. Care must be taken however for if £2,000 represents an overvaluation of the chattels, the avoidance of stamp duty land tax would amount to a fraud on the Inland Revenue both by the clients and ourselves. In this event the contract for the sale of the land would be construed as a contract to defraud the Inland Revenue and as such would be unenforceable by action (*Saunders v. Edwards* [1987] 2 All ER 651).

Any reduction in the purchase price of the property should be reported to and first approved by the clients' prospective mortgagee. It is a requirement of the CML Lenders' Handbook that the mortgagee must be informed if the purchase price for the property is different from that set out in the mortgage instructions. In any event we should check the terms of the mortgage offer and instructions carefully and ensure we comply with them fully.

Finally, we must give them appropriate advice regarding the likely costs and expenses of the transaction, including stamp duty land tax, search fees and Land Registry fees. In addition, client care and complaints procedures should be adhered to, pursuant to r. 15 of the Solicitors' Practice Rules 1990.

Question 4

Your firm has recently been instructed to act for Stuart Rush and his wife Harriet Rush in the sale of 'Saxifrage' and the related purchase of 'Bentley Lodge'. Your principal has passed you the two files from which you note the following:

(a) The sale price of Saxifrage is £175,000.

(b) The purchase price of Bentley Lodge is £185,000.

(c) The clients have an endowment mortgage on Saxifrage securing a loan of £120,000.

(d) The clients have received a mortgage offer on Bentley Lodge of £130,000. There is a retention of £30,000 on the mortgage advance until essential repairs have been carried out to the roof and chimney stacks.

(e) The clients wish to complete the purchase before the sale as Harriet's mother lives with them and they wish to carry out the repairs before they all move.

(f) The clients' bank has offered them a bridging loan of £30,000 to enable them to complete the purchase before the sale.

(g) The bank will only release the bridging loan upon receipt of a solicitor's undertaking to pay the net sale proceeds of Saxifrage to the bank.

(h) The estate agents' particulars relating to Saxifrage have arrived in this morning's post.

1. What advice will you give your clients in respect of their proposed financial arrangements and what factors should you consider before you give any undertaking to the bank? (10 marks)

2. Explain briefly whether Harriet's mother has an overriding interest within the meaning of the Land Registration Act 2002 and what effect, if any, this may have on the sale. (6 marks)

Commentary

The first part is an example of a Property Law and Practice question that involves a simple calculation of figures (calculator not essential!) and it will assist you and the marker, if you jot down a brief financial statement in your answer book before you start.

Conveyancing clients often arrive in the office armed with an inaccurate financial plan and it is essential that you check their figures carefully. The obvious point must be made that every conveyancer should at the stage of taking instructions check that the client has sufficient funds available not only to complete but also to cover all costs and expenses. You will notice the question states that estate agents are involved, so their commission will obviously be payable on the sale.

The clients are selling and buying and the two transactions are dependent upon each other so, even though the proposed completion dates are different, it is essential to synchronise exchange of contracts. If you hint in your answer at an exchange on one property before the other, the examiner will think you have misunderstood your clients' needs.

The question of the undertaking introduces another professional conduct issue and one of critical importance to property lawyers. You should be aware that professional undertakings turn up time and time again in subject assessments, so be prepared for them.

The second part of the question is more academic in nature and requires a good understanding of the Land Registration Act 2002. There are only six marks allocated so it is important to be concise in your answer.

Suggested answer

1. Before considering our advice, it may be helpful to prepare a brief financial statement:

Sale price	175,000
less mortgage redemption	120,000
sale proceeds	55,000

Purchase price	185,000
less net mortgage advance	100,000
	85,000
sale proceeds	55,000
add bridging loan	30,000
	85,000

At first glance the calculations appear to be correct, but a careful analysis of the clients' instructions will reveal that they have overlooked the following matters:

(a) The amount required to redeem the Saxifrage mortgage will not be exactly £120,000. This is the initial loan and does not take into account any outstanding interest charges, administration fees or redemption penalties. We must obtain an up to date redemption figure. (As the mortgage is an endowment rather than a repayment, the principal sum will not have been reduced.)

(b) We are told there are estate agents on the sale so the clients will be liable to pay their commission + VAT.

(c) They must pay 1% stamp duty land tax on the purchase (£1,850).

(d) They must pay legal fees on the sale and purchase, plus VAT and disbursements (e.g. Land Registry and search fees). They must also pay their surveyor's fee.

(e) The bridging loan will incur interest charges and probably an arrangement fee.

In the light of the above, the clients should be advised that the net sale proceeds of Saxifrage will be insufficient to repay the bridging loan. We cannot advise them to proceed unless they can increase their bridging loan or find additional funds. An alternative solution would be to try and negotiate a reduction in the purchase price of Bentley Lodge.

We would advise the clients that they will need to fund the 10% deposit on the purchase, payable on exchange of contracts. We could seek to utilise the deposit we receive on the sale (this is permitted under a contract incorporating the standard conditions of sale), but this would still leave a shortfall of £1,000. The clients would have to find this from their own resources or seek a further bridging loan. Alternatively, the owners of Bentley Lodge could be asked to accept a reduced deposit.

Saxifrage appears to be the clients' principal private dwelling house but if this is not the case then they must be advised of their potential liability to CGT.

In the event of the bridging loan proceeding we must consider several matters before giving an undertaking to the bank. Breach of a solicitor's undertaking is professional misconduct and will result in disciplinary action.

(a) Can we trust the clients and are they creditworthy?

(b) The clients must give us an express and irrevocable authority in writing to give the undertaking.

(c) Our undertaking should be in writing and signed by a partner.

(d) We must be sure that we can comply absolutely with the terms of the undertaking. To this end, the wording must be clear, unambiguous and wholly capable of performance by our firm.

(e) Are we satisfied that the anticipated net sale proceeds will be sufficient to discharge the bridging finance plus interest?

(f) In our undertaking we would state the sale price and itemise the anticipated deductions (e.g. mortgage redemption, agent's commission, legal fees, etc.) to calculate the approximate net proceeds of sale.

(g) As the undertaking is one to pay money, we would make it clear in the wording that payment by us of the net sale proceeds of Saxifrage will be made only if and when the sale proceeds are received by our firm. This safeguards against the possibility of us never receiving the proceeds of sale (e.g. because of client bankruptcy), but still being obliged to repay the bank.

(h) Ideally, the undertaking should not be given until after exchange of contracts. However as the clients will require a synchronised exchange we would in practice give it shortly before the point of exchange provided there are no unresolved problems.

2. In general terms overriding interests are interests which bind a transferee of registered land even though that they are not recorded on the register of title.

The categories of overriding interest in registered land are laid down in Sch. 3 of the Land Registration Act 2002. These were listed previously in s. 70(1) of the Land Registration Act 1925 which is now repealed. Paragraph 2 of Sch. 3 protects an interest belonging at the time of the disposition to a person in actual occupation. However importantly it does not offer protection (a) where the person's occupation would not have been obvious on a reasonably careful inspection of the land at the time of the disposition, or (b) where the transferee has actual knowledge of the interest. On the facts of this question we would require more information to assess whether these exceptions would apply here.

Although Harriet's mother is clearly in 'actual occupation', it should be noted that overriding interests do not apply to purely personal rights in the land, only proprietary interests which are capable of being overriding (see *Strand Securities Ltd v. Woosey* [1965] Ch 958). Thus if Harriet's mother has contributed towards the purchase price of Saxifrage (or any subsequent improvement), she would have acquired a beneficial interest under a trust (a proprietary interest) which would be capable of protection as an overriding interest (see *William & Glyn's Bank Ltd v. Boland* [1981] AC 487 where a wife contributed to the purchase price and became a beneficiary under a resulting trust of the land). But if Harriet's mother has not acquired a proprietary interest in the property then, notwithstanding her occupation, she cannot have an overriding interest.

Even if Harriet's mother has an overriding interest, it will be noted from a reading of Sch. 3, para. 2(b) of the 2002 Act that her interest will be defeated if the proposed buyer asks her what rights she has and she fails to disclose them when she could reasonably have been expected to do so. In order for this to occur the buyer must enquire directly of her. It is insufficient merely for the buyer to raise an enquiry with the registered proprietors (see *Hodgson v. Marks* [1971] Ch 892 per Russell LJ).

The mother's interest (if any) may also be defeated in another way, stemming from the fact that the property is held under a trust of land by two trustees. The house is registered in the joint names of her daughter and son-in-law and so a sale by them as trustees would overreach any equitable interest she may have acquired, and in this event her right of occupation would cease (see *City of London Building Society v. Flegg* [1988] AC 54).

Finally it should be noted that if Saxifrage has an unregistered title, Sch. 1 (not Sch. 3) of the 2002 Act is relevant. On first registration, Sch. 1 para. 2 protects simply 'an interest belonging to a person in actual occupation, so far as relating to land of which he is in actual occupation, except for an interest under a settlement under the Settled Land Act 1925'. Unlike with registered land there are no further qualifications as mentioned above.

2.3.2 MULTIPLE CHOICE QUESTIONS AND ANSWERS

We set out below examples of ten multiple choice questions that you might encounter in a subject assessment. Answers to these are set out in 2.3.3 below. Remember our initial guidance. Never leave multiple choice answers with a blank. If there are four possibilities and you are not sure of the answer select the one you think might be right; after all, you have a one in four chance of getting it right! Also look at the instructions on the paper. If it says select the right answer on the paper by circling the correct choice then do just that. Do not make a tick or underline your selection as the strict response would be to fail you even though the selection may be correct. Think carefully before selecting your answer and have correcting fluid to hand just in case you make a mistake or change your mind. To assist you, we have given brief explanations for the answers but generally this is not something you will be required to do (unless your exam paper says so!).

2.3.2.1 **Multiple choice questions**

Unless otherwise directed, select the right answer by circling it in each question. Should you think that none of the selections apply please explain why not in your answer book.

1. In which of the following circumstances can you NOT act for both parties in an arm's length conveyancing transaction where there is clearly no conflict between the parties involved:

   (a) both parties are established clients

   (b) the consideration is £10,000 or less

   (c) there is no other qualified conveyancer in the vicinity who can reasonably be consulted

   (d) the parties agree together in writing to instruct you

2. On a sale of registered freehold, which of the following is the seller obliged to supply to the buyer under the Land Registration Act 2002 and/or Land Registration Rules 2003:

   (a) copy of title plan

   (b) evidence of overriding interests known to the seller

   (c) copy of a conveyance containing restrictive covenants noted on the charges register

   (d) official copies of entries on the register

3. The Land Registration Act 2002 does NOT stipulate that first registration must take place within two months of completion of which of the following:

   (a) a conveyance on sale of a freehold estate

   (b) a grant of a new lease for a term of more than seven years

   (c) an assignment on sale of an existing lease where the term left to run is six years at completion

   (d) a first mortgage protected by deposit of title deeds

4. It is generally accepted that a solicitor should not give mortgage advice to a client because of the risk of contravening the Financial Services and Markets Act 2000.

   Is this statement TRUE/FALSE? Please delete the incorrect choice.

5. A registered lease with a good leasehold title means that:

   (a) the registration is such that there is no guarantee that the lease has been validly granted

   (b) the registration is such that there is a qualified guarantee that the lease has been validly granted

   (c) the registration is such that there is a lease that has been validly granted for a term of more than seven years

   (d) the registration is such that there is no lease plan to scale and that the lease has therefore not been validly granted

6. You have a client who owns and lives in a large house and garden extending to 1.5 hectares. It has been his family home for the last seven years. He wishes to sell off half, being the bottom of the garden, to a company developer for a small high-class housing estate. Which of the following will apply for tax purposes:

   (a) the sale is exempt from capital gains tax

   (b) the sale is not exempt from capital gains tax

   (c) the sale is subject to income tax

   (d) the sale is subject to corporation tax

7. A young married couple wishing to buy their first home instruct you to act for them. They are each contributing £5,000 and a mortgage advance will fund the rest of the purchase price. Generally, how will you advise them to hold the beneficial ownership in the property:

   (a) as legal and equitable co-owners

   (b) as tenants in common

   (c) as licensees

   (d) as joint tenants

8. You act for the purchaser of a 200-year-old cottage. Your client is buying with the aid of a building society mortgage. The survey you will recommend is:

   (a) the one suggested by the building society as being appropriate for this type of property

   (b) a full structural survey

   (c) a valuation report

   (d) a home buyer's valuation and survey report

9. In registered land the appropriate method of protecting a beneficial interest under an implied trust is to register a:

   (a) caution

   (b) charge

   (c) notice

   (d) restriction

10. Smith and Jones own adjoining unregistered properties. Smith claims that he is the true owner of a small strip of land just inside Jones's boundary. Smith, in order to protect his claim, would be advised to lodge at Land Registry a caution against first registration against Jones's title.

    Is this statement TRUE/FALSE? Please delete the incorrect choice.

2.3.2.2 *Answers to multiple choice questions (with brief explanations)*

1. The correct answer is (d). The first three are all exceptions to r. 6 of the Solicitors Practice Rules 1990 which prohibits a solicitor from acting for seller and buyer in the same arm's length transaction. Option (d) is not an exception but an additional requirement, i.e. the parties must also agree in writing that the same solicitor may act for them.

2. The correct answer is none! Under the old s. 110 of the Land Registration Act 1925 the seller was obliged to supply evidence of title. However there is no such requirement under the new legislation and the parties are free to make their own contractual arrangements.

3. The correct answer is (c). Under the Land Registration Act 2002 the grant of a lease of more than seven years is compulsorily registrable (formerly twenty-one years). Similarly the assignment of a lease with more than seven years to run is also compulsorily registrable. In option (c) the lease that is assigned has *less* than seven years to run.

4. The statement is false. A solicitor may give generic mortgage advice provided he or she does not give advice about a specific investment product. So for example, advising on the merits or otherwise of repayment, endowment or pension mortgages is fine. But advising a client to take up a mortgage linked to a pension with say, Standard Life as opposed to Norwich Union is not allowed (unless, unusually, the solicitor is authorised by the Financial Services Authority to give mainstream investment advice).

5. The correct answer is (a). This is a fairly straightforward question concerning the characteristics of a good leasehold title, but be sure to read it carefully—the word 'no' in option (a) is crucial.

6. The correct answer is (b). The principal private dwelling exemption for CGT does not apply here because the grounds being sold exceed half a hectare. Do not be drawn towards corporation tax simply because you see the word 'company'. Remember that it is the seller who prima facie pays CGT on the disposal of an interest in land.

7. The correct answer is (d). Only options (b) or (d) are relevant on these facts. As the couple are married and are contributing in equal shares, a joint tenancy is appropriate. You will however have explained to them the differences between a joint tenancy and a tenancy in common and have taken their instructions on the matter. Note the word 'generally' in the question. Occasionally married couples prefer to hold as tenants in common but generally this is not the case.

8. The correct answer is (b). This is a very straightforward question. The fact that the property is over 100 years old means you must recommend a full structural survey notwithstanding the extra cost involved. Note that the question asks for your recommendation—ultimately it will be up to the client to choose what to do. Be careful not to be drawn to option (a). Remember that the mortgagee is only interested in establishing that the value of the property is adequate security for the proposed loan.

9. The correct answer is (d). Remember that cautions against dealings have been abolished under the Land Registration Act 2002 and it is not possible to protect a beneficial interest by notice. The appropriate entry is a restriction in the proprietorship register. Before the Land Registration Act 2002 it was possible to lodge a caution to protect such an interest.

10. The statement is true. This is the purpose of cautions against first registration. They are designed to protect third party claims against unregistered titles and Land Registry will not register the land until the claim is settled. The weaker student might select 'false' on the basis that Land Registry is not concerned with unregistered title, but this is not the case here.

2.3.3 SHORT ANSWER QUESTIONS

Question 1

Mrs Megan Falenta is an established client of your firm and has made an appointment to see you regarding her proposed sale and a related purchase. You note from the official copies of the sale property that she and her husband Derek are registered as joint proprietors. She has told your secretary that she and her husband are divorcing and has asked whether it would be acceptable for your firm to act for them both on the sale. She has already received a mortgage offer on her purchase and so does not require any mortgage advice.

What key matters will you discuss with her in the interview?

Question 2

Your firm acts for a new client, Rachael Fletcher in her proposed purchase of freehold shop premises at 28 Longhurst Way, Fulham at a price of £300,000, subject to contract. You are a trainee solicitor with the firm. Following your general advice when taking instructions, Rachael has applied for a commercial loan and has told you that the balance of the purchase price will be coming from her savings. This morning your firm's cashier tells you that Rachael has just handed in £30,000 in cash in respect of the 10% deposit payable on exchange. Discuss.

Question 3

You act for Alicia Burrell, a new client who is buying with the aid of a repayment mortgage a leasehold flat, 13A Sandhurst Gardens London NW3. The purchase price is £275,000. The transaction is the assignment of an existing lease, which was granted four years ago and has 95 years left to run. The lease has a registered title. The National Protocol is being used. A graduate student is starting with your firm next week for some work experience. He has not studied law and so is unfamiliar with the conveyancing process. To assist him as he follows the progress of this file, you have been asked to list for him chronologically the key stages in the transaction.

2.3.3.1 *Suggested answers to short answer questions*

Question 1

This is a fairly straightforward question on taking instructions but you need to tailor your answer carefully to the facts. Do not write everything you know about the subject but confine your answer to relevant matters. One complication here is the client's impending divorce. Do not be put off by this, as you are not being tested on family law! However you will need to think through the conveyancing ramifications.

To begin with you are told that Megan is an established client so there is no need for you to give full client care advice or to verify her identity. However inform her that you will have the day to day running of the files and give her the name of the partner with overall responsibility. Note down her contact details, e.g., telephone number, and details of the estate agents involved. Ask her to confirm the agreed sale and, purchase price, whether she has paid any preliminary deposit and whether other terms have been agreed, e.g. sale of chattels. Inform her of your firm's fees plus VAT and any other relevant expenses, such as stamp duty land tax. Ask whether anyone else, apart from her and her husband, occupies the sale property. You could give her the Property Information Form for her to complete and return.

Explain that as her husband is joint proprietor you would need him to confirm that he wishes to proceed with the sale (remember the conduct rule that you must not receive instructions through a third party, in this case Megan). There appears to be no conflict of interest in acting for Derek on the sale provided both husband and wife are in agreement. He will no doubt be instructing his own solicitors in connection with the divorce and you will be in touch with his divorce solicitors regarding the distribution of his agreed share of the sale proceeds. His firm may indeed confirm on his behalf that he is happy for you to act on the sale.

As Megan has a related purchase you will ensure that the sale and purchase are synchronised so that exchange of contracts and then completion occur simultaneously. In particular you will ensure that Megan's financial arrangements are in order. She must have sufficient funds from her share of the proceeds and her new mortgage to finance the purchase (including costs, stamp duty, etc.). However this may be difficult given that her share of the sale proceeds will be determined only once the divorce settlement has been agreed. Prepare a brief financial statement for her in respect of both sale and purchase and give her an indication of any likely shortfall she must find in order to complete.

Tell her you will write to her existing mortgagee, requesting the deeds and asking for confirmation of the loan currently outstanding. Ask her for the mortgage account or roll number, which you will need to mention in your letter. On the purchase, establish the age of the property and give appropriate advice on survey. On the sale, check that the principal private dwelling exemption applies for CGT purposes.

Conclude the interview by informing her of the next steps and that you will be writing to confirm your advice. Give her some indication of how long the whole conveyancing process is likely to take (on average about two months).

Question 2

This question concerns the dangers of possible money laundering when taking instructions and subsequently when acting for a client in a property transaction. It is important that you or your firm do not assist unwittingly in the laundering of proceeds of any crime. Solicitors must be aware of the Criminal Justice Act 1993, the Proceeds of Crime Act 2002 and the Money Laundering Regulations 2003 and your firm must take the steps required by the Regulations to ensure that it cannot be used by money launderers. The firm should have in place a recognised procedure for obtaining satisfactory evidence of the identity of its clients.

As Rachael is a new client, you should in the first interview have verified her identity by inspecting her passport and keeping a copy for your file.

One sign of possible money laundering is a client who asks you to hold large sums of cash on her behalf and this has occurred here. Your firm will have appointed a partner to whom staff can report suspicions of money laundering. The partner will be responsible for making decisions on whether to report any suspicion to the appropriate authority, the National Criminal Intelligence Unit (NICS). It is not for you the trainee solicitor personally to make this decision.

It is a criminal offence for a firm to fail to disclose to the authorities knowledge or suspicion of others involved in money laundering. This is an exception to the normal solicitor/client confidentiality rule. It is also an offence to 'tip off' the client by telling her that your suspicions are being reported. You should therefore report the matter to the partner responsible and say nothing to the client at this stage. There may be a perfectly innocent explanation as to why Rachael has given you the cash but the nominated reporting partner must investigate it further and seek guidance from the NICS as to whether the cash can be paid into the firm's client account.

Question 3

This question tests your knowledge of the conveyancing process as a whole but expects you to be concise. Although it is a leasehold transaction, the stages in the conveyancing process are essentially no different from a freehold transaction, but with some added refinements. Do not make the mistake of writing about the contents of a lease or the possible defects in a lease. All that is required is a list of the essential conveyancing steps. Remember that this is a *short* answer so just use a bullet list—there will be insufficient time or marks available for a lengthy disposition on leasehold conveyancing!

Key stages in the purchase of 13A Sandhurst Gardens London NW3

- Take instructions—various matters to cover. As this is a new client, full client care advice must be given.
- Receive from seller's solicitors: the draft contract, official copies, copy lease and property information forms (including the leasehold form and the fixtures and fittings form).
- Study the official copies and possibly raise requisitions if necessary.
- Consider the property information forms and raise any queries or further enquiries where necessary.
- Make all appropriate pre-contract searches and consider results. Follow up any adverse matters.
- Study the lease for any defects having particular regard to the requirements of the CML Lenders' Handbook. Check whether the lessor's consent to the proposed assignment is necessary.
- Approve draft contract.
- Receive mortgage offer and check conditions.
- If required, ensure seller has obtained lessor's consent to the proposed assignment.
- Report to client in writing.
- Client to sign contract and give us her deposit cheque which must be cleared before exchange.
- Exchange contracts and agree completion date.
- Carry out pre-completion searches.
- Draft transfer deed.
- Draft mortgage deed.
- Send to seller's solicitors the completion information and requisitions on title questionnaire. Consider replies.
- Prepare bill and send it with financial statement to client. Obtain any required funds from client.
- Client to execute mortgage.
- Request mortgage advance from lender.

- Complete the purchase.

- Pay stamp duty land tax of 3% (£8,250).

- Give notice of assignment and mortgage to lessor (if required by lease).

- Register transfer and mortgage at Land Registry. No charge certificate will be issued.

- Forward original lease and other documents to mortgagee (check mortgagee's requirements).

2.4 REFERENCES TO WIDER READING INCLUDING PRACTITIONER TEXTS

- *A Practical Approach to Conveyancing* by Abbey R. and Richards M. (6th edn, OUP)—Chapter 1 (Introduction) and Chapter 2 (Taking Instructions and Other Initial Matters).

- *The Law Society's Conveyancing Handbook 10th edn*, by Silverman F.—Section A Dealing with Preliminary Conveyancing Matters.

- Generally—the *Law Society's Guide to the Professional Conduct of Solicitors*

- Ruoff and Roper Registered Conveyancing (Sweet and Maxwell)

- *Blackstone's Guide to The Land Registration Act 2002* by Abbey R. and Richards M. (OUP).

- *Textbook on Land Law* by MacKenzie J. A. and Phillips M. (9th edn, OUP)—Chapter 4 (Unregistered Land) and Chapter 5 (Registered Land).

- Emmet on Title: Chapters 1 and 9.

2.5 RELEVANT WEBSITES FOR MORE INFORMATION

- Acts of Parliament, http://www.hmso.gov.uk/acts.htm
  Keep up to date with statutory developments.

- Council of Mortgage Lenders, http://www.cml.org.uk
  There is an on-line version of the CML Lenders' Handbook available at this site and it should be referred to in cases of doubt about lenders' requirements.

- Financial Services Authority, http://www.fsa.gov.uk
  Obtain information on all aspects of financial regulation in the UK.

- Land Registry, http://www.landreg.gov.uk
  Further information on the Land Registration Act 2002 and the Land Registration Rules 2003.

- Law Society, http://www.lawsoc.org.uk

- National Association of Estate Agents, http://www.naea.co.uk

3 | THE DRAFT CONTRACT

3.1 INTRODUCTION

The draft contract is an enduring favourite with property law examiners and you can almost guarantee a question on it in some shape or form. The classic approach is for the examiner to reproduce a defective draft and ask the student to amend and explain; Standard question 1 follows this line. Another popular technique is to present a set of facts, similar to those in standard question 2, and ask the student to actually draft the contract. Standard forms of contract will normally be provided but often you will be asked just to draft the special conditions.

Since the introduction of the National Protocol, the form of contract most commonly used is the Law Society standard form incorporating the Standard Conditions of Sale (4th edition); indeed this must be utilised by the seller and buyer where the Protocol is being adopted. Accordingly you would do well to familiarise yourself with the contents of the form, including the standard conditions. Fortunately these days it is unlikely that you will be expected to recite the standard conditions parrot-fashion, but it is vital that you at least know your way around them and understand the points they cover. This will help you not only on this topic but throughout the Property Law and Practice course. The following standard conditions are of particular importance: 2.2 (the deposit),

3.4 (retained land on sales of part), 4.1 (proof of title), 4.6 (the Transfer), 5.1 (responsibility for property pending completion), 6 (completion) and 7 (remedies).

A contract for the sale of part of land is more complex than a contract for the sale of whole, and an example of the type of question you might encounter is set out in standard question 3. It is good practice to prepare and learn a checklist of the essential matters that may be relevant on a sale of part. Ask yourself the following questions: How will I describe the part being sold? (A plan is nearly always essential.) What new grant of easements will the buyer need? What new reservation of easements will the seller need? What new covenants should be imposed? Will the seller's mortgagee consent to the sale? These are all important matters you should consider when preparing for questions on the draft contract.

In commercial conveyancing you are likely to become involved with contracts that are different from the conventional unconditional contract, such as conditional contracts or option agreements. Standard question 4 considers these types of contracts.

3.2 AN OVERVIEW OF THE SUBJECT AND A LOOK AT SOME PROBLEM AREAS

Acting for the seller you will draft the contract and send it in duplicate to the buyer's practitioner. Before drafting the contract you should obtain the seller's title deeds and, if the title is registered, apply for official copies from Land Registry. The title to the property should be checked carefully. This is to ensure primarily that the seller's duty of disclosure is satisfied because you have to disclose any encumbrances in the contract. In addition, you must also check that the seller actually owns the legal estate and/or is otherwise entitled to sell it. You can also check for any discrepancies on the title plan, e.g. if any land is missing from it. Investigating your own client's title will enable you to identify any defects in the title and to anticipate (and hopefully remedy) the questions (or requisitions) which the buyer's practitioner is likely to raise.

3.2.1 OCCUPIERS AND TENANCIES

Be careful to check who occupies the property. This is important because, to fulfil a contractual obligation to give vacant possession, the seller must be satisfied before contracts are exchanged that all occupiers will vacate the property on or before the contractual completion date. In respect of a non-owning spouse or other adult occupier, always obtain a written release of any rights in the property together with an agreement to vacate. The spouse or other occupier must be informed that their rights may be affected by giving such consent and that they should obtain independent advice from another practitioner before signing the release.

If the property is to be sold subject to tenancies, full details of these must be disclosed in the contract. Standard condition 3.3 deals with leases affecting the property. It says that the seller is obliged to provide full particulars of lettings with copies of any documents relating thereto so as to ensure the buyer enters into the contract 'knowing and fully accepting those terms'. To give effect to this provision the seller should supply, with the draft contract, a copy of any relevant lease or tenancy agreement along with any deeds or documents that are supplementary to them, such as a deed of variation. The seller must inform the buyer of any lease or tenancy termination after exchange but before completion, as well as to act as the buyer reasonably directs, with the buyer indemnifying the seller against any consequent loss or damage. Similarly, the conditions prohibit the seller from agreeing any changes to the lease terms and require the seller to advise the buyer of any proposed or agreed changes. If there are tenants but the property is to be sold with vacant possession then the seller must take steps to terminate the tenancies.

3.2.2 SELLER'S DUTY OF DISCLOSURE

The seller is obliged to disclose in the contract all latent encumbrances and defects in title (see *Faruqi v. English Real Estates Ltd* [1979] 1 WLR 963 and standard condition 3.1). This duty does not extend to physical defects in the property to which *caveat emptor* (let the buyer beware) applies. However, wilful concealment of a physical defect may give rise to a claim in the tort of deceit (*Gordon v. Selico Co. Ltd* [1986] 1 EGLR 71, which concerned the covering up of dry rot). A breach of the seller's duty of disclosure will normally permit the buyer to rescind the contract and claim damages.

A latent encumbrance is one which is not apparent from an inspection of the property (a restrictive covenant is an example of a latent encumbrance). However, there is some doubt about the precise meaning of 'latent'. In *Yandle and Sons v. Sutton* [1922] 2 Ch 199 a right of way across land was held to be a latent encumbrance that the seller should have disclosed. The seller's conveyancer will therefore ensure that all non-physical defects and encumbrances which are known to the seller are disclosed in the contract. This includes matters apparent from an inspection of the title deeds, thus underlining the importance of a full title investigation by the seller's conveyancer.

3.2.3 FORMALITIES

Section 2 of the Law of Property (Miscellaneous Provisions) Act 1989 lays down the requirements for the creation of land contracts created on or after 27 September 1989. It provides that the contract must be in writing and incorporate all the agreed terms, either in one document or by reference to another document. The written contract must be signed by or on behalf of each party to the contract, although where contracts are to be exchanged, both sides need sign only their respective parts, not both parts.

3.2.4 CONTRACT RACES

A contract race arises when a seller decides to deal with more than one prospective buyer, thus creating a 'race' by the buyers to see who can secure the property by being first to exchange contracts. A contract race raises an issue of professional conduct for the seller's practitioner, who must comply with the Solicitors' Practice Rules 1990, r. 6A. This rule states that, provided your client consents, you must immediately inform the practitioners acting for each buyer (or the buyer direct if acting in person) of your client's decision, if possible by telephone or fax. Telephone conversations must be confirmed by letter or fax. If the seller refuses to consent to the disclosure, you must immediately cease to act for the seller.

3.2.5 CONTENTS OF THE CONTRACT

As well as the formal parts, that is, names and addresses of the parties, the contract will comprise the particulars of sale and the conditions of sale. The particulars describe the physical extent of the property being sold and its tenure, i.e. freehold or leasehold. The property may be described using a simple postal address, provided the land is easily identifiable from it. If not, a more detailed description is necessary, referring to a scale plan and/or measurements. (This applies particularly on a sale of part of an existing title where a new description will be required.) For registered land the description in the property register of the title can be used and the title number quoted, together with the class of title (absolute, good leasehold, etc.). For unregistered land the description in the previous conveyance to the seller can usually be used, although its accuracy should always be verified. A misdescription may of course entitle the buyer to rescind the contract or seek an abatement in the purchase price.

Due to the complexity of the common law rules concerning land contracts (known as the 'open contract rules'), property lawyers have devised their own standardised general conditions of sale. These are periodically updated, and the current edition is the 4th edition of the Standard Conditions of Sale, which is reproduced in Appendix 3.3. There is also a set of conditions for commercial property known as the Standard Commercial Property Conditions. The general conditions cover a variety of areas, such as time limits for submission and approval of the draft purchase deed, proof of title and remedies.

In addition, there are special conditions that are specific to the transaction in question. If the parties agree to delete or modify a general condition, this is done by an appropriate special condition (e.g. 'standard condition 5.1 shall not apply'). Some special conditions almost invariably apply in every transaction and for convenience they are printed on the last page of the Law Society standard form of contract (see Appendix 3.3). It should be noted that one of the alternatives in special condition 4 must be deleted depending on whether the property is to be sold with vacant possession or subject to tenancies. In every transaction the practitioner must consider whether any additional special conditions are necessary, over and above those on the printed form. This is particularly so in sales of part of an existing title where the parties often agree to create new easements and covenants, the precise terms of which should properly be expressed in the special conditions (see below).

3.2.6 DEPOSIT

The deposit, payable on exchange of contracts, is normally 10% of the purchase price, (although the parties sometimes agree less). The standard conditions provide for the deposit to be held as stakeholder except where the seller before completion agrees to buy another property in England or Wales for his residence (i.e. the seller has a related purchase). In this situation the seller may use all or any part of the sale deposit as a deposit on the related purchase provided it is used only for this purpose (standard condition 2.2.5). Effectively this permits a deposit to be passed along a chain of transactions and assists the operation of a telephonic exchange under Law Society formula C (see Chapter 6).

The buyer should be wary of allowing the deposit to be held as agent for the seller. This would mean that once exchange has taken place the seller's practitioner is free to release the deposit to the seller. But if this occurs, there is inherent risk for the buyer if the seller defaults. This is because although the buyer will be legally entitled to the return of the deposit if the seller defaults, the buyer may have practical difficulty in actually recovering the deposit from the seller (for instance because the seller is bankrupt or cannot be traced).

3.2.7 COMPLETION AND CONTRACT RATES

Where your client has a related sale and purchase you should seek to ensure that the agreed completion dates for both transactions are the same. If synchronisation is not possible the client must be advised in writing of the implications, financial or otherwise. By completing the sale first the client may have to move into temporary accommodation and incur other expenses such as furniture storage fees. By completing the purchase first the client will almost certainly require a bridging loan and the consent of the buyer's mortgagee.

If the seller has met all deadlines during the transaction and the buyer fails to pay the balance of the purchase price on the contractual completion date, the buyer will be liable to pay the seller interest on the amount outstanding. Interest is calculated at the 'contract rate' specified in the contract (normally 4% above the base rate of a high street bank). Care must be exercised where the client has a related sale and purchase. The practitioner should ensure that the contract rate in the purchase contract is no higher than the contract rate in the sale contract. Imagine a situation in which the contract rate on the sale is 4% above base while the contract rate on the purchase is 5% above base. If the client is dependent on the sale proceeds to finance the purchase but the client's buyer completes late, the client will as a consequence be forced to complete the purchase late. The compensation the client has to pay under the purchase contract will be 1% more than the compensation receivable under the sale contract; the client will therefore be out of pocket.

3.2.8 TITLE GUARANTEE

The seller must decide whether to give a full title guarantee, a limited title guarantee or no title guarantee at all. The importance of the title guarantee is that covenants for title on the part of the seller are implied into the purchase deed. By definition, a limited guarantee will imply less extensive covenants for title than a full guarantee, and no guarantee will imply none. A full title guarantee is given normally where the seller owns the whole legal and equitable interest in the property. A limited title guarantee is given normally where the legal owner/seller is a personal representative, or a trustee holding on trust for others. It is usual to give no title guarantee where the seller has little or no knowledge of the property or the title history, or if the disposition is by way of gift.

3.2.9 INDEMNITY COVENANTS

Under privity of contract, an owner of land may continue to be liable under a covenant affecting the land even after the control of the land has passed to someone else, namely, the buyer or buyer's successor in title. In this situation the seller's practitioner must ensure that the buyer gives the seller an indemnity covenant against any future breaches of the covenant because the seller could in future be sued for breach of contract. As the property continues to change hands a chain of indemnity covenants will be built up between successors in title.

Standard condition 4.6.4 provides that if, after completion, the seller will remain bound by any obligation affecting the property, the buyer will indemnify the seller against any future breach as well as perform the obligation. The indemnity covenant itself is given in the purchase deed. To determine whether your client seller requires an indemnity from the buyer, you need to ask yourself two questions:

- Did your client previously give any new covenants,
- When your client acquired the land, did he or she give the previous owner an indemnity covenant?

You can discover the answers to these questions as follows: if the land is unregistered, simply read the covenants (if any) given by your client in the most recent conveyance, namely, the one to your client. If the land is registered, inspect the Charges Register for details of any covenants given by the proprietor (i.e. your client) and inspect the Proprietorship Register for evidence of any indemnity covenant given by the proprietor. (If the proprietor is the first registered proprietor, it may be necessary to inspect the last pre-registration conveyance, i.e. the one to the present proprietor). If the answer to either of the two questions is yes, your client seller will require an indemnity covenant from the current buyer. So when you later approve the draft purchase deed after exchange, you will have to check that the buyer's practitioner has included the indemnity covenant in the draft (see Chapter 7).

3.2.10 SALES OF PART

Sales of part are generally more complex transactions than sales of whole and special considerations apply when dealing with the draft contract. First, it will be necessary to draft an entirely new description of the land being sold off, and for this purpose reference to a plan is essential. The plan should be of sufficient size and scale to enable the boundaries to be easily identified. Convention dictates that the land being sold should be edged red on the plan, while the land being retained by the seller (normally defined in the contract as 'the retained land') should be edged blue. Other features should also be clearly marked so that, for instance, if a right of way is being granted or reserved, the route would be shown by a broken line of a different colour or, if appropriate, by hatching.

On a sale of part the buyer may acquire certain rights over the seller's retained land by virtue of s. 62 of the Law of Property Act 1925 and the rule in *Wheeldon v. Burrows* (1879) 12 ChD 31. As the nature and extent of these implied rights is not always clear, it is prudent for the seller's practitioner to exclude the effect of the rules and set out expressly the rights and reservations required by the parties. If implied rights of light or air were granted to the buyer, this could hinder any future plans of the seller to develop the retained land. Standard condition 3.4 provides on a sale of part for the exclusion of implied rights of light or air in favour of the buyer. The condition also provides for the mutual grant of easements and reservations on a sale of part, but the condition is not exact and should be relied upon only as a fallback, i.e. if express easements are overlooked. Ideally the special conditions in the contract should deal with these matters expressly.

The seller's practitioner should always consider the covenants, if any, that the seller may wish to impose on the buyer, for instance, regarding the future use of the land being sold off. The buyer's practitioner in turn must determine whether the seller should enter into any new covenants, e.g. not to obstruct access to the property being sold or possibly a fencing obligation.

3.2.11 OPTION AGREEMENTS

A characteristic option agreement is a contract in which the grantee of the option (the buyer) is able, within a fixed period, to serve notice on the owner requiring the latter to transfer the land to the buyer. The option is a particularly useful tool for developers wishing to acquire several pieces of land from different owners in order to develop a larger site. Once the developer has secured options over all the pieces of land, it has effectively gained control of the development site and can safely apply for planning permission. Then once planning permission is obtained the developer can exercise all the options to ensure that it owns every part of the proposed development site.

The option agreement should state that title having been deduced the grantee shall not raise any requisition or objection to it. The agreement should provide for a completion date for the purchase, e.g. ten working days after service of the buyer's notice exercising the option. The method of service of the notice should also be made clear, e.g. 'notice in writing served on the grantor on or before . . .'. As with ordinary contracts, the agreement should also provide for the incorporation of general conditions of sale, e.g. the latest Standard Commercial Property Conditions. The grantee may require a warranty from the owner that it will not encumber the land without the grantee's consent.

Owners who grant options must of course appreciate that the land will be tied up for the length of the option period and any sale of the land by the owner will be subject to the rights under the option (provided the option is registered). Consequently, an option is an estate contract and as such the grantee must protect it by registration. This is done either by lodging an agreed or unilateral notice in registered land or, in unregistered land, registering a Class C(iv) land charge. Only registration of the option will make it binding on any subsequent purchaser of the land; actual notice of the option by a subsequent purchaser will be irrelevant (*Midland Bank Trust Co. Ltd v. Green* [1981] AC 513).

3.3 SUBJECT ASSESSMENTS

There now follows some examples of assessment questions in the subject area of the draft contract. Commentary and a suggested answer accompany the standard assessment questions. These are then followed by multiple choice questions (with answers) and short answer questions with suggested answers.

3.3.1 STANDARD QUESTIONS, COMMENTARY AND SUGGESTED ANSWERS

Question 1

You act for Sandra Ince and Martin Robson both of 24 Lady Jane Court, Blakey, Cornshire. They wish to buy with vacant possession a freehold house known as 19 Minster Yard, Blakey. They have agreed with the seller a price of £190,500 subject to contract. The price includes carpets, curtains and some items of furniture. You are also acting for your clients in their related sale of 24 Lady Jane Court.

The seller of 19 Minster Yard is the Reverend Giggs, rector of Blakey. He shares the house with his aged aunt, Connie Flowers.

19 Minster Yard is registered at Land Registry with absolute title under title number CL 58372. The registered proprietors are stated as the Reverend Julian Giggs and his wife Mildred Giggs. Up to date official copies of the title do not reveal any restrictions in the proprietorship register and the charges register is blank.

Reverend Giggs has instructed Shark & Co solicitors who offer the cheapest conveyancing service in town. They have sent you the attached draft contract [refer to Appendix 3.1].

List and explain fully any amendments you would make to the draft contract.

Commentary

This question is more difficult than it seems on first reading. A sound knowledge of conveyancing practice is required not only in relation to the drafting of the contract but also in other areas such as completion and the implied covenants for title. As we mentioned in the introduction, you will also need to know your way around the Standard Conditions of Sale. Moreover, good practical skills and a mastery of detail are essential if high marks are to be obtained. Notwithstanding all this, the question will suit many of you, especially those who thrive on attention to detail and adopt a methodical approach to your work. It will appeal also to those students who have already had some practical experience of conveyancing.

We cannot emphasise enough the importance of a careful reading of the question. You will see from the suggested answer that almost every fact in the question is relevant in some way or another. Notice that the purchase is with vacant possession. Notice the significance of the dependent sale transaction in relation to the special condition dealing with the time for completion. Notice that there are no restrictions in the proprietorship register which tells you that Mr and Mrs Giggs hold the property as joint tenants not tenants in common. This is crucial because if you discuss tenancy in common considerations the examiner will know that, from an inspection of a registered title, you cannot distinguish one from the other.

Similarly a weak answer might suggest that a plan should be attached to the contract as referred to in the property description. The reference to a plan is a red herring because the title plan at Land Registry is definitive and on the sale of whole of registered land a verbal description referring to the title number will be quite sufficient.

Mrs Giggs is shown in the official copies as a joint registered proprietor so it is unlikely that she has transferred her interest in the property to her husband. You would not be penalised though, for posing the question of whether such a transfer is in the course of registration. However if you do, you would also mention that the official copies would have revealed such an application, and the question is silent on this point.

Suggested answer

1. There are some typographical errors. The buyer's name is Robson not Dobson and the seller's address is 19 Minster Yard not 19 Minster Lane. The balance of the purchase price has been incorrectly calculated and should read £171,450.

2. The seller's full name as stated on the title register should be stated, not 'Reverend Giggs'.

3. Mildred Giggs is a joint registered proprietor and on the face of it her name should be added as joint seller with her husband. As there is no restriction on the proprietorship register this indicates that Mr and Mrs Giggs hold (or held) the property as joint tenants rather than tenants in common. If Mrs Giggs has died then a copy of her death certificate will be required as evidence of Reverend Giggs' entitlement to her interest by survivorship.

4. Enquiry should be made of the aunt to establish whether she has any interest in the property, perhaps by a contribution towards the purchase price. As she is in actual occupation and the land is registered she may have an overriding interest by virtue of the Land Registration Act 2002, Sch. 3, para. 2. She should be asked to formally release any rights and confirm that she will vacate the property on completion. The following is a suggested form of wording:

    'In consideration of your today entering into a contract with Julian Giggs for the purchase of the property known as 19 Minster Yard Blakey, I Constance Flowers agree to release any equitable interest I may have in the property, such interest, if any, being transferred to the proceeds of sale of the property. I also agree to vacate the property on or before completion.'

    If it transpires that Mrs Giggs is joined with her husband as co-seller then a sale to them as trustees would overreach any equitable interest Aunt Connie might have (*City of London Building Society v. Flegg* [1988] AC 54). However this case does not guarantee that the aunt will vacate. As a matter of good practice a release in the terms above should be sought.

5. The description is wrong. The alternative of leasehold should be deleted because we are told that the land is freehold. There is no need to refer to a plan (and it is unnecessary to attach one). The property description should read simply:

    'All that land known as 19 Minster Yard Blakey registered at Land Registry with title absolute.'

6. The title number CL 58372 should be written in place of the words 'Conveyance on sale' and the alternative 'Root of title' should be deleted as the land is registered not unregistered.

7. The title guarantee has been left blank. If the seller is the beneficial owner as well as the legal owner (as appears to be the case) it is appropriate for a full title guarantee to be given and this should be inserted (note that if it is left blank a full guarantee will be given anyway by standard condition 4.6.2).

8. The completion date is not introduced until contracts are exchanged, when a specific date is inserted.

9. The contract rate of interest is unreasonably high because the Law Society interest rate is normally set at 4% above the base rate of one of the clearing banks. The effect of this clause is to put the rate at 8% above base! A fairer suggestion would be the Law Society interest rate for the time being in force

(this can be achieved by leaving the clause blank—see standard condition 1.1.1(e)) or say, 4% above the base rate of one of the clearing banks.

10. We are told that the price includes some carpets, curtains and items of furniture and these should be itemised on an attached list (see special condition 3). The Law of Property (Miscellaneous Provisions) Act 1989 s. 2 requires all agreed terms to be incorporated into the contract, failing which the contract is rendered invalid. The buyer may also wish to consider an apportionment of the purchase price between the price for the land and the price for the chattels. This will bring about a small stamp duty saving because stamp duty land tax is not payable on the cost of chattels.

11. Delete the second alternative in special condition 4 as the property is being sold with vacant possession.

12. In special condition 5 the latest time for completion is far too early where, as is the case here, the clients' purchase price is being financed by the monies they are receiving on their sale. We are unlikely to receive the completion monies on the sale in time to pay over the completion monies on the purchase by 12 noon. Our clients would thus be in breach of contract and liable to pay Reverend Giggs interest on the balance of the purchase monies at the contract rate. Unless the clients' purchaser's solicitors can be persuaded to agree in the related sale contract a completion time of earlier than 12 o'clock (which is unlikely), we should insist on the deletion of special condition 5 so that the position is governed by standard condition 6.1.2. This provides for a latest completion time of 2 p.m. Alternatively we could compromise at say, 1.30 p.m. provided we ensure that the stipulated time in our related sale contract is earlier.

13. Delete special condition 6 and state that the deposit shall be held by the seller's conveyancer's as stakeholder. This is safer for the buyer because a stakeholder deposit must remain in the seller's solicitor's bank account until completion. It should thus be easily recoverable if the seller defaults.

   If the deposit is held by the solicitor as agent for the seller then the agent is entitled to hand over the money to the seller before completion. In this event, if the seller defaults the buyer may have difficulty in recovering the deposit.

   Alternatively special condition 6 could be deleted and not replaced with anything in which case standard condition 2.2.6. would govern the position. This provides for the deposit to be held as stakeholder unless the seller intends to use it as a deposit on a related purchase of a residence in England or Wales. The various options should be explained to the clients and their instructions sought.

14. Delete the final special condition or at least qualify it. As drafted, the clause prohibits the buyer from relying on *any* representations, even replies to solicitors' pre-contract enquiries. A reasonable qualification to the clause would be the addition of the words, 'other than the written replies of the seller's solicitors to the pre-contract enquiries of the buyer's solicitors'. This is acceptable to most property practitioners.

15. Finally, details of the parties' conveyancers should be entered.

Question 2

RICHARDS ABBEY AND PARTNERS, SOLICITORS

OFFICE MEMORANDUM

To   The Trainee Solicitor

From   The Property Partner

<u>Re our client Angela Dawkins: sale of 13 Augustine Way Kerwick</u>

I have acted for the above client for many years. Sadly her husband Paul died last month. Paul's will leaves everything he owns equally between his wife Angela and Paul's brother, Kevin and we have been instructed to wind up the estate. My probate partner is dealing with this aspect.

Angela has decided to sell 13 Augustine Way and buy a two-bedroomed flat in Kerwick. The owners of the flat have secured a property to buy and the chain above them is complete.

A prospective buyer for 13 Augustine Way has been found. He is Andrew Peach of 25 Woodlands Road Kerwick. His solicitors are Messrs Young & Price of 1A High Street Kerwick (Miss P Knight acting). The agreed price is £70,000 subject to contract, plus £500 for carpets and curtains. I have told Miss Knight that we intend to use the National Protocol although I have not yet confirmed this in writing.

The deeds to 13 Augustine Way are of course held by Angela's mortgagee.

I attach a photocopy of the title entries that I made after Mr and Mrs Dawkins bought the property back in 1990 [refer to Appendix 3.2].

As you know I am away on holiday from tomorrow so please progress matters in my absence.

1. Explain the matters you would consider and what action you would take before drafting the contract. (15 marks)

2. Draft the contract using the Law Society Contract. (10 marks)

3. Draft a letter to the buyer's solicitors enclosing the draft contract and any other enclosures. Include in your letter any information or enquiries that you consider to be relevant. (10 marks)

Commentary

First of all it is important to note the allocation of marks and apportion your time accordingly when answering the question. Secondly, the question takes the form of a memo from a partner in the firm and so the answer should also take the form of a memo.

The partner has told you that the National Protocol is being used and this is a clear pointer to the matters you should be considering in answering parts 1 and 3. There is no substitute for actually reading and digesting the *current* edition of the Protocol. The word current is stressed because various changes have been made since the inception of the Protocol. In particular, the original philosophy of the seller carrying out searches on behalf of the buyer has been reversed and this shows how important it is to keep up to date with changes in conveyancing practice. Do not rely on out of date textbooks!

There is no restriction in the Proprietorship Register stating that the survivor of joint proprietors cannot deal with the property, so you should appreciate that Mr and Mrs Dawkins held as joint tenants and that Angela takes her late husband's share in the property by survivorship. The terms of his will are therefore not relevant.

Parts 2 and 3 require you to demonstrate good drafting skills and remember that marks will be awarded for style as well as content. The drafting of the contract should be relatively straightforward provided attention is paid to the details of the transaction that you have been given. You will be provided with a blank form of contract to complete. The letter to the buyer's solicitor should be easy enough for those who have practised their letter writing skills, and of course instruction in letter writing will have been covered in the skills sessions on your Legal Practice Course.

Suggested answer

RICHARDS ABBEY AND PARTNERS, SOLICITORS
OFFICE MEMORANDUM

To   The Property Partner

From   The Trainee Solicitor

Re our client Angela Dawkins: sale of 13 Augustine Way Kerwick

I refer to your memo regarding the above and respond as follows.

1. Having regard to the requirements of The National Protocol we should consider the following:

(i) Write to mortgagee and obtain deeds

The first thing we should do is write to the mortgagee, Weyford Building Society for loan of the deeds and documents of title. Our firm is likely to be on their panel of solicitors, in which case they will instruct us to act for them on the discharge of the mortgage. In our letter we should undertake to hold the deeds to the order of the Society pending repayment of the loan. If unusually we were not instructed by the Society, we would write to the Society's solicitors asking for the deeds (or copies of them).

Obviously, it is intended that the mortgage in favour of Weyford Building Society will be discharged on completion, and thus the property will not be sold subject to it. In our letter to the Society we should request confirmation of the amount required to discharge the mortgage. We must ensure that Angela is not in a negative equity situation and we should therefore check that there will be sufficient sale proceeds to repay the Building Society loan in full.

(ii) Apply for official copies of the title

The Protocol requires the seller's solicitors to supply the buyer's solicitors with up-to-date official copies of the title and title plan. We cannot use the 1990 copy entries that are on file. Accordingly we must make an application for official copies on Land Registry Form OC1.

(iii) Incumbrances on the title

The covenants created in 1924 are listed in Entry 1 of the Charges Register but the buyer will also require full details of the restrictive covenants contained in the Transfer dated 29 July 1990 (see Entry 3 in the Charges Register). We should therefore apply to Land Registry for an official copy of the Transfer on Land Registry Form OC2.

(iv) Property Information Form

We should ask Angela to complete the Property Information Form (PIF) part I and Fixtures, Fittings and Contents Form. Where the latter is provided it will form part of the contract. We should ask Angela about any target date she may have for completion. We would also ask her for any of the following in her possession: original guarantees with any accompanying specification, planning decisions and building regulation approvals. Once we have inspected the deeds and checked her answers in PIF part I for any discrepancies, we would complete PIF part II.

(v) Occupiers

We would have to be sure that we can sell the property free from any third party interests and with vacant possession. Accordingly we must ask Angela for the identity of all people aged 18 and over living in the house. We must ask about any financial contribution they or anyone else may have made towards its purchase or subsequent improvement. All persons identified in this way should be asked to confirm their consent to the sale proceeding.

(vi) Draft contract and send package to buyer's solicitors

We would draft the contract as below and submit it in duplicate for approval to the buyer's solicitors accompanied by the other items in our package recommended by the Protocol (see letter below). We should bear in mind that if it becomes necessary to depart from Protocol procedures then we must give notice to the buyer's solicitors.

If and to the extent that Angela consents to the disclosure, we would supply to the buyer's solicitors information about her own purchase and the other transactions in the chain above.

2. The suggested form of draft contract is set out in Appendix 3.3.

3. The suggested draft letter to the buyer's solicitors is as follows:

RICHARDS ABBEY AND PARTNERS, SOLICITORS

4 Red Lion Square London WC1

Partners

M.B.Richards

R.M.Abbey

Messrs Young & Price
Solicitors
1A High Street
Kerwick
Maradon
Cornshire

For the attention Miss P. Knight

Our ref: MR/TS/PP

[Date]

Dear Sirs

13 Augustine Way Kerwick

We refer to Miss Knight's recent telephone conversation with our Mr Richards and confirm that we act for the intended seller of the above property, Angela Dawkins, to your client Andrew Peach for £70,000 plus £500 for carpets and curtains.

We confirm that the National Protocol will be used in this transaction and accordingly enclose the following documents for your consideration:

1. Draft contract in duplicate,

2. Official copies of title and title plan,

3. Seller's Property Information Form duly completed with supporting documents,

4. Fixtures Fittings and Contents Form duly completed.

Our client has a related purchase, which is in its early stages, and the chain above this is complete. Our client has in mind a completion date of six weeks from today. Please let us know whether this date is convenient for your client and also your client's position on any related sale. Please confirm that you will be paying a 10% deposit on exchange.

In our Mr Richards's absence on holiday [name of trainee] will be dealing with this matter.

Yours faithfully

RICHARDS ABBEY AND PARTNERS

Question 3

RICHARDS ABBEY AND PARTNERS, SOLICITORS
INTERNAL MEMORANDUM

To   The Trainee Solicitor

From   The Property Partner

Re land to the rear of 14 Wellington Road

We act for Philip Brown of 14 Wellington Road, Midchester who has recently obtained planning permission for the building of a dwellinghouse and garage at the rear of his garden. He has decided to sell this building plot to a property developer. The area in question is approximately half a hectare. A price has been agreed, subject to contract, and he has asked us to progress the sale as soon as possible. 14 Wellington Road is freehold and registered at Land Registry with title absolute under title number MB 34857. Mr Brown bought the property back in 1981. I attach a plan that the client has given me [refer to Appendix 3.4]. The proposed boundary between the building plot and the land Mr Brown is retaining is shown by a thick black line. We will use the Law Society form of contract incorporating the Standard Conditions of Sale.

Mr Brown has given me the following specific instructions:

1. Access to the building plot will be along the client's driveway, which runs from Wellington Road along the side of his garden. Mr Brown will share the use of the driveway with the buyer of the plot. The driveway is shown hatched black on the plan.

2. The buyer of the plot can lay new drains and sewers and connect them into the client's existing drains and sewers ('the existing services'). The existing services in turn connect into the mains drainage and sewage systems in Wellington Road. The run of the existing services is shown by a broken line on the plan.

3. Once the buyer's connection is made, the buyer can share the use of the existing services and come onto Mr Brown's retained land to carry out any necessary maintenance or repairs to the services.

4. There is a greenhouse on the building plot, the position of which is indicated on the plan. Once the sale is legally binding on the buyer, Mr Brown says he will relocate it in the part of the garden he is keeping.

5. The client does not want to be overlooked, so the new building must be no more than one storey high—this is very important. Mr Brown will also want to see and approve the plans for the new property before it is built.

6. The buyer will put up a suitable fence along the boundary between the plot and the land Mr Brown is keeping, and the buyer will maintain the fence.

    (a) We will have to prepare the draft contract for approval by the buyer's solicitors. Please explain the particular matters we should consider when drafting the contract and draft the special conditions of sale that you consider will meet the requirements of both our client and the buyer. (25 Marks)

    (b) In relation to Mr Brown's proposed sale please let me have a note of any tax advice we should give him. (5 Marks)

Commentary

The crucial point to appreciate in this question is that you are acting on a sale of part and by its nature it will necessitate a more complex contract than a sale of whole. There is the need in particular to consider a new accurate description of the part being sold, the grant and reservation of easements and the imposition of new covenants. Consequently, it is an area of Property Law and Practice that finds favour with examiners.

On the Legal Practice Course you should expect some drafting questions because drafting is one of the core skills of the course. Here is one that asks you to exhibit that skill in the context of Property Law and Practice—something that may fill some of you with unease!

Ideally you will need time to go away and consult a precedent book (or computer software) and unless the examiner is feeling particularly mean, you will not face part (a) in an examination room (although don't bank on it, especially in these days of open book exams!). Generally speaking, you are more likely to find this type of question as part of a writing and drafting skills assessment, with a return date of say—two or three weeks ahead.

Before searching for the precedent or precedent clauses, always stop, and ask yourself what is the client trying to achieve? Remember that a precedent is only your guide and it will have to be adapted to suit the client's specific needs and requirements. If the precedent is in a book, take a photocopy of it and amend it after careful thought. You will rarely satisfy your client's requirements by copying slavishly word for word from a precedent.

Fortunately your instructions here are quite common in a situation where land is sold off for development and you should have covered a scenario similar to this in class. Remember that part of your job as the seller's conveyancer is to ensure that your client is adequately protected in terms of receiving the benefit of appropriate covenants and the reservation of appropriate easements. A failure to do this on your part could adversely affect your client's ability to offer a good and marketable title to prospective buyers of the retained land. So again, do not slavishly follow your client's instructions—he is not a property lawyer and doubtless will not have thought of everything. Here for example, Mr Brown does not appear to have considered that if the buyer is permitted to share the use of the driveway and existing drains, then he ought at least to share the cost of maintaining them.

As well as the seller's requirements, the question also asks you to consider the needs of the buyer. From your instructions, anticipate the easements a buyer would want and include them as well. This is courteous to the buyer's solicitor and will avoid unnecessary delay. The question also invites you to explain the relevant points so you must understand what the clauses mean and why they are necessary. Give your explanation before each draft condition—that way it is easier to mark.

Part (b) raises the topic of revenue law which of course pervades Property Law and Practice and you have already encountered it in the preceding chapter. This problem is straightforward provided you spot that the relevant tax is Capital Gains Tax. Note the significance of the area being sold ('approximately half a hectare') and also the purchase in 1981 (this affects the calculation of the gain). Do not be drawn into a discussion about stamp duty land tax—this is only payable by purchasers—and advising the clients that they will be paying VAT on your costs is astute but really misses the point! Finally, note the apportionment of marks between parts (a) and (b); the tax advice need only be brief, so stick to general principles.

Suggested answer

RICHARDS ABBEY AND PARTNERS, SOLICITORS
INTERNAL MEMORANDUM

To   The Property Partner

From   The Trainee Solicitor

Re land to the rear of Wellington Road

(a)

1. Description

As this is a sale of part it is important to describe accurately the land being sold. This will be done by adapting the existing description of 14 Wellington Road on the title register and referring to a scale plan annexed to the contract. For example,

'All that freehold land shown edged red on the plan annexed hereto ('the Plan') being part of the land known as 14 Wellington Road Midchester registered at HM Land Registry with title absolute under title number MB 34857'

The land being retained by the client should also be described accurately in the contract by reference to blue edging on the plan. It should be defined as 'the Retained Land'.

2. Negate implied grant of easements in favour of buyer

On a sale of part the buyer may acquire certain rights over the Retained Land by virtue of the Law of Property Act 1925, s. 62 and the rule in *Wheeldon v. Burrows* [1879] 12 ChD 31. As the nature and extent of the implied rights is not always clear, it is prudent to exclude the effect of these rules and set out expressly the rights and reservations required by the parties. If implied rights of light or air were granted to the buyer here, this could hinder any plans Mr Brown may have in the future to build on the Retained Land.
A suggested negation of implied rights clause would be:

'The Transfer to the Buyer shall contain an agreement and declaration that the Buyer shall not by implication or otherwise become entitled to any rights of light or air which would restrict or interfere with the free use of the Retained Land for building or other purposes.'

Alternatively as the contract incorporates the Standard Conditions of Sale, we could rely on condition 3.4, which provides on a sale of part for the exclusion of rights of light or air.

3. The grant and reservation of new easements

Standard condition 3.4 also provides for the mutual grant of easements and reservations on a sale of part but the condition is not exact and should only be relied upon as a 'fallback' if express easements are overlooked. The special conditions should therefore deal with these matters expressly.

The creation of new easements in favour of the buyer are called 'grants'; the creation of new easements in favour of the seller are called 'reservations'. When acting for a seller wishing to *reserve* easements, reliance should never be placed upon s. 62 of the Law of Property Act 1925 or the rule in *Wheeldon v. Burrows* (1879) 12 ChD 31 because both of these relate to implied *grants* not implied reservations.

The following special condition is suggested to cover our instructions:

'The Transfer to the Buyer shall contain the following rights in favour of the Buyer and the Buyer's successors in title:

(a) A free and uninterrupted right of way at all times and for all purposes with or without vehicles over the accessway shown hatched black on the Plan leading across the Retained land ("the Accessway") subject to the Buyer paying a fair proportion according to user of the cost of maintaining repairing and renewing the said accessway;

(b) The right to lay maintain and use for all proper purposes connected with the Property a new drain and sewer ("the new services") to be laid within a period of eighty years from the date hereof under the Retained Land along the route marked with a broken [orange] line on the Plan;

(c) The right to connect into the Seller's existing drain and sewer ("the existing services") on the Retained Land and to use the existing services in common with the Seller subject to the Buyer paying a fair proportion of the cost of maintaining repairing and renewing the existing services and making good any damage caused to the satisfaction of the Seller;

(d) The right on giving reasonable notice and at reasonable times (except in the case of emergencies) to enter the Retained Land for the purpose of inspecting maintaining and repairing the new services and the existing services the person exercising such right causing as little damage as possible and making good any such damage caused'

The period of eighty years referred to in (b) above is necessary because if new easements are to be created in the future their grant must be limited to the perpetuity period (see the Perpetuities and Accumulations Act 1964).

It should be noted that the seller has been protected by the provision for the Buyer to make good any damage caused to the Retained Land and for repairs to be carried out only upon prior notice, save in the case of an emergency. The route of the new services has also been specified so as to avoid unnecessary intrusion onto the Retained Land.

From the information you have provided, it appears that the only reservation Mr Brown will require is the right to remove the greenhouse. The following special condition would cover the point:

'The Seller reserves the right to remove the greenhouse on the Property provided that the Seller shall exercise this right before completion and shall cause no unnecessary damage to the Property'

If the National Protocol is being used the right to remove the greenhouse could be taken care of by mentioning this on the standard Fixtures Fittings and Contents Form.

4. The imposition of new covenants

Mr Brown has imposed some specific conditions and each one will be the subject of a new covenant imposed on the buyer. Although not mentioned in our instructions it would be prudent in addition, (a) to restrict the use of the new property to residential only (this is probably a condition of the planning permission anyway), (b) to prohibit the buyer from obstructing the driveway and, (c) to impose a general covenant against causing a nuisance or annoyance to the owners and occupiers of the Retained Land.

Wherever possible when acting for a covenantor, the covenants should be drafted so as to be restrictive (i.e. negative) in nature because the burden of a *positive* covenant will not run with the land (*Tulk v. Moxhay* 1848 2 Ph 774). This will be done here in the case of the new building on the plot. Rather than say 'The buyer will build only a single storey dwelling . . .', say 'Not to erect any building save for . . .'. This cannot be done in the case of the obligation to build the fence, but we should stipulate a time limit, a minimum height and its type.

The benefit of the covenants should also be expressly annexed to the Retained Land.

The following special condition is suggested:

'The Buyer shall in the Transfer enter into a covenant with the Seller to the intent that the burden of such covenant shall run with and bind the Property and every part thereof and that the benefit of such covenant shall be annexed to and run with the Retained Land and every part thereof to observe and perform the following:

(a) Not to erect on the Property any building or other structure other than one bungalow and garage for residential use and occupation by one family in accordance with plans previously approved in writing by the Seller or the Seller's successors in title;

(b) Within three months from the date of completion to erect and forever thereafter maintain a close-boarded fence not less than six feet in height along the boundary between the Retained Land and the Property between the points marked A and B on the Plan;

(c) Not to park vehicles on or otherwise obstruct or cause or permit to be obstructed the Accessway;

(d) Not to do or permit to be done on the Property anything which may be or grow to be a nuisance or annoyance to the owners or occupiers of the Retained Land'

(b)

We should advise Mr Brown of his potential liability to Capital Gains Tax (CGT) that can arise on the disposal of an interest in land.

It should be noted that if the land he is retaining (14 Wellington Road and part garden) is his principal private dwelling house, he will enjoy an exemption from CGT provided the land being sold does not exceed 0.5 hectares. We are told that the area of the land is approximately half a hectare so it will be important to requisition a survey in order to establish the precise area.

If the land exceeds 0.5 hectares the gain will be calculated by taking the sale price and deducting from it the value of the land in 1982, incidental acquisition costs (including legal fees) and incidental disposal costs. The client has an annual exemption, which can be set against the chargeable gain. Any gain above the exemption figure will be charged to CGT at the highest rate at which Mr Brown pays income tax.

Question 4

RICHARDS ABBEY AND PARTNERS, SOLICITORS

INTERNAL MEMORANDUM

To   The Trainee Solicitor in the Property Department

From   The Litigation Partner

Re Harnham Pastures and other land

About 15 years ago our firm acted for Walter Maddocks when he purchased Harnham Pastures, a piece of farmland situated on the outskirts of Tamworth. I have acted for Mr Maddocks on a number of litigation matters since and he is a rather demanding client.

Yesterday I was contacted by Simon Walker the managing director of a local building company, Walker Developments Ltd. Simon has heard good things about our property department and would like us to act for his company in the proposed acquisition of Harnham Pastures. The company is intending to apply for planning permission to develop the land into a small industrial estate to serve the community of Tamworth. Once the development is completed they intend to lease the commercial units to business tenants.

In order to proceed with the development the company will need to acquire in addition two further parcels of land adjoining Harnham Pastures which are separately owned by other people.

Simon is coming to see me tomorrow afternoon and I would like to advise him generally on the possible contractual arrangements in this matter. As our property partner is away from the office for a few days perhaps you could prepare a short briefing paper outlining the advice I should give to Mr Walker.

I have not heard from Mr Maddocks but presumably, as an established client, he will want us to act for him on the sale. We have not acted for Walker Developments Ltd before and it looks like we could have a good client for the future.

Commentary

This question raises a number of issues, not least the clear professional conduct point about acting for both seller and buyer in a conveyancing transaction (something which has obviously been overlooked by the Litigation Partner!). The fact that the development company needs to acquire several pieces of land means that conditional contracts or option agreements are likely to be the preferred method of proceeding rather than the conventional unconditional contract. Note also the business awareness point—if you have to choose whom to act for, pick the client who is likely to generate more revenue for the firm.

You have been asked to prepare a briefing paper, so structure your answer in bullet format and respond in similar fashion to the question, i.e. by internal office memorandum.

Suggested answer

RICHARDS ABBEY AND PARTNERS, SOLICITORS
INTERNAL MEMORANDUM

To   The Litigation Partner

From   The Trainee Solicitor in the Property Department

Re Harnham Pastures and other land

In response to your memo I think the following issues are important:

- The company is intending to acquire several separate parcels of land owned by different people.

- The current use of the subject land is farmland. It will therefore be necessary for the company to apply for planning permission to change the use of the land and for permission to develop it as an industrial estate.

- Accordingly conventional unconditional contracts would not appear to be appropriate in this transaction.

- The grant of planning permission is obviously crucial to the company's plans. As this may take several months to finalise it is important that the company does not commit itself unconditionally to the acquisition until it can be certain that planning consent will be forthcoming.

- The company should therefore consider alternative contractual arrangements such as conditional contracts, option agreements or rights of pre-emption.

Conditional contracts

- One suggestion would be to have the contracts created conditionally upon satisfactory planning permission, i.e. a condition precedent to the performance of the contracts. This would mean that there could be no enforceable contract unless and until the condition is satisfied. The law in this area is complex and we must take care when drafting or approving any condition to ensure that the condition is not rendered void for uncertainty. As the condition relates to our client obtaining satisfactory planning permission we must specify the exact nature of the permission required and what conditions annexed to the consent would entitle our client to withdraw. Other important considerations are:

  - To define the client's proposed development.

  - To define the relevant planning permission as the planning permission for the buyer's proposed development, and to state whether the planning permission should be outline or detailed.

  - Our client will not want to complete if planning permission is granted subject to any unreasonable conditions. We should therefore define 'unreasonable conditions', e.g. one that materially affects the cost of construction or the marketability of the development. If the parties cannot agree whether a condition is unreasonable, then the matter should be referred to an independent surveyor for determination.

  - If the relevant planning permission is not granted by a pre-determined long-stop date then either party should be permitted to rescind the contract and the deposit be returned to our client.

Option agreements

- Another alternative would be for our client to enter into option agreements. These are contracts in which the grantee of the option (in this case, our client) is able, within a fixed period, to serve notice on the owner requiring the owner to transfer the land to it. An option is a particularly useful tool for developers wishing to acquire several pieces of land from different owners in order to develop a larger site. This is the situation faced by our client.

- Once our client has secured options over all the pieces of land, it has effectively gained control of the development site and can safely apply for planning permission. Then, once planning permission is obtained, our client would be able to exercise all the options to ensure that it owns every part of the proposed development site.

- In return for the grant of the options our client will probably have to pay the owners an option fee as consideration. The fee may be nominal, but is more likely to be substantial if the owners recognise the development potential of their land. The option fee may be deducted from the purchase price if and when the option is exercised and the land transferred. The method of calculating the purchase price for the land will normally be agreed at the time the option is granted. It will either be a fixed price, or the market value at the time the option is exercised, or the development value to be determined by a valuation formula in the option agreement. The option agreement may be liable to stamp duty land tax.

- As options are estate contracts we would have to protect them by registration. We would do this by lodging either an agreed or unilateral notice for registered land, or, for unregistered land, by registering a Class C(iv) land charge. Only by registering the option will it be binding on any subsequent purchaser of the land, so this would be a very important protection for our client.

Rights of pre-emption

- A right of pre-emption is slightly different from an option in that the grantee cannot force the grantor to sell the property to the grantee. It merely gives the grantee a right of first refusal so that if, and only if, the owner decides to sell during the currency of the pre-emption agreement, the owner must offer the land to the grantee first. I do not think a right of pre-emption would be suitable for our client in the present situation because it is too uncertain, i.e. the seller could not be forced to sell the land.

<u>Summary and other matters</u>

- In the circumstances, as there are several pieces of land involved, I believe that the most suitable contractual arrangement for Walker Developments Ltd would be to enter into separate option agreements with the respective owners of the subject property. Alternatively the company may wish to consider individual contracts with the owners in which satisfactory planning permission is a condition precedent i.e. conditional contracts.

- I would remind you that Rule 6 of the Solicitors Practice Rules 1990 prohibits us from acting for both sides in a conveyancing transaction. Accordingly if we accept instructions to act for the company we would be unable to act for Mr Maddocks in this transaction. We could however recommend him to another local firm.

- No doubt if we had to choose between our 'demanding' client Mr Maddocks and the development company we should select the latter on the basis of its likely future instructions in respect of the development and subsequent lettings of the industrial units.

- Lastly, a reminder that as the company is a new client we would need to comply with the Law Society's client care and complaints procedures under Rule 15 of the Solicitors Practice Rules 1990.

3.3.2 MULTIPLE CHOICE QUESTIONS AND ANSWERS

We set out below examples of ten multiple choice questions that you might encounter in a subject assessment. Answers to these then follow. Remember our initial guidance. Never leave multiple choice answers with a blank. If there are four possibilities and you are not sure of the answer select the one you think might be right; after all, you have a one in four chance of getting it right! Also look at the instructions on the paper. If it says select the right answer on the paper by circling the correct choice then do just that. Do not make a tick or underline your selection as the strict response would be to fail you even though the selection may be correct. Think carefully before selecting your answer and have correcting fluid to hand just in case you make a mistake or change your mind. To assist you, we have given brief explanations for the answers but generally this is not something you will be required to do (unless your exam paper says so!).

3.3.2.1 **Multiple choice questions**

Unless otherwise directed, select the right answer by circling it in each question. Should you think that none of the selections apply please explain why not in your answer book.

1. Under the Standard Conditions of Sale (4th edition), where the buyer of a freehold or leasehold property is allowed by the seller into occupation before completion, the buyer:
   - (a) must not alter the property
   - (b) cannot permit anyone else to occupy the property
   - (c) must advise the buyer's mortgagee (if any)
   - (d) assumes the risk in the property after serving notice on the seller

2. On the sale of a freehold commercial property subject to leases, in which the contract incorporates the Standard Commercial Property Conditions, the seller must inform the buyer without delay if any tenancy ends between exchange and completion and the buyer must not serve any notice to end any tenancy.

   Is this statement TRUE/FALSE? Please delete the incorrect choice.

3. If the seller wishes to use the deposit after exchange towards the deposit on his new yacht, the seller's solicitor must ensure that the contract provides for it to be held as:
   - (a) stakeholder
   - (b) agent for the seller

    (c) agent for the buyer

    (d) by the estate agent

4. Under a contract for the sale of land which excludes standard condition 5.1, the risk of post-exchange damage to the property remains with the seller.

    Is this statement TRUE/FALSE? Please delete the incorrect choice.

5. The form of contract that should be used in National Protocol cases when selling/buying an unregistered freehold title that is subject to compulsory first registration is:

    (a) any form that the parties agree

    (b) the unregistered freehold title form

    (c) the Law Society form incorporating the Standard Conditions of Sale

    (d) the National Protocol form incorporating the National Conditions of Sale

6. In a transaction where the seller owns the whole legal and equitable interest in the subject property the draft contract should normally provide that the seller will give the buyer a limited title guarantee.

    Is this statement TRUE/FALSE? Please delete the incorrect choice.

7. Acting for a client who is selling his home 'Sunnylands' and buying a new home 'Green Willows', which of the following would you NOT normally include in the draft contract for Sunnylands (both properties have registered titles):

    (a) a special condition ensuring that on the day of completion the latest time for completion of the sale is earlier than the corresponding provision in the purchase contract

    (b) a reference to Sunnylands' registered title number

    (c) that the purchaser of Sunnylands will be responsible for any stamp duty land tax that is properly payable

    (d) that Sunnylands is sold with vacant possession

8. Manuel has for some time permitted his neighbour Basil to walk through his garden as a short cut to the local shops. Manuel subsequently purchased Basil's property for himself. Manuel is now selling his original property and instructs you to draft the contract (which will incorporate the Standard Conditions of Sale). Manuel wishes to keep the right to walk through the garden ('the right'). Which of the following statements is correct:

    (a) section 62 of the Law of Property Act 1925 will imply the right

    (b) the rule in *Wheeldon v. Burrows* will imply the right

    (c) standard condition of sale 3.4 will enable Manuel to acquire the right

    (d) Manuel will not acquire the right unless express provision is made in the contract

9. If your client instructs you to submit a draft contract to another prospective buyer without informing the original buyer's conveyancer of this fact, you should:

    (a) refuse your client's instructions and cease to act

    (b) carry out your client's instructions with reasonable promptness

    (c) inform the original buyer's conveyancer in any event

    (d) advise both buyers' conveyancers that there is a contract race

10. Following exchange of contracts for the purchase of an unregistered title (with an agreed completion date two weeks hence) it is standard practice for the buyer's conveyancer to protect his or her client's contract by registering it as a C(iv) land charge at the Land Charges Registry.

    Is this statement TRUE/FALSE? Please delete the incorrect choice.

3.3.2.2 *Answers to multiple choice questions (with brief explanations)*

1. The correct answer is (a). In the unusual situation of the buyer entering into occupation before completion the position is governed by standard condition 5.2. This provides expressly that the buyer must not alter the property (5.2.2(f)). Standard condition 5.2.2(b) permits the buyer to allow members of his or her household to occupy the property. Standard condition 5.2.2(g) provides for the buyer to assume the risk in the property but without any requirement of serving notice on the seller. The standard conditions make no reference to the duties owed by the buyer to the buyer's mortgagee; these are covered by the terms of the mortgage offer.

2. The statement is true and is covered by Standard Commercial Property Condition 3.3.6.

3. The correct answer is (b). If the deposit is held as agent for the seller then following exchange the seller is free to do what he likes with it (including buying a yacht!).

4. The statement is false. If standard condition 5.1 is excluded then the position at common law applies. This is that the risk of post-exchange damage to the property passes to the buyer on exchange of contracts, and the buyer should therefore insure the property from exchange. However the seller is a qualified trustee and owes a duty to exercise reasonable care in respect of the property (*Clarke v. Ramuz* [1891] 2 QB 456).

5. The correct answer is (c). The reference to unregistered freehold title subject to compulsory registration is a red herring. In *any* transaction in which the conveyancers agree to adopt the National Protocol unamended, the parties should use the Law Society contract incorporating the Standard Conditions of Sale.

6. The statement is false. If the seller owns the whole legal and equitable interest in the subject property then the buyer would expect to receive a *full* title guarantee. This implies more comprehensive implied covenants for title than would be the case with a limited title guarantee.

7. The correct answer is (c). Although the buyer of Sunnylands will be responsible for any stamp duty land tax, this is not something that need concern the seller and so no mention of it should be made in the contract.

8. The correct answer is (c). This is quite a difficult question and requires knowledge of how s. 62 of the Law of Property Act 1925 and the rule in *Wheeldon v. Burrows* operate, together with an understanding of standard condition 3.4. Remember that s. 62 and the rule in *Wheeldon v. Burrows* only assist a *buyer* (by implying grants of easements). This case concerns a purported reservation in favour of a seller (Manuel). Although standard condition 3.4(b) is rather vague and imprecise, it will help a seller in this situation (by allowing s. 62 and *Wheeldon v. Burrows* effectively to act in reverse). Thus strictly speaking a special condition is unnecessary (although good practice would dictate the inclusion of one).

9. The correct answer is (a). If you carry out any of the other alternatives in the question you will be in breach of Solicitors' Practice Rule 6A. You may only inform the buyers' conveyancers of the contract race if your client consents to it. If however your client refuses to consent to the disclosure you must cease to act.

10. The statement is false. It sounds sensible enough but in practice registration of the contract rarely happens unless there are exceptional circumstances, e.g. an extended completion date (which is not the case here).

3.3.3 SHORT ANSWER QUESTIONS

Question 1

Eloise is planning to sell off roughly half of her garden situated to the rear of her dwellinghouse. The prospective purchaser is Newbuild Limited, a developer who plans to erect a new detached two-storey house and garage on the land. Eloise's existing dwellinghouse fronts onto a public highway and is connected to all mains services located beneath the highway. On completion of the sale Eloise wishes to remove some rare plants from the land she is selling. There is no access to the land she is selling other than over her retained land.

Without actually drafting them list:

(a) any special conditions Newbuild Limited might expect to be included in the draft contract, and

(b) any special conditions Eloise might expect to be included in the draft contract.

Limit your answer to those special conditions that are specific and relevant to the facts of the question.

Question 2

Patel is selling a registered freehold property known as High Trees to Mary and has instructed you to act for him. In respect of each of the following matters affecting the property, state whether or not you should disclose them in the contract, giving a brief explanation of your answer:

(a) The property has several missing roof tiles.

(b) Entry number one in the charges register refers to a right of way over Blackacre which benefits an adjacent property.

(c) The property is subject to a registered charge in favour of Barclays Bank plc.

(d) A tenant is in occupation under a lease for a fixed term of five years granted by deed by Patel last year.

(e) Entry number two in the charges register refers to a fencing covenant along the rear boundary of Blackacre which benefits a property to the rear.

Question 3

Two years ago when Lesley acquired part of Greenacre, she entered into a restrictive covenant with the vendor in which she agreed not to use Greenacre for any purpose other than as agricultural land. Lesley has now found a buyer for Greenacre and you have been instructed to prepare a draft contract incorporating the Standard Conditions of Sale. Explain whether she needs an indemnity covenant from the buyer and, if so, whether the contract should contain a special condition to this effect.

3.3.3.1 *Suggested answers to short answer questions*

Question 1

Before writing your answer, note how the question asks you to limit your special conditions to those that are specific and relevant to the facts of the question. You should therefore avoid referring to special conditions of a more general nature, such as those listed on the back of the Law Society contract or those which are commonly used to amend the standard conditions, e.g. the latest time for completion.

(a)

On these facts the special conditions Newbuild Limited might expect to be included in the draft contract are as follows:

- As the land being sold comprises land to the rear of Eloise's existing property, the developer will require a right of way with or without vehicles over Eloise's retained land to enable it to gain access to and from the public highway.

- The developer will also require a right to lay, maintain and use new services which will no doubt pass through Eloise's retained land and connect into the mains services beneath the public highway fronting the property.

- A further right may be needed to connect into Eloise's existing services that currently serve her dwelling-house and to use them in common with Eloise.

- Finally the developer will require a right to enter Eloise's retained land (on reasonable notice and at reasonable times, except for emergencies) to inspect, maintain and repair the new and existing services as when necessary.

(b)
The special conditions Eloise might expect to be included in the draft contract are as follows:

- Eloise should reserve the right to remove her rare plants from the land being sold.

- Eloise should consider imposing a covenant on Newbuild Limited restricting development on the land to one two-storey dwellinghouse and garage for residential use only. The design and construction should be in accordance with plans previously approved in writing by Eloise.

- Eloise should consider imposing a covenant on Newbuild Limited to erect and maintain a fence along the boundary between the land being sold and Eloise's retained land. Ideally the fence should be close-boarded and not less than two metres in height.

- There should be negated any implied grant of easements in favour of the developer (e.g. under s. 62 of the Law of Property Act 1925 or the rule in *Wheeldon v. Burrows* (1879) 12 ChD 31). Although mention of this is made in standard condition 3.4, in practice, the point is often highlighted by special condition as well. The grant of any new easements should be dealt with expressly as special conditions (see (a) above).

Question 2

(a) There is no need for the seller to volunteer information concerning the missing roof tiles and no reference should be made to it in the draft contract. The Latin maxim *caveat emptor* (let the buyer beware) applies and the purchaser should rely on her survey. However if the purchaser raises a pre-contract enquiry regarding the condition of the roof the seller should ensure that no misrepresentation is made.

(b) Yes, the right of way is clearly a latent incumbrance, which is noted on the charges register, and should be disclosed in the contract as a specified incumbrance subject to which the property is to sold.

(c) Although the registered charge is an incumbrance noted on the charges register, it will be discharged on completion out of the proceeds of sale. It is therefore not an incumbrance subject to which the property is sold and there is no need to disclose it in the contract. The purchaser will of course seek an assurance from the seller that it will be discharged on or before completion.

(d) The legal lease is an unregistered interest which overrides a registered disposition under the Land Registration Act 2002, Sch. 3, para. 1. As the tenant is in actual occupation the tenant's interest will also be overriding under Sch. 3, para. 2 of the same Act. The lease should be disclosed as an incumbrance subject to which the property is sold.

(e) The positive fencing covenant is another latent incumbrance, which should be disclosed in the contract as a specified incumbrance subject to which the property is to sold.

Question 3

Yes, Lesley requires a personal indemnity covenant from her buyer because under the doctrine of privity of contract she will remain liable under the user covenant as the original covenantor. This liability will remain even after she has disposed of the land and effectively lost control over how the land may be used. The aim of the indemnity covenant is to protect Lesley in the future should the person with the benefit of the user covenant seek to enforce it against her. It will enable her to seek an indemnity from her buyer in respect of any loss she may suffer as a result of enforcement proceedings being taken against her.

It is not strictly necessary to provide for the indemnity covenant as a special condition in the contract. This is because we are told the contract will incorporate the Standard Conditions of Sale. Condition 4.6.4 provides that the buyer will covenant in the transfer deed to indemnify the seller against liability for any future breach of the obligation and to perform it from then on.

3.4 REFERENCES TO WIDER READING INCLUDING PRACTITIONER TEXTS

- *A Practical Approach to Conveyancing* by Abbey R. and Richards M. (6th Edition, OUP)—Chapter 3 (The Draft Contract).
- *The Law Society's Conveyancing Handbook 10th edn*, by Silverman F.—Section B Dealing with Pre-exchange and Section J Dealing with Sales of Part.
- *Emmet on Title*: chapter 2.
- Ruoff and Roper Registered Conveyancing (Sweet and Maxwell)
- *Textbook on Land Law* by MacKenzie J.A. and Phillips M. (9th edn, OUP)—Chapter 3 (The Contract) and Chapter 16 (Resulting and Constructive Trusts and Proprietary Estoppel).

3.5 RELEVANT WEBSITES FOR MORE INFORMATION

- Acts of Parliament, http://www.hmso.gov.uk/acts.htm
  Keep up to date with statutory developments.
- Council of Mortgage Lenders, http://www.cml.org.uk
  There is an on-line version of the CML Lenders'Handbook available at this site and should be referred to in cases of doubt about the requirements of the lender in relation to the contract.
- House of Lords judgments, http://www.parliament.the-stationery-office.co.uk/pa/ld199697/ldjudgmt/ldjudgmt.htm
  Keep up to date with important new cases.
- Inland Revenue, http://www.inlandrevenue.gov.uk/home.htm
  The site for information on any problems about the possible payment of stamp duty land tax (in particular the apportionment of price in the contract between land and chattels).
- Land Registry, http://www.landreg.gov.uk
- Land Registry Internet register access, http://www.landregistrydirect.gov.uk
  The location for on-line applications for official copies of registered title.
- Law Commission, http://www.lawcom.gov.uk
  Keep up to date on proposals for law reform.
- Law Society, http://www.lawsoc.org.uk
- Location statistics, http://www.upmystreet.com
- National Association of Estate Agents, http://www.naea.co.uk
- Ordnance Survey, http://www.ordnancesurvey.co.uk
  It might be useful to consult a detailed Ordnance Survey map when drafting descriptions of land in the draft contract (e.g. sales of part).
- A street map anywhere in the UK, http://www.streetmap.co.uk
- Valuation Office, http://www.voa.gov.uk

APPENDIX 3.1
DRAFT CONTRACT FOR SALE OF 19 MINSTER YARD, BLAKEY

CONTRACT
Incorporating the Standard Conditions of Sale (Fourth Edition)

Date	:	
Seller	:	Reverend Giggs of 19 Minster Lane Blakey Cornshire
Buyer	:	Martin Dobson and Sandra Ince of 24 Lady Jane Court Blakey Cornshire
Property (freehold/leasehold)	:	All that land and building erected thereon known as 19 Minster Yard Blakey Cornshire which is more particularly delineated on the plan annexed hereto and thereon edged red
Title number/root of title	:	Conveyance on sale
Specified incumbrances	:	
Title guarantee (full/limited)	:	
Completion date	:	4 weeks from the date hereof
Contract rate	:	4% above the Law Society interest rate for the time being in force
Purchase price	:	£190,500
Deposit	:	£19,050
Chattels price (if separate)	:	Nil
Balance	:	£171,550

The Seller will sell and the Buyer will buy the Property for the Purchase price.

SPECIAL CONDITIONS

1. (a) This contract incorporates the Standard Conditions of Sale (Fourth Edition).

   (b) The terms used in this contract have the same meaning when used in the Conditions.

2. Subject to the terms of this contract and to the Standard Conditions of Sale, the seller is to transfer the Property with either full title guarantee or limited title guarantee, as specified on the front page.

3. The chattels which are on the Property and are set out on any attached list are included in the sale and the buyer is to pay the chattels price for them.

4. The Property is sold with vacant possession.

(or) 4. The Property is sold subject to the following leases or tenancies:

5. The latest time for completion shall be 12 noon.

6. The deposit shall be held by the Seller's conveyancers as agent for the Seller.

7. The buyer having previously inspected the Property admits entering into this Contract in reliance upon the knowledge gained from such inspection and not from any statement or representation made by the Seller or any person on behalf of the Seller before the date hereof.

Seller's conveyancers*:

Buyer's conveyancers*:

*Adding an e-mail address authorises service by e-mail: see condition 1.3.3(b)

APPENDIX 3.2

Copy title entries of 13 Augustine Way, Kerwick
Specimen Register

TITLE NUMBER: CS72510

HM Land Registry

Edition date: 31 August 1990

Entry No.	A. PROPERTY REGISTER containing the description of the registered land and the estate comprised in the Title
	COUNTY DISTRICT CORNSHIRE MARADON
1.	(19 December 1989) The Freehold land shown edged with red on the plan of the above Title filed at the Registry and being 13 Augustine Way, Kerwick.
2.	(19 December 1989) The land has the benefit of a right of way on foot only over the passageway at the rear leading into Monks Mead.

Entry No.	B. PROPRIETORSHIP REGISTER stating nature of the Title, name, address and description of the proprietor of the land and any entries affecting the right of the disposing thereof TITLE ABSOLUTE
1.	(31 August 1990) Proprietor(s): PAUL JOHN DA WKINS and ANGELA MARY DAWKINS both of 13 Augustine Way, Kerwick, Maradon, Cornshire.
2.	(31 August 1990) RESTRICTION: Except under an order of the registrar no disposition by the proprietor(s) of the land is to be registered without the consent of the proprietor(s) of the Charge dated 29 July 1990 in favour of Weyford Building Society referred to in the Charges Register.

Entry No.	C. CHARGES REGISTER containing charges, incumbrances etc. adversely affecting the land and registered dealings therewith
1.	(19 December 1989) A Conveyance of the land in this title and other land dated 19 May 1924 made between (1) Allen Ansell (Vendor) and (2) Frances Amelia Moss (Purchaser) contains the following covenants:- "And the purchaser for herself her heirs executors administrators and assigns hereby covenants with the Vendor his heirs and assigns that she will perform and observe the stipulations set out in the First Schedule hereto so far as they relate to the hereditaments hereby assured THE FIRST SCHEDULE above referred to (a) No caravan shall be allowed upon the premises and the Vendor or owner or owners of adjoining premises may remove and dispose of any such caravan and for that purpose may forcibly enter upon any land upon which a breach

Specimen Register

TITLE NUMBER: CS72510

HM Land Registry

Entry No.	C. CHARGES REGISTER (continued)
	of this stipulation shall occur and shall not be responsible for the safe keeping of any such caravan or for the loss thereof or any damage thereto or to any fence or wall
	(b) No earth gravel or sand shall at any time be excavated or dug out of the land except for the purpose of excavations in connection with the buildings erected on the land and no bricks or tiles shall at any time be burnt or made nor any clay or lime be burnt on the land."
2.	(19 December 1989) The passageway at the side included in the title is subject to rights of way on foot only.
3.	(31 August 1990) A Transfer of the land in this title dated 29 July 1990 made between (1) JOHN EDWARD CHARLES BROWN and (2) PAUL JOHN DAWKINS and ANGELA MARY DAWKINS contains restrictive covenants. *NOTE:- Copy in Certificate*
4.	(31 August 1990) REGISTERED CHARGE dated 29 July 1990 to secure the moneys including the further advances therein mentioned.
5.	(31 August 1990) Proprietor(s): WEYFORD BUILDING SOCIETY of Society House, The Avenue, Weymouth, Cornshire.

*****END OF REGISTER*****

NOTE A:	A date at the beginning of an entry is the date on which the entry was made in the Register.
NOTE B:	This certificate was officially examined with the register on 31 August 1990. This date should be stated on any application for an official search based on this certificate.

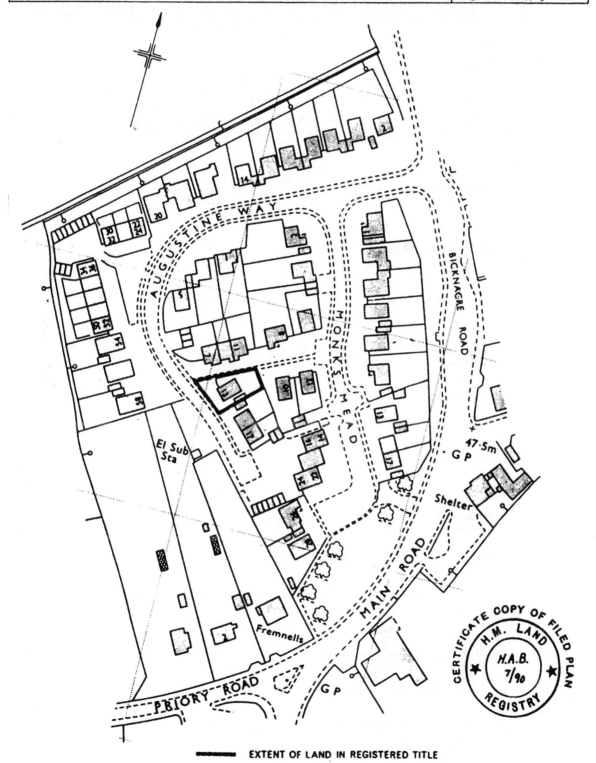

H.M. LAND REGISTRY		TITLE NUMBER	
		CS72510	
ORDNANCE SURVEY PLAN REFERENCE	TL 7802	SECTION U	Scale 1/1250 Enlarged from 1/2500
COUNTY CORNSHIRE	DISTRICT MARADON		© Crown copyright 1977

EXTENT OF LAND IN REGISTERED TITLE

APPENDIX 3.3

CONTRACT
Incorporating the Standard Conditions of Sale (Fourth Edition)

Date	:	
Seller	:	ANGELA MARY DAWKINS of 13 Augustine Way Kerwick Maradon Cornshire
Buyer	:	ANDREW PEACH of 25 Woodlands Road Kerwick Maradon Cornshire
Property (freehold/leasehold)	:	13 Augustine Way Kerwick Maradon Cornshire registered at HM Land Registry with Title Absolute
Title number/root of title	:	CS 72510
Specified incumbrances	:	Entries 1, 2 and 3 in the Charges Register of the Title
Title guarantee (full/limited)	:	Full Title Guarantee
Completion date	:	
Contract rate	:	The Law Society's interest rate from time to time in force
Purchase price	:	£70,000
Deposit	:	£7,000
Chattels price (if separate)	:	£500
Balance	:	£63,500

The seller will sell and the buyer will buy the property for the purchase price.

WARNING	Signed
This is a formal document, designed to create legal rights and legal obligations. Take advice before using it.	Seller/Buyer

STANDARD CONDITIONS OF SALE (FOURTH EDITION)
(NATIONAL CONDITIONS OF SALE 24th EDITION, LAW SOCIETY'S CONDITIONS OF SALE 2003)

1.   GENERAL

1.1   Definitions

1.1.1   In these conditions:
(a)   "accrued interest" means:
   (i)   If money has been placed on deposit or in a building society share account, the interest actually earned
   (ii)   otherwise, the interest which might reasonably have been earned by depositing the money at interest on seven days' notice of withdrawal with a clearing bank less, in either case, any proper charges for handling the money
(b)   "chattels price" means any separate amount payable for chattels included in the contract
(c)   "clearing bank" means a bank which is a shareholder in CHAPS Clearing Co. Limited.
(d)   "completion date" has the meaning given in condition 6.1.1
(e)   "contract rate" means the Law Society's interest rate from time to time in force
(f)   "conveyancer" means a solicitor, barrister, duly certified notary public, licensed conveyancer or recognised body under sections 9 or 23 of the Administration of Justice Act 1985
(g)   "direct credit" means a direct transfer of cleared funds to an account nominated by the seller's conveyancer and maintained by a clearing bank
(h)   "lease" includes sub-lease, tenancy and agreement for a lease or sub-lease
(i)   "notice to complete" means a notice requiring completion of the contract in accordance with condition 6
(j)   "public requirement" means any notice, order or proposal given or made (whether before or after the date of the contract) by a body acting on statutory authority
(k)   "requisition" includes objection
(l)   "transfer" includes conveyance and assignment
(m)   "working day" means any day from Monday to Friday (inclusive) which is not Christmas Day, Good Friday or a statutory Bank Holiday.

1.1.2   In these conditions the terms "absolute title" and "official copies" have the special meanings given to them by the Land Registration Act 2002.

1.1.3   A party is ready, able and willing to complete:
(a)   if he could be, but for the default of the other party, and
(b)   in the case of the seller, even though the property remains subject to a mortgage, if the amount to be paid on completion enables the property to be transferred freed of all mortgages (except any to which the sale is expressly subject).

1.1.4   These conditions apply except as varied or excluded by the contract.

1.2   Joint parties
   If there is more than one seller or more than one buyer, the obligations which they undertake can be enforced against them all jointly or against each Individually.

1.3   Notices and documents

1.3.1   A notice required or authorised by the contract must be in writing.

1.3.2   Giving a notice or delivering a document to a party's conveyancer has the same effect as giving or delivering it to that party.

1.3.3   Where delivery of the original document is not essential, a notice or document is validly given or sent if it is sent:
(a)   by fax, or
(b)   by e-mail to an e-mail address for the intended recipient given in the contract.

1.3.4   Subject to conditions 1.3.5 to 1.3.7, a notice is given and a document is delivered when it is received.

1.3.5   (a)   A notice or document sent through a document exchange is received when it is available for collection
(b)   A notice or document which is received after 4.00pm on a working day, or on a day which is not a working day, is to be treated as having been received on the next working day
(c)   An automated response to a notice or document sent by e-mail that the intended recipient is out of the office is to

be treated as proof that the notice or document was not received.

1.3.6   Condition 1.3.7 applies unless there is proof:
(a)   that a notice or document has not been received, or
(b)   of when it was received.

1.3.7   A notice or document sent by the following means is treated as having been received as follows:

(a) by first-class post:	before 4.00pm on the second working day after posting
(b) by second-class post:	before 4.00pm on the third working day after posting
(c) through a document exchange:	before 4.00pm on the first working day after the day on which it would normally be available for collection by the addressee
(d) by fax:	one hour after despatch
(e) by e-mail:	before 4.00pm on the first working day after despatch.

1.4   VAT

1.4.1   An obligation to pay money includes an obligation to pay any value added tax chargeable in respect of that payment.

1.4.2   All sums made payable by the contract are exclusive of value added tax.

1.5   Assignment
   The buyer is not entitled to transfer the benefit of the contract.

2.   FORMATION

2.1   Date

2.1.1   If the parties intend to make a contract by exchanging duplicate copies by post or through a document exchange, the contract is made when the last copy is posted or deposited at the document exchange.

2.1.2   If the parties' conveyancers agree to treat exchange as taking place before duplicate copies are actually exchanged, the contract is made as so agreed.

2.2   Deposit

2.2.1   The buyer is to pay or send a deposit of 10 per cent of the total of the purchase price and the chattels price no later than the date of the contract.

2.2.2   If a cheque tendered in payment of all or part of the deposit is dishonoured when first presented, the seller may, within seven working days of being notified that the cheque has been dishonoured, give notice to the buyer that the contract is discharged by the buyer's breach.

2.2.3   Conditions 2.2.4 to 2.2.6 do not apply on a sale by auction.

2.2.4   The deposit is to be paid by direct credit or to the seller's conveyancer by a cheque drawn on a solicitor's or licensed conveyancer's client account.

2.2.5   If before completion date the seller agrees to buy another property in England and Wales for his residence, he may use all or any part of the deposit as a deposit in that transaction to be held on terms to the same effect as this condition and condition 2.2.6.

2.2.6   Any deposit or part of a deposit not being used in accordance with condition 2.2.5 is to be held by the seller's conveyancer as stakeholder on terms that on completion it is paid to the seller with accrued interest.

2.3   Auctions

2.3.1   On a sale by auction the following conditions apply to the property and, if it is sold in lots, to each lot.

2.3.2   The sale is subject to a reserve price.

2.3.3   The seller, or a person on his behalf, may bid up to the reserve price.

2.3.4   The auctioneer may refuse any bid.

2.3.5   If there is a dispute about a bid, the auctioneer may resolve the dispute or restart the auction at the last undisputed bid.

2.3.6   The deposit is to be paid to the auctioneer as agent for the seller.

3.   MATTERS AFFECTING THE PROPERTY

3.1   Freedom from incumbrances

3.1.1   The seller is selling the property free from incumbrances, other than those mentioned in condition 3.1.2.

3.1.2   The incumbrances subject to which the property is sold are:
(a)   those specified in the contract

(b) those discoverable by inspection of the property before the contract

(c) those the seller does not and could not reasonably know about

(d) entries made before the date of the contract in any public register except those maintained by HM Land Registry or its Land Charges Department or by Companies House

(e) public requirements.

3.1.3 After the contract is made, the seller is to give the buyer written details without delay of any new public requirement and of anything in writing which he learns about concerning a matter covered by condition 3.1.2.

3.1.4 The buyer is to bear the cost of complying with any outstanding public requirement and is to indemnify the seller against any liability resulting from a public requirement.

3.2 Physical state

3.2.1 The buyer accepts the property in the physical state it is in at the date of the contract unless the seller is building or converting it.

3.2.2 A leasehold property is sold subject to any subsisting breach of a condition or tenant's obligation relating to the physical state of the property which renders the lease liable to forfeiture.

3.2.3 A sub-lease is granted subject to any subsisting breach of a condition or tenant's obligation relating to the physical state of the property which renders the seller's own lease liable to forfeiture.

3.3 Leases affecting the property

3.3.1 The following provisions apply if any part of the property is sold subject to a lease.

3.3.2 (a) The seller having provided the buyer with full details of each lease or copies of the documents embodying the lease terms, the buyer is treated as entering into the contract knowing and fully accepting those terms.

(b) The seller is to inform the buyer without delay if the lease ends or if the seller learns of any application by the tenant in connection with the lease; the seller is then to act as the buyer reasonably directs, and the buyer is to indemnify him against all consequent loss and expense.

(c) Except with the buyer's consent, the seller is not to agree to any proposal to change the lease terms nor to take any step to end the lease.

(d) The seller is to inform the buyer without delay of any change to the lease terms which may be proposed or agreed.

(e) The buyer is to indemnify the seller against all claims arising from the lease after actual completion; this includes claims which are unenforceable against a buyer for want of registration.

(f) The seller takes no responsibility for what rent is lawfully recoverable, nor for whether or how any legislation affects the lease.

(g) If the let land is not wholly within the property, the seller may apportion the rent.

3.4 Retained land

Where after the transfer the seller will be retaining land near the property:

(a) the buyer will have no right of light or air over the retained land, but

(b) In other respects the seller and the buyer will each have the rights over the land of the other which they would have had if they were two separate buyers to whom the seller had made simultaneous transfers of the property and the retained land.

The transfer is to contain appropriate express terms.

4. TITLE AND TRANSFER

4.1 Proof of title

4.1.1 Without cost to the buyer, the seller is to provide the buyer with proof of the title to the property and of his ability to transfer it, or to procure its transfer.

4.1.2 Where the property has a registered title the proof is to include official copies of the items referred to in rules 134(1)(a) and (b) and 135(1)(a) of the Land Registration Rules 2003, so far as they are not to be discharged or overridden at or before completion.

4.1.3 Where the property has an unregistered title, the proof is to include:

(a) an abstract of title or an epitome of title with photocopies of the documents, and

(b) production of every document or an abstract, epitome or copy of it with an original marking by a conveyancer either against the original or an examined abstract or an examined copy.

4.2 Requisitions

4.2.1 The buyer may not raise requisitions:

(a) on the title shown by the seller taking the steps described in condition 4.1.1 before the contract was made

(b) in relation to the matters covered by condition 3.1.2.

4.2.2 Notwithstanding condition 4.2.1, the buyer may, within six working days of a matter coming to his attention after the contract was made, raise written requisitions on that matter. In that event, steps 3 and 4 in condition 4.3.1 apply.

4.2.3 On the expiry of the relevant time limit under condition 4.2.2 or condition 4.3.1, the buyer loses his right to raise requisitions or to make observations.

4.3 Timetable

4.3.1 Subject to condition 4.2 and to the extent that the seller did not take the steps described in condition 4.1.1 before the contract was made, the following are the steps for deducing and investigating the title to the property to be taken within the following time limits:

Stop	Time Limit
1. The seller is to comply with condition 4.1.1	Immediately after making the contract
2. The buyer may raise written requisitions	Six working days after either the date of the contract or the date of delivery of the seller's proof of title on which the requisitions are raised, whichever is the later
3. The seller is to reply in writing to any requisitions raised	Four working days after receiving the requisitions
4. The buyer may make written observations on the seller's replies	Three working days after receiving the replies

The time limit on the buyer's right to raise requisitions applies even where the seller supplies incomplete evidence of his title, but the buyer may, within six working days from delivery of any further evidence, raise further requisitions resulting from that evidence.

4.3.2 The parties are to take the following steps to prepare and agree the transfer of the property within the following time limits:

Stop	Time Limit
A. The buyer is to send the seller a draft transfer	At least twelve working days before completion date
B. The seller is to approve or revise that draft and either return it or retain it for use as the actual transfer	Four working days after delivery of the draft transfer
C. If the draft is returned the buyer is to send an engrossment to the seller	At least five working days before completion date

4.3.3 Periods of time under conditions 4.3.1 and 4.3.2 may run concurrently.

4.3.4 If the period between the date of the contract and completion date is less than 15 working days, the time limits in conditions 4.2.2, 4.3.1 and 4.3.2 are to be reduced by the same proportion as that period bears to the period of 15 working days. Fractions of a working day are to be rounded down except that the time limit to perform any step is not to be less than one working day.

4.4 Defining the property

4.4.1 The seller need not:

(a) prove the exact boundaries of the property

(b) prove who owns fences, ditches, hedges or walls

(c) separately identify parts of the property with different titles further than he may be able to do from information in his possession.

4.4.2 The buyer may, if it is reasonable, require the seller to make or obtain, pay for and hand over a statutory declaration about facts relevant to the matters mentioned in condition 4.4.1. The form of the declaration is to be agreed by the buyer, who must not unreasonably withhold his agreement.

4.5 Rents and rentcharges

The fact that a rent or rentcharge, whether payable or receivable by the owner of the property, has been, or will on completion be, informally apportioned is not to be regarded as a defect in title.

4.6 Transfer

4.6.1 The buyer does not prejudice his right to raise requisitions, or to require replies to any raised, by taking any steps in relation to preparing or agreeing the transfer.

4.6.2 Subject to condition 4.6.3, the seller is to transfer the property with full title guarantee.

4.6.3 The transfer is to have effect as if the disposition is expressly made subject to all matters covered by condition 3.1.2.

4.6.4 If after completion the seller will remain bound by any obligation affecting the property which was disclosed to the buyer before the contract was made, but the law does not imply any covenant by the buyer to indemnify the seller against liability for future breaches of it:

(a) the buyer is to covenant in the transfer to indemnify the seller against liability for any future breach of the obligation and to perform it from then on, and

(b) if required by the seller, the buyer is to execute and deliver to the seller on completion a duplicate transfer prepared by the buyer.

4.6.5 The seller is to arrange at his expense that, in relation to every document of title which the buyer does not receive on completion, the buyer is to have the benefit of:

(a) a written acknowledgement of his right to its production, and

(b) a written undertaking for its safe custody (except while it is held by a mortgagee or by someone in a fiduciary capacity).

5. PENDING COMPLETION

5.1 Responsibility for property

5.1.1 The seller will transfer the property in the same physical state as it was at the date of the contract (except for fair wear and tear), which means that the seller retains the risk until completion.

5.1.2 If at any time before completion the physical state of the property makes it unusable for its purpose at the date of the contract:

(a) the buyer may rescind the contract

(b) the seller may rescind the contract where the property has become unusable for that purpose as a result of damage against which the seller could not reasonably have insured, or which it is not legally possible for the seller to make good.

5.1.3 The seller is under no obligation to the buyer to insure the property.

5.1.4 Section 47 of the Law of Property Act 1925 does not apply.

5.2 Occupation by buyer

5.2.1 If the buyer is not already lawfully in the property, and the seller agrees to let him into occupation, the buyer occupies on the following terms.

5.2.2 The buyer is a licensee and not a tenant. The terms of the licence are that the buyer:

(a) cannot transfer it

(b) may permit members of his household to occupy the property

(c) is to pay or indemnify the seller against all outgoings and other expenses in respect of the property

(d) is to pay the seller a fee calculated at the contract rate on a sum equal to the purchase price and the chattels price (less any deposit paid) for the period of the licence

(e) is entitled to any rents and profits from any part of the property which he does not occupy

(f) is to keep the property in as good a state of repair as it was in when he went into occupation (except for fair wear and tear) and is not to alter it

(g) is to insure the property in a sum which is not less than the purchase price against all risks in respect of which comparable premises are normally insured

(h) is to quit the property when the licence ends.

5.2.3 On the creation of the buyer's licence, condition 5.1 ceases to apply, which means that the buyer then assumes the risk until completion.

5.2.4 The buyer is not in occupation for the purposes of this condition if he merely exercises rights of access given solely to do work agreed by the seller.

5.2.5 The buyer's licence ends on the earliest of: completion date, rescission of the contract or when five working days' notice given by one party to the other takes effect.

5.2.6 If the buyer is in occupation of the property after his licence has come to an end and the contract is subsequently completed he is to pay the seller compensation for his continued occupation calculated at the same rate as the fee mentioned in condition 5.2.2(d).

5.2.7 The buyer's right to raise requisitions is unaffected.

6. COMPLETION

6.1 Date

6.1.1 Completion date is twenty working days after the date of the contract but time is not of the essence of the contract unless a notice to complete has been served.

6.1.2 If the money due on completion is received after 2.00pm, completion is to be treated, for the purposes only of conditions 6.3 and 7.3, as taking place on the next working day as a result of the buyer's default.

6.1.3 Condition 6.1.2 does not apply and the seller is treated as in default if:

(i) the sale is with vacant possession of the property or any part of it, and

(ii) the buyer is ready, able and willing to complete but does not pay the money due on completion until after 2.00pm because the seller has not vacated the property or that part by that time.

6.2 Arrangements and place

6.2.1 The buyer's conveyancer and the seller's conveyancer are to co-operate in agreeing arrangements for completing the contract.

6.2.2 Completion is to take place in England and Wales, either at the seller's conveyancer's office or at some other place which the seller reasonably specifies.

6.3 Apportionments

6.3.1 Income and outgoings of the property are to be apportioned between the parties so far as the change of ownership on completion will affect entitlement to receive or liability to pay them.

6.3.2 If the whole property is sold with vacant possession or the seller exercises his option in condition 7.3.4, apportionment is to be made with effect from the date of actual completion; otherwise, it is to be made from completion date.

6.3.3 In apportioning any sum, it is to be assumed that the seller owns the property until the end of the day from which apportionment is made and that the sum accrues from day to day at the rate at which it is payable on that day.

6.3.4 For the purpose of apportioning income and outgoings, it is to be assumed that they accrue at an equal daily rate throughout the year.

6.3.5 When a sum to be apportioned is not known or easily ascertainable at completion, a provisional apportionment is to be made according to the best estimate available. As soon as the amount is known, a final apportionment is to be made and notified to the other party. Any resulting balance is to be paid no more than ten working days later, and if not then paid the balance is to bear interest at the contract rate from then until payment.

6.3.6 Compensation payable under condition 5.2.6 is not to be apportioned.

6.4 Amount payable

The amount payable by the buyer on completion is the purchase price and the chattels price (less any deposit already paid to the seller or his agent) adjusted to take account of:

(a) apportionments made under condition 6.3

(b) any compensation to be paid or allowed under condition 7.3.

6.5 Title deeds

6.5.1 As soon as the buyer has complied with all his obligations on completion the seller must hand over the documents of title.

6.5.2 Condition 6.5.1 does not apply to any documents of title relating to land being retained by the seller after completion.

6.6 Rent receipts

The buyer is to assume that whoever gave any receipt for a payment of rent or service charge which the seller produces was the person or the agent of the person then entitled to that rent or service charge.

6.7 Means of payment

The buyer is to pay the money due on completion by direct credit and, if appropriate, an unconditional release of a deposit held by a stakeholder.

6.8 Notice to complete

6.8.1 At any time on or after completion date, a party who is ready, able and willing to complete may give the other a notice to complete.

6.8.2 The parties are to complete the contract within ten working days of giving a notice to complete, excluding the day on which the notice is given. For this purpose, time is of the essence of the contract.

6.8.3 On receipt of a notice to complete:
   (a) if the buyer paid no deposit, he is forthwith to pay a deposit of 10 per cent
   (b) if the buyer paid a deposit of less than 10 per cent, he is forthwith to pay a further deposit equal to the balance of that 10 per cent.

7. **REMEDIES**

7.1 Errors and omissions

7.1.1 If any plan or statement in the contract, or in the negotiations leading to it, is or was misleading or inaccurate due to an error or omission, the remedies available are as follows.

7.1.2 When there is a material difference between the description or value of the property, or of any of the chattels included in the contract, as represented and as it is, the buyer is entitled to damages.

7.1.3 An error or omission only entitles the buyer to rescind the contract:
   (a) where it results from fraud or recklessness, or
   (b) where he would be obliged, to his prejudice, to accept property differing substantially (in quantity, quality or tenure) from what the error or omission had led him to expect.

7.2 Rescission

If either party rescinds the contract:
   (a) unless the rescission is a result of the buyer's breach of contract the deposit is to be repaid to the buyer with accrued interest
   (b) the buyer is to return any documents he received from the seller and is to cancel any registration of the contract.

7.3 Late completion

7.3.1 If there is default by either or both of the parties in performing their obligations under the contract and completion is delayed, the party whose total period of default is the greater is to pay compensation to the other party.

7.3.2 Compensation is calculated at the contract rate on an amount equal to the purchase price and the chattels price, less (where the buyer is the paying party) any deposit paid, for the period by which the paying party's default exceeds that of the receiving party, or, if shorter, the period between completion date and actual completion.

7.3.3 Any claim for loss resulting from delayed completion is to be reduced by any compensation paid under this contract.

7.3.4 Where the buyer holds the property as tenant of the seller and completion is delayed, the seller may give notice to the buyer, before the date of actual completion, that he intends to take the net income from the property until completion. If he does so, he cannot claim compensation under condition 7.3.1 as well.

7.4 After completion

Completion does not cancel liability to perform any outstanding obligation under this contract.

7.5 Buyer's failure to comply with notice to complete

7.5.1 If the buyer fails to complete in accordance with a notice to complete, the following terms apply.

7.5.2 The seller may rescind the contract, and if he does so:
   (a) he may
      (i) forfeit and keep any deposit and accrued interest
      (ii) resell the property and any chattels included in the contract
      (iii) claim damages
   (b) the buyer is to return any documents he received from the seller and is to cancel any registration of the contract.

7.5.3 The seller retains his other rights and remedies.

7.6 Seller's failure to comply with notice to complete

7.6.1 If the seller fails to complete in accordance with a notice to complete, the following terms apply.

7.6.2 The buyer may rescind the contract, and if he does so:
   (a) the deposit is to be repaid to the buyer with accrued interest

   (b) the buyer is to return any documents he received from the seller and is, at the seller's expense, to cancel any registration of the contract.

7.6.3 The buyer retains his other rights and remedies.

8 **LEASEHOLD PROPERTY**

8.1 Existing leases

8.1.1 The following provisions apply to a sale of leasehold land.

8.1.2 The seller having provided the buyer with copies of the documents embodying the lease terms, the buyer is treated as entering into the contract knowing and fully accepting those terms.

8.1.3 The seller is to comply with any lease obligations requiring the tenant to insure the property.

8.2 New leases

8.2.1 The following provisions apply to a contract to grant a new lease.

8.2.2 The conditions apply so that:
"seller" means the proposed landlord
"buyer" means the proposed tenant
"purchase price" means the premium to be paid on the grant of a lease.

8.2.3 The lease is to be in the form of the draft attached to the contract.

8.2.4 If the term of the new lease will exceed seven years, the seller is to deduce a title which will enable the buyer to register the lease at HM Land Registry with an absolute title.

8.2.5 The seller is to engross the lease and a counterpart of it and is to send the counterpart to the buyer at least five working days before completion date.

8.2.6 The buyer is to execute the counterpart and deliver it to the seller on completion.

8.3 Consent

8.3.1 (a) The following provisions apply if a consent to let, assign or sub-let is required to complete the contract
   (b) In this condition "consent" means consent in the form which satisfies the requirement to obtain it.

8.3.2 (a) The seller is to apply for the consent at his expense, and to use all reasonable efforts to obtain it
   (b) The buyer is to provide all information and references reasonably required.

8.3.3 Unless he is in breach of his obligation under condition 8.3.2, either party may rescind the contract by notice to the other party if three working days before completion date (or before a later date on which the parties have agreed to complete the contract):
   (a) the consent has not been given, or
   (b) the consent has been given subject to a condition to which a party reasonably objects. In that case, neither party is to be treated as in breach of contract and condition 7.2 applies.

9. **COMMONHOLD LAND**

9.1 Terms used in this condition have the special meanings given to them in Part 1 of the Commonhold and Leasehold Reform Act 2002.

9.2 This condition applies to a disposition of commonhold land.

9.3 The seller having provided the buyer with copies of the current versions of the memorandum and articles of the commonhold association and of the commonhold community statement, the buyer is treated as entering into the contract knowing and fully accepting their terms.

9.4 If the contract is for the sale of property which is or includes part only of a commonhold unit:
   (a) the seller is to apply for the written consent of the commonhold association at his expense and is to use all reasonable efforts to obtain it
   (b) either the seller, unless he is in breach of his obligation under paragraph (a), or the buyer may rescind the contract by notice to the other party if three working days before completion date (or before a later date on which the parties have agreed to complete the contract) the consent has not been given. In that case, neither party is to be treated as in breach of contract and condition 7.2 applies.

10. **CHATTELS**

10.1 The following provisions apply to any chattels which are included in the contract, whether or not a separate price is to be paid for them.

10.2 The contract takes affect as a contract for sale of goods.

10.3 The buyer takes the chattels in the physical state they are in at the date of the contract.

10.4 Ownership of the chattels passes to the buyer on actual completion.

SPECIAL CONDITIONS

1. (a) This contract incorporates the Standard Conditions of Sale (Fourth Edition).

   (b) The terms used in this contract have the same meaning when used in the Conditions.

2. Subject to the terms of this contract and to the Standard Conditions of Sale, the seller is to transfer the property with either full title guarantee or limited title guarantee, as specified on the front page.

3. The chattels which are on the property and are set out on any attached list are included in the sale and the buyer is to pay the chattels price for them.

4. The property is sold with vacant possession.

~~(or) 4 x x The property is sold subject to the following leases or tenancies:~~

5. The Buyer having inspected the Seller's title shall raise no objection to it or requisition on it.

Seller's conveyancers*: Rodgers & Co

Buyer's conveyancers*: Young & Price

*Adding an e-mail address authorises service by e-mail: see condition 1.3.3(b)

APPENDIX 3.4

Appendix 4: Chapter 3, Question 4

Plan of 14 Wellington Road, Midchester

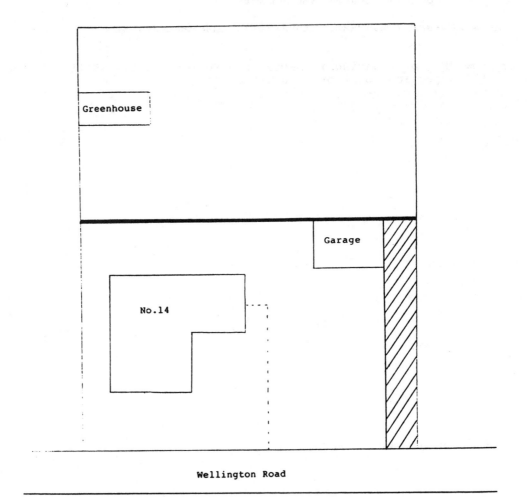

4 PRE-CONTRACT SEARCHES, ENQUIRIES AND TOWN AND COUNTRY PLANNING

4.1 INTRODUCTION

The topics covered by this chapter seem on the face of it to be straightforward. However, as is usually the case with conveyancing, topics that seem simple generally turn out to be quite complex. The main difficulty for you will be the broad variety of questions that candidates can expect to encounter. These questions can extend from the very wide, touching upon several areas within the topics down to very particular questions focusing on one area. The questions provided are examples of both these extremes. Your difficulties spread further in that other areas will be involved as will be seen in the questions in 4.3.1 below. Because conveyancing is an ongoing, forward rolling process you must expect questions to incorporate several subjects not just limited to the chapter headings. This is inherent in the nature of the subject generally.

You should also note the wide diversity of style of questions displayed in these examples. In one the examiner is looking in the answer for a memorandum, in another a file note and in another a letter of advice. In all your answers you should provide exactly what the examiner wants. It is important for you to realise that this is of crucial importance to your success and that essay answers to all the questions will not suffice. There will be occasions when an essay is appropriate and the style of question will readily identify when this is so. However because an essay format is not called for does not mean you should abandon the tried and tested examination technique that is the pathway to success. In preparing your answer you should still draw up a plan of how you are going to structure your answer, then make sure you stay with your plan and then make your points in a clear and concise way. Always make sure you give a cogent conclusion so that the examiner can appreciate that there is style, form and content to your answer.

What will be immediately clear from the following questions and answers, and indeed from this entire book is that case law knowledge is really secondary in importance to knowledge and in-depth understanding of the conveyancing process. Indeed there is one answer in this chapter where there is a complete absence of cited cases. Do not be perturbed, you can still obtain high marks by exhibiting a thorough knowledge of the process of conveyancing and by making sure that your knowledge of the process is properly applied to the problem contained within the question. Of course statutes will apply in almost all answers and are arguably more important to a Conveyancer.

This chapter will first look at pre-contract searches. This is an interesting and important topic within the conveyancing process and covers a lot of points that can be of considerable consequence to a buyer. So far as enquiries are concerned they have been greatly affected by changes ushered in by the Law Society's National Conveyancing Protocol. This being the case you should expect questions to arise that are concerned with this area of considerable change to the traditional system. You should acquaint yourself with the contents of the old style pre-printed traditional forms of enquiries before contract as well as the newer property information forms. By doing this you will come to appreciate the ways in which the forms differ and how the system has been streamlined with the adoption of the Protocol approach. Finally there is some overlap between enquiries and planning in that there should always be planning enquiries in most transactions. You should be aware of this and be able to demonstrate your knowledge of this possible combination of topics. Furthermore all three items, searches enquiries and planning are all topics that will be important to both sides of property practice, i.e. commercial and residential.

Finally we set out at 4.2.4 below a decision tree that covers the whole of the topics covered in this chapter but in diagrammatic format. This should help you to understand the area from the perspective of an overview and enable you to make selections according to the nature of a particular transaction be it commercial or residential.

4.2 AN OVERVIEW OF THE SUBJECT AND A LOOK AT SOME PROBLEM AREAS

Caveat emptor (let the buyer beware) remains a cornerstone of conveyancing in England and Wales. As such a buyer will need to find out as much as possible about the subject property before contracts are exchanged. This being so it will inevitably lead to a buyer's practitioner making pre-contract searches and pre-contract enquiries. This process will include searches and enquiries that will cover planning matters. These three aspects of pre-contract conveyancing will now be examined in turn.

4.2.1 PRE-CONTRACT SEARCHES

With regard to pre-contract searches, the first concern for a practitioner is—have I completed all the searches I need to for a particular property? The following chart should assist—

Q. 1 Is the property registered	
Yes Go to Q.2	No Do a map index search and if you have title details a land charges search
Q. 2 Is the property in an urban area?	
Yes Go to Q.3	No If it is rural or on the edge of town or a recent development do a commons registration search
Q. 3 Have you checked the location in the Coal Mining Directory and is it affected?	
Yes Complete a coal mining search	No Go to Q. 4
Q. 4 Are you buying from a company?	
Yes Complete a company search	No Go to Q. 5
Q. 5 Have you completed an environmental search?	
Yes Go to Q.6	No Check your client's instructions and always advise that one is necessary
Q. 6 Have you completed a local authority search, a water company search?	
Yes Go to Q.7	No Do them now. Both searches should be made in all transactions
Q. 7 Have you advised your client to inspect the property prior to exchange	
Yes Go to Q.8	No This should be done to check the state of the property, whether there any unlawful occupiers, etc.
Q. 8 Have you checked for other location dependant searches	
Yes Go and do something else!	No Complete all other such searches, e.g. Tin mining in Cornwall, Brine extraction in Cheshire, etc.

4.2.1.1 **Searches summary**

The following searches should be considered, all or some of which may be required prior to an exchange of contracts:

(a) *Local authority search and enquiries*. This is of such importance that no conveyancing matter be it commercial or residential should proceed without one. A practitioner will need to carefully review both the results of the search on the local land charges register as well as the replies to standard enquiries completed by the local authority. The two items together are accepted in practice as constituting the local authority search result.

(b) *Water company search and enquiries*. Once again this will be of relevance to all types of conveyancing cases. Commercial property searches should be specifically marked as such on the search form to gain the benefit of extra insurance cover against mistakes by the issuing water company.

(c) *Commons registration search*. Of particular relevance when buying a new property.

(d) *Coal mining search*. Affects all types of conveyancing cases when they are located in an area currently or previously affected by coal mining. The subject property might be a victim of subsidence or could be a potential victim. A buyer needs to know this before deciding on the merits of the proposed purchase.

(e) *Index map search*. Used particularly to see if the title to the subject property is partially or completely registered and if so what tenures are registered.

(f) *Land charges search*. Of use in unregistered land when you have seen all the title before exchange and you are taking the prudent step of checking for undisclosed encumbrances at an early stage in the transaction.

(g) *Company search*. This search is relevant if you are buying from a company and want to make sure that it is properly registered at Companies House and is not subject to any winding up or liquidation proceedings.

(h) *Other searches dependent upon the location of the property*. See the section on extra searches at 4.2.1.2 below.

(i) *Physical search or inspection of the property*. To check the condition of the property just before exchange and to make sure that any contents or fixtures and fittings mentioned in the contract are where they should be at the time the contract becomes binding. Accordingly, when considering searches it is always appropriate for domestic conveyancing and probably for many types of commercial con-veyancing matters to advise the buyer to inspect the subject property prior to exchange. In detail the reasons for the inspection are fivefold and are to check:

- the state and condition of the property,
- who is in actual occupation of the property,
- the boundaries,
- on rights and easements affecting or benefiting the property, and,
- that the fixtures and fittings contracted to be sold are in the subject property just prior to exchange

(j) *Environmental searches (including flooding)*. This has only recently joined the list of pre-contract searches. The need for this search has arisen out of recent legislation making land owners responsible for contamination remediation on land that they own. Similarly, the recent increase in the frequency of the flooding of property has affected the insurability of some premises located near to or adjacent to sources of flooding. Accordingly, in every transaction, a conveyancer must consider whether contamination is a relevant issue. Searches and enquiries should be made about environmental concerns. Hence the need for environmental searches including enquiries about flooding.

4.2.1.2 Extra searches

In addition, you should also appreciate that other searches may be necessary and you can only decide on what others are required by looking closely at the address and location of the subject property. England and Wales can be viewed as a patchwork of exclusive localities. The use of exclusive comes from the possibility that each locality can have a speciality, a peculiarity, all to itself. Consequently searches can be specialised or localised depending on the location of the subject property. An examiner could quite easily place a subject property in the Greater Manchester area and ask about pre-contract searches. In doing so you would be expected to know that coal mining and brine extraction might affect the property and consequently searches would be required to address these potential concerns. Examples of some of these less common localised searches are:

(a) *Limestone mining searches.* If the property is located in Dudley, Sandwell, Walsall or Wolverhampton, a search should be sent to the local council asking about limestone mining. The result will reveal the presence, or indeed absence, of disused underground workings that could cause subsidence.

(b) *Clay mining searches.* If the property is located in Devon or Cornwall, a search should be sent to English China Clay Company asking about clay mining. The result will reveal the presence or absence of any operations that could cause subsidence.

(c) *Brine extraction searches.* If the property is located in Cheshire or Greater Manchester, a search should be sent to the Cheshire Brine Subsidence Compensation Board asking about brine extraction works in the locality. The result will reveal the presence or absence of old workings that could cause subsidence.

(d) *Tin mining searches.* If the property is located in Devon or Cornwall, a search should be sent to the Cornish Chamber of Mines asking about tin mining. The search result will reveal the presence or absence of disused mines that could cause subsidence.

(e) *The New Forest.* If the property is located in Hampshire (and parts of Dorset too), and is in or near to the New Forest, then a search must be carried out with the Verderers of the New Forest. This is because by s. 11 of the Commons Registration Act 1965 the New Forest is excluded from the provisions of that Act. This search will confirm if the land is common land or is affected by common rights.

4.2.1.3 The National Land Information Service

The modernisation of the process of making searches has been ushered in with the creation of the National Land Information Service. The idea behind the NLIS is to create an environment that will allow speedy and simple access to a wide range of land and property information, held on the databases of many different public and private sector groups. The objective is that this wide range of data will be available from a single point of enquiry. This is because it brings together in one point of enquiry almost all the different agencies involved in a conveyance, such as the local authority, the Land Registry, the local water companies, Companies House, the Environmental agency and the Coal Authority. The NLIS is now operative (having gone live in February 2001) in all of England and Wales through three NLIS licensed channels. Practitioners can set up facilities to carry out searches via these companies, whose web site addresses are set out in section 4.5 below. Eventually the NLIS will use Britain's first comprehensive gazetteer of addressable properties: *The National Land and Property Gazetteer.* All addresses will be given a unique identifier, called a 'Unique Property Reference Number' (UPRN), which will be used to cross-reference data for conveyancing searches. Indeed, there is already a section in the new CON 29 for practitioners to insert the NLPG UPRN to assist in identifying the subject property.

4.2.2 PRE-CONTRACT ENQUIRIES

The buyer must carry out all appropriate enquiries before entering into a binding contract to purchase the subject property. If a buyer does make all necessary enquiries of the seller, and gets sensible answers, an informed decision can then be taken about the nature and suitability of the property based on all the information obtained prior to exchange. So a buyer will need to find out as much as possible about the subject property before contracts are exchanged. The simple yet compelling reason for this is that the buyer must take the property in whatever condition it is in, at the point when there is a binding contract for the purchase. Consequently, the law imposes a clear obligation upon the buyer to find out as much about the property because the common law recognises that the seller has only a limited duty of disclosure.

Pre-contract enquiries, otherwise called preliminary enquiries can, in domestic transactions, take two different forms. The first type is the orthodox traditional form in the style of a list of far reaching questions aimed at the seller and intended to seek out as much detail via the seller's solicitor. In commercial transactions traditional lists of questions are commonly used as specific questions will be necessary for non-domestic transactions. The reason being that commercial properties will usually be more complicated than a house or flat and in may cases involve leaseholds that require particular enquiries about the nature of the tenancy. The second modern style form emanates from changes made by the Law Society. Preliminary enquiries have been greatly affected by procedural changes ushered in by the Law Society's National Conveyancing Protocol. Practitioners should acquaint themselves with the contents of the old-style printed traditional forms of enquiries before contract as well as with the new Protocol Property Information Forms. By doing this you will come to appreciate the ways in which the forms differ and how the conveyancing process has been, to a limited extent, streamlined with the adoption of the Protocol approach.

The old style preliminary enquiry forms have been replaced by client questionnaires that form an integral part of the Protocol. The 4th Edition of the Protocol brought with it a revision of these questionnaires. The 4th Edition forms are:

(i) The Seller's Property Information Form (2nd Edition), called Form Prop 1. It has two parts, one to be completed by the seller and the other to be completed by the seller's practitioner.

(ii) The Seller's Leasehold Information Form (2nd Edition), called Form Prop 4. This also has two parts, completed in the same way as the previous form.

(iii) Fixtures Fittings and Contents New Form (3rd Edition) (Form Prop 6).

Many conveyancing practitioners have adopted the Protocol 'enquiry' forms even when they are not actually using the full Protocol process. They will also use the Protocol forms specifically dedicated to leaseholds. However, others remain traditionally minded and use pre-printed forms, or their own in-house preliminary enquiry forms. These questions, sometimes actually entitled preliminary enquiries and sometimes enquiries before contract, are listed in duplicate and submitted to the seller. (Two copies are issued as a convenient and helpful practice, enabling the seller's practitioner to retain a copy of the questions with replies as a file copy.) Whatever form is used, the intention remains the same: to seek out answers from the seller, about any matters that affect or could affect the subject property.

When using Protocol forms, there still remains the difficulty of reconciling the professional obligation on the buyer's conveyancing practitioner to make all proper and reasonable enquiries on behalf of their client with the aim of the Protocol, that of streamlining the enquiry process. The difference between this aspect of the Protocol procedures and the buyer's conveyancing practitioner's overriding duty to the client now appears to be very slender. It seems inevitable that either the printed Protocol forms will continue to expand, or they will be accompanied by copious extra enquiries raised by anxious or perhaps prudent conveyancing practitioners. It is only natural for them to incline towards more rather than fewer questions. This is of course in the perhaps vain hope that, notwithstanding the Property Information Forms, by asking as many questions as possible, practitioners might be able to avoid negligence claims by dissatisfied clients.

It is clear that when a conveyancer is involved in the buying or selling of tenanted properties, the heavier burden rests with the buyer's practitioner. This is because the buyer will want to have full details of the title approved, as well as details of the tenancy or tenancies affecting the subject property. A buyer will expect a good and marketable title to the subject property, as well as a letting that is upon terms that the buyer deems acceptable. This will of course centre on the rental due, but will also cover other terms of the tenancy or letting. Therefore, this particular form of conveyancing transaction in particular requires extra care when raising preliminary enquiries. This is also the case when looking at the title and when raising requisitions. In summary, the following matters should always form the subject of preliminary enquiries:

(a) *Disputes*. No buyer would willingly buy a property that is subject to an ongoing dispute. Furthermore it is incumbent upon a seller to advise a buyer of any dispute particularly one that involves a neighbour.

(b) *Notices*. A buyer will want to know about notices served upon the seller from say the local authority or central government or the landlord of the subject premises.

(c) *Boundaries and fences*.

(d) *Services and conducting media*. Does the property have the benefit of all the main services such as gas and electricity? Is there main drainage or does the property have a private drainage arrangement?

(e) *Exclusive facilities*.

(f) *Shared facilities*.

(g) *Occupiers*. This might cover both tenants as well as licencees.

(h) *Use and planning*.

(j) *Service charges*. This can cover both leaseholds as well as freeholds paying an estate rentcharge and will therefore cover both commercial and residential properties.

(k) *Insurance arrangements*.

(l) *Covenants*. On the title and possibly in a lease.

(m) *Flooding and general environmental concerns*.

There will be a need for additional core topics for leasehold matters. For example, it is a great help for the buyer and the buyer's conveyancer if the seller can accurately confirm the names and addresses of the lessor, any superior lessor, the superior lessor's managing agent, if any, and the superior lessor's solicitors. If there is a management company mentioned in any of the leases of the subject property, full details of the management company, its officers, agents and solicitors should be requested.

4.2.2.1 Commercial Property Standard Enquiries

The Commercial Property Standard Enquiries (CPSEs) are a set of documents that have been drafted by members of the London Property Support Lawyers Group under the sponsorship of the British Property Federation, (BPF). Contributions were also made by a number of other firms and individuals. The CPSEs are endorsed by the BPF and it is anticipated that they might become industry standard pre-contract enquiries for commercial property conveyancing. Form CPSE.1 is designed to cover all commercial property transactions and will (together with any additional enquiries relevant to the particular transaction) be sufficient if the transaction deals only with a freehold sold with vacant possession. The following supplemental enquiries are intended to be used in conjunction with CPSE.1. Which particular additional form or forms will be required will depend upon the individual circumstances of each transaction. The following supplemental forms are available:

1. *CPSE.2*: where the property is sold subject to existing tenancies.
2. *CPSE.3*: where a lease of a property is being granted.
3. *CPSE.4*: where the property being sold is leasehold.

The enquiries set out in CPSE1 cover the following topics all of which will normally be of concern when buying a commercial property and can therefore be used whether the property is subject to a letting or not:

1. boundaries and extent	2. party walls
3. rights benefiting the property	4. adverse rights affecting the property
5. title policies (by way of indemnity)	6. access to neighbouring land
7. access to and from the property	8. physical condition
9. contents	10. utilities and services
11. fire certificates and means of escape	12. planning and building regulations
13. statutory agreements and infrastructure	14. statutory and other requirements
15. environmental (to include flooding)	16. occupiers and employees
17. insurance	18. rates and other outgoings
19. capital allowances	20. Value Added Tax (VAT) registration information
21. transfer of a business as a going concern (TOGC)	22. other VAT treatment
23. standard-rated supplies	24. exempt supplies
25. zero-rated supplies	26. transactions outside the scope of VAT (other than TOGCS)
27. notices	28. disputes

Finally as a general word of warning, the seller and the seller's solicitor should be aware of the risks of qualifying a reply to an enquiry with words like 'not so far as the seller is aware' or 'not to our knowledge but no warranty can be given'. These and similar phrases are treated by the courts as an implied representation that the seller and the seller's solicitors have no actual knowledge of a matter and that they have made all the investigations that a prudent conveyancer would be expected to have made (*William Sindall PLC v. Cambridgeshire County Council* [1994] 1 WLR 1016). Clearly, an answer of this type is intended to avoid making the effort to research the true answer. The decision makes it clear that the answer will infer that the work was done even if in reality it was not!

4.2.3 TOWN AND COUNTRY PLANNING

Town and country planning legislation seeks to control the development of land and buildings, (see s. 57(1) of the Town and Country Planning Act 1990). In particular, this section stipulates that 'planning permission is required for the carrying out of any development of land'. Development is defined by s. 55 as being of two kinds:

1. 'the carrying out of building, engineering, mining or other operations in, on, over or under land'; and,
2. 'the making of any material change in the use of any buildings or other land'.

Types of use are defined within the Town and Country Planning (Use Classes) Order 1987, which lists sixteen separate classes. If a client intends to carry out development in the manner defined by the Act then planning permission, and a planning consent, will be required. This can be obtained in one of two ways:

1. by a permission deemed to have been given as a consequence of the effects of the Town and Country Planning (General Permitted Development) Order 1995; or
2. by a formal application for planning permission submitted to the local planning authority. If the Town and Country Planning (General Permitted Development) Order 1995 does not apply then an express application will be needed.

(You should be aware that general permissions for change across different use classes are authorised by the Town and Country Planning (General Permitted Development) Order 1995.) If the local planning authority becomes aware of a breach of planning control, they have the power to issue and serve an enforcement notice. Failure to comply with an enforcement notice can amount to a criminal offence for which magistrates can impose a fine of up to £20,000.

Where enforcement action is contemplated it must be taken within four years of any operational development (i.e. such as the erection of a new building). The four-year period runs from when the operations were substantially completed. Similarly, a four-year period for enforcement operates for changes of use of any building to use as a single dwellinghouse, running from when the fresh use commenced. In the case of any other breach of planning law, the enforcement action period is ten years from the date of any breach. Any other breach will be all breaches including changes of use other than operational development or a change of use to a single dwellinghouse. The four-year rule therefore applies to the change of use of a building to a single dwellinghouse. The four-year rule also applies to building works such as a flat conversion. If a notice is validly served then the recipient can appeal to the Secretary of State on one or more of the grounds for appeal set out in s. 174 of the Town and Country Planning Act 1990. These grounds include indicating that planning permission ought to be granted and that the proposals, if they occur, do not constitute a breach of planning control.

While an enforcement notice is under appeal it has no effect. The consequence of this is that the alleged improper use can continue. If the authority wishes to terminate the use forthwith upon service of an enforcement notice then they must also issue and serve a stop notice. The planning authority can rely upon s. 183 of the Town and Country Planning Act 1990, which empowers them to issue stop notices that effectively prohibit any use or activity contained or mentioned in the allied enforcement notice. A stop notice will not prohibit the use of any building as a dwellinghouse (s. 183(4) of the Town and Country Planning Act 1990). Accordingly, a stop notice will arise only in the context of an enforcement notice.

4.2.4 A PRE-CONTRACT DECISION TREE

Please see the diagram opposite for the different branch-decisions and selections you need to make for searches, enquiries and planning concerns. There are three clear strands to the diagram and each represents the approach you will need to consider for each part covered by this chapter. The decision tree can apply equally to commercial as well as domestic property transactions.

4.3 SUBJECT ASSESSMENTS

It is inevitable that you will encounter some or all of the topics covered in this chapter in a subject assessment of property law and practice or conveyancing. Pre-contract searches and enquiries are problem areas in practice and if for no other reason examiners will want to be sure that students have a thorough grounding in these complex areas.

4.3.1 SUBJECT ASSESSMENT QUESTIONS AND A COMMENTARY UPON THE TYPE AND CONTENT OF SUBJECT ASSESSMENT QUESTIONS

Question 1

RICHARDS ABBEY AND PARTNERS, SOLICITORS
OFFICE MEMORANDUM

From   The Training Partner

To   The Trainee solicitor

Purchase of Red Lion House—New Offices

I have had a brief look at this commercial conveyancing file and understand you are familiar with it having assisted Ms Brownlow, your principal, with the matter since our firm was first instructed by the buyer. As you know, the seller's solicitors have produced full title details by deducing title on the basis of an unregistered title, and it would seem that because of the commercial nature of the transaction the Law Society's National Conveyancing Protocol is not being used. When I looked at the file I particularly noted that the property is located on the edge of town adjoining open countryside and fields.

   In the circumstances, I would like you to let me know what searches should we and/or our clients make before exchange and why? Where should those searches be made? Please let me have an explanatory note on this before close of business today. If there are any incidental points arising, please let me know.

Commentary

This is a typical question to be found in modern conveyancing examination or subject assessment papers. It is in the form of an Office Memorandum from a Principal to the Trainee Solicitor and is in fact seeking to replicate just the kind of note a trainee might receive in the office. This should immediately make you realise that the answer must be in the form of a Memorandum in reply. Style marks could be available if you remember to reply in this uncomplicated way. An essay answer is not appropriate; you must direct your answer in the form of a memorandum dealing with the practical problems point by point. By failing to adopt

Pre-contract decision tree

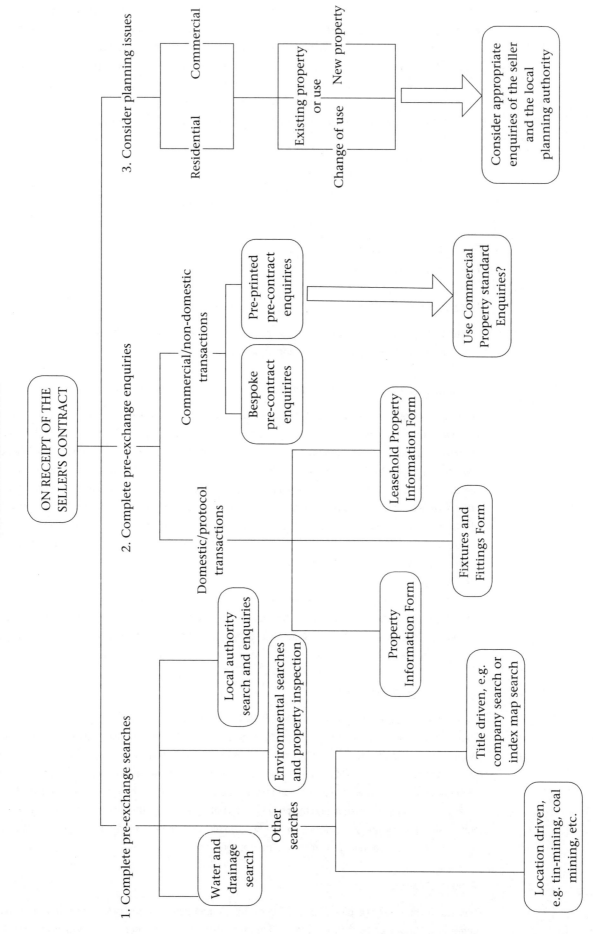

a memorandum answer form you might lose all important style marks that are otherwise easily attained. The question is deceptively simple in that you might be tempted to just consider the main local authority search. Of course the answer requires you to consider this along with some of the more unusual but nevertheless important searches. The question is in two parts; first you are required to suggest appropriate searches and secondly you need to show where these searches should be made. To get full marks you should make sure you deal fully with both aspects of the question. Finally, reference is made to searches the client may need to make. Clearly this is mentioned in the question for a reason as the following answer demonstrates.

Suggested answer

RICHARDS ABBEY AND PARTNERS, SOLICITORS
OFFICE MEMORANDUM

To   The Training Partner

From   The Trainee solicitor

<u>Purchase of Red Lion House</u>

I write to reply to your memorandum enquiring about what searches might be necessary in this case and set out below all the searches I consider appropriate to this matter:

1. <u>Local land charges search and enquiries of local authority and water and drainage searches</u>

Every buyer should make a local search before exchanging contracts. It will disclose public charges many of which are not matters of title and so not within the seller's duty of disclosure. These charges will be registered by the local authority whose obligation it is to record the same. Standard condition 3 of the Standard Conditions of Sale (4th Edition) makes a sale subject to local land charges. Accordingly the buyer must search to make sure full details are obtained from the council of all relevant information affecting the property concerned. The search is made at the local authority accompanied by a plan if the land is not easily identifiable from the postal address. The search also directs important enquiries to the local authority concerned with subjects within their control such as road schemes, notices or planning matters. The search and enquiries are usually sent by post but if the matter is urgent you can carry out a personal search of the Local Land Charges Register and ask questions of other relevant departments such as highways and planning. Unfortunately not all councils will answer all the enquiries on a personal basis. If a complete set of answers is not available a personal search should be avoided. The client should also be warned that the results of personal searches will not have the authenticated stamp of the local authority, so if the council give an incorrect verbal answer, it may later be difficult to prove an error on the council's part.

2. <u>Water and drainage search</u>

Local authorities have abdicated the responsibility for answering water and drainage enquiries and now refer questions about water supplies and drainage to the local water company. Details of the English Water Service Companies can be obtained from Water UK 1 Queen Anne's Gate London SW1H 9BT (www.water.org.uk). Water UK represents the water companies. There is now a new drainage search and all the water companies use it in a common format. The search covers water and drainage items including detail on water supply, metering and the proximity of a public sewer. We therefore need to complete a separate water and drainage search for this property. To obtain an increase level of indemnity cover, the search should be marked up as being a commercial transaction.

3. <u>Index map search</u>

This search should always be made when purchasing unregistered land. It will confirm that the land is unregistered because if by chance the land is registered then the title number (and tenure) will be revealed.

It will also reveal any caution against first registration registered at the Land Registry. The search is made at a Land Registry local office accompanied by a plan although the registry will issue a search result without a plan if the property can be clearly identified from the postal address. The search is in the Index Map maintained at the Registry for the relevant locality. As this property is at the edge of town I assume a plan will be required. You mentioned in your memorandum that the title to this property is unregistered. You should bear in mind that all of England and Wales is now an area of compulsory registration. Accordingly, if the last conveyance to the seller was for value (and therefore compulsorily registrable), and this was after 1 December 1990, then the seller must rectify this defect by registering the title. In these circumstances the seller must ensure that the property is offered for sale with a proper and fully registered title.

4. A search in the Land Charges Register

Again this is relevant to unregistered land only. (Although even with registered land it would be prudent to carry out a bankruptcy search to make sure the seller was not an undisclosed bankrupt!) It is recommended that a land charges search should be made before exchange of contracts as well as before completion. A land charge (e.g. D(ii) restrictive covenant) duly registered will be binding on a purchaser for value. A prudent purchaser will therefore want to be aware of it before exchange, notwithstanding any subsequent cause of action he may have against the seller for non-disclosure. It should be noted that a land charges search against the seller would reveal any bankruptcy/liquidation registration. In this way any such problems can be addressed before exchange when there is sufficient time rather than after when time is limited by the impending contractual completion date. The search is made at the Government Land Charges Department in Plymouth against the names of the estate owners not the land and for their periods of ownership.

5. Commons registration search

This search should be made in any case where the land to be purchased adjoins a village green or common land, or is in open country. This is irrespective of whether the land has a registered title or not. It is unlikely that Red Lion House was built on common land but, given the property's position, it would be prudent to search as there could be rights concerning the use of common land that affect the property. It should be noted that in the case of *G & K Ladenbau (UK) Ltd. v. Crawley and de Reya (a firm)* [1978] 1 All ER 682; it was held that failure to make a commons search in circumstances where one ought properly to be made could be grounds for an action in negligence against the solicitor. You make the search at the county council accompanied by a plan.

6. Physical inspection of the property

This is of the subject property and should be undertaken by the client purchaser in all cases. There are three particular reasons for this. First, to check that there are no undisclosed occupants within the property who could claim rights of occupation and thereby delay or indeed defeat completion. Secondly, to check that there have been no material changes to the property that might adversely affect it or its value since the buyers put in their offer. Thirdly if the purchase includes fixtures and fitting it is always sensible to check that those items are still at the property and properly listed on the contract. In this way there can be no doubt as to what is actually being purchased and whether or not it actually exists!

7. Mining search

I am not personally acquainted with the locality of the subject property and I am therefore not sure whether it is or has been affected by mining. To be on the safe side I would suggest that you carry out a coal mining search. This kind of search is necessary in an area of coal mining or an area that has been so affected in the past. If you are not sure whether the property is so affected British Coal maintains a detailed list of each and every area that has been concerned with coal mining either presently or in the past. The main concern is of course subsidence that might affect the property and whether or not compensation has been paid or indeed whether or not there are any relevant claims pending. The search should be sent to British Coal with a plan.

8. Other uncommon searches

Should the property be affected by an adjacent river or canal a search should be directed to the appropriate water authority to check on matters relevant to the water way such as fishing rights and bank side ownership. The search is made by letter to the relevant water authority.

Local mineral extraction searches can also be considered although they may not be relevant to this particularly property as they are very much limited to the localities where the mineral is to be found. The minerals concerned include brine, tin and limestone. As I am not acquainted with the area could you please decide if any of these are necessary although if in doubt a search should be made. Where they should be made depends on each type of mineral.

9. Finally an environmental search is also recommended

A practitioner acting for a buyer is required to make all prudent searches and enquiries and this should certainly include an environmental search. (Although this is a commercial matter, it is noteworthy that the CML Lenders' Handbook says a buyer's practitioner should 'carry out any other searches which may be appropriate to the particular property, taking into account its locality and other features'.) We cannot merely rely upon any contaminated land information obtained from the local authority in the reply to the enquiries in the local authority search. This is because the detail supplied is likely to be insufficient, being limited to land identified by the local authority as contaminated or potentially affected by nearby contaminated land. It is possible to make a search with the Environment Agency but the results can take time to be issued and the information likely to be available may not be widespread enough to be of real benefit. However, environmental searches can be obtained from the Landmark Information Group (www.landmark-information.co.uk) and they can assist with both residential and commercial properties. The search will cover historical land use, current contaminating and polluting processes, coal-mining areas, radon affected areas as well as risk of subsidence and flooding. Furthermore the Environment Agency has made maps available on the Internet that show areas potentially liable to flooding. This is a free service and can be accessed using a property postcode at www.environment-agency.gov.uk. The maps however do not indicate the level of risk. There is an alternative approach. Countrywide Legal Indemnities offer an insurance solution. The insurance policy on offer is intended to cover homeowners against the potential liability for remediation costs of any contaminants found on their land. Full details can be found at www.helpforconveyancers.com. The cover includes any shortfall in the market value of the property as a result of the remediation work having been carried out.

I do hope this explanatory note is of assistance but if there is anything else I can assist with please let me know.

TIME ENGAGED 45 MINUTES

TRAINEE SOLICITOR

Question 2

Your Principal's secretary has taken a telephone call from Ms Alexandra Temple, a long-established and important client of the firm, who needs some urgent advice. Alexandra would like someone from the firm to ring her back before 3 p.m. as she is leaving for her summer holiday this afternoon and wants peace of mind before going. Your Principal is out at a meeting for the rest of the day. It is your responsibility to provide cover for your Principal during this afternoon.

The secretary's note of the telephone conversation is as follows:

'12.25 p.m. Attending Ms Temple on the telephone.

Now that her car restoration business is so successful she is thinking of buying a detached house (about eleven years old) on a small and exclusive residential estate. The house is on the edge of the estate occupying a good-sized corner site. It seems that the side road is a private unmade road. The side road is very quiet and is used infrequently as it leads down to a private paddock. She especially wants this particular house because the present owner, a Mr Brownlow, has built a large double garage and rear workroom for his own cars five years ago at the bottom of the garden and fronting right onto the side road. For the last four years he has been using the garage for repairing renovating re-spraying and servicing all sorts of vehicles and Ms Temple wishes to do the same. When Ms Temple asked about planning permission the owner Mr Brownlow said as far as he was concerned he didn't think it was a problem and anyway no one so far as he knew has objected. In any event it was only a single storey garage that was entirely in keeping with the general style of buildings on the estate.

Can someone ring her back as soon as possible to advise her if there are any unforeseen problems?'

You duly rang the client after considering all the circumstances and after reading through the client file.

Consider the issues that concerned you and prepare an attendance note for the file of the advice you gave the client when you rang her back.

Commentary

This is another searching question that, on the face of it, seems simple. Do not be deceived. There are several difficult areas of concern that need to be considered and analysed. However your first decision is about the format of your answer. You have been asked for an attendance note and you must adopt this form to ensure your answer is on the right lines. Conveyancing is a system that relies heavily upon rigorous file management along with the accurate recording of events and details. An attendance note being a record of a telephone conversation or a meeting between the client and the solicitor is a fundamental constituent element of just such a file. The areas of concern should be considered in turn and especially the planning issue which patently merits careful examination. However the question is not just about planning, it actually touches upon other important issues highlighted in the following answer. In conveyancing it is common to find that competent answers will require a broad base stretching over several topics. Finally remember this is a practical matter and in practice you must always record your time. This being the case end your attendance note with an indication of how long you think the conversation was. For any solicitor or licensed conveyancer, time is money.

Suggested answer

Suggested telephone attendance note of advice:

RICHARDS ABBEY AND PARTNERS, SOLICITORS
INTERNAL MEMO

Re Alexandra Temple and her proposed residential house purchase with garage

Subsequently telephoning back Ms Temple and advising her as follows:

1. Planning

There are two potential planning difficulties, first was the garage built with planning consent and secondly has there been a material change of use of that garage from a mere garage for the storage of cars conveniently close by the house into commercial garage premises? (s. 55(1) Town and Country Planning Act 1990).

(i) So far as the building of the garage is concerned I advised the client that this appeared to be a building that would have required a planning consent from the local planning authority, usually the local authority, prior to erection. However, there is a time limit for enforcement action of four years and this has passed so no enforcement notice can be served by the local authority requiring its demolition (s. 172(4) Town and Country Planning Act 1990).

(ii) I further advised Ms Temple that there has been a material change of use in relation to the garage from residential to business use. This would have required planning permission that it seems was not granted. There is a ten-year time limit for the service of an enforcement notice by the local authority in these circumstances and the council could therefore serve an enforcement notice upon the owner of the property at any time requiring the business use to cease (s. 4 Planning and Compensation Act 1991). A buyer would buy subject to the breach and the possibility of an enforcement notice affecting them in the future. A local search would reveal the existence or otherwise of an enforcement notice. Failure to comply with an enforcement notice is a criminal offence.

There is a third difficulty allied to planning and that is whether or not the seller obtained building regulations approval from the local authority for the garage at the time it was built. Indeed even assuming the garage did not need a planning consent it would have had to comply with building regulations that have been issued to ensure that buildings comply with precise and detailed standards of construction. In the case of *Cottingham v. Attey Bower & Jones (A firm)* [2000] EGCS 48 it was noted that injunction proceedings under s. 36(6) of the Building Act 1984 enable a local authority to take enforcement proceedings at any time after the works have been carried out. This provision in effect creates an unlimited obligation upon conveyancers to seek copy building regulation approvals. Proper approvals are required. Indeed, the concern must remain that without building regulations approval the premises may have been erected in a substandard condition. If this was the case then there could be grave potential problems for a purchaser who would be responsible for the maintenance of the structure.

2. Title

The title will need to be checked to establish whether the land is subject to a restrictive covenant prohibiting business use. It is very likely that the developer of the estate would have imposed such a covenant when he sold the house to the first purchaser. He may have created a building scheme so that the covenants are enforceable by the owners of the other houses on the estate. Furthermore, there is the distinct possibility that there was another restrictive covenant imposed at the same time requiring the original developers' permission for the erection of new buildings on the estate, such as the double garage. There is the possibility that a restrictive covenant indemnity policy could be obtained to protect Ms Temple in the light of a claim against her for breach of covenant, although the premium for this could be expensive.

3. Side road

A local search of the property will reveal whether the road is a public highway. If not, the deeds must be checked to see if the owner has the right to walk and drive cars along it. Clearly if there is not such express legal right of way there are very real difficulties for a proposed purchaser who might face the daunting prospect of being lawfully denied access to the garage by the legal owner of the side road. If the local authority decide to adopt the road in the future then the cost of making up the road to an adoptable standard will fall on the frontagers, who would include the owner of the property in question.

4. Advice

In the light of the above I advised Ms Temple against making any firm plans to proceed until we were in receipt of further information and in particular until we knew precisely the position concerning planning issues, building regulations, the ownership of the road and whether or not there were any adverse restrictive covenants affecting the property. She was informed that a local authority search would reveal information about the side road that would inform her decision as to whether or not she should proceed. I went on to say that planning consents relating to the property would be referred to in the search result and that furthermore specific enquiries could be directed to the local planning authority. I also indicated that we would carefully check the seller's title deeds to see if there were any such problematic restrictive covenants but that if there were there could be the possibility of obtaining a restrictive covenant indemnity policy from an insurance company. Insurance cover might also be possible in the absence of a building regulations approval. It was difficult to be optimistic about the business use question and we would probably be advising her not to go ahead if this aspect was crucial to her.

TIME ENGAGED 20 MINUTES

TRAINEE SOLICITOR

Question 3

Ms Benazir Khan has instructed you in connection with her proposed purchase of a house in West Manchester. She has just come from the agents and has told you that she wants to buy the house as quickly as possible because she considers the price to be considerably under the true market value. The last person to live in the house died at the end of last year and the deceased's executors are selling the house. She intends to let the building to students in bed-sits. However, she has mentioned to you some concerns she has being:

1. That the house is on a main road which has been widened a few miles further on and wants to know about future widening plans.

2. That the basement seems to be capable of being lived in but at the moment it is all boarded up and she wants to use it for bed-sits.

3. That some of the houses nearby have been pulled down by the local authority to enable them to build some new council accommodation.

4. That she thinks the house has been occupied by one family for many years.

5. That she knows that just around the corner the same kind of houses are very expensive and are similar fine examples of Victorian architecture that the local authority are keen to preserve.

6. That she wants to put in some modern aluminium double glazing and remove the old original sash and stained-glass windows.

She has asked you to write to her to let her know how you might check on these points. She is particularly concerned because she does not think much information will come from the sellers who are only executors with little or no personal knowledge of the property or the locality.

Commentary

This is another example of a question that is based on a specific and narrow area of the conveyancing process namely the local authority search and enquiries made of the local authority. The question requires a detailed knowledge of the kind of information that might be disclosed in a search result and how that information might be of use to a client in deciding whether or not to purchase a property. In this particular example the points in the question are all there for several good reasons. Each raises an issue that might affect a client and whether or not a property is suitable. The answer must be in the form of a letter of advice and needs to highlight what might be disclosed in the search and should therefore address each point in turn. The client's intentions should be borne in mind at all times, namely the proposed use of the property as bed-sits. Mention should also be made of the seller's limited duty of disclosure even when the sale is by executors. See the case of *Rignall Developments Ltd. v. Halil* [1988] Ch 190.

Remember this assessment could be a test of your writing and drafting skills as well as your knowledge of the conveyancing process. This being so ensure your letter is well structured, written in plain English and avoids legal jargon where possible. Plan your answer before starting and make sure you keep to the plan.

If necessary adopt numbered paragraphs or headings. Remember good legal writing will come from clear legal thinking. The outcome should be concise, clear and to the point.

Suggested answer

Dear Ms Khan,

<u>Your proposed purchase</u>

I refer to your recent instructions concerning your proposed purchase of the house in West Manchester and write to provide you with the information you require. I particularly note that you intend to use the property for student bed-sits and I will refer to this subsequently.

I can confirm that most if not all the concerns you have can be addressed by a local search sent to the appropriate local authority. The local search is actually a local land charge search together with enquiries of the local authority. Section 3 Of the Local Land Charges Act 1975 requires local authorities (usually the district, metropolitan or London Borough Council) to maintain a local land charges register. There are various matters capable of registration but bearing in mind your express concerns it should be noted that the register will contain details of planning charges. The effect of registration is that a buyer is bound by the registrations whether or not a search is made. Accordingly a search of this kind is an absolute necessity for a prudent buyer. The items capable of registration are limited and as a consequence other important details can be sought from the local authority by means of pre-printed enquiry forms. There are lengthy standard enquiries that question the council about road schemes, outstanding notices, compulsory purchase, and areas designated for slum clearance and planning applications and consents.

Turning to your specific requirements, you are firstly concerned with road widening schemes in view of the fact that the property is on a main road that has been widened a few miles further on. Question 3.4 that the council must answer specifically asks if there are any such schemes that may affect the property. Clearly if there are then details must be sought before any decision is made to exchange contracts. Apart from road widening question 3.4 also discloses new road schemes as well that might similarly affect the property concerned.

You say you would like to use the basement for bed-sits although it is at present boarded up. Indeed your intention is to change the use of the whole of the property from a single dwelling house in the occupation of one family to multiple occupation in the form of bed-sits. Two points arise, first can you use the house in this way and secondly can you use the basement? I am of the view that your proposed use would be a material change of use for planning purposes and without any consent authorising the change the multiple occupation would be a breach of planning law. However the local authority search and enquiries would, from the answer to question 1.1, reveal planning applications and consents and if there was a consent for the property to be used in this way then there is no difficulty, otherwise you will need to make a planning application and you will have to decide whether or not you will want to exchange whilst awaiting the outcome of the application. The risk is of course that your application is unsuccessful notwithstanding you may well have already exchanged. As to the basement there is a possibility that due to its condition the council have made a closing order declaring the area to be unfit for human habitation. If this is the case the council search and enquiries will reveal whether or not this is the case. If it is then you may well want to renegotiate the price or withdraw from the transaction altogether.

You have mentioned that nearby the council have demolished houses to make way for a new area of council houses and you are clearly concerned to ensure that your proposed property is not similarly affected. Question 3.11 asks if the property is subject to a compulsory purchase order and orders will be registered as a land charge. Accordingly a local search result will indicate if a property is or is likely to be the subject of compulsory acquisition by the council and if this is the case then of course my advice would have to be that you should not proceed.

Finally, you have mentioned that there are similar houses nearby that the council are keen to preserve and you have also mentioned the fact that you are considering making some external alterations by way of double-glazing. I have taken these two items together because in fact they are interrelated so far as my advice and the council search is concerned. If councils want to preserve a neighbourhood they can do so by declaring a conservation area. If the property is so affected this will be seen as a land charge being a restriction on the use of the land and will be disclosed in the local land charge search result. Indeed if the property is covered by a conservation order then there are severe restrictions placed on an owner which include a prohibition on external alterations such as new windows. Accordingly if the property is in a conservation area you will need to enquire of the council to see if they would allow new aluminium windows otherwise you would be in breach of planning law if you went ahead with the changes without council consent.

I know you do not think that the sellers will provide much information because they are mere executors. However, I can tell you that notwithstanding their capacity the sellers are still obliged to disclose a local land charge if they are aware of it. So if the executors have become aware of a local land charge from the deceased's papers then they will be obliged to provide details failing which you may be entitled to damages or rescission.

To sum up, I am of the view that your concerns will be addressed by the result of a local land charge search and the council's replies to enquiries. I therefore suggest that the search be sent to the local authority as a matter of priority and that I will then let you know the result that should be available two to three weeks from the date of dispatch.

Yours sincerely

TRAINEE SOLICITOR

Question 4

You have been consulted by Istvan Kermes in connection with his proposed sale of his bachelor flat within a large mansion block of flats in the fashionable area of London called Knightsbridge. He has asked you to provide some preliminary advice with a view to him perhaps instructing your firm in connection with the sale. He has decided to sell for two reasons, first, that he wants to move to Hampstead, and secondly, he has been told by his former neighbour Glenys Gould what a quick and efficient job you did recently for Ms Gould when she recently sold her flat in the same block. On coming to see you Mr Kermes indicated that his previous neighbour had explained to him that the reason for her sale going through so quickly was that a lot of the usual questions normally asked by the buyer before exchange of contracts had been avoided by you adopting something called 'The Protocol'. As a consequence Mr Kermes wants to know more about the Protocol and in particular how it changes the system of asking questions before exchange of contracts takes place.

Would you please make a written file note of the advice you gave Mr Kermes summing up the way in which enquiries are dealt within the context of the Protocol and the manner in which this differs from the traditional approach.

Commentary

This is a very specific question in that the area concerned is very precise and narrow. Accordingly you should only attempt questions of this type if you have a comprehensive understanding of the relevant area. In this question you will be required to show a detailed understanding of the way in which preliminary enquiries have been affected and altered by the introduction of the National Conveyancing Protocol. Arguably, this has been the most successful element of the whole Protocol and the one most commonly adopted by practitioners throughout England and Wales. It is therefore not surprising to see a question of this very specific nature that seeks to identify the candidate's knowledge of not only Protocol enquiries but also orthodox preliminary enquiries as well. The answer required will not comprise a detailed examination of the whole of

the Protocol. What is called for is just an examination of the area of enquiries only although a brief introduction to the Protocol is appropriate. A good answer will clearly highlight the differences between the old
and the new systems and their strong and weak aspects. On a practical basis ensure the note contains a file
reference and that you record your time.

Suggested answer

File Note for Client matter No. 505245:

Attended upon Mr Istvan Kermes to provide him with some preliminary advice in the hope that he will
instruct the firm in connection with his proposed flat sale. He asked about conveyancing in general and
preliminary enquiries in particular with special reference to the National Conveyancing Protocol and how its
implementation might speed up the sale of his flat. I advised him in general terms about the process of conveyancing and in particular about pre-contract enquiries. I pointed out that the buyer will want to find out
as much as possible about his flat before contracts are exchanged. I mentioned that in the main 'caveat
emptor' still applies to a conveyance and that there were therefore compelling reasons for a buyer to raise
as many questions as possible. Indeed I explained that the buyer's solicitor had a duty to make all usual and
necessary enquiries and if they were not made a solicitor might be liable in negligence.

I went on to mention that in the orthodox form of conveyancing the system of asking questions is normally
by standard pre-printed questionnaires issued by the buyer's solicitor and to be answered by the seller. These
standard enquiries will include amongst others questions about boundaries, disputes, notices, alterations to
the property and planning matters. These are all material, relevant and important matters that a buyer will
want to know about before proceeding with a purchase. I pointed out that buyers' solicitors will raise vast
numbers of enquiries on the basis that if they do not they might be seen as acting negligently. It is not unusual
to see such enquiries stretching over twenty or more pages and comprising dozens of multi-sectioned questions. Of course a seller can refuse to give answers but if this happens then any sensible buyer will immediately
back out of the proposed transaction on the basis that the seller must have something to hide. I carried on to
indicate that this system can be particularly time consuming because the seller must wait for the buyer to raise
preliminary enquiries even though they will probably be in a standard pre-printed format.

I then referred to the modern system of conveyancing ushered in by the Law Society in 1990 in the form
of the National Conveyancing Protocol. The intention of the Protocol was to streamline the system of conveyancing, the Law Society to limit the time between the buyer making the offer and contracts being
exchanged. To ensure that their intention was fulfilled the Protocol envisages the adoption of standardised
documentation. In the case of pre-contract enquiries I explained that this meant the introduction of new
enquiry forms that were to be used in all Protocol conveyancing cases. These were called by the Law Society
'Property Information Forms'. The critical change and indeed the novel element brought in by the Protocol
was that these were issued and completed by the seller's solicitor with the seller and then sent off to the
buyer with the contract and other supporting documentation such as the title details. In this way a great
deal of time is saved by the seller issuing standard enquiries with answers at the very earliest opportunity
and in particular along with the contract and title details. I pointed out that the client would be expected
to help in the completion of these forms as they are in two parts, one for the seller to complete and the
other for the solicitor. I made it clear I would of course check his answers and let him peruse mine to make
sure that the answers were as accurate as possible. I also noted that because the property he intended to
sell was a flat it was most probably leasehold and that consequently there would be an additional form to
complete, the Seller's Leasehold Information Form. This was used to provide extra information applicable
to leasehold properties only and calls for the provision of further documents such as the last ground rent
receipt.

I went on to explain that because of the provisions of section five of the Protocol the buyer's solicitor can
only raise extra or additional enquiries that fulfil specific conditions defined by the Law Society. First, they
must be necessary to clarify something within the documentation supplied, and secondly they must be relevant to the nature or location of the property. It is also accepted that specific questions raised by the buyer

can be asked expressly of the seller. However I made it clear that it is also the case that no enquiry should be made that is about the condition of the property or which could be answered elsewhere such as from the buyer's own searches, survey or inspection. In this way clearly defined limits have been fixed to the extent of the enquiries that can be required. I pointed out that it should be noted that there is no such limitation in the traditional approach where anything goes, right down to questions about the type of telephones in the house or other matters more properly dealt with elsewhere. I made it clear to Mr Kermes that we would be under no obligation to answer any additional enquiries that did not come within the above parameters especially if they are pre-printed on standard forms other than those contemplated by the Protocol.

I summed up by advising Mr Kermes that the Protocol procedure could speed up the process but he would have to assist by helping with the completion of the relevant forms and by providing all necessary documents. I indicated that the traditional system was open to delay and involved the possibility of unnecessary and irrelevant questions being raised that could delay the forward progress of the sale. I made it clear that the fact that the Protocol seeks to limit the number and nature of the buyer's enquiries must assist and I finally pointed out that as we will be issuing the forms with answers at the earliest opportunity it will enable us to control the progress of the sale from the very start of transaction. Mr Kermes said he would think about it and would get back to me later this week.

TIME ENGAGED 45 MINUTES

THE TRAINEE SOLICITOR

4.3.2 MULTIPLE CHOICE QUESTIONS AND ANSWERS TO MUTIPLE CHOICE QUESTIONS

We set out below examples of ten multiple choice questions that you might encounter in a subject assessment. Thereafter you will find some typical short answer questions that can also feature in a subject assessment and which cover pre-contract searches and enquiries. Answers to both are also set out below. Remember our initial guidance. Never leave multiple choice answers with a blank multiple choice. If there are four possibilities and you are not sure of the answer select the one you think might be right, you have a one in four chance of getting it right! Also look at the instructions on the paper. If it says select the right answer on the paper by circling the correct choice then do just that. Do not make a tick or underline your selection as the strict response would be to fail you even though the selection may be correct.

4.3.2.1 Multiple choice questions

Unless otherwise directed, select the right answer by circling it in each question. Should you think that none of the selections apply please explain why not in your answer book.

1. You are buying for a client a commercial unit in Hackney in the Centre of London. Which of the following pre-contract searches would you not complete?

   (a) local authority search

   (b) coal mining search

   (c) water and drainage search

   (d) environmental search

2. When applying for a local authority search which registry deals with the application and issues the result of the search?

   (a) the land charges registry

   (b) the land registry

(c) the local land charges registry

(d) the district land registry

3. 'Where planning law enforcement action is contemplated it must be taken within four years of any development.'

Is this statement TRUE/FALSE? Please delete the incorrect choice.

4. 'Because s. 55(5) of the Town and Country Planning Act 1990 states that the use of an external part of a property for advertising will require planning consent, if there is any advertising on a subject property, then a pre-contract enquiry should be raised about planning consents for any advertising hoarding.'

Is this statement TRUE/FALSE? Please delete the incorrect choice.

5. Why is the case of *Cottingham v. Attey Bower & Jones (A firm)* [2000] EGCS 48 of importance to conveyancing practitioners? Is it because—

   (a) it confirmed that solicitors have a duty to mortgagees as a trustee of the mortgage advance?

   (b) it highlighted the need to register titles before the expiry of a search priority period?

   (c) it confirmed the need for planning consents even when demolishing a property without replacing it with another?

   (d) it confirmed that solicitors would be acting negligently by failing to take all reasonable steps to obtain copies of building regulation consents?

6. The National Land Information Service allows conveyancing practitioners to apply over the Internet for pre-contract searches. Which of the following pre-contract searches cannot be obtained through this service?

   (a) a coal mining search report

   (b) a drainage and water search

   (c) the local land charge or local authority search

   (d) the land registry index map search

7. A buyer should always be advised to inspect a subject property prior to exchange. The reasons for the inspection are listed below. Please indicate which is not relevant:

   (a) to arrange for contracts to be signed in readiness for exchange

   (b) to check who is in actual occupation of the property

   (c) to check on rights and easements affecting or benefiting the property

   (d) to check that the fixtures and fittings contracted to be sold are in the subject property just prior to exchange

8. Your client has asked you if you can tell from the pre-contract papers whether there are any road schemes that might affect her proposed purchase. Where would you normally expect to find the answer?

   (a) in the draft contract?

   (b) in the drainage and water search result?

   (c) in the land registry index map search result?

   (d) in the local land charge or local authority search result?

9. Your local authority search result confirms that the council for this property has paid an improvement grant. What should you do about this entry?

   (a) ignore it, because it is for the benefit of the property being purchased, as it is an improvement

(b) advise the client about this benefit for the property before moving to exchange of contracts

(c) check to see if it is repayable and if so whether this liability might accrue to your client

(d) check to see if other grants are available in respect of this or other property in the locality

10. Question 3.12 of a local authority search covers contaminated land. There is sufficient information in the answers for a buyer of residential property.

    Is this statement TRUE/FALSE? Please delete the incorrect choice.

4.3.2.2 *Answers to multiple choice questions*

1. The correct selection is (b). The reason for this is that there is no coal mining in London, nor has there ever been and it is a reasonable assumption to make that this is common knowledge enabling the correct answer to be made on this basis. Clearly all the other searches listed will be relevant to a transaction of the kind described in the question.

2. The correct answer is (c). Students always get confused about which registry is which and who does what. Remember the local searches are of the local land charges registry while the land charges registry deals with land charge searches as well as bankruptcy searches. Just to confuse you further the land charges service operates under the umbrella of the land registry!

3. The correct answer is that the statement is false. The reason being that while there is a four-year rule there is also a ten-year rule, i.e. the four-year rule does not apply to **any** development but only to specific parts of planning law. The statement is half right and is written in this way to catch the hasty candidate who has not thought through to the correct answer. Always pause and think about an answer to avoid being caught by this all too familiar trap.

4. The correct answer is that the statement is true. If there are adverts on a building then s. 55(5) will apply and enquiries should be made about possible planning consents.

5. The correct selection is (d). Regrettably, injunction proceedings under s. 36(6) of the Building Act 1984 enable local authorities to take enforcement proceedings at any time after building works have been carried out. This provision in effect creates an unlimited obligation upon Conveyancers to seek copy building regulation approvals.

6. The correct answer is in fact that none of the selections apply! This is a 'trick' question in that all of these searches can be applied for through the National Land Information Service. Indeed, there are very few searches that cannot be obtained through this electronic facility. Always be on guard for the possibility of just such a question appearing in your subject assessment where you have to have the courage to say that none are correct and explain why.

7. The correct answer is (a). The other three selections are all highly relevant reasons why a buyer should always be advised to inspect a subject property prior to exchange. Selection (a) has little or no relevance as they will normally be dealt with between a solicitor and client.

8. The correct selection is (d). This is just the kind of information you would expect to find in this search. Question 3.2 in this search asks about land to be acquired for road works. A positive answer in the result will be concerned with land to be acquired for highway construction or improvement. Question 3.4 asks about nearby road schemes. Answers will draw attention to road schemes within 200 metres of the property, including alterations and improvements to existing roads as well as flyovers and underpasses.

9. The correct answer is (c). It can be the case that there are conditions attaching to such a grant and that they require repayment possibly on change of ownership and that repayment call fall upon a buyer to pay. To avoid this liability the seller should be made to repay on or before completion.

10. The correct answer is that the statement is false. Practitioners should not merely rely upon any contaminated land information obtained from the local authority in the reply to question 3.12 of the enquiries in the local authority search. This is because the detail supplied is likely to be insufficient, being limited to land identified by the local authority as contaminated or potentially affected by nearby contaminated land. A detailed environmental search report should be obtained for the buyer and the buyer's surveyor.

4.3.3 SHORT ANSWER QUESTIONS WITH ANSWERS

We set out below answers to this type of assessment with brief explanations where required highlighting either the purpose of the question or the nature of the answer.

4.3.3.1 Short answer questions

Question 1

You act for Kevin Scott who intends to purchase some freehold offices in a converted residential property in Edgware in North London. He has asked you to make sure that he can use the premises for his public relations business bearing in mind he is buying the property for £750,000. He also thinks that there might be a problem with traffic as the property is right on a main road.

Please indicate how you intend to advise your client and what documentation and any relevant parts or sections you will reply upon for that advice.

Question 2

You act for Dean and Angela Richards, the proposed purchasers of a residential property called 69 Pottery Lane Burmantoft Leeds. You have completed your local authority search and there is nothing onerous or unusual in the result of the search made of the local land charges registry. The replies to the accompanying enquiries are attached with the actual questions. (see Appendix 4.1) Where necessary please comment upon the replies given to the standard questions.

Question 3

You act for Bazlur Rashid in connection with his purchase of a freehold property in Leicester. It is a three bedroom terraced house with both small front and rear gardens. The seller is Leslie King. The Protocol has been adopted. You have received the seller's replies to the Property Information Form although the solicitors for the seller have not completed Part II saying that it is not their policy to do so. The replies to Part I are attached (see Appendix 4.2). Where necessary please comment upon the replies given to the standard questions.

4.3.4.2 *Answers to the short answer questions*

Question 1

This question is concerned with making searches and enquiries on behalf of a purchaser and advising him about the contents of the search results as well as the replies to enquiries. There are two topics upon which to give advice. First, the use of the premises, and secondly, the potential; traffic problem. Information about both of these topics will be forthcoming from pre-contract searches as well as enquiries made of the seller. Dealing first with pre-contract searches, we will need to obtain a local authority search result. This will give us information about planning matters. The search in the local land charges register will disclose planning charges covering various planning entries in the register including planning consents. Accompanying the search of the local land charges register there is a list of questions posed of the local authority. Question 1 covers planning and building regulations and in particular planning decisions, pending applications and certificates of lawfulness of use. Furthermore question 3.9 will give details of notices, orders, directions and proceedings under planning acts. If there are or have been planning enforcement proceedings then this will be highlighted in answers given to this question.

With regard to the potential traffic problem, information about this will also been found in this search result. Question 3.2 covers land to be acquired for road works, question 3.4 covers nearby road schemes and more importantly question 3.6 covers traffic schemes such as traffic calming works or pedestrianisation.

Pre-contract enquiries can also cover both topics. Specific questions can be directed to the seller asking for copy planning consents permitting the conversion of the property and the use as offices together with information about any conditions attaching to those consents. Similarly the seller can be asked to give details of any traffic schemes directly affecting the property or near to it of which the seller is aware. Indeed, almost all pre-printed preliminary enquiry forms contain questions that will cover these two topics and when the seller gives replies the buyer can be given the details along with advice on the information from the search result.

Question 2

This question requires you to do what any Conveyancer must do for each transaction, check the replies to a local search questionnaire and consider what steps must be taken to deal with various entries. Where a search result discloses an entry you need to review the disclosure and decide upon the gravity of it. You will then have to consider the need to refer the information to the client. Clearly anything that might affect the use or enjoyment of the property should be mentioned to the buyer.

The first reply of concern relates to question 1.1 (c). This concern also links to the answer given by the council to question 3.10. In both answers the council have indicated that the property is in a conservation area. In the case of this kind of disclosure, the client will need to be advised of the restrictive nature of the registration and how it might affect the property and its neighbourhood. Question 3.10 will confirm if a conservation area not disclosed in the official certificate of search affects the subject property. This will cover all such areas that were designated before 31 August 1974. The reason for this is that after that date conservation areas became land charges and are disclosed in searches of the local land charges registry. A buyer will want to know if the property is in a conservation area as there will, as a result, be limitations on development. Even minor alterations can be disallowed in a conservation area and consequently this information may be critical to a buyer intending to alter, demolish or improve the property.

The answer to question 2(a) should be referred to the client as the buyer may be under a duty to maintain or pay for the maintenance of the alleyway. You will need to check the title for possible details.

The answers to questions 3.4, 3.5 and 3.6 should all be referred to the client as they might all adversely affect the property. The first disclosure mentions a nearby traffic improvement, the second a future travel proposal and the third an imminent scheme for the road that could mean the banning of cars and lorries. The buyer needs to consider if this is likely to be adverse. You should write to the council for full details of all these matters for onward transmission to the buyer.

Question 3

This question requires you to do what any Conveyancer must do for each transaction, check the replies to a property information form or questionnaire and consider what steps must be taken to deal with various entries. The same will be true for pre-contract enquiries where the Protocol does not apply. Where a reply discloses a matter of concern, you need to review the disclosure and decide upon the gravity of it. You will then have to consider the need to refer the information to the client. Clearly anything that might affect the use or enjoyment of the property should be mentioned to the buyer.

There are not many answers that are problematic. The answer to question 2 needs to be immediately referred to the buyer. The problem might arise again and the reason for them stopping needs to be investigated. Has the noisy neighbour moved? If so then perhaps the problem has gone as well. In question 4 work for damp course treatment and rot or infestation has been carried out but there is no mention of a guarantee certificate. You need to ask for the report and estimate and the guarantee so that full copies can be sent to the buyer.

Question 8 is of concern to you as the solicitor for the buyer. You are on notice of a non-owning occupier who may have an equitable interest in the property and who must be required to sign the contract to confirm her willingness to vacate on the day of completion. You need to ensure that the contract is amended to take into account this requirement.

The answer to question 12 makes it clear that the buyer may be delayed in obtaining early possession of the property, as the seller does not yet have a property to buy. You should copy the full form to the buyer and advise him of the likelihood of delay. You also need to consider the terms of the contract relating to the deposit bearing in mind the stated intention of the seller to use the deposit on an allied purchase. In particular you need to ensure that the deposit is protected so far as is possible where it is being used along a chain of transactions.

Finally you should ask the seller's solicitors to reconsider their policy and to complete Part II of the form. At the very least they should say if the replies are consistent with the information in their possession and whether there is an indemnity policy with the deeds.

4.4 REFERENCES TO WIDER READING INCLUDING PRACTITIONER TEXTS

1. Chapter 1 'Matters Before Contract' in *'Emmet on Title'*; Farrand J. (Longman Sweet & Maxwell).
2. Chapter 4 'Pre-Contract Searches and Enquiries, Town and Country Planning' in *'A Practical Approach to Conveyancing'*; Abbey R. and Richards M. (6th edn, Oxford University Press).
3. Section B covering Pre-Contract Concerns in the *Law Society's Conveyancing Handbook (10th edn)*; Silverman.
4. Chapter 9 'Selling and Buying Tenanted Properties' in *'A Practical Approach to Commercial Conveyancing and Property'*; Abbey R. and Richards M.; (2nd edn; Oxford University Press).

4.5 RELEVANT WEBSITES FOR MORE INFORMATION

- Environmental searches can be obtained from the Landmark Information Group. They can assist with both residential and commercial properties— http://www.landmark-information.co.uk
- Environmental risk can be checked without cost at another site— http://www.homecheck.co.uk.
- On-line environmental searches can be carried out at the following site. It will also provide a certificate, where possible, confirming that the subject property is not likely to be described as 'contaminated land' as defined by s. 78 of the Environmental Protection Act 1990—http://www.homecheckpro.co.uk
- The Environment Agency has made maps available on the Internet that show areas potentially liable to flooding. This is a free service and can be accessed using a property postcode at http://www.environment-agency.gov.uk

- Countrywide Legal Indemnities offer an insurance solution when there are concerns about contamination. The insurance policy on offer is intended to cover homeowners against the potential liability for remediation costs of any contaminants found on their land. Full details can be found at http://www.helpforconveyancers.com

- Details of the English Water Service Companies can be obtained from Water UK 1 at Queen Anne's Gate, London SW1H 9BT, http://www.water.org.uk

- Details of land registry services and the search facilitites available on-line can be found at http://www.landreg.gov.uk

- On-line company searches are available from the Companies House website at http://www.companies-house.gov.uk

- The National Land Information Service that was set up to facilitate on-line searches has its own site at http://www.nlis.org.uk

- The NLIS having gone live in February 2001 in all of England and Wales offers a search service through three NLIS licensed channels. Practitioners can set up facilities to carry out searches via these companies, whose web site addresses are:

  (a) http://www.transaction-online.co.uk
  (b) http://www.territorium.co.uk
  (c) http://www.searchflow.co.uk

- The Royal Town Planning Institute website is at http://www.rtpi.org.uk

- Finally, the new Land Registry e-conveyancing website is on http://www.landregistry.gov.uk/e-conveyancing/ and contains details of how e-conveyancing will affect all the topics covered in this chapter.

APPENDIX 4.1
STANDARD ENQUIRIES OF LOCAL AUTHORITY
(2002 EDITION)

Re: 69 Pottery Lane Burmantoft Leeds

1.1

(a) none

(b) none

(c) Property in Burmantoft Conservation Area made 12.12.89

(d) none

(e) none

(f) none

(g) none

Copies from Planning Dept. Civic Centre Leeds LS1 2NS

1.2 None

2

(a) Pottery Lane. Side passage and rear alleyway is private

(b) none

(c) none

(d) none

3 See below, copies from the Civic Centre Leeds LS1 2NS

3.1 None

3.2 None

3.3 None

3.4 Headrow Underpass improvement scheme 175 metres away

3.5 Leeds City tramway scheme proposed 2010, not in this road

3.6 Cycle way proposed for Pottery Lane, 2004

3.7 None

3.8 None

3.9 None

3.10 Property in Burmantoft Conservation Area made 12.12.89

3.11 None

3.12 None

3.13 None

CON 29 Part I Standard Enquiries of Local Authority (2002)

PLANNING AND BUILDING REGULATIONS

1.1. Decisions and Pending Applications

What applications for any of the following (if applicable) have been granted, refused or are now pending?

(a) planning permissions
(b) listed building consents
(c) conservation area consents
(d) certificates of lawfulness of use or development
(e) building regulation approvals
(f) building regulation completion certificates
(g) certificate of compliance of a replacement window, rooflight, roof window or glazed door.

How can copies of any of the above be obtained?

1.2. Planning Designations and Proposals

What designations of land use for the property or the area, and what specific proposals for the property, are contained in any current adopted or proposed development plan?

ROADS

2. Which of the roads, footways and footpaths mentioned in boxes B and C are:

(a) highways maintainable at public expense;
(b) subject to a current legal agreement for adoption and, if so, is the agreement supported by a bond or other financial security;
(c) to be made up at the cost of the frontagers under a current Council resolution;
(d) to be adopted without cost to the frontagers under a current Council resolution.

OTHER MATTERS

Apart from matters entered on the registers of local land charges, do any of the following matters apply to the property? How can copies of relevant documents be obtained?

3.1. Land required for Public Purposes

Inclusion of the property in a category of land required for public purposes within Schedule 13 paras 5 & 6 of the Town & Country Planning Act 1990.

3.2. Land to be acquired for Road Works

Inclusion of the property in land to be acquired for an approved scheme of Highway construction or improvement.

3.3. Drainage Agreements and Consents

(a) An agreement under the Building Act 1984, s.22 for drainage of any part of the property in combination with another building through a private sewer?
(b) Statutory agreement or consent for a building or extension to a building on the property to be constructed over or in the vicinity of a drain, sewer or disposal main.
    Note: The sewerage undertaker for the area should also be asked about 3(b) and drainage generally.

3.4. Nearby Road Schemes

Location of any part of the property within 200 metres of:

(a) the centre line of a new trunk road or special road specified in an order, draft order or scheme notified to the Council by the appropriate Secretary of State; or
(b) the centre line of a proposed alteration or improvement to an existing road, notified to the Council by the appropriate Secretary of State, involving the construction of a subway, underpass, flyover, footbridge, elevated road or dual carriageway (whether or not within the existing highway limits); or
(c) the limits of construction of a proposed alteration or improvement to an existing road, notified to the Council by the appropriate Secretary or State, involving the construction of a roundabout (other than a mini-roundabout) or widening by the construction of one or more additional traffic lanes; or
(d) the limits of construction of an approved new road to be constructed by the Council or an approved alteration or improvement by the Council to an existing road involving the construction of a subway, underpass, flyover, footbridge, elevated road or dual carriageway (whether or not within existing highway limits) or the construction of a roundabout other than a mini-roundabout) or widening by the construction of one or more additional traffic lanes; or
(e) the centre line of the possible route of a new road under proposals published for public consultation by the Council or by the appropriate Secretary of State; or
(f) the limits of construction of a possible alteration or improvement to an existing road involving the construction of a subway, underpass, flyover, footbridge, elevated road or dual carriageway (whether or not within existing highway limits) or the construction of a roundabout (other than a mini-roundabout) or widening by the construction of one or more additional traffic lanes, under proposals published for public consultation by the Council or by the appropriate Secretary of State.
    Note: A mini-roundabout is a roundabout having a one-way circulatory carriageway around a flush or slightly raised circular marking less than 4 metres in diameter and with or without flared approaches.

3.5. Nearby Railway Schemes

Location of any part of the property within 200 metres of the centre line of a proposed railway, tramway, light railway or monorail.

3.6. Traffic Schemes

Approval by the Council of any of the following, not yet implemented, in respect of such of the roads, footways and footpaths mentioned in Box B (and, if applicable, Box C) which abut the boundaries of the property:

(a) permanent stopping up or diversion
(b) waiting or loading restrictions
(c) one way driving
(d) prohibition of driving
(e) pedestrianisation
(f) vehicle width or weight restriction
(g) traffic calming works e.g. road humps
(h) residents parking controls
(i) minor road widening or improvement
(j) pedestrian crossings
(k) cycle tracks
(l) bridge construction

3.7. Outstanding Notices

Current statutory notices relating to the property under legislation relating to building works, environment, health and safety at work, housing, highways or public health, other than those falling elsewhere within 3.1. to 3.13.

3.8. Infringement of Building Regulations

Proceedings authorised by the Council for infringement of the Building Regulations in respect of the property.

3.9. Notices, Orders, Directions and Proceedings under Planning Acts

Subsisting notices, orders, directions, or proceedings, or those which the Council has decided to issue, serve, make or commence in the following categories (other than those which are shown in the Official Certificate of Search or which have been withdrawn or quashed) relating to the property:

(a) enforcement notice
(b) stop notice
(c) listed building enforcement notice
(d) breach of condition notice
(e) planning contravention notice
(f) other notice relating to breach of planning control
(g) listed building repairs notice
(h) order for compulsory acquisition of a listed building with a minimum compensation provision
(i) building preservation notice
(j) direction restricting permitted development
(k) order revoking or modifying a planning permission or discontinuing an existing planning use
(l) tree preservation order
(m) proceedings for breach of a statutory planning agreement

3.10. Conservation Area

Creation of the area before 31 August 1974 as a Conservation Area or a subsisting resolution to designate the area as a Conservation Area.

3.11. Compulsory Purchase

Inclusion of the property in land which is subject to an enforceable order or resolution for compulsory purchase.

3.12. Contaminated Land

(a) Entry relating to the property in the register maintained under s.78R(1) of the Environmental Protection Act 1990,
(b) Notice relating to the property served or resolved to be served under s.78B(3).
(c) Consultation with the owner or occupier of the property having taken place, or being resolved to take place under s.78G(3) in relation to anything to be done on the property as a result of adjoining or adjacent land being contaminated land.
(d) Entry in the register, or notice served or resolved to be served under s.78B(3) in relation to any adjoining or adjacent land, which has been identified as contaminated land because it is in such a condition that harm or pollution of controlled waters might be caused on the property.

3.13. Radon Gas

Location of the property in a Radon Affected Area.

Notes:

This form must be submitted in duplicate and should be read in conjunction with the guidance notes available separately.

(1) Unless otherwise indicated, matters will be disclosed only if they apply directly to the property described in Box B.

(2) "Area" means any area in which the property is located.

(3) References to 'the Council' include any predecessor Council and also any council committee, sub-committee or other body or person exercising powers delegated by the Council and their 'approval' includes their decision to proceed. The replies given to certain enquiries cover knowledge and actions of both the District Council and County Council.

(4) References to the provisions of particular Acts of Parliament or Regulations include any provisions which they have replaced and also include existing or future amendments or re-enactments.

(5) The replies will be given in the belief that they are in accordance with information presently available to the officers of the replying Council, but none of the Councils or their officers accept legal responsibility for an incorrect reply, except for negligence. Any liability for negligence will extend to the person who raised the enquiries and the person on whose behalf they were raised. It will also extend to any other person who has knowledge (personally or through an agent) of the replies before the time when he purchases, takes a tenancy of, or lends money on the security of the property or (if earlier) the time when he becomes contractually bound to do so.

SELLER'S PROPERTY INFORMATION FORM (3rd edition)

Address of the Property:

IMPORTANT NOTE TO SELLERS - PLEASE READ THIS FIRST

* **Please complete this form carefully. If you are unsure how to answer the questions, ask your solicitor before doing so.**

* **This form in due course will be sent to the buyer's solicitor and will be seen by the buyer who is entitled to rely on the information.**

* For many of the questions you need only tick the correct answer. Where necessary, please give more detailed answers on a separate sheet of paper. Then send all the replies to your solicitor. This form will be passed to the buyer's solicitor.

* The answers should be those of the person whose name is on the deeds. If there is more than one of you, you should prepare the answers together.

* It is very important that your answers are correct because the buyer is entitled to rely on them in deciding whether to go ahead. Incorrect or incomplete information given to the buyer direct through your solicitor or selling agent or even mentioned to the buyer in conversation between you, may mean that the buyer can claim compensation from you or even refuse to complete the purchase.

* If you do not know the answer to any question you must say so.

* The buyer takes the property in its present physical condition and should, if necessary, seek independent advice, e.g. instruct a surveyor. You should not give the buyer your views on the condition of the property.

* If anything changes after you fill in this questionnaire but before the sale is completed, tell your solicitor immediately. THIS IS AS IMPORTANT AS GIVING THE RIGHT ANSWERS IN THE FIRST PLACE.

* Please pass to your solicitor immediately any notices you have received which affect the property, including any notices which arrive at any time before completion of your sale.

* If you have a tenant, tell your solicitor immediately if there is any change in the arrangement but do nothing without asking your solicitor first.

* You should let your solicitor have any letters, agreements or other documents which help answer the questions. If you know of any which you are not supplying with these answers, please tell your solicitor about them.

* Please complete and return the separate Fixtures, Fittings and Contents Form. It is an important document which will form part of the contract between you and the buyer. Unless you mark clearly on it the items which you wish to remove, they will be included in the sale and you will not be able to take them with you when you move.

* You may wish to delay the completion of the Fixtures, Fittings and Contents Form until you have a prospective buyer and have agreed the price.

Part I - to be completed by the seller

1 | Boundaries

"Boundaries" mean any fence, wall, hedge or ditch which marks the edge of your property.

1.1 Looking towards the house from the road, who either owns or accepts responsibility for the boundary:

Please mark the appropriate box

(a)   on the left?

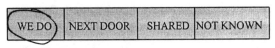

(b)   on the right?

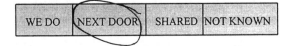

(c)   across the back?

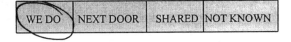

1.2 If you have answered "not known", which boundaries have you actually repaired or maintained?

(Please give details)

1.3 Do you know of any boundary being moved in the last 20 years?

(Please give details) NO

2 | Disputes and complaints

2.1 Do you know of any disputes or anything which might lead to a dispute about this or any neighbouring property?

Noisy parties next door. Now stopped

Please mark the appropriate box

2.2 Have you received any complaints about anything you have, or have not, done as owner?

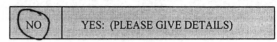

2.3 Have you made any such complaints to any neighbour about what the neighbour has or has not done?

see above

---

3 | Notices

3.1 Have you either sent or received any letters or notices which affect your property or the neighbouring property in any way (for example, from or to neighbours, the council or a government department)?

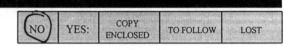

3.2 Have you had any negotiations or discussions with any neighbour or any local or other authority which affect the property in any way?

---

4 | Guarantees

4.1 Are there any guarantees or insurance policies of the following types:

(a) NHBC Foundation 15 or Newbuild?

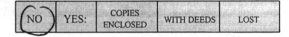

(b) Damp course?

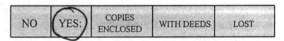

(c) Double glazing, roof lights, roof windows, glazed doors?

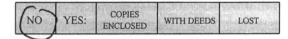

(d) Electrical work?

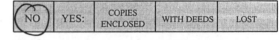

(e) Roofing?

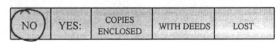

Prop 1/3

Please mark the appropriate box

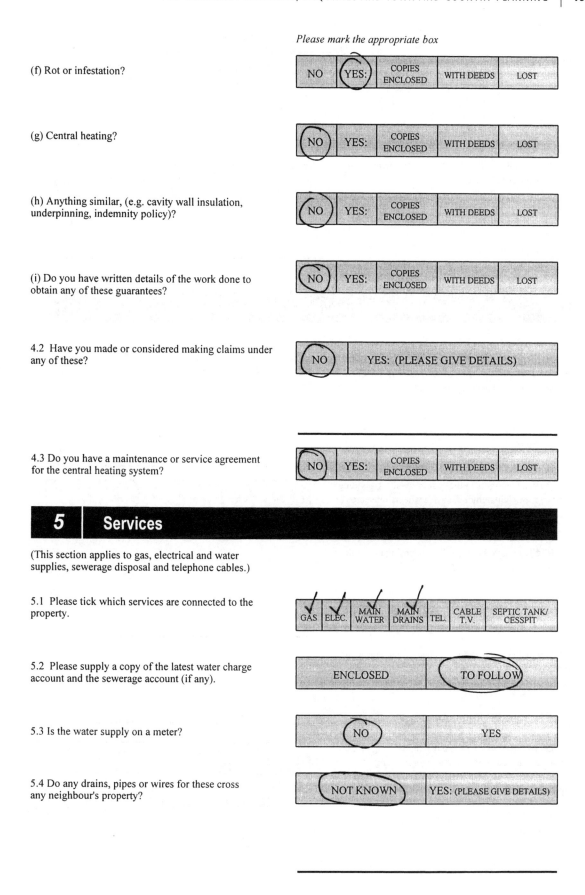

(f) Rot or infestation?

| NO | YES: | COPIES ENCLOSED | WITH DEEDS | LOST |

(g) Central heating?

| NO | YES: | COPIES ENCLOSED | WITH DEEDS | LOST |

(h) Anything similar, (e.g. cavity wall insulation, underpinning, indemnity policy)?

| NO | YES: | COPIES ENCLOSED | WITH DEEDS | LOST |

(i) Do you have written details of the work done to obtain any of these guarantees?

| NO | YES: | COPIES ENCLOSED | WITH DEEDS | LOST |

4.2 Have you made or considered making claims under any of these?

| NO | YES: (PLEASE GIVE DETAILS) |

4.3 Do you have a maintenance or service agreement for the central heating system?

| NO | YES: | COPIES ENCLOSED | WITH DEEDS | LOST |

5 | Services

(This section applies to gas, electrical and water supplies, sewerage disposal and telephone cables.)

5.1 Please tick which services are connected to the property.

| GAS | ELEC. | MAIN WATER | MAIN DRAINS | TEL. | CABLE T.V. | SEPTIC TANK/ CESSPIT |

5.2 Please supply a copy of the latest water charge account and the sewerage account (if any).

| ENCLOSED | TO FOLLOW |

5.3 Is the water supply on a meter?

| NO | YES |

5.4 Do any drains, pipes or wires for these cross any neighbour's property?

| NOT KNOWN | YES: (PLEASE GIVE DETAILS) |

Please mark the appropriate box

5.5 Do any drains, pipes or wires leading to any neighbour's property cross your property?

| NOT KNOWN | YES: (PLEASE GIVE DETAILS) |

5.6 Are you aware of any agreement or arrangement about any of these services?

| NOT KNOWN | YES: (PLEASE GIVE DETAILS) |

6 | Sharing with the neighbours

6.1 Are you aware of any responsibility to contribute to the cost of anything used jointly, such as the repair of a shared drive, boundary or drain?

| YES: (PLEASE GIVE DETAILS) | NO |

6.2 Do you contribute to the cost of repair of anything used by the neighbourhood, such as the maintenance of a private road?

| YES | NO |

6.3 If so, who is responsible for organising the work and collecting the contributions?

6.4 Please give details of all such sums paid or owing, and explain if they are paid on a regular basis or only as and when work is required.

6.5 Do you need to go on to any neighbouring property if you have to repair or decorate your building or maintain any of the boundaries or any of the drains, pipes or wires?

| YES | NO |

House walls (terrace)

Prop 1/5

Please mark the appropriate box

6.6 If "Yes", have you always been able to do so without objection by the neighbours?

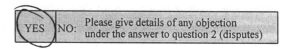

6.7 Do any of your neighbours need to come onto your land to repair or decorate their building or maintain their boundaries or any drains, pipes or wires?

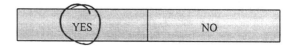

6.8 If so, have you ever objected?

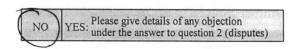

7 | Arrangements and rights

7.1 Is access obtained to any part of the property over private land, common land or a neighbour's land? If so, please specify.

7.2 Has anyone taken steps to stop, complain about or demand payment for such access being exercised?

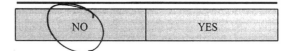

7.3 Are there any other formal or informal arrangements which you have over any of your neighbours' property?

(Examples are for access or shared use.)

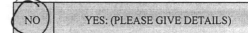

7.4 Are there any other formal or informal arrangements which someone else has over your property?

(Examples are for access or shared use.)

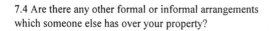

Please mark the appropriate box

8 | Occupiers

8.1 Does anyone other than you live in the property?

NO	YES
	(YES)

If "NO" go to question 9.1.
If "YES" please give their full names and (if under 18) their ages.

Selina Stott
(girl-friend)

8.2(a)(i) Do any of them have any right to stay on the property without your permission?

(These rights may have arisen without you realising, e.g. if they have paid towards the cost of buying the house, paid for improvements or helped you make your mortgage payments.)

NO	YES: (PLEASE GIVE DETAILS)

She helped with the deposit and mortgage

8.2(a)(ii) Are any of them tenants or lodgers?

NO	YES: (Please give details and a copy of any Tenancy Agreement)

8.2(b) Have they all agreed to sign the contract for sale agreeing to leave with you (or earlier)?

NO	YES: (PLEASE GIVE DETAILS)

She will

9 | Changes to the property

9.1 Have any of the following taken place to the whole or any part of the property (including the garden) and if so, when?

(a) Building works (including loft conversions and conservatories)

NO	YES: In the year ....

(b) Change of use

NO	YES: In the year ....

(c) Sub-division

NO	YES: In the year ....

(d) Conversion

NO	YES: In the year ....

Please mark the appropriate box

(e) Business activities

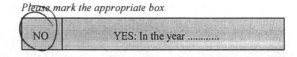

(f) Replacement windows, roof lights,
roof windows, glazed doors?

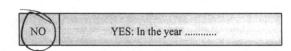

If "YES" what consents were obtained under any
restrictions in your title deeds?

(*Note:* The title deeds of some properties include
clauses which are called "restrictive covenants".
These may, for example, forbid the owner of the
property from carrying out any building work or from
using it for business purposes or from parking a caravan
or boat on it unless someone else (often the builder of
the house) gives consent.)

9.2 Has consent under those restrictions been
obtained for anything else done at the property?

YES	NO

9.3 If any consent was needed but not obtained:

(a) Please explain why not.

(b) From whom should it have been obtained?

(*Note*: Improvement can affect council tax
banding following a sale.)

10 | Planning and building control

10.1 Is the property used only as a private home?

10.2(a) Has the property been designated as a Listed
Building or the area designated as a Conservation Area?
If so, when did this happen?

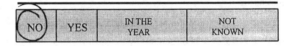

10.2(b) Was planning permission, building regulation
approval or listed building consent obtained for each
of the the changes mentioned in 9?

NO	YES:	COPY ENCLOSED	TO FOLLOW	LOST

(*Please list separately and supply copies of the
relevant permissions and, where appropriate,
certificates of completion.*)

10.2(c) If any of the changes in 9.1(f) have taken place,
and the work completed after 1 April 2002, please
supply either a FENSA certificate or a building
regulation certificate.

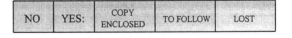

Prop 1/8

Please mark the appropriate box

11 | Expenses

Have you ever had to pay for the use of the property?

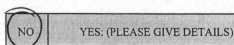

| NO | YES: (PLEASE GIVE DETAILS) |

(Note: Ignore council tax, water rates, and gas, electricity, and telephone bills. Disclose anything else: examples are the clearance of cesspool or septic tank, drainage rate, rent charge.)

(If you are selling a leasehold property, details of the lease's expenses should be included on the Seller's Leasehold Information Form and not on this form.)

12 | Mechanics of the sale

12.1 Is this sale dependent on your buying another property?

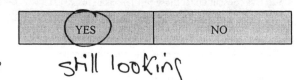

| YES | NO |

12.2 If "YES", what stage have the negotiations reached?

still looking

12.3 Do you require a mortgage?

| YES | NO |

12.4 If "YES", has an offer been received and/or accepted or a mortgage certificate obtained?

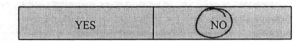

| YES | NO |

13 | Deposit

Do you have the money to pay a 10% deposit on your purchase?

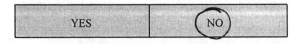

| YES | NO |

If "NO" are you expecting to use the deposit paid by your buyer to pay the deposit on your purchase?

| YES | NO |

Prop 1/9

Please mark the appropriate box

14 | Moving Date

Please indicate if you have any special
requirement about a moving date.

*(Note: This will not be fixed until contracts
are exchanged i.e. have become binding. Until
then you should only make provisional removal
arrangements.)*

YES	NO

Signature(s): _____

Date: _____

Prop 1/10

Part II - to be completed by the seller's solicitor

Please mark the appropriate box

A. Is this information provided by the seller in this form consistent with the information in your possession?

YES	NO

If "NO" please specify.

B. Do you have any information in your possession to supplement the information provided by the seller?

YES	NO

If "YES" please specify.

C. Is there an indemnity policy?

If "YES" please supply a copy.

YES	NO

Reminder to solicitor

1. The Fixtures, Fittings and Contents Form should be supplied in addition to the information above.

2. Copies of all planning permissions, building regulations consents, certificates of completion, engineer's certificates, guarantees, assignments, certificates and notices should be supplied with this form.

3. If the property is leasehold, also supply the Seller's Leasehold Information Form.

Seller's solicitor: _____

Date: _____

The Law Society

This form is part of the Law Society's TransAction scheme. © The Law Society 1994 and 2002
The Law Society is the professional body for solicitors in England and Wales

Laserform International Ltd is an Approved Law Society Supplier

5 | DEDUCING AND INVESTIGATING TITLE

5.1 INTRODUCTION

This is the part of the Property Law and Practice syllabus that invariably seems to cause LPC students the most difficulty, in particular the deduction and investigation of title to unregistered land. The statutory and common law rules and procedures can appear, in theory at least, extremely complex and many students understandably find them difficult to grasp. The position is compounded by the fact that until these rules are put into practice, the explanation on the written page can at times seem almost incomprehensible. That is why this topic more than any other warrants the phrase, albeit hackneyed, 'practice makes perfect'. Indeed, if there is one part of the Property Law and Practice syllabus where practising past questions really pays dividends, this is it.

In comparison, the investigation of registered title is relatively straightforward in that the entries on the register will be definitive, and the conveyancer can be guided quite easily by the Land Registration Act 2002 and the accompanying rules. You will appreciate that all areas of England and Wales are now in a compulsory area of registration and so the majority of titles you will come across in practice will be registered. That at least may be some comfort to you but it does not hide the fact that in practice you will encounter unregistered titles and, more importantly for you right now, you may have to cope with one in your subject assessment. The secret, as always, is to be prepared.

Here are some preliminary tips when faced with an unregistered title:

- Before plunging headlong into the minutiae of each document, pause a moment and take an overall view of the title.

- Check first that the proposed root of title is 'good' (see 5.2.2 below).

- Then trace the chain of ownership from the root document right down to the present owner and ask yourself some basic questions. Are there any gaps in the chain of title? Are there any missing documents? Have the names of the parties changed? Are the dates in order? Have the land charges searches been made correctly against all the estate owners? Did the individual estate owners have the ability to sell? Should the title have been substantively registered following an earlier disposition?

- Check whether there has in the past been a sale of part. If there has, look out for obvious defects such as an inadequate property description, no memorandum on the previous conveyance, no acknowledgement for production of earlier deeds and no evidence of copy documents having been examined against originals.

- Consider whether any other special considerations apply, e.g. has there been a sale by mortgagee; sale by personal representatives; sale by surviving co-owner? If so, make the necessary checks.

- Having taken a global view of the title, you can now begin to consider the detailed provisions of each document. Check for such matters as missing clauses, any failure to stamp, references to earlier deeds, incorrect plans and imperfect execution of deeds.

We suggest that you try this approach for yourself in standard question 3 below. Sometimes the examiner will give you an epitome of title without actually attaching the documents of title. Standard question 4 follows this format.

5.2 AN OVERVIEW OF THE SUBJECT AND A LOOK AT SOME PROBLEM AREAS

The accepted practice today is for the parties to deduce and investigate title before contracts are exchanged. Put simply, deducing title is the process by which the seller demonstrates to the buyer that the seller owns the property and can convey it. On the other hand, the process of investigating title is the means by which the buyer ensures that the seller owns the land and can convey it. This is done by examining the title that the seller has deduced. Alternatively the seller is entitled to show that the land is owned by another person whom the seller can compel to convey, e.g. in the case of a sub-sale.

If the Protocol is being used, the seller must deduce title at the same time as the draft contract and other pre-contract documents are forwarded to the buyer's solicitor, i.e. the title documents will be part of the 'pre-contract package'. Indeed this is the normal procedure in practice today even if the Protocol is not being used.

5.2.1 DEDUCING TITLE TO REGISTERED LAND

When deducing title to registered land, the parties to the contract are free to agree whatever contractual provisions they like regarding deduction of title. Of course title is invariably deduced prior to exchange of contracts which makes it unnecessary for the contract to regulate the manner in which title is deduced. In practice, after taking instructions, you will simply apply to Land Registry on Form OC1 for up to date official copies of the registered title(s) being sold (and if appropriate on Form OC2 for official copies of documents referred to in the register). You will then forward these to the buyer as part of the 'pre-contract package'.

5.2.2 DEDUCING TITLE TO UNREGISTERED LAND

When deducing title to unregistered land you should supply the buyer with particulars of the deeds, tracing a chain of ownership through to the current seller (or someone whom the seller can compel to convey). This can be done either by a traditional abstract or, the preferred method today, an epitome of title. An epitome involves the preparation of a list or schedule, in chronological order, of all the material title deeds and events which form the chain of title, for example a conveyance, a mortgage or a death. You then attach to the schedule photocopies of all the relevant documents. The photocopies must of course be legible with copy plans correctly coloured.

The buyer should insist that the seller deduces title from at least fifteen years before the date of the contract (this applies both at common law and under the standard conditions), and the chain of title must commence with a 'good root' (i.e. the starting point for the period of ownership) duly stipulated in the sale contract. A good root must satisfy the following criteria. It should:

(a) deal with or show ownership of the whole legal and equitable interest in the property (the buyer will normally be concerned only with the legal estate; if the proper conveyancing procedures are adopted, any equitable interests should be overreached and thus will not bind the buyer; see *City of London Building Society v. Flegg* [1988] AC 54);

(b) contain an adequate, identifiable description of the property. A mortgage will fail this test if it lacks a full description of the property (mortgages often refer to a fuller description in the conveyance to the mortgagor). Similarly, an assent will fail if it simply vests the property, 'for all the estate or interest of the deceased';

(c) do nothing to cast doubt on the title. A document will cast doubt if it depends for its effect on an earlier instrument, such as a power of attorney (see *Re Copelin's Contract* [1937] 4 All ER 447), but such doubt can be overcome if the seller can prove that the earlier document still subsisted at the time of its execution;

(d) at the date of the contract be at least fifteen years old (s. 44, Law of Property Act 1925 as amended by s. 23, Law of Property Act 1969).

The best document for the root is a conveyance on sale. This is preferable to a gift of title, such as a voluntary conveyance or an assent, where it is unlikely that any prior title investigation was made before completion of the gift. As a general rule, a buyer should always insist on a conveyance on sale as the root of title (assuming one is available). If unusually a conveyance on sale is not available, the buyer must ensure that the alternative root document does in fact satisfy the good root criteria.

5.2.3 INVESTIGATING TITLE TO REGISTERED LAND

If your client is buying registered land you must check carefully the official copies and other documents referred to on the register and compare them against the information given in the draft contract. Remember that the official copies should be as up to date as possible (ideally just a few weeks old and certainly no more than twelve months old). You should in particular consider the following:

- Confirm whether the estate is freehold or leasehold.
- Is the title number correct?
- Consider the class of title; is it absolute, possessory, good leasehold or qualified? (Anything less than absolute title will generally be considered as adverse.)
- Does the land being bought correspond with the title description? (Consider the title plan—does it indicate that land has been removed from the title?)

- Is the seller in the contract the same as the registered proprietor?
- Are there any incumbrances in the charges register and how will these affect the buyer?

If there are discrepancies or if other adverse entries are present which protect third party interests, for example, a unilateral notice or a pre-October 2003 caution, you should raise these as requisitions with the seller's practitioner. Other examples might be the presence of a Family Law Act notice, an apparent breach of covenant or possibly covenants referred to on the title but details of which were not given to Land Registry on first registration. Your requisition should identify the defect/problem and require the seller to remedy it (if necessary, at the seller's cost).

In addition to the above, you should before completion carry out a Land Registry search to up-date the information in the official copies (see Chapter 8 regarding pre-completion searches). You must also check for any overriding interests which are not entered on the register but which will bind the buyer irrespective of notice (e.g. rights of persons in actual occupation, local land charges, etc.).

5.2.4 INVESTIGATING TITLE TO UNREGISTERED LAND

If your client is buying unregistered land, first check that the root of title offered by the seller is a good one and is at least fifteen years old at the date of the contract (see 5.2.2 above for what constitutes a good root). You must then trace chronologically from the root document, a chain of ownership all the way down to the current seller; a chain which is complete and without missing links. So, if Jones and Clark bought the land previously, make sure it is they who later sell, not Jones and Smith or even Jones and Clarke (spelling discrepancies should always be raised).

Ensure that you see evidence of any change of name. For example, if a previous owner purchased the property as an unmarried woman using her maiden name, and then after her marriage sold using her married name, you would want to see a certified copy of the marriage certificate. Also make sure that you see evidence of the death of any estate owner. For example, if a joint tenant has died and the survivor(s) has subsequently sold, you would want to see a certified copy of the death certificate.

Having traced the chain of ownership you should now examine carefully each document in the abstract or epitome, checking for any deficiencies or omissions. Examples of defects might be a mortgage taken out by a previous estate owner which has not been discharged, or an improperly executed or stamped document.

Ensure that the description of the property in the most recent conveyance or other document accords with that which the client is buying (this is a fundamental point which will always be thoroughly checked by Land Registry on first registration). Ensure that the property benefits from all necessary easements. If there has been a sale of part, ensure that an acknowledgement for future production of retained original documents has been given, and that a sale-off memorandum has been endorsed on the previous conveyance. Check that all appropriate documents have been stamped. Lastly, check whether the property should already have been registered—was it in a compulsory area on the date of a previous conveyance?

Any defects should be raised with the seller's practitioner as requisitions on title. You should identify the defects and require the seller to remedy them, if necessary at the seller's cost. For further reading on the often-complex area of investigating unregistered title see Abbey R. and Richards M., *A Practical Approach to Conveyancing*, chapter 5 (OUP).

Flowchart—Investigating an unregistered title

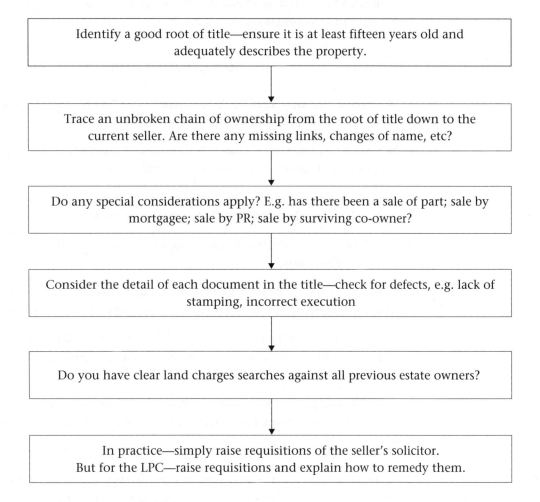

Identify a good root of title—ensure it is at least fifteen years old and adequately describes the property.

Trace an unbroken chain of ownership from the root of title down to the current seller. Are there any missing links, changes of name, etc?

Do any special considerations apply? E.g. has there been a sale of part; sale by mortgagee; sale by PR; sale by surviving co-owner?

Consider the detail of each document in the title—check for defects, e.g. lack of stamping, incorrect execution

Do you have clear land charges searches against all previous estate owners?

In practice—simply raise requisitions of the seller's solicitor. But for the LPC—raise requisitions and explain how to remedy them.

5.3 SUBJECT ASSESSMENTS

As in previous chapters there now follows some examples of assessment questions in the subject area of deducing and investigating title. Commentary and a suggested answer accompany the standard assessment questions. These are then followed by multiple choice questions (with answers) and short answer questions with suggested answers.

5.3.1 STANDARD QUESTIONS, COMMENTARY AND SUGGESTED ANSWERS

Question 1

Your principal has passed you the deeds of factory premises known as The Old Forge, Ridgewood Industrial Estate, Seatown. Your firm is acting for the owners, Christopher and Jill Browning, in the sale of the property with vacant possession. The property is freehold and has an unregistered title. Seatown came within an area of compulsory registration on 1 December 1990.

The property is presently mortgaged to the Cornshire Building Society who have forwarded the deeds to your firm to be held to order on the usual terms.

Your principal has asked you to deduce title to the buyer's solicitors. She has handed you the file and the deeds packet. The deeds packet contains several documents; each listed in the schedule below.

Identify with reasons which document or documents would be suitable as the root of title and then deduce title by drafting an epitome. Explain your reasons for including or excluding the following listed documents in your epitome:

<u>SCHEDULE OF DOCUMENTS</u>

1. A conveyance on sale dated 20 July 1963 from Richard Tyler to Ashley Perryman containing a restrictive covenant imposed on Ashley Perryman.

2. A conveyance on sale dated 3 July 1971 from Ashley Perryman to John Little, stating that the property is sold subject to the covenant in the 1963 conveyance.

3. A legal mortgage dated 3 July 1971 given by John Little to the Westhampton Building Society, with a receipt endorsed on it dated 5 October 1974.

4. A business lease of part of the property dated 9 July 1971 by John Little to Wendy Webb for a term of twelve years.

5. A land charges search dated 29 September 1974 against Richard Tyler, Ashley Perryman and John Little, revealing no entries save for a D(ii) entry against Ashley Perryman.

6. A conveyance on sale dated 5 October 1974 from John Little to Mary Ann Jessop, stating that the property is sold subject to the covenant in the 1963 conveyance and also subject to and with the benefit of the lease dated 9 July 1971.

7. A legal mortgage dated 5 October 1974 given by Mary Ann Jessop to the Cornshire Building Society with a receipt endorsed on it dated 1 October 1979 sealed by the Society.

8. A general power of attorney dated 15 September 1979 given by Guy Budd to Steven Cox.

9. An examined copy grant of probate of the estate of Mary Ann Jessop deceased dated 23 September 1979 to her executors Guy Budd and Ann Budd.

10. A land charges search dated 25 November 1979 against Mary Ann Jessop, Guy Budd and Ann Budd revealing no entries save for a C(i) entry against Mary Ann Jessop.

11. An assent dated 30 November 1979 from Guy Budd (executed on his behalf by his attorney Steven Cox) and Ann Budd to Philip Ross.

12. A business lease of the whole of the property dated 28 February 1985 by Philip Ross to Peter Kay for a term of twenty-five years.

13. A copy of a planning permission dated 14 March 1988.

14. A deed of surrender dated 11 April 1988 of the lease to Peter Kay.

15. A local land charges search dated 4 May 1990.

16. A land charges search dated 8 June 1990 against Philip Ross, Peter Kay, Christopher Browning and Jill Browning revealing no entries.

17. A conveyance on sale dated 12 June 1990 from Philip Ross to Christopher Browning and Jill Browning as joint tenants stating that the property is sold subject to the covenant in the 1963 conveyance.

18. A legal charge dated 12 June 1990 given by Christopher Browning and Jill Browning to the Cornshire Building Society.

Commentary

This question will exercise your skill in spotting the relevant from the irrelevant, the hallmark of any competent lawyer. Modern questions will endeavour to mirror real life and so, unlike most law degree or postgraduate diploma in law questions, you will sometimes be given facts or documents which bear no direct relevance to the answer required. This process of sifting for relevant material will be carried out by a solicitor in practice almost on a daily basis.

Do not be put off by the fact that the subject premises are industrial and that business leases have been granted. Remember that when deducing and investigating title, the same principles of good conveyancing practice apply irrespective of whether the premises are used for residential or commercial purposes. The aim for the buyer ultimately in each case is to secure a good and marketable title free from defects.

Those of you who understand the concept of 'root of title' and are proficient in finding your way around unregistered titles should have little trouble in achieving high marks on this question. Conversely those with thin knowledge are likely to flounder!

A careful reading of the question ('. . . or excluding . . .') should alert you to the fact that not all documents are to be included in the epitome.

Choose your root of title and explain succinctly why you have chosen it. The choice of root may not be straightforward and there may be more than one document which could qualify, so do not be afraid to discuss possible alternatives.

Once you have dealt with the root, run down the list of documents and tick those you intend to include in the epitome whilst at the same time making a rough note of the reasons why each document should or should not be included. It may be safer to deal with your explanation first before attempting to draft the epitome. That way you will have more time to think through your reasoning fully (and perhaps change your mind to the good without recourse to the correcting fluid!).

You may decide that some documents strictly do not need to be included but that it is courteous and customary to do so. For example, land charges searches are normally abstracted (and indeed must be if the National Protocol is being used). Do not be afraid to make these points in your explanation; it will help the examiner to appreciate your understanding of the question.

Finally, draft the epitome clearly and legibly. Do not forget to complete the heading and all columns, just as you would in a property department of a solicitors' office.

The far right-hand column of the epitome form often confuses students. Generally, unless there has been a sale of part or administration of an estate, all original documents will be handed over to the purchaser's solicitor on completion. The grant of probate in this case is not the original (which is probably still held by the executors) but an examined copy. This is sufficient to deduce title and thus the original grant will not be handed over on completion.

Suggested answer

The suggested draft epitome is set out in Appendix 5.1.

Explanation of draft epitome

It is first necessary to determine which document will constitute the root of title. The following criteria should be noted:

(a) It must be at least fifteen years old (Law of Property Act 1969, s. 23 amending Law of Property Act 1925, s. 44(1)).

(b) It must deal with the ownership of the whole legal and equitable estate.

(c) It must contain a description by which the property can be identified.

(d) It must show nothing to cast any doubt on the title of the disposing party.

The 1979 assent is the latest document that may be used but it should be checked as it may fail test (c) above. Assents often describe the land transferred by reference to a full description in an earlier deed, e.g. here possibly the 1974 or earlier conveyances. Moreover, it may fail to specify the estate assented to, simply vesting the property for all the estate or interest of the deceased. If the description is inadequate then the 1974 conveyance should be used as the root (assuming this also satisfies the criteria for a good root). There is nothing to prevent any of the earlier conveyances (or even the 1971 mortgage) being used as the root, provided the above criteria are met.

It should be noted that where assents or mortgages are used as roots of title Land Registry may insert a protective entry on the charges register of the subsequent registered title. This is because restrictive covenants are rarely mentioned in assents or mortgages and Land Registry is warning that they may exist. Notwithstanding these potential pitfalls the draft epitome in this answer assumes that the assent is a good root and will be used as such. The 1979 grant of probate is also deduced as proof of the assentors' title to make the assent. A memorandum of the 1979 assent should have been endorsed on the rear of the original grant before this copy was made and examined, so this should be checked.

Having established the root of title it is then necessary to deduce all the links in the chain of the freehold title from the root document to the document by which ownership became vested in the seller, i.e. the 1990 conveyance.

Can the documents created earlier than the root be disregarded and excluded from the epitome? Not without checking whether any of them fall within Law of Property Act 1925 s. 45(1), which lists the exceptions to the general rule that precludes a buyer from requiring production of or raising requisitions about the pre-root title.

There are two documents here which do fall within the exceptions. First, the power of attorney of 15 September 1979 granted to Steven Cox under which the abstracted 1979 assent is executed. This exception was confirmed in the case of *Re Copelin's Contract* [1937] 4 All ER 447. Secondly, the 1963 conveyance although dated pre-root, imposes a restrictive covenant which, as it is protected by registration (see D(ii) entry in Land Charges Search of 29 September 1974), will bind a purchaser of the legal estate for money or money's worth. (Land Charges Act 1972, s. 4(6)). Accordingly, both the power and the 1963 conveyance should be abstracted by inclusion in the epitome.

The land charges search certificates are also included. Although a seller is generally not obliged to deduce these (because they are not documents of title) it is standard practice and courteous to do so, because it saves the buyer's solicitor from having to repeat them. If the National Protocol is being used then the seller's solicitor *must* provide a certificate of search against 'appropriate' names. The 1974 search certificate is pre-root but it confirms that the 1963 covenant has been protected by registration.

The land charges search against Mary Ann Jessop reveals a C(i) puisne mortgage. Presumably Mary Ann took out a second mortgage after her first mortgage to Cornshire Building Society. This could be a potential problem and we would need to check that the puisne mortgage has been discharged. We could do this by requesting an office copy of the C(i) entry from the Land Charges Registry in Plymouth (which would reveal the name of the mortgagee), and then by writing to the mortgagee requesting confirmation of discharge (it is hoped!). If it is discharged our client would then be entitled to require the mortgagee to remove the C(i) entry.

The property is being sold with vacant possession, so do the leases have to be abstracted? The 1971 lease, although still subsisting post-root, does not have to be abstracted because it has expired by effluxion of time. However, some conveyancers may choose to include it in the epitome on the basis that it is still part of the post-root title. The 1985 lease is no longer subsisting but it has not expired by effluxion of time; it has been surrendered. Consequently, the lease and the surrender will be deduced to enable the buyer to check the validity of the surrender.

The 1988 planning permission and the 1990 local land charges search are not documents of title and have no place in an epitome of title.

The 1990 conveyance to the seller is included to complete the chain of title. The legal charge of the same date is also listed. Although the seller on completion will no doubt discharge the latter, it is still a subsisting mortgage affecting title to the property and as such must be deduced.

Question 2

RICHARDS ABBEY AND PARTNERS, SOLICITORS
OFFICE MEMORANDUM

To   The Trainee Solicitor

From   The Senior Partner

Re our clients Sam and Jane Cluanie: purchase of Flat 3, 125 Clothier Street Kemptville Cornshire

Sam and Jane are old friends and clients who have put in an offer to buy the above leasehold property from Provincial Finance Ltd, a mortgagee in possession. Our clients are buying with the aid of a mortgage. We are also instructed by their mortgagee and the CML Lenders' Handbook is being used. Apparently the owner of the flat was mortgaged up to the hilt. The seller is second in a line of three mortgagees and we shall obviously have to make sure that Sam and Jane get good title. It is some time since I acted on a purchase from a mortgagee. Please would you research the following points and let me have your brief report by this evening. In particular:

1. Do we have to investigate the seller's entitlement to sell?

2. As matters stand, how do we ensure that Sam will buy the property free from any of the mortgages?

We shall be using the Law Society contract incorporating the Standard Conditions of Sale. The seller's solicitors have deduced title by sending me a copy of the entries inside their client's Charge Certificate, which I attach [refer to Appendix 5.2]. In your report, please mention any problem regarding the title and the deduction of it. I have to say I am a little concerned about the presence of the restriction and caution—can you reassure me?

Commentary

You have received a memorandum from the senior partner who requires a 'brief report by this evening' so you will need to act quickly! A busy senior partner will not appreciate a long-winded diatribe on the finer points of sales by mortgagee or registered leasehold titles. The partner has told you specifically what is required so stick to the matters in question and make your memorandum in response short and to the point.

You will need to demonstrate a clear understanding of the principles of overreaching in the context of a sale by a mortgagee. There are a number of entries on the register to consider. You should appreciate that the third mortgage and caution registered after the seller's charge will be overreached by the mortgagee's sale, and so may be ignored. The restriction is also something of a red herring. Although this affects future dispositions by a survivor of one of the registered proprietors, it does not prevent a disposition by a mortgagee under its power of sale.

This is a classic case for P.A.T. (Pause and Think). Unless you think the question through, you run the risk of setting off on the wrong track, for instance by writing at length about the restriction and caution which is completely uncalled for. You will not want to find after writing perhaps a page about cautions, that you realise only then that the presence of a caution *on these facts* will be no obstacle to a sale.

You will notice also the reference to the copy (not *official* copy) entries of title and the standard conditions of sale, with the specific query concerning deduction of the title—easy marks should be gained here if you appreciate the fundamentals of deduction of title to registered land.

Lastly, whenever you are given a registered leasehold title, always check its class—you can virtually guarantee it will be good leasehold, thus inviting an appraisal of the deficiencies of this class of title. Note the reference to the CML Lenders' Handbook, a clear sign that you are expected to refer to it. In this case, you will have to check what the Handbook says about good leasehold title.

Suggested answer

RICHARDS ABBEY AND PARTNERS, SOLICITORS
OFFICE MEMORANDUM

To   The Senior Partner

From   The Trainee Solicitor

Re our clients Sam and Jane Cluanie: purchase of Flat 3, 125 Clothier Street Kemptville Cornshire

I refer to your memorandum on the above and report as follows:

Sale by mortgagee

1. A purchaser from a mortgagee must be satisfied on the following two counts:
    (a) That the mortgagee's power of sale exists,
    (b) That the mortgagee's power of sale has arisen.

2. A power of sale is implied into every legal mortgage unless expressly excluded in the mortgage deed (LPA 1925 s. 101). We shall need to inspect the second mortgage deed to check this.

3. We must also check the second mortgage to ensure that the selling mortgagee's power of sale has arisen, i.e. that the principal monies have become due for repayment. This is normally stated to be a date early on in the mortgage term (e.g. one month after the date of the mortgage).

4. It is not necessary for a purchaser from a mortgagee to check that the power of sale has become exercisable (although the mortgagee must check this, otherwise the mortgagee may be liable in damages to the mortgagor).

5. A sale by a second mortgagee cannot affect the security of a prior mortgagee. Therefore Mr and Mrs Cluanie will take subject to the first mortgage unless the selling mortgagee agrees to discharge the first mortgage from the proceeds of sale. We must obviously insist on this by requiring the seller's solicitors to give an undertaking on completion to discharge the charge in favour of Cornshire Building Society and to send us Form DS1 upon receipt.

6. The buyers will take free of the seller's registered charge although on completion, the charge technically is not discharged.

7. The third mortgage was registered after the registration of the seller's charge and thus will be overreached by the sale. Mr and Mrs Cluanie will therefore take free of it.

The Title

8. A seller's solicitor should deduce title to registered land by means of official copies, so the photocopies we have of the entries inside the Charge Certificate are not sufficient. We must insist that the seller's solicitors deduce title by providing us with up to date official copies of the registered title.

9. Entry number 4 in the Property Register reveals a Deed of Covenant dated 8 March 1984 which is supplemental to the registered lease. The register indicates that a copy of the Deed is filed at Land Registry. We must ask the seller's solicitors to produce an official copy of it, so that we can establish the nature and extent of the rights and obligations contained in the deed and see how they may affect our client's proposed use and enjoyment of the property.

10. We should be concerned that the leasehold title is only registered with a good leasehold title. This means that although Land Registry is satisfied that the lease itself is good, the Registry has not approved the superior freehold title. Consequently the right of the landlord to grant the lease is not

guaranteed and our clients, once registered as proprietors, would take subject to any right in derogation of the landlord's title to grant the lease. I note that the CML Lenders' Handbook is being used. Paragraph 5.4.2 of the Handbook stipulates that good leasehold title is acceptable to the lender if a marked abstract of the superior title is provided, or we are prepared to certify that the title is good and marketable, or we arrange indemnity insurance in accordance with paragraph 9 of the Handbook. In order for the leasehold title to be become fully good and marketable, ideally it should be upgraded to an absolute title as soon as possible. Accordingly we should ask the seller's solicitors to deduce the whole title to the freehold (which is presumably unregistered). Once we are happy with the freehold title and are satisfied that Land Registry will approve it and will upgrade the leasehold title to absolute, then we can accept the title. Alternatively if this is not feasible, we could arrange good leasehold indemnity insurance (at the seller's expense) in accordance with the requirements of paragraph 9 of the Handbook. However these requirements are quite strict and the best course would be to ensure that the title will be upgraded.

The Restriction

11. This indicates that Mr and Mrs Logsdail hold the property as tenants in common in equity and prevents a disposition by the survivor of them except by order of the registrar or court. However the restriction will not prevent a sale by the mortgagee under its power of sale (nor indeed any sale by *both* proprietors) so we need not be concerned by it.

The Caution

12. This protects a third party interest in the property (possibly an equitable mortgage) in favour of the cautioner, Stephen Longman (Finance) Ltd. The nature of the interest need be of no concern to us however, as it will be overreached by the sale by Provincial Finance Ltd, the proprietor of an earlier registered charge.

TIME ENGAGED 30 MINUTES

TRAINEE SOLICITOR

Question 3

Your client is purchasing The Corner House, Chiltern Road, Pitton. The property has an unregistered title which your principal has asked you to investigate. In the draft contract, the root of title is expressed to be a Conveyance of 13 January 1980 and the seller is stated as Flora Nicholson. The property came within an area of compulsory registration on 1 December 1990.

Investigate the attached Abstract of Title [refer to Appendix 5.3] and list and explain the requisitions you would raise on the title deduced.

Commentary

You will need no reminding to read the introductory paragraph carefully. It is likely to, and does, contain information which will have a crucial bearing on the requisitions you will raise. Note especially that the title in question is unregistered. Different considerations apply to the investigation of an unregistered as opposed to a registered title.

The question asks you to raise requisitions 'on the title deduced' so it is important that you confine your requisitions exclusively to the title you have been given. Do not be drawn into a discussion of generalities concerning such matters as local searches, standard pre-contract enquiries or requisitions of an administrative nature commonly found on the Completion Information Form (e.g. what are the arrangements for release of keys?).

This is a traditional abstract. It takes the form of a precis of the documents and events which constitute the title. In the interests of brevity an abstract is often abbreviated (which can make it virtually indecipherable to non-conveyancers!) but in this question the text is set out in full. These days the traditional form is not as commonly used in practice as an epitome of title with copy documents attached, but it does crop up from time to time so you should know how to deal with it.

Before putting pen to paper it is vital that you spend enough time familiarising yourself with the abstract. The first thing many students do when faced with an abstract or epitome is to start writing before thinking through a logical plan of action. Don't panic! Just read it carefully and jot down on a piece of rough paper the defects and discrepancies which will form the subject matter of your requisitions. For instance, you will note from a careful reading of the January 1994 conveyance that the buyers purchased as tenants in common. If you fail to spot this you may be drawn into an irrelevant discussion of the Law of Property (Joint Tenants) Act 1964, which is relevant only when buying unregistered land from a surviving joint tenant (see standard question 4).

Notice that the question says 'list *and explain*'. A buyer's solicitor will raise requisitions by submitting to the seller's solicitor a list of numbered questions, in the same way as enquiries before contract. In an LPC subject assessment however, you must demonstrate that you understand why you are raising the requisitions; that is the reason for having to explain them as well.

The preferred approach is to write the requisition and then follow it with your explanation before moving on to the next requisition, and so on. You should not attempt an essay-style answer which will be harder to write and take the examiner longer to mark.

We recommend that you familiarise yourself with abstracts and epitomes and practice this type of question as much as possible before sitting a Property Law and Practice subject assessment. In this way you should become adept at coping with unregistered titles and will tackle them with confidence.

Suggested answer

1. 'Please supply a copy of the conveyance dated 18 January 1975.'

   The abstract of title as deduced does not contain an adequate description of the property. It is clear from the contents of the 1980 Conveyance that the property is fully described in the 1975 Conveyance. This conveyance also creates a right of way and imposes covenants and conditions which, provided they are registered as D(ii) land charges, will bind a purchaser for value. Accordingly we are entitled to examine the 1975 Conveyance, notwithstanding that it is dated prior to the root of title.

2. 'The 1990 land charges search certificate is out of date. Please supply copies of all land charges search certificates in your possession.'

   The June 1990 Conveyance was not completed within fifteen working days of the April 1990 search certificate and so the latter cannot be relied upon as evidence that there are no subsisting entries against Benjamin Edwards. The seller's solicitors will be asked to see whether the search was renewed, and also to check for other search certificates which, if they exist and are valid, will obviate the need for the buyer's solicitor to carry them out now.

3. 'The Conveyance of 20 June 1990 does not appear to have been stamped. Please clarify and, if necessary, confirm that it will be stamped before completion at the seller's expense.'

   The 1990 Conveyance is the only conveyance abstracted which does not indicate a stamp beneath the date in the margin. The conveyance does not contain a certificate for value so it seems likely that the *ad valorem* stamp and particulars delivered (PD) stamp were overlooked. The importance of this requisition is that an improperly stamped document is not admissible in evidence (Stamp Act 1891, s. 14). A buyer is entitled to have every deed forming a link in the chain of title properly stamped (see *Whiting v. Loomes* (1881) 17 Ch D 10, CA).

4. 'The Mortgage dated 20 June 1990 does not appear to have been discharged. Please confirm that a receipt for all money due under the mortgage, naming Sharon Munro and properly executed by Blakey Bank Ltd, is endorsed on the mortgage deed.'

The buyer's solicitor must ensure that all mortgages revealed by the abstract have been properly discharged. The receipt referred to above is that prescribed by the Law of Property Act 1925, s. 115 for unregistered land. The section also provides that the receipt should name the person making the payment. Here, we should check that the person named in the receipt as making the payment was the then owner of the property (Sharon Munro), otherwise the receipt may not discharge the mortgage but instead operate to transfer ownership of it from the original mortgagee (Blakey Bank Ltd) to the person named as making the payment. (See also *Cumberland Court (Brighton) Ltd v. Taylor* [1964] Ch 29.)

5. 'Please supply a copy of the Grant of Probate dated 19 January 1991 and confirm that the original or an examined copy will be handed over on completion.'

It is likely that the original Grant has been retained by the personal representatives. However, the Grant is still a document of title and as such, a subsequent buyer is entitled to receive at least an examined copy of it.

We will need to see a copy of the Grant to be sure that all proving personal representatives named therein duly joined in the subsequent Assent in favour of Elizabeth Campbell. This is a requirement imposed by the Administration of Estates Act 1925, s. 68.

We must also check the Grant for any memoranda endorsed on it. There should be one endorsement only, namely that of the assent to Elizabeth Campbell. The absence of such an endorsement would constitute a defect in title as the assent may theoretically have been defeated by a later sale of the land by the personal representatives to a buyer who took from them a written statement that they had made no previous assent or conveyance of the land (i.e. a statement under the Administration of Estates Act 1925, s. 36(6)).

6. 'Please confirm that the Assent dated 29 July 1991 contains an acknowledgement for production of the Grant of Probate dated 19 January 1991.'

Whenever an original document of title is retained on completion (in this case, the Grant of Probate) the buyer (or in this case the assentee) and successors in title are entitled to an acknowledgement of the right to production of the original (*Cooper v. Emery* (1884) 1 Ph 388). This is because a subsequent owner of the land may need to inspect the original at a later date. The benefit of the acknowledgement runs with the land.

7. 'Please explain why the title was not registered following completion of the Conveyance dated 14 January 1994 and confirm that the sellers will register the title with Title Absolute at their own expense before completion.'

The question tells us that the land became compulsorily registrable on 1 December 1990. Accordingly, the 1994 Conveyance would have induced compulsory registration and the seller must therefore regularise the position immediately. It is noted that the 1991 Assent did not induce first registration as assents have induced first registration only since the Land Registration Act 1997, which came into force on 1 April 1998. (Our other requisitions will be rendered superfluous if the seller can achieve registration with Title Absolute but this seems unlikely at present given the apparent defects in title!)

8. 'Why is Alastair Nicholson not selling the property in conjunction with Flora Nicholson? Please deduce devolution of title from them jointly to Flora alone.'

Unless Alastair also joins in the contract there will be a break in the chain of ownership and a consequent defect in title. It is apparent from the Conveyance of 14 January 1994 that Alastair and Flora purchased the property as tenants in common. Accordingly, if Alastair has died then a second trustee will need to be appointed to overreach the equitable interests under his will or intestacy. Alternatively, he may have conveyed his interest to Flora (perhaps pursuant to a divorce settlement), in which case a copy of the conveyance to Flora will be required.

9. 'Please confirm that the Mortgage dated 14 January 1994 will be discharged on or before completion.'

It is essential that all subsisting mortgages are discharged on or before completion. Normally, the seller's solicitors give the buyer's solicitors on completion an undertaking in Law Society format to discharge the mortgage from the proceeds of sale. It is therefore prudent to raise this point at the requisitions stage.

Question 4

Your firm acts for Wilderness Estates and Developments Ltd, a major commercial client who have expressed interest in acquiring an option to purchase a greenfield site on the outskirts of Westport, Cornshire. The company's ultimate intention, provided appropriate planning permission is forthcoming, is to acquire the site for development as a shopping centre, with a view subsequently to letting the individual shop units on full repairing and insuring business leases.

You have been asked to investigate the title to the greenfield site on behalf of your client. The land has a single unregistered freehold title and you have received the epitome of title, which is set out below. The intended seller is Mr Walter Smith, who is claiming to be the beneficial owner of the land. Explain with reasons the matters which from a perusal of the epitome will concern you. You may assume that the documents are in the correct form, have been properly executed and (where appropriate) are correctly stamped. Cornshire became an area of compulsory registration on 1 December 1990. In addition, from your examination of the title deduced consider whether Walter Smith has acquired the legal estate as beneficial owner.

EPITOME OF TITLE
RELATING TO FREEHOLD LAND AT WESTPORT CORNSHIRE

DATE	DOCUMENT/EVENT	WHETHER ORIGINAL TO BE HANDED OVER
31 May 1979	Conveyance on sale by Ian Kerr Gregory Kerr and Trevor Kerr to Gregory Kerr	Yes
7 February 1972	Power of attorney by Gregory Kerr to Neil Harvey	Yes
10 November 1983	Conveyance on sale by Gregory Kerr (acting by his attorney Neil Harvey) to Jack Collins and Jill Collins as joint tenants in equity	Yes
3 July 1985	Death of Jack Collins	N/A
4 August 1990	Conveyance on sale by Jill Collins to Dennis Williams	Yes
4 April 1994	Death of Dennis Williams	N/A
24 June 1994	Letters of administration of estate of Dennis Williams granted to Walter Smith	No

Commentary

Those of you heading for firms who act for large commercial property clients may encounter this scenario quite often; the developer client wishing to acquire and build on a greenfield site, i.e. land that has not been built on before. The ownership of the land in question has not changed hands for many years and so it still has an unregistered title, which it is now your job to investigate. Do not assume that simply by securing a training contract with a large commercial firm you can forget about unregistered land! On the contrary, you may find yourself considering unregistered titles rather frequently, especially where your firm acts for property developers.

The information provided here is sufficient to answer the question so do not worry that you have not been given copies of the documents. Similarly, you have been told that the documents are all in order so it is important not to waste time raising hypothetical technical points about the form, execution or stamping of the documents.

You will note that the suggested answer begins by listing the relevant areas of discussion and then goes on to deal with each one in turn. A well-structured approach will naturally appeal to the examiner who will immediately see that you have grasped the important points. Try not to ramble around the issues, but meet them head on, clearly and concisely.

Lastly, a mention about evidencing the death of estate owners (you will notice two deaths in this title). It is our experience that students sometimes fail to appreciate that production of a death certificate as evidence of death is unnecessary where a grant of representation has been obtained to the estate; the grant itself is quite acceptable evidence of the death. One occasion however when a request for a death certificate would be appropriate is on the death of a joint tenant in equity, a situation that has arisen here.

Suggested answer

The areas of concern arising from this question are essentially fourfold and relate to: a conveyance by trustees to one of themselves; an out of date power of attorney; the operation of the Law of Property (Joint Tenants) Act 1964, and the transfer of a legal estate to a beneficiary who is also the personal representative of the deceased's estate. Each area will be considered in turn.

1. By the conveyance of 31 May 1979 it appears that the co-owners Ian, Gregory and Trevor Kerr conveyed the property to one of themselves, namely Gregory Kerr. From the information provided it is unclear in what capacity the three of them held the equitable interest in the property, although they would have held the legal estate as personal representatives or trustees of land. Under s. 1(2) of the Trusts of Land and Appointment of Trustees Act 1996 a trust of land is defined as including trusts of any kind whether express, implied, resulting or constructive, whether arising before or after 1 January 1997 (the date on which the 1996 Act came into force).

   Prima facie, the sale by trustees to one of their number is in breach of trust and the conveyance is voidable by the beneficiaries under the trust. The principle is that a trustee must not place himself in a position where his interest and duty would clash (see generally *Re Bulmer* [1937] Ch 499 and *Holder v. Holder* [1968] Ch 353 CA). However this potential difficulty can be resolved if one of the following can be proven:

   (i)   proof of a pre-existing contract to purchase, or a right of pre-emption or option to purchase in favour of Gregory;

   (ii)   proof that all the legally competent beneficiaries consented to the conveyance to Gregory;

   (iii)   that the conveyance to Gregory was made pursuant to a court order;

   (iv)   that the conveyance to Gregory was sanctioned by the trust instrument or,

   (v)   that Gregory was a beneficiary under a will or intestacy.

   We should therefore request our seller's solicitor to provide evidence (in the form of one of the above) that the transaction by the trustees to one of their number was not in breach of trust.

2. The conveyance by Gregory Kerr dated 10 November 1983 was executed on his behalf by his attorney, Neil Harvey. We may assume from a reading of the question that the power of attorney was in the correct

form and the sale was therefore within the attorney's authority. However it is vital to determine whether the power was revoked before the attorney executed the conveyance of 10 November 1983. The purchasers in that conveyance would only have taken good title if they bought in good faith without knowledge of revocation of the power (Powers of Attorney Act 1971, s. 5(2)). Our client being a subsequent buyer will obtain the protection of s. 5(4) of the Powers of Attorney Act 1971 if either:

(i) the transaction between the attorney, Neil Harvey, and Jack and Jill Collins took place within twelve months of the grant of the power; or

(ii) the purchasers Jack and Jill Collins made a statutory declaration within three months of completion of the transaction stating that they had no knowledge of any revocation of the power.

As more than twelve months elapsed between the granting of the power, on 7 February 1982, and the conveyance to Jack and Jill Collins on 10 November 1983, a statutory declaration must be obtained. If one was not signed at the time this could be a problem as Jack is dead and the whereabouts of Jill may be unknown. However, even if Jill cannot be found, the position may not be irretrievable if the solicitors who acted for Jack and Jill on their purchase can be located. The reason for this is that a certificate of lack of knowledge of revocation given by *that person's solicitor* may be sufficient for Land Registry purposes.

3. The epitome states that Jack and Jill Collins held the property on trust for themselves as joint tenants in equity. Provided the joint tenancy was not severed prior to Jack's death, it appears that the only evidence of Jack's death we shall require is a certified copy of his death certificate. This is because Jill was entitled to Jack's share by survivorship and on Jack's death, Jill became beneficially entitled to the whole legal estate and equitable interest in the land. Once the legal and equitable interests merged and vested in Jill, the trust of land became extinguished and Jill was able to convey as sole beneficial owner (see The Law of Property (Amendment) Act 1926, s. 7). In this event, the terms of Jack's will or intestacy are of no relevance to the title, and will not concern us.

However, as the land is unregistered we must check against the possibility of Jack and Jill's joint tenancy having been severed before Jack's death. If this had occurred, Jack's equitable interest would not have passed to Jill by survivorship but would have passed instead under the terms of Jack's will or intestacy. In this event, the trust of land would have continued and, unless it could be shown that Jill was entitled to the whole equitable estate anyway (for which we would want to see the grant of representation to Jack's estate and an assent made in favour of Jill), another trustee should have been appointed to sell jointly with Jill (in the conveyance of 4 August 1990). A sale by two trustees would have overreached the equitable interests under Jack's will or intestacy.

A severance of a joint tenancy can occur in several ways. For example, by one joint tenant serving on the other a written notice of severance or, on the bankruptcy of a joint tenant. How can we be sure that Jack and Jill's joint tenancy has not been severed? The answer lies in the Law of Property (Joint Tenants) Act 1964 which offers protection to a purchaser of unregistered land where there has been a sale by a sole surviving joint tenant since 1925 (interestingly the 1964 statute acted retrospectively). The 1964 Act provides that a purchaser in these circumstances may assume that no severance of the joint tenancy has occurred provided:

(i) no memorandum of severance has been endorsed on or annexed to the conveyance under which the joint tenants bought the property; and

(ii) no bankruptcy proceedings are registered against the names of either of the joint tenants; and

(iii) the conveyance by the survivor either contained a statement (usually in the recitals) that the survivor was solely and beneficially entitled to the property, or that the survivor actually conveyed as beneficial owner.

Points (i) and (iii) above can be checked by examining the conveyance by Jill Jones to Dennis Williams dated 4 August 1990, but point (ii) can only be verified by carrying out a land charges search against both Jack Jones and Jill Jones to ensure there were no bankruptcy proceedings. We could do this ourselves or ask to see the search made at the time of the 1990 Conveyance on behalf of the purchaser, Dennis Williams.

4. Lastly, the question asks whether Walter Smith acquired the legal estate as beneficial owner. The epitome does not support the contention that the seller is beneficially entitled to the land. Walter is the personal representative of Dennis's estate as evidenced by the grant of letters of administration dated 24 June 1994. As such we cannot accept that Walter has acquired beneficial ownership unless this is proven. To this end we would ask to see a copy of the assent that Walter should have executed in favour of himself. The point here is that even if Walter is beneficially entitled to the property under Dennis's intestacy, Walter cannot properly sell as beneficial owner unless he first executes an assent in favour of himself (see *Re King's Will Trusts* 1964 Ch 542). If this has not been done Walter would have to sell in his capacity as personal representative and this has ramifications as to the type of title guarantee to be given to the buyer. Whereas a beneficial owner would normally give a full title guarantee, a personal representative should, at most, give only a limited title guarantee. The importance of this to the buyer is that the implied covenants for title under a limited title guarantee are less extensive than those under a full title guarantee (see Law of Property (Miscellaneous Provisions) Act 1994).

It is noted from the far right-hand column of the epitome that the original Grant of letters of administration is not being handed over to us on completion. Any assent by Walter to himself should therefore contain an acknowledgement for future production of the Grant. This acknowledgement will run with the land thus benefiting future estate owners. In addition, a memorandum of any assent by Walter to himself should be endorsed on the Grant, and we should check this.

On completion of our client's purchase, the land will become compulsorily registrable and our client will wish to receive an Absolute Title, being the best class of title that can be granted. This is particularly important, as our client is a developer who we are told will be granting business leases, which will themselves become registrable (if granted for more than seven years). The title as deduced is defective and Land Registry will not grant an Absolute Title to the freehold or the leaseholds until all the above points have been resolved. In conclusion therefore, we would want to be satisfied on all these matters before we could advise our client to proceed with the intended acquisition of the greenfield site. If matters cannot be resolved, we could consider the possibility of defective title indemnity insurance to be arranged at the seller's cost.

5.3.2 MULTIPLE CHOICE QUESTIONS AND ANSWERS

We set out below examples of ten multiple choice questions that you might encounter in a subject assessment. Answers to these then follow. Remember our initial guidance. Never leave multiple choice answers with a blank. If there are four possibilities and you are not sure of the answer select the one you think might be right; after all, you have a one in four chance of getting it right! Also look at the instructions on the paper. If it says select the right answer on the paper by circling the correct choice then do just that. Do not make a tick or underline your selection as the strict response would be to fail you even though the selection may be correct. Think carefully before selecting your answer and have correcting fluid to hand just in case you make a mistake or change your mind. To assist you, we have given brief explanations for the answers but generally this is not something you will be required to do (unless your exam paper says so!).

5.3.2.1 Multiple choice questions

Unless otherwise directed, select the right answer by circling it in each question. Should you think that none of the selections apply please explain why not in your answer book.

1. A solicitor acting for a buyer in relation to a sale by a mortgagee in possession should ensure that the mortgagee's power of sale has arisen and become exercisable.

   Is this statement TRUE/FALSE? Please delete the incorrect choice.

2. The following restriction in a registered title—

'No disposition by a sole proprietor of the land (not being a trust corporation) under which capital money arises is to be registered except under an order of the Registrar or of the court.'—means that:

   (a) the sole proprietor is bankrupt

   (b) the sole proprietor is a surviving joint tenant

   (c) the sole proprietor is a surviving tenant in common

   (d) the sole proprietor is a debtor with a registered court judgment on the property.

3. Mr Hutton sold his house to Mrs Sutcliffe in December 2003. Mr Hutton's attorney, Miss Gooch, executed the transfer deed. The power of attorney is dated 30 November 2002. A statutory declaration of non-revocation of the power of attorney should be given by:

   (a) Mr Hutton

   (b) Mrs Sutcliffe

   (c) Miss Gooch

   (d) Mr Hutton's solicitor

4. A statement under s. 36(6) of the Administration of Estates Act 1925 should be included in:

   (a) an assent

   (b) a conveyance from personal representatives

   (c) a power of attorney

   (d) a grant of representation

5. Under the Land Registration Act 2002 which of the following is the seller obliged to supply to the buyer when deducing title on the sale of a registered freehold property:

   (a) evidence of overriding interests known to the seller

   (b) copy of a conveyance containing restrictive covenants noted on the charges register

   (c) official copies of entries on the register

   (d) copy of title plan

6. In order to ensure that a buyer obtains a good title from the survivor of joint tenants in relation to registered land, the buyer's solicitor must ensure that:

   (a) the terms of any restriction are complied with

   (b) a written assent is used

   (c) the death certificate of the deceased is produced

   (d) there is no memorandum of severance endorsed on the grant

7. In which of the following documents would you find an acknowledgement for production of deeds:

   (a) conveyance of part of unregistered land by sole owner

   (b) conveyance of whole of unregistered land by trustees

   (c) transfer of part of registered land by sole owner

   (d) transfer of whole of registered land by trustees

8. When investigating an unregistered title the buyer's solicitor should, before advising his or her client to proceed, always ensure that any land charges registered against the estate owners in the title have been discharged.

Is this statement TRUE/FALSE? Please delete the incorrect choice.

9. You act for a wealthy buyer of a registered freehold property. Your client informs you that following completion she intends to convert the property into a commercial Internet café. While investigating the title you discover a covenant from 1910 in the charges register restricting the use of the property to a single private dwelling house. Which of the following are NOT appropriate for you to at least consider:

    (a) arranging restrictive covenant indemnity insurance

    (b) applying to the Lands Tribunal to have the covenant removed

    (c) contacting the person who currently has the benefit of the covenant to ask for consent to your client's proposed user

    (d) discussing with your client the possibility that she may wish to consider buying elsewhere

10. When preparing an epitome of title in unregistered land it is strictly unnecessary to include prior land charges search certificates against previous estate owners. However to assist the buyer's solicitor it is courteous to do so.

    Is this statement TRUE/FALSE? Please delete the incorrect choice.

5.3.2.2 *Answers to multiple choice questions (with brief explanations)*

1. The statement is false. To obtain good title it is correct to say that the buyer's solicitor must ensure that the mortgagee's power of sale has arisen, i.e. that the legal date of redemption has passed. But it is *not* necessary to check that the power has become exercisable, i.e. that the borrower is in default. This is a matter between the lender and borrower and does not affect the title.

2. The correct answer is (c). This is the classic co-ownership restriction, which is entered on the register when joint proprietors hold the equitable estate as tenants in common. It protects the interests of the deceased co-owner's estate by preventing the sole survivor from selling the property on his own. Typically a second trustee is appointed by the survivor to satisfy the restriction.

3. The correct answer is (b). The statutory declaration is required because the power is granted more than twelve months before the sale to Mrs Sutcliffe. Remember however that the declaration should be made by the person who dealt with the attorney, i.e. the buyer, not the attorney herself.

4. The correct answer is (b). The s. 36(6) statement protects a purchaser in a conveyance of unregistered land who accepts it as evidence that there has been no previous assent or conveyance by the personal representatives. It is not necessary to include the statement in an assent because the assentee is not a 'purchaser' but a beneficiary.

5. The correct answer is none! Under the old law, s. 110 of the Land Registration Act 1925 laid down minimum requirements as to what the seller of registered land should produce to the buyer. The Land Registration Act 2002 is silent on the point; so the seller is not obliged to supply any of these items (although a prudent buyer would insist on seeing them!).

6. The correct answer is (c). Note that the question says the land is registered so we need not concern ourselves with the Law of Property (Joint Tenants) Act 1964 which is relevant only to unregistered land. In registered land the buyer from a surviving joint tenant simply needs to see evidence of the deceased co-owner's death to be satisfied that the survivorship principle will apply.

7. The correct answer is (a). An acknowledgement for production is required in a conveyance of *part* of unregistered land because the seller is retaining part and needs to keep the original deeds to show title to the retained part in the future. As the buyer receives only examined copies of the deeds on completion, the seller acknowledges that s/he will produce the original deeds in future if the buyer (or the buyer's successor) needs them (e.g. in connection with a boundary dispute). An acknowledgement is not required in a conveyance of whole (because the buyer receives the original deeds), nor in a transfer of registered land.

8. The statement is false. It is not the case that *every* land charge will be adverse to the prospective buyer's use or enjoyment of the land. There may be entries protecting covenants or easements disclosed in the contract that the buyer is quite happy about, for example, a covenant preventing business use in a residential neighbourhood or a neighbour's right of way over the property.

9. The answer is none. You should at least consider all of these matters before advising your client of the best alternative suited to her individual circumstances. There is a good chance that indemnity insurance is appropriate but that is not what the question asks!

10. The statement is true. This is good conveyancing practice and it will endear you to the buyer's solicitor as it saves him or her having to repeat the searches.

5.3.3 SHORT ANSWER QUESTIONS

Question 1

A client William McKnight instructs you concerning a problem he has with some unregistered land he has inherited. His father, James McKnight, died ten years ago. His will appointed James McKnight's two brothers to be his executors and the land in question was left to William. The two brothers obtained probate and executed an assent to vest the land in William. It has now come to light that the executors, instructing another firm of solicitors, subsequently and erroneously purported to sell the land to a friend and neighbour of the deceased, Claire Henderson. She has been to see William McKnight and is claiming that the land is legally hers. Explain how you will establish whether or not she is correct.

Question 2

Your senior partner has asked you to prepare a briefing paper for the junior property lawyers in your firm. You are required to set out as bullet points the important matters that should be considered by a buyer's solicitor when investigating official copies of a registered title.

Question 3

You act for a prospective buyer of an unregistered title in November 2004. The seller's solicitor has deduced title specifying the root of title as a deed of gift to the seller dated 14 October 1992. What risks or disadvantages are there to your client if you accept this deed of gift as the root of title?

5.3.3.1 *Suggested answers to short answer questions*

Question 1

The executors first executed an assent of the land in favour of our client William McKnight. The Administration of Estates Act 1925, s. 36(5), enables a person in whose favour an assent or conveyance of a legal estate is made by a personal representative to have notice of it endorsed on the grant of representation. Thus a memorandum of this assent should have been endorsed on the grant of probate at the time of completion of the assent. We must check the grant for this endorsement and, if it is present, our client will have good title to the land.

If however the endorsement is not present our client may have a problem. Under the Administration of Estates Act 1925, s. 36(6) where a conveyance by personal representatives contains a declaration that there has been no previous assent or conveyance, the purchaser (in this case Claire Henderson) is entitled to rely on this statement *even if it is wrong* as sufficient evidence that no assent has been given—unless of course there is an endorsement on the grant. If this is the case here then s. 36(6) will operate to transfer the legal estate to Claire Henderson as if no previous assent had been made to William McKnight.

Thus Claire Henderson's claim will succeed if:

(i) the conveyance to her contained the above declaration, and

(ii) there is no endorsement of the assent on the grant.

However it is important to appreciate that a declaration under s. 36(6) of the Administration of Estates Act 1925 is merely sufficient evidence that no assent has been given. It is not conclusive evidence, and as such if Claire had actual knowledge of the prior assent or was aware of suspicious circumstances a court would be unlikely to allow her to rely on the s. 36(6) statement.

If our firm failed to ensure that a memo was endorsed on the grant at the time of the assent then regrettably this raises the possibility of professional negligence. If this is the case we should immediately advise the client to take independent advice and inform our professional indemnity insurers of the situation.

Question 2

<u>Briefing Paper</u>

To   The Property Department

From   Trainee Solicitor

When acting for a buyer of a registered title the following matters should be considered when inspecting copies of the seller's title:

<u>Generally:</u>

• Check that the copies are *official* copies not merely photocopies.

• Ensure that they are up to date, i.e. the 'search from date' should be within the last twelve months.

• Check that there are no pages missing.

<u>Property register:</u>

• Is the land freehold or leasehold?

• Does the description of the land correspond with the description in the draft contract?

• Is the title number the same as that given in the draft contract?

• What easements (if any) are noted as being enjoyed by the property?

• Has any land been removed from the title? If so, does this affect the land being bought?

<u>Proprietorship register:</u>

• Is the seller in the draft contract the same as the registered proprietor? If not, ask the seller's solicitor who has the ability to transfer the land and obtain evidence of this.

• Are there any entries in the register and, if so, what is their effect? (Examples of such entries might be restrictions, unilateral notices and old cautions entered prior to 13 October 2003).

• Check that the class of title is Absolute. Any lesser title, e.g., Good Leasehold or Possessory may be unacceptable to a lender. If appropriate, check the relevant parts of the CML Lenders' Handbook.

<u>Charges register:</u>

• Are there any encumbrances noted on the register (e.g. restrictive covenants, registered charges)?

• If so, how do they affect the buyer? In particular will they adversely affect your client's proposed use and enjoyment of the land?

• Which of the encumbrances will be removed or discharged on completion and how will their removal be achieved?

- Registered charges should be discharged on or before completion—ensure that you receive the seller's solicitors' undertaking to do so.

<u>Title plan:</u>
- Check that the land your client is buying is included within the red edging shown on the title plan.
- Check for any hatchings or colourings, which may show the extent of covenants, rights of way, or land that has been removed from the title (e.g. following a sale of part).

Question 3

This is a straightforward question concerning a root of title in unregistered land. Do not be drawn into a discussion of the Insolvency Act 1986. Although you are told there is a disposition by gift, a court cannot set aside the transaction as the gift took place more than five years ago. (However it would still be prudent to carry out a bankruptcy search against the donor from the date when the donor acquired the property until five years after the donor disposed of it.)

There are in fact just two aspects to this question; the nature of the proposed root of title and the age of the document. Dealing first with the deed of gift (or voluntary conveyance) as the proposed root. It is generally acknowledged that a deed of gift is an inferior root to a conveyance on sale. This is because on completion of a gift it is unlikely that any prior title investigation was made (i.e. the donee just accepts the gift). However with a conveyance on sale there is a perceived 'double guarantee' because of the assumption that the buyer under the root conveyance would have investigated title himself over a fifteen-year period. This effectively provides the current buyer with certainty of title going back at least thirty years.

Secondly, and more importantly, the proposed root will be less than fifteen years old at the date of the contract. The Law of Property Act 1925, s. 44(1) as amended by the Law of Property Act 1969 provides that the buyer can require the title to be deduced for at least the last fifteen years.

There are several risks and disadvantages for a buyer in accepting a short root. Briefly these are:

(i) The buyer will be bound by equitable interests (e.g. restrictive covenants) that would have been discoverable had the buyer investigated for the full fifteen years. In accepting a short title the buyer is deemed to have constructive notice of them (see *Re Nisbet and Pott's Contract* [1906] 1 Ch 386, CA).

(ii) The buyer will lose any rights to compensation from the State under s. 25 of the Law of Property Act 1969. This compensation is for loss arising from undiscovered land charges registered against an estate owner who owned the land before the date of the document which should have been used as the root. This compensation is only available if a prudent buyer who investigated a proper fifteen-year title would not have discovered such encumbrances.

(iii) An important practical issue is that Land Registry will probably refuse to grant absolute title on the buyer's application for first registration following completion. The Registry may also place a 'protective' entry in the Charges Register to cover the possibility of undisclosed restrictive covenants, i.e. 'subject to such restrictive covenants as may have been imposed thereon and are still subsisting'.

(iv) As a result of the above, the title to the property will become less marketable and unattractive to potential buyers and lenders.

To conclude, the buyer should insist on an earlier root of title (preferably a conveyance on sale) which is at least fifteen years old at the date of the contract.

5.4 REFERENCES TO WIDER READING INCLUDING PRACTITIONER TEXTS

- *A Practical Approach to Conveyancing* by Abbey R. and Richards M. (6th edn, OUP)—chapter 5 (Deduction and Investigation of Title).

- *The Law Society's Conveyancing Handbook 10th edn*, by Silverman F.—Section D dealing with title.
- *Emmet on Title*:

    —good root of title—Chapter 5, Part 2

    —abstract of title—Chapter 5, Part 3

    —mortgagee's power of sale—Chapter 25, Part 3

    —co-ownership and sale by surviving joint tenant—Chapter 11

    —execution of deeds—Chapter 20

    —acknowledgements for production—Chapter 12, Part 3

    —requisitions on title generally—Chapter 5, Part 4.

- Ruoff and Roper Registered Conveyancing (Sweet and Maxwell).
- For more detail on the changes introduced by the Land Registration Act 2002 see *Blackstone's Guide to The Land Registration Act 2002* by Abbey R. and Richards M. (OUP).
- *Textbook on Land Law* by MacKenzie J.A. and Phillips M. (9th edn, OUP)—Chapter 4 (unregistered land); Chapter 5 (registered land); Chapter 15 (co-ownership) and Chapter 19 (mortgages).

5.5 RELEVANT WEBSITES FOR MORE INFORMATION

- Acts of Parliament, http://www.hmso.gov.uk/acts.htm
  Keep up to date with statutory developments.
- Council of Mortgage Lenders, http://www.cml.org.uk
  There is an on-line version of the CML Lenders' Handbook available at this site and should be referred to in cases of doubt about the requirements of the lender in relation to title matters.
- House of Lords judgments, http://www.parliament.the-stationery-office.co.uk/pa/ld199697/ldjudgmt/ldjudgmt.htm.
  Keep up to date with important new cases.
- Inland Revenue, http://www.inlandrevenue.gov.uk/home.htm.
  The site for information on any problems about the possible payment of stamp duty
- Land Registry, http://www.landreg.gov.uk/
- Land Registry Internet register access, http://www.landregistrydirect.gov.uk
  The location for on-line pre-completion registered land searches.
- Landmark Information group, property and environmental risk information, http://www.landmark-information.co.uk
  Environmental searches can be obtained from the Landmark Information Group. These might shed light on former uses of the land perhaps revealed by covenants in the deeds.
- Lands Tribunal On-Line, http://www.landstribunal.gov.uk
  The Lands Tribunal considers applications to discharge or modify restrictive covenants
- Law Commission, http://www.lawcom.gov.uk
  Keep up to date on proposals for law reform.
- Law Society, http://www.lawsoc.org.uk
- Location statistics, http://www.upmystreet.com
- Ordnance Survey, http://www.ordnancesurvey.co.uk
  It might be useful to consult a detailed Ordnance Survey map when considering boundary problems and to compare with title deed plans.
- A street map anywhere in the UK, http://www.streetmap.co.uk

APPENDIX 5.1

Epitome of Title [a]

Relating to ___The Old Forge, Ridgewood Industrial Estate, Seatown_____

_____ which is a ___free hold property

Date	Nature of document or event (b)	Parties (c)	Whether abstract or photographic copy (d)	Document number (e)	Whether original document to be handed over on completion
20 July 1963	Conveyance	(1) Richard Tyler (2) Ashley Perryman	Copy	1	Yes
29 Sept 1974	Land charges search Certificate number	against names of Richard Tyler, Ashley Perryman and John Little	Copy	2	Yes
15 Sept 1979	Power of Attorney	(1) Guy Budd (2) Steven Cox	Copy	3	Yes
23 Sept 1979	Examined copy grant of probate of estate of Mary Ann Jessop deceased	granted to Guy Budd and Ann Budd	Copy	4	No
25 Nov 1979	Land charges search Certificate number	against names of Mary Ann Jessop, Guy Budd, Ann Budd	Copy	5	Yes
30 Nov 1979	Assent	(1) Guy Budd and Ann Budd (2) Philip Ross	Copy	6	Yes
28 Feb 1985	Lease	(1) Philip Ross (2) Peter Kay	Copy	7	Yes
11 Apr 1988	Deed of surrender	(1) Peter Kay (2) Philip Ross	Copy	8	Yes
8 June 1990	Land charges search Certificate number	against names of Philip Ross, Peter Kay, Christopher Browning and Jill Browning	Copy	9	Yes
12 June 1990	Conveyance	(1) Philip Ross (2) Christopher Browning and Jill Browning	Copy	10	Yes
12 June 1990	Legal Charge	(1) Christopher Browning and Jill Browning (2) Cornshire Building Society	Copy	11	Yes

EPT Epitome of title

APPENDIX 5.2

Copy title entries of Flat 3, 125 Clothier Street, Kemptville

SPECIMEN

Edition date : 20 January 1995　　　　　　　　　　　**TITLE NUMBER : CS92148**

Entry No.	A. PROPERTY REGISTER
	containing the description of the registered land and the estate comprised in the Title
	Unless the contrary is indicated below any subsisting legal easements granted by the under-mentioned lease(s) for the benefit of the land in this title are included therein. The registration takes effect subject to any rights excepted and reserved by the said lease(s) so far as such rights are subsisting and affect the land in this title.

	COUNTY　　　　　　　　　　　　　DISTRICT
	CORNSHIRE　　　　　　　　　　　KEMPTVILLE
1.	(30 August 1960) The Leasehold land shown edged with red on the plan of the above Title filed at the Registry and being Flat 3, 125 Clothier Street, Kemptville, (KV3 8LU).
2.	Short particulars of the lease(s) (or under-lease(s)) under which the land is held: DATE　　　　:　　17 August 1960 TERM　　　　:　　99 years from 27 July 1960 RENT　　　　:　　£25 PARTIES　　:　　1. Marian Bell 　　　　　　　　　　2. Margaret Elsie Logsdail and 　　　　　　　　　　　　Constance Logsdail
3.	There are excepted from the effect of registration all estates, rights, interests, powers and remedies arising upon, or by reason of, any dealing made in breach of the prohibition or restriction against dealings therewith inter vivos contained in the Lease.
4.	Deed of Covenant dated 8 March 1984 made between (1) Margaret Elsie Logsdail and Constance Logsdail and (2) James Dawkins supplemental to the registered lease. *NOTE:- Copy filed.*

Entry No.	B. PROPRIETORSHIP REGISTER
	stating nature of the Title, name, address and description of the proprietor of the land and any entries affecting the right of disposing thereof **TITLE GOOD LEASEHOLD**

1.	(30 August 1960) Proprietor(s) : MARGARET ELSIE LOGSDAIL and CONSTANCE LOGSDAIL both of Flat 3, 125 Clothier Street, Kemptville, Cornshire KV3 8LU.
2.	(30 August 1960) RESTRICTION : No disposition by a sole proprietor of the land (not being a trust corporation) under which capital money arises is to be registered except under an order of the registrar or of the Court.
3.	(14 October 1994) CAUTION in favour of Stephen Longman (Finance) Ltd., care of Messrs. Parsley and Lion, Solicitors, Herb House, High Street, Kemptville, Cornshire.

Continued on the next page

SPECIMEN

Entry No.	C. CHARGES REGISTER
	containing charges, incumbrances etc., adversely affecting the land and registered dealings therewith
1.	(30 August 1960) REGISTERED CHARGE dated 17 August 1960 to secure the moneys including the further advances therein mentioned.
2.	(30 August 1960) Proprietor(s): CORNSHIRE BUILDING SOCIETY of 3 Church Street, Kemptville, Cornshire.
3.	(14 June 1986) REGISTERED CHARGE dated 8 June 1986 to secure the moneys including the further advances therein mentioned.
4.	(14 June 1986) Proprietor(s): PROVINCIAL FINANCE LIMITED of 10 High Street, Kemptville, Cornshire.
5.	(29 January 1991) REGISTERED CHARGE dated 4 January 1991 to secure the moneys including the further advances therein mentioned.
6.	(29 January 1991) Proprietor(s): LENDALOT LIMITED of 12 Market Place, Kemptville, Cornshire.

**** END OF REGISTER ****

NOTE : A date at the beginning of an entry is the date on which the entry was made in the Register.

APPENDIX 5.3—
ABSTRACT OF TITLE

ABSTRACT OF THE TITLE of Flora Nicholson to freehold property known as 'The Corner House' Chiltern Road Pitton in the County of Cornshire

7 January 1980	OFFICIAL CERTIFICATE of search in HM Land Charges Register No. 217432 against Charles Lane revealing no subsisting entries

13 January 1980
Stamp £1,000
PD Stamp

BY CONVEYANCE of this date made between CHARLES LANE of The Corner House Chiltern Road Pitton in the County of Cornshire (thereinafter called 'the vendor') of the one part and BENJAMIN EDWARDS of 24 Rothesay Avenue Pitton in the County of Cornshire (thereinafter called 'the purchaser') of the other part

RECITING seisin of the vendor and agreement for sale

IT WAS WITNESSED as follows:-
1. IN pursuance of the said agreement and in consideration of the sum of £50,000 paid to the vendor by the purchaser (receipt acknowledged) the vendor as beneficial owner thereby conveyed unto the purchaser

ALL THAT premises fronting Chiltern Road Pitton aforesaid comprising 1.9 acres or thereabouts and delineated and described on a plan annexed to a Conveyance dated 18th January 1975 made between (1) Mark Ellins and (2) Charles Lane (hereinafter called 'the said Conveyance') AND ALSO ALL THAT messuage or dwelling house erected thereon and known as 'The Corner House' Chiltern Road Pitton aforesaid TOGETHER with the full benefit and advantage of the right of way granted by the said Conveyance over and along the road shown coloured brown on the said plan

TO HOLD unto the purchaser in fee simple SUBJECT to the covenants and the conditions contained in the said Conveyance
2. COVENANT by the purchaser with the vendor to observe and perform the said covenants and conditions and to indemnify EXECUTED by both parties and ATTESTED

24 April 1990

OFFICIAL CERTIFICATE of search in HM Land Charges Register No. 328557 against Benjamin Edwards revealing no subsisting entries

20 June 1990

BY CONVEYANCE of this date made between the said BENJAMIN EDWARDS of 'The Corner House' Chiltern Road Pitton in the County of Cornshire (thereinafter called 'the vendor') of the one part and SHARON MUNRO of 49 Nobbs Hill Pitton in the County of Cornshire (thereinafter called 'the purchaser') of the other part

RECITING seisin of the vendor and agreement for sale

IT WAS WITNESSED as follows:-

1. IN pursuance of the said agreement and in consideration of the sum of £65,000 paid to the vendor by the purchaser (receipt acknowledged) the vendor as beneficial owner thereby conveyed unto the purchaser

ALL THAT the before abstracted premises together with the said dwellinghouse built thereon TOGETHER with the full benefit and advantage of the before abstracted right of way

TO HOLD unto the purchaser in fee simple SUBJECT to the covenants and the conditions contained in the said Conveyance

2. COVENANT by the purchaser with the vendor to observe and perform the said covenants and conditions and to indemnify EXECUTED by both parties and ATTESTED

20 June 1990   BY MORTGAGE of this date made between the said SHARON MUNRO (thereinafter called 'the mortgagor') of the one part and BLAKEY BANK LTD of 10 High Street Blakey (thereinafter called 'the mortgagee') of the other part

After reciting seisin of Mortgagor in fee simple IT WAS WITNESSED that in consideration of sum of £40,000 paid by the mortgagee to the mortgagor (receipt acknowledged) the mortgagor as beneficial owner thereby charged unto the mortgagee

ALL THAT before abstracted property

PROVISO for cesser and other usual clauses
EXECUTED by mortgagor and ATTESTED

17 November 1990   WILL made on this date by said SHARON MUNRO appointing DUNCAN MUNRO and SHEILA MUNRO, her parents, to be her executors

12 December 1990   Death of the said SHARON MUNRO

19 January 1991   Grant of Probate to the said will issued out of Blakey District Probate Registry on this date to the said DUNCAN MUNRO and SHEILA MUNRO

29 July 1991   BY ASSENT of this date the said DUNCAN MUNRO and SHEILA MUNRO assented to the vesting of the before abstracted property in ELIZABETH CAMPBELL

14 January 1994
Stamp £900
PD Stamp

BY CONVEYANCE of this date made between the said ELIZABETH CAMPBELL of The Corner House Chiltern Road Pitton in the County of Cornshire (thereinafter called 'the vendor') of the one part and ALASTAIR NICHOLSON and FLORA NICHOLSON of 2 Mill Road Pitton in the County of Cornshire (thereinafter called 'the purchasers') of the other part

RECITING seisin of the vendor and agreement for sale

IT WAS WITNESSED as follows:-

1. IN pursuance of the said agreement and in consideration of the sum of £90,000 paid to the vendor by the purchaser (receipt

acknowledged) the vendor as beneficial owner thereby conveyed unto the purchasers

ALL THAT the before abstracted premises together with the said dwellinghouse built thereon TOGETHER with the full benefit and advantage of the before abstracted right of way

TO HOLD unto the purchasers in fee simple as tenants in common in equity SUBJECT to the covenants and the conditions contained in the said Conveyance

2. COVENANT by the purchasers with the vendor to observe and perform the said covenants and conditions and to indemnify EXECUTED by both parties and ATTESTED

14 January 1994 BY MORTGAGE of this date made between the said ALASTAIR NICHOLSON and FLORA NICHOLSON (thereinafter called 'the mortgagors') of the one part and CORNSHIRE BUILDING SOCIETY of 14 Broad Street Blakey (thereinafter called 'the mortgagee') of the other part

After reciting seisin of mortgagors in fee simple IT WAS WITNESSED that in consideration of sum of £65,000 paid by the mortgagee to the mortgagors (receipt acknowledged) the mortgagors as beneficial owners thereby charged unto the mortgagee

ALL THAT before abstracted property

PROVISO for cesser and other usual clauses
EXECUTED by mortgagors and ATTESTED

6 | EXCHANGE OF CONTRACTS

6.1   INTRODUCTION

Exchange of contracts is recognised as being the most critical stage in the conveyancing process, the moment when the parties become legally bound to proceed. If the property law practitioner makes a mistake here the consequences for the client (and the practitioner) can be very grave indeed.

Where your client is selling one property and buying another (assuming the two transactions are dependent upon each other) the importance of synchronising the two exchange of contracts cannot be overstated. It is of course routinely the case that many clients selling a house or flat will also be buying another, and *vice versa*. In these cases, the conveyancer must ensure that exchange of contracts on both transactions is synchronised so that the client does not end up with two properties or none at all. Remember that either seller or buyer in a conveyancing transaction can withdraw without liability at any time prior to exchange of contracts (unless unusually a 'lock-out' agreement is in place).

Many students overlook the importance of synchronisation when answering a question on exchange of contracts and get bogged down in the minutia of the formulae for telephonic exchange. We cannot emphasis enough the importance of this one word—*synchronisation*. You may be able to recite perfectly the formulae for telephonic exchange (and you should be able to), but you will probably fail the question unless you can demonstrate the significance of synchronisation. Look carefully at the suggested answers to standard questions 2 and 4 in this chapter.

In the context of commercial conveyancing, such as the grant or assignment of a business lease, or the transfer of a freehold property which is tenanted, you should appreciate that synchronisation is likely to be of less significance. This is because there is usually no chain; only one property is involved and your client is dealing with just one other company or person, e.g., a commercial freehold with seller and buyer, or a landlord granting a business lease to a commercial tenant. Indeed in many commercial leasehold transactions, when the landlord and tenant are ready to proceed they may simply go straight to completion without exchanging contracts at all. Nevertheless in each transaction it is always important that you check whether your client has a related transaction in which synchronisation is required.

Naturally questions on exchange of contracts are not limited to the physical act of exchange itself. You should anticipate questions concerning the requisite conveyancing steps immediately before exchange (such as arrangements for bridging finance) and also steps you should take following exchange, for example, arranging insurance or whether the contract should be protected by registration.

Insurance is a common feature in Property Law and Practice assessments and is a topic you would do well to revise thoroughly. Standard condition 5.1 deals with risk and insurance and has come in for much criticism from the profession; you should be aware of its failings. Question 3 is typical of the subject matter you might receive on an insurance question, namely a consideration of the legal position when a property is damaged by fire between exchange and completion.

Death and insolvency of the contracting parties is also mentioned briefly in this Chapter. You will need to know what to do in the event of either of these events occurring between exchange and completion.

As you read this Chapter, notice how the style of standard questions differs, thus inviting different ways of answering. You will see how two questions take the form of internal office memoranda, another requires a direct answer in point form, whilst another is more general in nature and requires an answer in the form of a letter to a client.

6.2 AN OVERVIEW OF THE SUBJECT AND A LOOK AT SOME PROBLEM AREAS

There are three distinct and important areas in the subject area of exchange of contracts: (a) pre-exchange, i.e. checking that you are ready to exchange; (b) the exchange process itself; and (c) what to do when supervening events occur after exchange, i.e. death or insolvency. We shall examine each of these in turn and consider some problem areas.

6.2.1 PRE-EXCHANGE

Whether buying or selling the period immediately before exchange is all about being sure that you are ready to commit your client to the transaction. As a buyer's solicitor you have more to do because of all the searches and enquiries, title investigation, and the verification of the buyer's financial arrangements. If the buyer is obtaining a mortgage it is crucial that you inspect the formal written offer and ensure that all conditions can be met before you exchange. In particular watch out for any retention from the advance, e.g. in respect of essential repairs to the property, or a mortgage indemnity guarantee premium.

The buyer's practitioner also needs to approve the draft contract and ensure that cleared funds are received from the client in respect of the deposit payable on exchange. If your client has a related sale it may be possible to fund the deposit in other ways. He or she may be able to utilise the deposit receivable on a related sale. Perhaps your client might consider offering a deposit guarantee instead of a money deposit. A bridging loan might also be a possibility. Do remember that where bridging finance is offered, the client's bank will invariably require your firm's undertaking to repay the bridging loan from the proceeds of the related sale (note that a bridging loan will normally only be available where the client has a related sale). Indeed, the *whole* of the net proceeds is normally requested, so that the balance received, after the bridging loan has been repaid, is credited to the client's bank account. Before giving the undertaking you will need to consider its terms very carefully to ensure that you can comply with them.

Reporting to the client is an essential part of the pre-exchange procedure. You have a duty to use reasonable care and skill in giving such advice as the particular transaction demands, having regard to the level of knowledge and expertise of your client (see *Sykes v. Midland Bank Executor and Trustee Co Ltd* [1971] 1 QB 113). You would therefore generally give fuller advice to a first time buyer than you would, say, to an experienced property developer (see *Aslan v. Clintons* (1984) 134 NLJ 584). Your advice to the client may be given orally or in writing, or by using both methods. For the avoidance of doubt it is best practice to report in writing.

The seller's solicitor has rather less to do but important matters should never be overlooked. In particular, you must be certain that the net proceeds of sale will be sufficient to pay off any existing mortgage(s) on the subject property. Obtain redemption statements from the mortgagee(s) yourself and check the figures carefully. If only part of the seller's property is being sold, it will probably be unnecessary to discharge fully any mortgage(s) on the property (although the seller may choose to do so if sufficient monies are available). The buyer will merely be concerned to ensure that the part of land being bought is released from the mortgage(s). The seller's conveyancer should therefore inquire of the existing mortgagee(s) as to how much is required for the release of the part being sold, and ensure that this sum at least will be available on completion to forward to the mortgagee(s). As far as the deposit is concerned, 10% of the sale price is the norm but parties sometimes agree less, so do check the terms of the contract. If there is a chain of transactions the deposit is sometimes forwarded directly from the bottom of the chain to the top. Check what arrangements have been agreed.

Both parties will of course need to sign the contract before exchange, although the signature need not be witnessed. As you should know, it is standard conveyancing practice to have two identical contracts, one signed by the seller and the other signed by the buyer. These are then exchanged so that the buyer receives the seller's signed contract, and vice versa. If you are reporting to the client in person this is a good time for the client to sign the contract in your presence (assuming the terms are agreed). You can then hold the signed but undated contract on file in readiness for exchange. If it is not practicable for you to see the client then the contract can be sent for signature with your written report. Ask the client to return the signed contract as soon as possible together with, if required, a cheque for the deposit (or the balance of it). Some clients may now prefer to transfer the deposit monies by bank transfer. Emphasise that the contract should *not* be dated when signed.

One problem area for students is synchronisation of exchange. If your client has a related transaction it is vital that you synchronise exchange of contracts on both the sale and purchase transactions. If you fail to do so and your client suffers loss, you will be negligent (see *Buckley v. Lane Herdman & Co.* [1977] CLY 3143). Consider the following disastrous chain of events:

- You exchange on the purchase before the sale.
- Your client's purchaser withdraws before you can exchange on the sale.

- Your client is legally bound to complete the purchase but is unable financially to do so.
- Your client is thus in breach of the purchase contract.
- Even if your client can secure alternative funds to complete (e.g. bridging loan), your client will end up with two properties (and a negligence claim against you).

Or alternatively:

- You exchange on the sale before the purchase.
- Your client's seller withdraws before you can exchange on the purchase.
- Your client is legally bound to complete the sale and does so.
- Your client has no property to move into and will have to find temporary accommodation and arrange furniture storage.
- Once again, your client has a negligence claim against you.

6.2.1.1 Insurance

If the buyer is to insure the property after exchange, then arrangements should be put in place before exchange, so that all that is needed after exchange is, at most, a simple telephone call to put the policy on risk. Some buyer's mortgagees will do this without the need for a phone call, i.e. the insurance is put in place automatically from the moment of exchange. The seller's insurance policy should always be maintained until completion in case the buyer does not complete. Remember that standard condition 5.1 reverses the open contract position by keeping the risk with the seller. However, check the contract carefully—standard condition 5.1 may have been excluded by special condition, in which case the risk passes to the buyer under the open contract rule. Also, if it is a commercial property and the commercial conditions are being used, similarly the risk also passes to the buyer on exchange.

Following exchange, the buyer's solicitor should consider whether registration of the contract is required. This takes the form either of a notice in registered land or a C(iv) estate contract in unregistered land. Remember that it is standard practice not to register a contract unless there are exceptional circumstances. Examples might be:

(i)   Where a dispute arises between the parties, or

(ii)   The buyer becomes suspicious of the seller possibly seeking to dispose of the property to someone else, or

(iii) Where there is a long period of time between exchange and completion, e.g. in excess of six weeks. This will be the case on a newly built property where the construction is at an early stage at the time of exchange.

As a study aid we set out below two pre-exchange flow-charts; one for the buyer and one for the seller. Do remember that in residential conveyancing your client is likely to be selling one house and buying another, so you will need to consider both. Although checklists and flowcharts are useful, it is important not be a slave to them; always check your file carefully to ensure that everything in the subject transaction is in order and that there are no unresolved issues.

6.2.2 THE EXCHANGE PROCESS ITSELF

There are three methods by which exchange of contracts can be effected: in person, by post (or document exchange) and by telephone. Exchange in person is rarely used these

Acting for the buyer

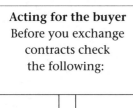

Acting for the buyer
Before you exchange contracts check the following:

Completion
Agree a completion date in principle with the other side.

Exchange
Decide which method of exchange to use. If by telephone, decide which formula to use.

Searches & Enquiries
Have all pre-contract searches & enquiries been made and are the results satisfactory?

Contract
Is the final form agreed? If so, get your client to sign it. Check the post exchange insurance position.

Synchronisation
If your client has a related sale make sure exchange of contracts on the two transactions is synchronised. This is important!

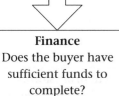

Finance
Does the buyer have sufficient funds to complete?

Report to your client
Always submit a full written report and if possible advise in interview as well.

Register the contract?
It is not normal practice to register the contract following exchange unless circumstances are unusual.

Mortgage Offer
Have you seen and approved the buyer's written mortgage offer, including any special conditions?

Title
Is the title good and marketable? Have all requisitions been answered satisfactorily?

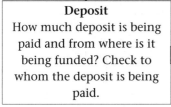

Deposit
How much deposit is being paid and from where is it being funded? Check to whom the deposit is being paid.

Survey
Is the result of the survey satisfactory?

Acting for the seller

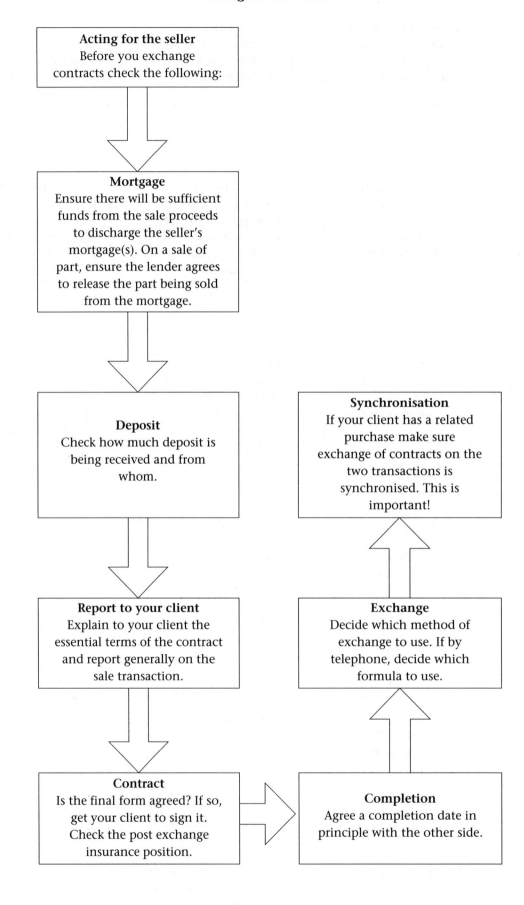

days unless the two offices are situated nearby. Pressures of time and the need for synchronisation in chain transactions make personal exchanges largely incompatible with the requirements of modern conveyancing.

For exchange by post the buyer's practitioner posts the buyer's signed contract and the cheque for the deposit to the seller's practitioner. Upon receipt, the seller's practitioner posts the seller's signed contract to the buyer's practitioner. It may also happen the other way round by the seller sending his contract first. If the standard conditions are being used, standard condition 2.1 confirms the common law postal rule on acceptance laid down in *Adams v. Lindsell* (1818) 1 B & Ald 681, namely that the contract comes into existence not when the second copy is received but when the second copy is *posted* (or deposited at the document exchange). Thus even if the contract is lost in the post a binding contract still exists. Postal exchange is not recommended where either party has a linked transaction, i.e. a dependant sale or purchase. The reason for this is the time lag between the first contract being posted and the second contract being posted, and during this time either party is of course free to change their mind and withdraw.

Telephonic exchange is the most common method of exchange today. This is a particular problem area for students who have no practical experience in a property practitioner's office. The moment of exchange occurs at the point in the telephone conversation when the practitioners agree that contracts are actually exchanged. The decision in *Domb v. Isoz* [1980] Ch 548 formally endorsed the practice of telephonic exchange and, following a recommendation by Templeman LJ, the Law Society subsequently produced formulae for use by practitioners. As the formulae involve the use of professional undertakings they should only be used between firms of solicitors and licensed conveyancers, i.e. not where unqualified persons are involved. Any variations of the formulae should be recorded on the practitioners' files and confirmed in writing, in case of any later disputes. The facts in short answer question 1 below illustrate how a failure to appreciate the importance of the rules about undertakings can cause problems for the unwary practitioner on exchange.

Telephone formula A is used when one party's practitioner (usually the seller's) holds *both* signed parts of the contract, together with the deposit cheque. (The buyer's practitioner will have forward the buyer's contract and deposit cheque to the seller's practitioner to be held to order in readiness for exchange.) On the assumption that it is the seller's solicitor who holds both parts of the contract, formula A works as follows (S = seller's practitioner, B = buyer's practitioner):

1. S confirms holding both signed contracts and the deposit cheque;
2. S and B agree that S will insert the agreed completion date in each contract;
3. Exchange is formally agreed by B releasing the buyer's contract and S agreeing to hold the seller's contract to B's order;
4. S undertakes to forward the seller's contract to B that day, either by first-class post, personal delivery or document exchange.

Following exchange, the practitioners must write file memos recording: their own names, the date and time of exchange, the formula used (and any variations to it), the completion date and the amount of the deposit being paid.

Formula B is used when both practitioners hold their own client's signed contracts (and the buyer's practitioner also holds the deposit cheque). Analogous to formula A, the practitioners confirm that they hold the signed contracts, they insert the agreed completion date, they agree to hold their client's contracts to the other's order and they undertake to send the contracts out that day (plus, for the buyer, the deposit cheque). As with formula A, file memos should be made after exchange recording the details of the conversation.

Formula C is used where there is a chain of transactions and the deposit monies are to be sent directly to another firm further up the chain. The practitioner at one end of the chain (X) telephones the practitioner next in line (Y). Both parties confirm that they hold their clients' signed contracts. X undertakes that X will definitely exchange with Y if Y rings back X before a specified time later that day requesting X to exchange. The same undertakings are then given to the other practitioners in the chain until the penultimate one in the chain is reached. Now at the end of the chain, a formula B exchange can occur between the penultimate practitioner and the practitioner at the end (assuming they are both ready). Thereafter the other contracts can be exchanged, one by one, back down the chain as the return calls are made. Thus the first call (e.g. by X to Y) activates formula C part 1; the return call (e.g. by Y to X)—when the exchange occurs—activates formula C part II. File memos should be made in respect of the conversations in parts I and II respectively. The part I memo will record the date and time of the conversation, the names of the practitioners speaking, any agreed variations to formula C, the final time later in the day for exchange, the completion date and the name of the practitioner to whom the deposit is to be paid (formula C assumes a 10% deposit). The part II memo will record the request to exchange, the time of exchange and the identities of the speakers.

This is a good area of the Property Law and Practice course for a 'hands-on' small group session in which students can learn the art of perfecting a synchronised exchange. In our experience many 'mock clients' go through the frightening stage of owning two houses or none at all. However, there can be no doubt that it is better to learn in the classroom by making your mistakes with fellow students than with real clients!

6.2.3 DEATH OR INSOLVENCY FOLLOWING EXCHANGE

We list below some key reminders of the essential points you would do well not to forget:

6.2.3.1 Death

- The contractual obligations are unaffected and the deceased's personal representatives are bound to complete.
- Advise the other side. It may be necessary to seek either a termination of the contract (unlikely) or a postponement of the completion date.
- If the other side do not agree to the above and completion is likely to be delayed apply for an expedited or limited grant of representation, advising the Probate Registry that the estate risks incurring liability for breach of contract.
- If one of three or more co-sellers dies the sale can proceed as normal.
- If one of two co-sellers dies check whether they held as joint tenants or tenants in common. If the latter, it will be necessary to appoint a second trustee.
- Unless the deceased's share passed by survivorship enabling a surviving co-seller(s) to sell the whole beneficial estate, do not complete until the grant of representation has been issued.
- On the death of a sole buyer, any mortgage offer is likely to be withdrawn, so the personal representatives will have to find alternative funding.
- If you need to serve notice on a deceased estate owner, address it to the deceased and the deceased's personal representatives at the deceased's last known address; also send a copy to the Public Trustee.

6.2.3.2 **Insolvency**

- On a registered title a notice will alert the buyer that a petition in bankruptcy has been presented against the registered proprietor; a bankruptcy restriction (or, prior to 13 October 2003, a bankruptcy inhibition) will alert the buyer that a bankruptcy order has been made.

- The bankruptcy proceedings will also be registered at the land charges department. These registrations are relevant for buyers of unregistered land only—it is not necessary to conduct a land charges search against the seller when buying registered land.

- A buyer who has relevant notice of bankruptcy proceedings should wait to take a transfer from the trustee in bankruptcy, not the seller.

- The buyer's practitioner should ask to see a copy of the bankruptcy order together with documentary proof of the trustee's appointment. Similarly, a buyer from a liquidator or administrative receiver of a company requires written evidence of the appointment.

- Any disposition by a bankrupt (including payment of purchase money) after the presentation of the petition is void. The same rule applies on company insolvency.

- A bankruptcy order will sever an equitable joint tenancy. The bankrupt co-owner's beneficial interest vests in the trustee who must execute the purchase deed with the surviving co-owner(s).

- Anyone buying from, or selling to, a company being wound up should deal with the liquidator of the company. A person dealing with a liquidator must ensure that the formalities of the liquidator's appointment have been observed.

- The appointment of an administrative receiver will normally crystallise a floating charge so that it becomes a fixed charge on the company's property. A buyer must ensure that the property is released from the fixed charge.

6.3 **SUBJECT ASSESSMENTS**

As in previous Chapters there now follow some examples of assessment questions in the subject area. Commentary and a suggested answer accompany the standard assessment questions. These are then followed by multiple choice questions (with answers) and short answer questions with suggested answers.

6.3.1 **STANDARD QUESTIONS, COMMENTARY AND SUGGESTED ANSWERS**

Question 1

Your firm is acting for Charlotte Mathysse on a dependent sale and purchase. The Standard Conditions of Sale (4th Edition) are being adopted in both contracts. The sale price is £50,000, the purchase price is £70,000. The solicitor in your office handling the two transactions is away ill. Charlotte has telephoned to raise two matters upon which she requires your advice:

(a) Charlotte has insufficient funds to finance the deposit on her purchase. What are her options and what advice would you give her? (12 Marks)

(b) Subject to the deposit problem being resolved, she would like you to exchange contracts immediately. What other matters should you consider before you exchange? (10 Marks)

Commentary

This question concerns the preparations for exchange, a stage of critical importance for both solicitor and client. Part (a) asks you to consider the client's arrangements for the deposit in which you will need to discuss the 'pros and cons' of bridging finance and the ways of circumventing it. One method commonly adopted to avoid bridging is to utilise the deposit on the related sale (note that the Standard Conditions are being used), but do not overlook the deposit guarantee scheme as well.

There are a few more marks for part (a) so you can afford to spend a little longer on it. Part (b) can be dealt with competently by simply listing the points that need checking. As well as the obvious things like the contract being signed and the results of searches being acceptable, do not forget practical points like making sure other people in the chain are ready.

Suggested answer

(a)
Charlotte has three main options:

(i)   to agree a reduced deposit on the purchase and utilise her sale deposit;

(ii) to borrow the deposit (or part of it) by way of bridging loan; or

(iii) to offer her seller a deposit guarantee instead of cash.

Each option will be considered in turn.

(i) Utilising her sale deposit

The first thing Charlotte should try (with our assistance) is to use the deposit she receives on her sale as the deposit on her purchase. Whether she can do this will depend on the capacity in which we as her solicitors hold the sale deposit. If we hold it as agent for the seller it can be done, but if we hold it as stakeholder, we are obliged to retain the sale deposit in our stakeholder account until completion. The simplest way of achieving the 'agent' capacity is to agree a special condition in the sale contract stating that we hold the deposit as agent for the seller. In this way, Charlotte will be free to use the deposit after exchange in any way she chooses. However this may not be acceptable to Charlotte's buyer who is likely to prefer the security of paying a stakeholder deposit. In this event the Standard Conditions (which we are told are being used) will assist Charlotte. Assuming Charlotte's purchase is in England or Wales and she is buying it as her residence, standard condition 2.2.5 will permit her to utilise her sale deposit towards the deposit on her purchase, provided ultimately the deposit is held by a solicitor as stakeholder.

The amount of the deposit is normally 10% of the purchase price. Although Charlotte will have £5,000 available from the sale deposit, the deposit payable on her purchase is £7,000, and so she still has the problem of finding a further £2,000. The practical answer to this is to negotiate the payment of a reduced deposit on her purchase which is equivalent to the deposit she will receive on her sale. Provided Charlotte can persuade her seller to accept this and provided Charlotte insists that her buyer pays a full 10% deposit, the problem of finding the further £2,000 will be overcome.

What should Charlotte do if her seller insists on a full 10% deposit? Where will she find the additional £2,000? She has two clear options: bridging finance or the deposit guarantee scheme.

(ii) Bridging finance

After taking into account the money she has available, Charlotte could borrow the shortfall from her bank (or another lender) on a short-term bridging loan. Most banks will be happy to help their customers in this way, especially where the loan is for only a short period. However before releasing any funds, the bank will normally require, from their borrower's solicitor, an undertaking to repay the bridging loan from the net proceeds of the related sale.

We should advise Charlotte that her bank will probably charge an arrangement fee for the bridging loan. We should also advise her that the interest charges on the loan will be high and, in the unlikely event of a delay on completion of the sale, the bridging loan could prove ultimately to be expensive.

(iii) <u>Deposit guarantee scheme</u>

Instead of offering her buyer a cash deposit, Charlotte could offer a deposit guarantee from an insurance company. If this is agreed then an appropriate provision would be needed in the contract. The scheme operates in the following way. Charlotte would pay a single premium to the insurance company, which in turn would provide a guarantee to Charlotte's buyer for the amount of the deposit. If Charlotte were to default under the purchase contract entitling her seller to forfeit the 'deposit', the insurance company would pay the seller the amount of the deposit. The insurance company would then exercise its right of recovery against Charlotte. The scheme is intended for use where a buyer enters into a simultaneous exchange of contracts on a sale, and so would be appropriate in this case. However, Charlotte's seller has of course to agree! Many sellers would prefer to have the security of 'cash' rather than a claim against an insurance company, and it should also be borne in mind that Charlotte's seller may have a dependent purchase, the deposit for which is to be financed from Charlotte's cash deposit.

In conclusion, we would advise Charlotte to pursue the first option of negotiating a reduction in the deposit on her purchase to £5,000 and utilising the sale deposit. If this is not successful, she would have to consider the other alternatives and weigh up the respective costs of each, for example, by comparing the cost of bridging against the amount of the deposit guarantee premium. Ultimately the decision could lie in her seller's hands, for if the seller insists on a full 10% cash deposit, Charlotte will be forced to borrow funds.

(b)

An exchange of contracts will commit Charlotte to binding and irrevocable legal obligations to buy and sell and so before exchange it is vital that we check the following matters:

(i)   Both sale and purchase contracts should contain all the agreed terms and be signed by the relevant parties. Charlotte should have signed her two parts in readiness for exchange, and these should be on file. Note that we should not sign on Charlotte's behalf without her express authority (*Suleman v. Shahisavari* [1989] 2 All ER 460). We would check that any non-owning occupiers who are required to sign the contracts have also done so.

(ii)   The deposit arrangements (including, if necessary, bridging finance and any requirement to give a solicitor's undertaking) would have to be finalised. If we are to draw a cheque for the deposit monies to her seller's solicitor, we would need to be put in cleared funds by the client.

(iii)   If Charlotte requires a mortgage to finance her purchase, she and we must see and approve the written mortgage offer. We should check in particular that the conditions of the intended mortgage are satisfactory. We would check generally that Charlotte's financial arrangements are in order.

(iv)   If she has a mortgage on her existing property, we would make sure that there is a redemption figure on file from her mortgagee, and that the sale proceeds will be sufficient to discharge it.

(v)   We would ensure that the local authority search and all other relevant searches have been made and that the results are satisfactory and do not reveal anything adverse.

(vi)   We would check that we have on file satisfactory replies to all relevant pre-contract enquiries, and that there are no adverse replies.

(vii)   We must be satisfied that the client is happy with the result of her surveyor's report and her own inspection of the property.

(viii) It is vital that the title to the purchase property is good and marketable and free from any onerous or unusual incumbrances. If the title is registered, there should be up to date official copies in the file which we would inspect. If the title is unregistered we would consider the abstract or epitome. If the solicitor who has the conduct of the file has raised any requisitions on the title, we should check that these have been answered satisfactorily.

(ix)   Following on from the above, we would as a matter of good practice always read the entire corres-pondence files to verify that there are no unresolved issues between the solicitors and that we are entirely happy.

(x) We would check the files and make sure that our firm has reported fully to Charlotte on the results of our pre-contract searches and investigations, and the terms of the contracts. Preferably the report should have been written, in which case there should be a copy on file. If the report was delivered orally, e.g. at a meeting with the client, then an attendance note of the meeting should have been placed on the correspondence file.

(xi) If we have any doubts at all, we should not exchange but refer the matter to a partner. In the event of uncertainty it may be necessary to contact our colleague in his or her sick bed!

(xii) Even if we are happy that everything is in order, we obviously cannot exchange until Charlotte's buyer and seller are also ready to exchange. Charlotte's sale and purchase are dependent upon each other and so the exchange of contracts and completion dates for each property must be synchronised. We shall therefore have to contact the other solicitors by telephone to discuss exchange and any proposed completion dates.

Question 2

RICHARDS ABBEY AND PARTNERS, SOLICITORS
INTERNAL MEMORANDUM

To   The Trainee Solicitor

From   The Training Partner

Re Jack Brinicombe: Green Willows and 15 Lingfield Avenue

Our firm has acted for Jack and Mabel Brinicombe for many years. Our first dealing with them was more than 30 years ago when they bought Green Willows, a four-bedroomed Victorian freehold house. Sadly, last year Mabel died and since then Jack has realised that Green Willows is really far too much for him on his own.

He came to see me a few weeks ago to say that he had found a small freehold bungalow he wanted to buy. The address is 15 Lingfield Avenue and it has a registered title. The owners have retired to the coast and moved out already so the bungalow is unoccupied and Jack is very keen to move in as soon as possible. There is no chain above Jack's seller.

Fortunately Jack has also secured a buyer for Green Willows. The buyer does not have a place to sell so both Jack's sale and purchase have proceeded quickly. The pre-contract conveyancing work on both properties has been done to my satisfaction.

I attach the files for each property. Green Willows is being sold for £100,000. The price for 15 Lingfield Avenue is £70,000. You will note that Green Willows is not mortgaged and Jack does not require a loan to finance his purchase. The 4th Edition of the Standard Conditions of Sale is incorporated into both contracts save that in the purchase contract standard condition 5.1 is excluded. The National Protocol is being used in both transactions.

We are ready to exchange contracts. We have received from Jack's purchaser's solicitors their client's signed part of the contract and cheque for the 10% deposit. We hold on file Jack's sale and purchase contracts duly signed by him. Jack will be out of the country for a couple of months and so has instructed me to exchange and complete 10 weeks today.

Please advise me, on these facts:

(a) How you will effect a telephonic exchange of contracts today; and

(b) What action you will take (if any) immediately following exchange.

Commentary

The question tells us that you are ready to exchange so there will be no marks for discussing whether pre-contract matters have been attended to, for example searches, enquiries, etc. The question requires you to demonstrate how you will effect a telephonic exchange, so stick to that—and a telephonic exchange at that, not any other kind.

When a sale and purchase are interdependent, as they here, then unless otherwise agreed, the client will expect to move out of one property and into the other on the same day. So, the completion dates must be the same, i.e. synchronised. Moreover, the physical act of exchange must be synchronised so that the two moments of binding legal obligation are as close together as possible. Remember that until exchange occurs either party is free to withdraw and consequently, unless synchronisation is achieved the client is in danger of ending up with two properties or none at all.

The post-exchange action, including possible registration of the contract, should be a source of easy marks for most students, but read the facts carefully—note the significance of the proposed ten-week completion and the fact that 15 Lingfield Avenue is registered land.

Suggested answer

RICHARDS ABBEY AND PARTNERS, SOLICITORS

INTERNAL MEMORANDUM

To   The Training Partner

From   The Trainee Solicitor

<u>Re Jack Brinicombe: Green Willows and 15 Lingfield Avenue</u>

I refer to your memo regarding our above client's sale and purchase and report as follows.

(a) <u>Procedure to effect exchange of contracts today</u>

First, we will telephone the firm of solicitors acting for Jack's seller and the firm acting for his buyer to verify that they are both ready to exchange today. A convenient completion date for all parties will also have to be agreed. The suggested ten-week completion is an unusually long time between exchange and completion and the client should appreciate that this may not be acceptable to either his buyer or seller. I appreciate that the client is going abroad but it may be necessary to take his instructions on an earlier completion date. He may need to consider granting a power of attorney to allow documents to be signed on his behalf in his absence.

Once a completion date has been agreed in principle, we must check that the solicitor acting on the sale of 15 Lingfield Avenue has in his or her possession a signed contract in identical form to the part signed by our client. We will advise the solicitor that we have a signed contract and deposit for 10% of the purchase price. The Standard Conditions of Sale permit our client to use the sale deposit for the deposit on his related purchase provided it is held ultimately by a solicitor as stakeholder (standard condition 2.2.5). Accordingly, we must check that there is no special condition in the 15 Lingfield Avenue contract providing for the deposit to be held as agent for the seller.

Once we are satisfied on this point, we will ask the seller's solicitor to release the seller's part of the contract to us until a time later in the day. The effect of this will be that the seller's solicitor undertakes to exchange if, by an agreed time later that day, we ring back to request an exchange. This will allow us time to exchange on our client's related sale and subsequently to telephone the seller's solicitor again to exchange. The 'release' is important to aid synchronisation, which is essential where, as in this case, there is a dependent sale and purchase.

Following the 'release' of the 15 Lingfield Avenue contract, we will telephone the solicitor acting on the purchase of Green Willows to effect a telephonic exchange under Law Society formula A. This is the appropriate formula where one solicitor (our firm) holds both signed parts of the contract. We will advise the other side's solicitor that our client's signed contract is identical to the purchaser's part. We will then formally agree the exchange and, as a result, undertake to send to the solicitor that day (by first-class post, document exchange or hand delivery) our client's signed part of the contract.

We will then ring back immediately the solicitor acting on the sale of 15 Lingfield Avenue to effect a formula B exchange. This is the appropriate formula where each solicitor holds his or her own client's signed part of the contract. Each solicitor will undertake to send their respective client's signed contract to each other that night. In addition, we will send the other side our firm's client account cheque for the deposit of £7,000. The remaining £3,000, being the balance of the Green Willows deposit, must remain in our stakeholder account because we hold it as stakeholder under the Standard Conditions of Sale (2.2.6). Our client will be entitled to receive interest on the stakeholder monies.

(b) Action immediately following exchange

We should draft a memorandum on each of the sale and purchase files noting the following: names of those who agreed the exchange; date and time of exchange; amount of deposit; completion date; the Law Society formula used.

We should telephone Jack to inform him that exchange has occurred and further advise him to insure the property from exchange. Standard condition 5.1 has been excluded from the 15 Lingfield Avenue contract so the open contract position prevails, which is that the risk in the property passes to the buyer from exchange. Normally a buyer's mortgagee would insure, but it is noted that Jack does not require a mortgage. We could offer to help him arrange the insurance. We should confirm our advice in writing.

We should inform the estate agents (if any) of the exchange of contracts and the completion date and ask them to send us their commission account.

We should enter the completion date in our diary so that it is not overlooked.

We should consider whether the purchase contract requires protection by registration. This is not normally done in practice unless the circumstances are unusual. In this case, if a ten-week completion were agreed, this would be unusual enough to contemplate registration. As the title is registered, our client's interest under the contract will be an interest required to be protected by an entry on the register (known before 13 October 2003 as a 'minor interest'). To protect our client's interest we should apply to register against the seller's title either a unilateral notice or, with the seller's consent, an agreed notice. This will preserve the priority of our client's interest in the unlikely event of any subsequent disposition of the title by the seller.

We should also consider registration of the contract if we believe the seller to be untrustworthy, or if a dispute arises between the seller and our client.

TIME ENGAGED 35 MINUTES

TRAINEE SOLICITOR

Question 3

For many years your firm has acted for Whitehead and Co, a local firm of estate agents and chartered surveyors. Mr Nicholas Brown, the senior partner of Whitehead and Co. wrote to your senior partner on 27 August asking for advice on a general point. He wants clarification on the legal position if, between exchange of contracts and completion, a dwellinghouse suffers damage by fire as a result of faulty electrical wiring.

Please draft a letter to Mr Brown giving general legal advice on this question. The letter should be written in your senior partner's name (Harriet Richards) who will approve and sign the letter before it is sent out. Your senior partner is on first name terms with Mr Brown and the address of Whitehead and Co. is 27 Hemdean Road, Blakey Cornshire CL1 2EG.

Note—five of the allocated marks for this question will be attributed to the writing and drafting quality of your letter.

Commentary

This question appears deceptively easy but is in fact very wide-ranging and requires you to demonstrate a thorough and broad knowledge of the subject area. The scarcity of factual information leaves all kinds of possibilities, and a very competent answer would consider each of these in turn. For example, is it an open contract or are the Standard Conditions being used? Is the property freehold or leasehold? Is the dwelling-house occupied or vacant?

If you have revised the topic of insurance thoroughly and appreciate and understand the recent criticisms of standard condition 5.1, this is definitely the question for you and you should score high marks. Those of you who prefer to answer questions of a more specific and practical nature would do well to leave this one alone (provided you have the choice!).

You have been asked to write your answer in the form of a letter. Note how five marks are allocated for the writing and drafting quality of your letter. Accordingly it is important that you write clearly and appropriately remembering all you have learnt in your writing and drafting skills sessions! The suggested draft encloses a copy of the Standard Conditions of Sale for the client's ease of reference.

Your letter should include your firm's letter heading, reference, date and subject heading. If you are not given a reference then simply make one up. Remember that a letter which starts 'Dear Sir' should end 'yours faithfully' while 'Dear Mr Brown' or 'Dear Nicholas' should end 'yours sincerely' (not 'yours Sincerely'). In our experience a small number of students still get confused over these elementary conventions of letter writing. In this question you are told that your senior partner and Mr Brown are on first name terms so begin the letter, 'Dear Nicholas' and end it 'yours sincerely'.

Suggested answer

Richards Abbey and Partners
East Chamber
Blakey
Cornshire CL1 2EG

Mr N Brown
Whitehead and Co.
27 Hemdean Road
Blakey
Cornshire CL1 4EG

Our ref: MBR/TS

4 August 2004

Dear Nicholas

Residential property—fire damage between exchange and completion

Thank you for your letter of 27 August requesting advice as to the legal position if, between exchange of contracts and completion, a dwellinghouse suffers damage by fire as a result of faulty electrical wiring. As you have asked for general advice I shall consider in the alternative (a) where the contract is an open contract, i.e., subject to common law rules and (b) where the Standard Conditions of Sale are being used. I will also advise you of the problem of double insurance and the position regarding leasehold property.

The open contract position

At common law the beneficial ownership in the property passes to the buyer on exchange of contracts and consequently the risk in the property passes to the buyer at the same time. The onus is on the buyer to insure the property from exchange because if the property is damaged by fire, the buyer will still be contractually bound to complete. However, if the property is damaged by fire after exchange and the buyer has failed to insure, the buyer may still be able to recover his loss in certain circumstances, which are as follows.

The first case is where the buyer's loss is due to a lack of proper care on the part of the seller. Between exchange and completion, the seller holds the legal estate as qualified trustee for the buyer and as such owes a duty of care to look after the property. If the seller breaches that duty and loss is caused as a result, the seller will be liable to the buyer in damages (*Clarke v. Ramuz* [1891] 2 QB 456). This would apply for example if the wiring had become faulty as a result of the seller's neglect. If the seller happens to have moved out and the house is empty, the seller is not released from this responsibility (*London & Cheshire Insurance Co Ltd v. Laplagrene Property Co Ltd* [1971] Ch 499). Similarly, if the buyer has moved in before completion, the seller's duty to take care is unaffected (unless the parties expressly agree otherwise, e.g. as part of a licence to occupy).

Secondly there is s. 47 of the Law of Property Act 1925. This section enables a buyer to claim loss from the seller's insurance policy, if one exists. It provides that insurance money payable to the seller after the date of the contract in respect of loss or damage to the property shall be payable to the buyer on completion (or upon receipt, if later) as long as:

(i)   the contract does not exclude s. 47;

(ii) the buyer pays a proportionate part of the insurance premium; and

(iii) the insurance company gives its consent.

Thirdly there is s. 83 of The Fires Prevention (Metropolis) Act 1774. Under this Act, if there is damage to a property by fire, a 'person interested' in the property can compel the insurance company to apply the insurance proceeds towards the re-instatement of the property. There is some doubt as to whether a buyer under a contract for sale would constitute an interested person for the purposes of the Act. In *Rayner v. Preston* [1881] 18 Ch 1 there is *obiter dicta* indicating that a buyer of land would be included within the definition. The operation of the Act is not confined solely to the metropolis of London (*Ex parte Gorely* (1864) 4 De GJ & S 477).

Lastly, the buyer may have recourse against his solicitor in negligence, under the principles enunciated in *Hedley Byrne & Co Ltd v. Heller & Partners Ltd* [1964] AC 465, if the solicitor failed to properly advise the buyer to insure on exchange of contracts.

The position under the Standard Conditions of Sale

I enclose a copy of the Standard Conditions for ease of reference. Standard condition 5.1 reverses the open contract position and provides that the seller retains the risk until completion. It also excludes s. 47 of the Law of Property Act 1925.

Standard condition 5.1.2 provides that if at any time before completion the physical state of the property makes it unusable for its purpose at the date of the contract then the buyer may rescind the contract. The seller may also rescind if it is damage against which the seller could not reasonably have insured, or damage which it is not legally possible for the seller to make good. In the present circumstances (damage by fire to a residential property), the seller is unlikely to be entitled to rescind, but there is every possibility that the buyer could rescind if the fire damage is severe.

Under standard condition 5.1.1 the seller must transfer the property in the same physical state as it was in at the date of the contract (except for fair wear and tear), but interestingly standard condition 5.1.3 states that the seller is under no obligation to insure the property. In the circumstances you envisage, the buyer could sue the seller for damages for breach of contract, but this is no guarantee for the buyer that he will recover his loss if in fact the property is not insured for its full re-instatement value. Accordingly, if the buyer has been well advised, the contract may well include a special condition varying standard condition 5.1.3 so that the seller is obliged to insure to the full re-instatement value.

Another option for the buyer is to exclude standard condition 5.1 altogether and revert to the open contract rule where the risk will pass to the buyer on exchange. In this way the buyer (or if the buyer requires mortgage finance, the buyer's mortgagee) controls the insurance arrangements and does not have to rely on a claim against the seller. The special conditions of the contract should therefore be read in each case to establish whether standard condition 5.1, or any part thereof, has been amended or deleted.

If the buyer has moved into occupation between exchange and completion, the terms of the occupation are set out in standard condition 5.2.2. The buyer is required, inter alia, to insure the property in a sum not less than the purchase price against all risks in respect of which comparable premises are normally insured. Unlike the open contract position when a buyer occupies before completion, standard condition 5.2.3 provides that standard condition 5.1 ceases to apply and the buyer assumes the risk until completion.

Double insurance

There is also the potential problem of double insurance. If the parties agree to adopt the open contract position, the buyer should obviously be advised to insure from exchange. The seller will also be advised to keep his existing policy on foot until completion in case the buyer defaults and the sale does not complete. In this event, whose insurance company will meet the claim? Each company may say that the other should meet it, and, in any event, they will not pay out twice for the same damage. This could result in the unhappy situation of the buyer and seller receiving only part of the whole claim.

The dilemma of double insurance can be circumvented by the parties agreeing a special condition whereby in the event of damage, the buyer will complete but receive an abatement in the price. This abatement would be equivalent to the amount by which the buyer's insurance proceeds are reduced by reason of the existence of the seller's insurance policy.

Leasehold property

I will conclude by considering the position of leasehold property. A well-drafted lease should state clearly whether it is the landlord or the tenant who insures. If the tenant insures, the same issues apply as above, with the additional consideration that, if the Standard Conditions are being used, standard condition 8.1.3 provides that the tenant/seller must comply with any lease provisions requiring the tenant to insure. The landlord normally has to approve the policy first, and it is usually simpler for the buyer/assignee to take over the seller/assignor's policy, rather than take out a new one. If the landlord insures, a claim will be made under the landlord's policy. If the fire was the tenant's fault and as a result, the landlord's insurance is invalidated, the tenant may, depending on the terms of the lease, be in breach of covenant under the lease.

I trust that this information has been helpful to you. If you have any queries or require further advice please do not hesitate to contact me or my assistant Mandy Sheeley.

Yours sincerely

Harriet Richards

Question 4

RICHARDS ABBEY AND PARTNERS, SOLICITORS
INTERNAL MEMORANDUM

To   The Trainee Solicitor

From   The Training Partner

We act for Tom Hayward who is selling 'Wickets', The Hyde, Eastminster to a first time buyer. Tom has a related purchase: he is buying (with the aid of a mortgage) Peartree Cottage, Hailey Lane,

Great Amwell, a town some forty miles away from our office. The seller of Peartree Cottage has instructed a firm of solicitors in Great Amwell. The sale and purchase are part of a large chain of transactions, of which 'Wickets' is at the bottom.

Each solicitor in the chain holds his or her client's signed part of the contract and—save obviously for the seller's solicitor at the top of the chain—deposit cheque. All parties are ready to exchange today although a completion date has yet to be finalised. Both Tom's contracts incorporate the Standard Conditions of Sale and the National Protocol is being used. Tom has asked whether he can complete his sale and purchase at the end of this week.

(a) Please advise me of the methods by which an exchange of contracts could be achieved and the moment at which the contract would become binding in each case. Explain which method would be most suitable and why other methods may not be suitable. (15 Marks)

(b) What matters should we consider before answering Tom's question about the completion date? (5 Marks)

Commentary

This question will appeal to those students who have had some practical experience of conveyancing. To score high marks it is important to answer the question according to how exchange ought *properly* to be carried out. Bear in mind that the prescribed methods of exchange (in particular the telephone formulae) do not always correspond with general practice!

Those students who rush into their answer may fail to appreciate that the question does not ask you to appraise the different formulae for telephonic exchange. It asks you to discuss the various *methods* of exchange, i.e. personal, postal or telephone. Notwithstanding that you can show your expertise on the Law Society formulae for telephonic exchange, you will regrettably fail the question if you discuss only the telephone method.

As well as covering the relevant ground, you must give your opinion as to the suitability or otherwise of each method as it applies to the facts, and indicate the time at which the contract under each method will become binding. The fact that the Standard Conditions of Sale and National Protocol are being used is relevant.

Part (b) also raises practical issues concerning the considerations a solicitor should have before agreeing a completion date on exchange of contracts. Those students who have had practical experience of conveyancing should find this straightforward, but others may experience difficulty. Do try to keep focused on the facts of the case, which inevitably will offer clues. For example, here note the existence of a long chain and the fact that the client needs a mortgage.

Finally, as always, note the allocation of marks and apportion your time accordingly.

Suggested answer

RICHARDS ABBEY AND PARTNERS, SOLICITORS
INTERNAL MEMORANDUM

To   The Training Partner

From The Trainee Solicitor

(a)

There are three methods of exchanging contracts:

 (i) in person;

 (ii) by post (or document exchange); or

 (iii) by telephone.

(i) In person

Both parties' solicitors meet at the office of the seller's solicitors. Each have their own clients' signed contracts and the buyer's solicitor holds a cheque for the deposit. The solicitors check that the two contracts are identical and that the seller's contract has been signed by the seller and the buyer's contract signed by the buyer. When both solicitors are ready to proceed, the contracts are physically exchanged—the buyer's solicitor receives the seller's signed part and *vice versa*. The buyer's solicitor also hands over the deposit cheque. It is at this moment of physical exchange that the contract becomes legally binding.

A personal exchange is recognised as being the safest method because it is an instant exchange and both parties can check there and then that the contracts are identical. However, in Tom's case there is a chain and he must synchronise his sale and purchase. An exchange in person will therefore not be suitable. We must also bear in mind that Tom's seller's solicitor's office is forty miles away, making a personal exchange on Peartree Cottage impracticable.

(ii) By post or document exchange

The buyer's solicitor sends to the seller's solicitor, by post or document exchange, the buyer's signed part of the contract and cheque for the deposit. Upon receipt, the seller's solicitor inserts the agreed completion date on both signed contracts and dates them. To effect the exchange, the seller's signed part is posted or sent in the document exchange to the buyer's solicitor.

As the contract incorporates the Standard Conditions of Sale, condition 2.1.1 provides that the contract will come into existence when the seller's part is actually posted or deposited at the document exchange. An exchange by this method will not be suitable in Tom's situation (where there is a chain), because there is a danger that Tom's buyer may withdraw between the time when Tom's seller's contract is posted and the time we receive it. This would leave Tom with two houses.

(iii) By telephone

This is the most popular method of exchange and was given judicial acknowledgement by the Court of Appeal in *Domb v. Isoz* [1980] Ch 548. It will nearly always be appropriate where there is a chain of transactions and will be the most suitable method for us to use in Tom's sale and purchase. The contract will become binding as soon as the parties' solicitors agree over the telephone that exchange has taken place.

The National Protocol is being used so if we decide to exchange by telephone, we must adopt one of the three telephonic exchange formulae introduced by the Law Society to avoid uncertainty. They are as follows:

(1) Formula A

The seller's solicitor holds both signed parts of the contract and the buyer's deposit. In the telephone conversation the seller's solicitor confirms to the buyer's solicitor that both parts of the contract are identical. The solicitors agree a completion date, which the seller's solicitor inserts in the contracts. The solicitors then effect the exchange and, by doing so, the seller's solicitor undertakes from that moment to hold the seller's signed part to the buyer's order, and to send to the buyer's solicitor that day by first-class post, document exchange or hand delivery, the seller's signed contract. Formula A can also work in reverse where the buyer's solicitor holds both parts, but this is less common.

(2) Formula B

This is where each solicitor holds his or her own client's signed contract. In the telephone conversation they confirm that the respective parts are identical and insert the agreed completion date. They then effect the exchange and by doing so undertake to hold the contract in their possession to the other's order and to send it to the other that day by first-class post, document exchange or hand delivery. The buyer's solicitor must also send the deposit cheque. Formula B is the most commonly used formula.

Following exchange under formula A or B the solicitors must record on file the following: names of the persons who agreed the exchange; date and time of exchange; completion date; the formula used and any agreed variations; amount of deposit.

(3) Formula C

This is designed for use where there is a long chain of transactions and would be suitable in our case. As with formula B, both solicitors hold their own client's signed contracts but, to aid synchronisation along the chain, the formula is in two parts. First, the buyer's solicitor undertakes to exchange by an agreed time later in the day, if the seller's solicitor so requests in a call back (the client's authority should be obtained before the undertaking is given). Each solicitor makes a detailed written note of the conversation. The seller's solicitor then activates the same procedure in the next link up the chain, and so on, to the top.

The second part of formula C occurs when, starting at the top and working down, the respective seller's solicitors ring back their respective buyer's solicitors by the appointed time to effect the exchange. The contracts are then sent out that day as with the other formulae. The parties may agree (on specified terms) that the buyer's deposit is sent directly to a solicitor further up the chain. Following exchange, the solicitors should make a second note, recording the actual exchange.

In conclusion I recommend that we exchange by using one or more of the telephone formulae.

(b)

The traditional period between exchange of contracts and completion is twenty-eight days but these days the parties normally agree a much shorter period. As the contract incorporates the Standard Conditions of Sale, condition 6.1.1 stipulates that the completion date shall be twenty working days after the date of the contract. It is more usual however for the parties to agree a specific date, which is then written into the contract and overrides standard condition 6.1.1. If Tom requires a quick completion this is the procedure we must adopt.

Tom is asking for completion within a matter of days. Although it is possible to agree such a short period (in some cases exchange and completion can take place on the same day), it is unlikely to be feasible in Tom's situation. The reasons for this are as follows:

(i) The long chain of dependent transactions. Unless Tom is prepared to incur the expense of bridging finance (which we would not recommend in the present case), every person in the chain would have to agree the short completion. As the chain is very long, I doubt whether unanimity could be achieved (bearing in mind also that the other conveyancers would be considering points (ii) and (iii) below), but to help Tom we could at least ask the rest of the chain to consider it.

(ii) We must allow ourselves sufficient time to carry out the post-contract conveyancing work, for example, the preparation, approval and execution of the purchase deed and mortgage deed. We will also have to carry out pre-completion searches, the results of which must be received before completion and, although there are telephone, fax and computer terminal search facilities available, it is possible that we may not achieve this by the end of the week.

(iii) Finally, and most crucially, Tom needs a mortgage to assist in his purchase. I note that we are ready to exchange today, so Tom will have received and we will have approved his mortgage offer, but we have to report on title to the mortgagee and request drawdown of the mortgage advance. Most mortgagees require three or four days or longer notice to release funds. This would have to be checked immediately with the mortgagee.

We should inform Tom of our reservations about the short completion and perhaps, in the circumstances, ask him to consider a slightly later date, which is mutually convenient to everyone in the chain.

TIME ENGAGED 45 MINUTES

TRAINEE SOLICITOR

6.3.2 **MULTIPLE CHOICE QUESTIONS AND ANSWERS**

We set out below examples of ten multiple choice questions that you might encounter in a subject assessment. Answers to these then follow. Remember our initial guidance. Never leave multiple choice answers with a blank. If there are four possibilities and you are not sure of the answer select the one you think might be right; after all, you have a one in four chance of getting it right! Also look at the instructions on the paper. If it says select the right answer on the paper by circling the correct choice then do just that. Do not make a tick or underline your selection as the strict response would be to fail you even though the selection may be correct. Think carefully before selecting your answer and have correcting fluid to hand just in case you make a mistake or change your mind. To assist you, we have given brief explanations for the answers although generally this is not something you will be required to do (unless your exam paper requires it).

6.3.2.1 **Multiple choice questions**

Unless otherwise directed, select the right answer by circling it in each question. Should you think that none of the selections apply please explain why not in your answer book.

1. When exchange of contracts occurs by post the contract becomes legally binding when:
   (a) the first contract is posted
   (b) the first contract is received
   (c) the second contract is posted
   (d) the second contract is received

2. The correct Law Society formula to use for telephonic exchange where each solicitor holds his or her own client's signed contract is formula A.

   Is this statement TRUE/FALSE? Please delete the incorrect choice.

3. You act for a first time purchaser who is buying a freehold cottage from an old man, Zaheer Abbas. Having yesterday exchanged contracts for completion in ten days' time you are today told by your client that the seller Mr Abbas sadly died this morning. You should refuse to complete until:
   (a) the death certificate is supplied
   (b) a second trustee is appointed
   (c) a grant of representation is issued
   (d) the beneficiaries are notified

4. In normal conveyancing practice, before exchanging contracts the solicitor for the buyer should ensure that the agreed form of contract held in his or her file is signed by:
   (a) the seller
   (b) the buyer
   (c) the seller and the buyer
   (d) the solicitor

5. When exchange of contracts occurs by telephone formula C which of the following is NOT a Law Society requirement:
   (a) that the conveyancer expecting to be telephoned back later in the day should give the name of other conveyancers in the office who could take the call if the first solicitor is otherwise engaged

    (b) that file memos should be made by each conveyancer recording the details of the telephone conversations constituting parts 1 and 2 of formula C

    (c) that the conveyancer ensures that he or she has the client's express authority to exchange contracts using formula C

    (d) that if contracts are not exchanged on the day that the conveyancers initiate formula C then the whole process must start again the next working day

6. Following exchange of contracts a buyer who acquires relevant notice of bankruptcy proceedings against the seller should insist on taking a transfer of the property from:

    (a) the seller

    (b) the petitioning creditor

    (c) the trustee in bankruptcy

    (d) the bankruptcy court

7. Following exchange of contracts, which of the following would generally NOT be carried out by the seller's solicitor?

    (a) conducting a bankruptcy search against the buyer

    (b) making a diary note of the completion date

    (c) requesting a redemption statement from the seller's mortgagee

    (d) preparing a financial statement for the client

8. You act for the seller of freehold factory premises. Following exchange of contracts but before completion (next week) your client informs you that the managing director of the purchasing company has asked if he can move his company's heavy plant and machinery into the factory a few days before completion. You would advise your client that:

    (a) this is normal practice in a commercial conveyancing transaction and your client should allow it

    (b) this should not be allowed as it may invalidate the contract

    (c) this is acceptable but you must first draw up a tenancy agreement so that the purchaser's occupation can be formalised

    (d) the purchaser should be asked to wait until completion

9. Under both the Standard Conditions of Sale and the Standard Commercial Property Conditions of Sale the seller is under no obligation to insure the subject property.

    Is this statement TRUE/FALSE. Delete the answer that is incorrect.

10. High winds have blown off a large number of roof tiles from a house, which is the subject of a conveyancing transaction in which the National Protocol is being utilised. The incident occurred after contracts were exchanged but before completion. The person who bears the responsibility for the damage is:

    (a) the seller

    (b) the buyer

    (c) the seller's solicitor

    (d) the buyer's solicitor

6.3.2.2   *Answers to multiple choice questions (with brief explanations)*

1. The correct answer is (c). The well-established common law rule on acceptance of contracts is that the contract comes into existence when the second copy is posted (*Adams v. Lindsell* (1818) 1 B & Ald 681). This is confirmed by standard condition 2.1.

2. The statement is false. This question is about as straightforward as it gets and tests your basic know-ledge of the Law Society telephone formulae. Where each solicitor holds their own client's signed part of the contract the relevant formula is of course B, not A.

3. The correct answer is (c). Note that there is no surviving co-owner here—you are told there is just one owner, Mr Abbas. Where a single seller dies between exchange and completion, the deceased's per-sonal representative(s) must complete the sale, and a personal representative cannot give good title until the grant of representation has been issued.

4. The correct answer is (b). It is acceptable for a solicitor to sign on the client's behalf with the client's authority, but this is not 'normal conveyancing practice' (read the question carefully). Also, both parties could legitimately sign one contract but again, normal practice is to exchange identical contracts.

5. The correct answer is none. This question is quite difficult and requires a thorough knowledge of formula C. In considering each point carefully you will appreciate that *all* of them are formula C requirements!

6. The correct answer is (c). If the buyer's searches reveal that the seller is bankrupt, the buyer should wait for the appointment of the trustee in bankruptcy and take a transfer from the trustee. The buyer's solicitor should also request a copy of the bankruptcy order together with documentary proof of the trustee's appointment.

7. The correct answer is (a). It is the buyer's solicitor on behalf of the buyer's mortgagee who conducts a bankruptcy search against the buyer.

8. The correct answer is (d). Completion is only a few days' away and in these circumstances it would be most unusual to accede to such a request. The prudent course is simply to wait until completion. Under no circumstances should the buyer be allowed to occupy early under a tenancy agreement as this may confer on the buyer security of tenure.

9. The statement is true. Both the Standard Commercial Property Conditions and the Standard Conditions of Sale impose no obligation on the seller to maintain insurance prior to completion. (They differ how-ever on the question of risk. Under the standard conditions the risk remains with the seller, while the commercial conditions preserve the common law rule that the buyer assumes the risk after exchange.)

10. The correct answer is (a). If the National Protocol is being utilised it is a requirement that the parties use the Law Society form of contract, which incorporates the Standard Conditions of Sale. Standard condition 5.1 provides that the risk of damage remains with the seller prior to completion.

6.3.3 SHORT ANSWER QUESTIONS

Question 1

Newly qualified solicitor Sally Rush acts for William Jellicoe, a first time buyer of 19 Trueman Street, a freehold house in Didsbury, Manchester. Sally has carried out her pre-contract searches and enquiries, investigated title and approved her client's mortgage offer. After receiving a full report from Sally, William has signed the agreed form of contract, which Sally is currently holding in her file. William has also put Sally's firm in funds for the 10% deposit.

At 10 a.m. today Sally telephones the seller's solicitor to inform him that she is ready to exchange contracts. The seller's solicitor explains that there is a long chain above him and he wishes to exchange using telephone formula C. Under part 1 of formula C he asks Sally to agree a time later in the day before which he may ring her back to exchange. Sally agrees a time of 4 p.m. and releases her client's contract to the other solicitor until that time.

At 3 p.m. today William telephones Sally to say that he has had a change of heart and no longer wishes to proceed with the purchase. In fact he expressly instructs Sally not to proceed with the exchange. Five minutes later the seller's solicitor telephones Sally to say that he has exchanged contracts on his client's related purchase and now wishes to exchange on 19 Trueman Street under formula C part 2. When Sally tells him that her client has pulled out the solicitor angrily informs her that unless she exchanges within the next 15 minutes he will have no hesitation in reporting her to the Law Society.

What are Sally's options and what lessons can she learn from what has happened?

Question 2

You act for Simon Diamond who has exchanged contracts to sell 'Big Surf', a freehold commercial premises used for the manufacture of surfing and windsurfing equipment. The purchaser is Conor Deasey and the contractual completion date is two months today. Simon has rung you to say that, as Conor has been able to arrange his finance sooner than expected, they have agreed to complete four weeks early. What action should you take, if any?

Question 3

You act for Luke Robinson who has exchanged contracts for the sale of his leasehold flat. The contract incorporates the Standard Conditions of Sale (4th Edition). A few days before completion Luke is tragically killed in a car accident. What action should you take, if any?

6.3.3.1 *Suggested answers to short answer questions*

Question 1

Although this question is about exchange of contracts it concerns an important area of professional conduct, namely the solicitor's professional undertaking. It is a classic illustration of the difficulty a solicitor can get into if s/he fails to follow the golden rules before giving an undertaking. Sally's undertaking was given when she 'released' her client's contract to the other solicitor. In doing so she impliedly undertook that if he rang her back before 4 p.m. she would definitely exchange contracts. Having received this assurance, the seller's solicitor committed his client on his client's related purchase.

Unfortunately Sally is now stuck in 'no man's land'. If she goes ahead and exchanges she will be acting contrary to her client's instructions. But if she refuses to exchange she will be in breach of undertaking and may be reported to the Law Society. (The chances of the seller's solicitor showing any sympathy with Sally's predicament are very slim indeed, given that the other contracts in the long chain are now exchanged.) Sally's only sensible option would appear to be to persuade her client to go ahead with the purchase after all. (She might indicate to William that in signing the contract he has given a clear indication of his intent upon which she has relied.)

What lessons can Sally learn? Clearly she should have explained to William the exchange procedure and then, importantly, obtained his *prior irrevocable authority* to give the undertaking. If she had done this, William could not have changed his mind at the last minute. An example of the written authority Sally might have asked William to sign would be as follows:

'I William Jellicoe understand that my purchase of 19 Trueman Street Didsbury Manchester is part of a chain of linked property transactions, in which all parties want the security of contracts which become binding on the same day. I agree that you should make arrangements with the other solicitors or licensed conveyancers involved to achieve this. I understand that this involves each property-buyer offering, early on one day, to exchange contracts whenever, later that day, the seller so requests, and that the buyer's offer is on the basis that it cannot be withdrawn or varied during that day. I agree that when I authorise you to exchange contracts, you may agree to exchange contracts on the above basis and give any necessary undertakings to the other parties involved in the chain and that my authority to you cannot be revoked throughout the day on which the offer to exchange contracts is made.'

Signed William Jellicoe

Question 2

This question is concerned with the variation of a contract between exchange and completion. Many conveyancers in this situation would simply do nothing and complete on the earlier date agreed by the clients. Other practitioners might decide to formally record the change of date in correspondence between them. However there are inherent dangers in this latter approach should the parties fall out and find themselves in a dispute over the terms of the contract.

In *McCausland v. Duncan Lawrie Ltd* [1997] 1 WLR 38 the parties exchanged contracts for completion on 26 March but the solicitors subsequently realised that this date was a Sunday. The solicitors then exchanged correspondence agreeing 24 March instead. Following a dispute on the contract the Court of Appeal held that the purported variation by exchange of letters was unenforceable because it did not comply strictly with the provisions of s. 2 of the Law of Property (Miscellaneous Provisions) Act 1989.

Thus in order to satisfy s. 2, we should ensure that there is a further exchange of documents, signed by Simon and Conor respectively. This further document would refer to the original contract and the subsequent variation of the completion date. In this way both parties would be protected in the event of any later dispute on the contract.

Question 3

This is a straightforward question concerning the death of a sole seller between exchange and completion. (Students should note the words 'sole seller'; on these facts clearly there is no need to consider the position of a surviving joint tenant or tenant in common.)

The death of a contracting party does not invalidate the contract, nor the obligations contained within it. Luke's personal representatives are therefore bound to complete the transaction in accordance with the terms of the contract just as if they were themselves the contracting party.

On the assumption that we are acting on the deceased's estate, we should apply as soon as possible to the Probate Registry for a grant of representation. Until the grant is issued the buyer of the flat can lawfully refuse to complete. This might cause completion to be delayed beyond the contractual completion date and any resultant liability for compensation and damages would fall upon Luke's estate. To speed up matters we could ask the Probate Registry to issue an expedited grant or possibly a grant limited to dealings with the subject property. We could always have a word with the Probate Registry to see what they suggest.

We should also notify the buyer's solicitor of our client's death. Once the other side (and possibly others in the chain) have been appraised of the situation they may be willing to postpone completion in the knowledge that a grant will be issued shortly.

If delay in completion is inevitable, Luke's personal representatives may wish to consider allowing the buyer into possession of the property on the contractual completion date under licence, whilst postponing actual completion until the grant is received. Although the estate may still be liable for compensation in respect of delayed completion, at least the personal representatives would be permitted to claim a licence fee from the buyer in occupation under Standard condition 5.2 of the contract.

6.4 REFERENCES TO WIDER READING INCLUDING PRACTITIONER TEXTS

- *A Practical Approach to Conveyancing* by Abbey R. and Richards M. (6th edn, OUP)—Chapter 6 (Exchange of contracts; death or insolvency).
- *The Law Society's Conveyancing Handbook 2003* by Silverman F.—Section C (Exchange of contracts) and Section E6 (Death and insolvency).
- Generally—the *Law Society's Guide to the Professional Conduct of Solicitors* (8th edn, 1999)—in particular Professional Undertakings.

- Ruoff and Roper Registered Conveyancing (Sweet and Maxwell).
- *Textbook on Land Law* by MacKenzie J. A. and Phillips M. (9th edn, OUP)—Chapter 2 (Buying a house) and chapter 3 (The Contract).
- Emmet on Title: Insurance—Chapter 1, Part 6.

6.5 RELEVANT WEBSITES FOR MORE INFORMATION

- Council of Mortgage Lenders, http://www.cml.org.uk
  There is an on-line version of the CML Lenders' Handbook available at this site and it should be referred to in cases of doubt about lenders' requirements.
- House of Lords judgments, http://www.parliament.the-stationery-office.co.uk/pa/ld199697/ldjudgmt/ldjudgmt.htm
  Keep up to date with important new cases.
- Law Commission, http://www.lawcom.gov.uk
  Keep up to date on proposals for law reform.
- Law Society, http://www.lawsoc.org.uk

7 | THE PURCHASE DEED AND MORTGAGE

7.1 INTRODUCTION

The purchase deed tends to be a fairly popular topic with students. This may have something to do with the fact that question spotting in this area is relatively straightforward. As the questions in this chapter will demonstrate, very often the examiner will simply present a set of facts and ask you what form the purchase deed should take, and ask you to explain (or possibly draft) its contents. Accordingly, if you can master the form and content of the different purchase deeds, you should do well when a question like this comes up.

Remember that all land in England and Wales is now an area of compulsory registration, so a sale, gift or mortgage of unregistered land will induce first registration. Land Registry are happy to accept a transfer of unregistered land instead of the traditional form of conveyance but, having said that, do not disregard the contents of the conveyance. This is because many questions specifically require a knowledge and understanding of it. You should also be aware that a few practitioners still prefer to draft a conveyance in preference to a Land Registry transfer, especially where the purchase deed is not straightforward (e.g. on a sale of part). In such cases, drafting a conveyance from a full precedent can actually be easier than starting from scratch with a blank form of transfer.

Another reason for mastering the contents of a conveyance is that it will help you to understand some of the complexities of another topic—investigation of unregistered title, where of course conveyances will have to be read and their essential ingredients (or lack of them!) understood. See Chapter 5 for practical examples.

Whereas students normally enjoy getting to grips with the purchase deed, the related topic of mortgages is a different matter altogether and many students make the mistake of paying too little attention to it. Remember that a conveyancer acting for a mortgagee will be just as concerned to ensure that the property in question has a good and marketable title, in the same way as another property lawyer would be if acting for the buyer. The mortgagee will, after all, want the comfort of knowing that the property is good security for the loan and that if it becomes necessary to exercise its power of sale, there is no technical impediment to prevent it from doing so.

As always, do not be surprised if a question on conflict (or potential conflict) of interest and/or client confidentiality crops up in a subject assessment. Matters of professional conduct are obviously very relevant for property law practitioners and problems and queries occur frequently in practice. As a Legal Practice Course student, you will need no reminding that professional conduct is a pervasive topic and therefore ripe for inclusion in subject assessments. You will note that professional conduct considerations play a part in the suggested answer to standard question 4 in this Chapter.

The questions on mortgages may well overlap with other Property Law and Practice topics, such as taking instructions and completion, and you will find frequent references to mortgages throughout this book.

7.2 AN OVERVIEW OF THE SUBJECT AND A LOOK AT SOME PROBLEM AREAS

7.2.1 THE PURCHASE DEED

The main purpose of the purchase deed is to transfer the legal estate in the property from the seller to the buyer. As you should be aware, the transfer of a legal estate is void unless it is made by deed (s. 52(1) of the Law of Property Act 1925).

7.2.1.1 Drafting the deed

The buyer's practitioner will draft the purchase deed once exchange of contracts has taken place. Its contents are governed by the terms of the contract. Whereas the contract sets out what the parties have agreed, the purchase deed actually puts those terms into effect. Sometimes the seller may prefer to draft the purchase deed, for example, when selling new properties on an estate where uniformity of documentation is important.

The standard procedure is for the buyer's practitioner to submit two copies of the draft purchase deed to the seller's practitioner for approval, and to keep an extra copy on file for reference (in case minor points are raised over the telephone). If the draft is approved as drawn, the top copy can be used as the engrossment. If the seller requires extensive amendments, these should be written clearly in red ink on one copy of the draft, which should be returned to the buyer's practitioner while a copy of the amended draft is kept on the file for reference. A seller's amendment typically arises where the buyer has overlooked the inclusion of a clause required by the contract, e.g. an indemnity covenant.

If the National Protocol is being used, it provides for the practitioners to submit, approve and engross the draft purchase deed as soon as possible and in any event within the time limits laid down by the standard conditions. These time limits are set out in standard condition 4.3.2, which of course will apply whenever the contract incorporates the standard conditions (even if the Protocol is not being used). A breach of the time limits may be of importance if one of the contracting parties later claims compensation for delay in completion. Under standard condition 7.3.1 if there is default by the parties in performing their obligations under the contract (e.g. the buyer submits the draft purchase deed out of time) then the party whose total period of default is the greater must pay compensation to the other.

In essence, the time limits are as follows. The draft deed must be submitted at least twelve working days before the completion date; the seller's practitioner then has four working days to approve it; the buyer's practitioner must then send out the engrossment at least five working days before completion. Standard condition 4.3.4 provides that if the period between the date of the contract and the completion date is less than fifteen working days, the time limits are reduced pro rata. Fractions of a working day are rounded down (but cannot be less than one working day). For example, if the completion date is ten working days after exchange, the time limits are reduced by two-thirds (i.e. ten divided by fifteen) so that the draft deed must be submitted at least eight working days before the completion date.

In order to transfer the legal estate the seller must *always* execute the purchase deed (s. 52(1) of the Law of Property Act 1925). However, the buyer need only execute the deed if the buyer is either making a declaration (e.g. as to co-ownership), or entering into new obligations (e.g. giving the seller an indemnity covenant, or agreeing new covenants on a sale of part).

As we have seen, the transfer of the legal estate must be by deed and, to be a valid deed, the document must state clearly on its face that it is a deed (Law of Property (Miscellaneous Provisions) Act 1989, s. 1). It is no longer necessary for a deed to be sealed (although a company may still use its seal), but it must be signed by the necessary parties in the presence of a witness, and delivered. Although the deed takes effect on delivery, the word 'delivered' is not necessary in the attestation clause. A typical attestation clause for execution by an individual would read as follows:

'Signed as a deed by [full name of seller]
in the presence of

[signature, name and address of witness]'

A typical attestation clause for execution by a limited company would read as follows:

'The common seal of ABC Ltd was affixed in the presence of:

[Signature] . . . Director of the above-named company
[Signature] . . . Secretary of the above-named company'

7.2.1.2 **Form of deed**

For registered land the purchase deed must be in the form prescribed by r. 58 of the Land Registration Rules 2003. For unregistered land there is no prescribed form and the practitioner may use either the traditional form (a conveyance for freeholds; an assignment for leaseholds), or alternatively where the title is subject to first registration, a Land Registry transfer. The two main Land Registry forms, which both feature in subject assessments in this chapter, are:

- TR1: Transfer of *whole* of registered land, or *whole* of unregistered land where the title is subject to first registration;
- TP1: Transfer of *part* of registered land, or *part* of unregistered land where the title is subject to first registration.

Remember that the contents of the purchase deed are governed by the contents of the contract. For example, on a sale of part, if new easements or covenants are to be created, the actual wording of these will have been agreed in the contract and it will simply be a matter of reproducing substantially the same clauses in the purchase deed. Likewise the description of the property, including reference to any plan, will have been settled at the contract stage and can be copied from the contract. Plans are generally necessary only where *part* of the seller's property is being sold. The plan must be accurate with all colourings and markings correctly made, and it must be tightly bound into the engrossed deed. Metric measurements must be used on the plan (Unit of Measurement Regulations 1995 (SI 1995/1804)). The verbal description of the property in the main body of the document should naturally refer to any plan. The plan should be to a stated scale and must not be merely for identification purposes. If any discrepancy arises between the plan and the verbal description in the deed, it is a matter of construction as to which should prevail. If the plan is described as being 'for identification purposes only' then the verbal description prevails. If the property is 'more particularly delineated or described' on the plan then the plan will prevail (see *Neilson v. Poole* (1969) 20 P & CR 909).

There may be some clauses in the purchase deed that will not be reproduced word for word from the contract. Reference to them may instead have been made in the standard conditions. For example, standard condition 4.6.5 provides for the seller to give an acknowledgement and undertaking in respect of documents, which the buyer will not receive on completion of an unregistered land transaction. Accordingly the buyer's practitioner will have to draft this clause and best practice would be to consult a precedent. As always, it is important not simply to copy the precedent slavishly; adapt it to suit your needs and make sure it is up to date. Lastly, remember that punctuation is generally not used in the drafting of a deed. The reason for this is to help prevent any fraudulent alteration of the deed (e.g. by inserting a comma) which could change its meaning.

7.2.2 THE MORTGAGE

7.2.2.1 Acting for lender and borrower

In most non-commercial transactions the lender will instruct you to act for it as well as the borrower (in a commercial property transaction the lender often instructs its own solicitors). You are permitted to act for borrower and lender provided the lender is an institutional lender that provides mortgages in the normal course of its business and provided no conflicts of interest arise. One difficulty is that the nature of any relevant information (e.g. a bankruptcy entry) will be confidential to the borrower client. As a matter of conduct, therefore, you will need to obtain the borrower's consent before passing on any confidential information to the lender. If the borrower refuses to give such consent then in accordance with the rules of professional conduct you must cease to act.

A conflict of interest will also arise if you discover that the borrower intends to breach a condition of the mortgage offer (e.g. to use the property for business purposes when such use is prohibited). In this situation you must explain to the borrower that a conflict has arisen and you can no longer act for the borrower or lender unless the lender permits you to continue to act for the borrower alone. As you can no longer act for the lender, the lender's papers should be returned. However, due to your duty of confidentiality to the borrower (which continues even after termination of the borrower's retainer) you cannot disclose the reason why you can no longer act. You must simply inform the lender that a conflict of interest has arisen and leave it at that.

You will need to acquaint yourself with the Council of Mortgage Lender's Handbook which contains standardised lenders' instructions for solicitors. You can access the handbook via the CML website at http://www.cml.org.uk. The handbook is divided into two parts. Part 1 sets out the main instructions and guidance, which must be disclosed by the conveyancers. Part 2 details each lender's specific requirements which arise from those instructions. The instructions from individual lenders will indicate whether the conveyancer is being instructed in accordance with the Handbook, in which case the conveyancer should follow the instructions in the Handbook.

7.2.2.2 The mortgage deed

A legal mortgage must be made by deed (Law of Property Act 1925, s. 85). Apart from this requirement, it need take no other prescribed form, although in registered land r. 103 of the Land Registration Rules 2003 provides that a legal charge may be in Form CH1.

Although not compulsory at present, Form CH1 is seen as something of a 'stepping-stone' towards a standard compulsory form of charge when e-conveyancing is introduced. Typically the institutional lender will supply its own printed mortgage form, which is sent to the practitioner along with the 'instructions pack'. The practitioner will then simply complete the blanks (name of borrower, property address, etc.) in readiness for execution by the borrower before completion.

Before your client signs the mortgage deed it is important that you explain to him or her the nature and effect of its contents. For example:

(a) Point out the initial rate of interest and amount of the first monthly repayment; explain that the lender may vary them at any time (unless the mortgage is fixed rate).

(b) Explain the borrower's covenants, such as the covenant to keep the property in good repair, not to make alterations without the lender's consent and any prohibition against letting or sharing possession without the lender's consent (lodgers often help to pay the mortgage).

(c) The borrower must understand that if there is any default on mortgage repayments or breach of covenant, the lender has the right to call in the loan and sell the property.

(d) Any penalty charges for early repayment should be explained (this is often the case in initially attractive looking fixed-rate packages).

(e) If the mortgage secures 'all monies' owed to the lender, a breach of this mortgage would entitle the lender to call in other loans (if any) made to the borrower. Most mortgages are all monies charges. Where there are joint borrowers, this would include sums advanced to them individually on sole mortgages on other properties (see *AIB Group UK plc v. Martin* [2002] 1 WLR 94 (HL)).

(f) The lender's right to insure the property and recover the premiums from the borrower should be explained; the mortgage deed normally contains an express power for the lender to insure, extending the statutory power under the Law of Property Act 1925, s. 101(1)(ii).

Any guarantor signing the deed should be told to take independent legal advice before signing. This is because the guarantor may become liable instead of, or as well as, the borrower for all the money owing under the deed.

If the mortgage monies are being used to finance a contemporaneous purchase, the relevant parties must properly execute the mortgage deed before completion of the purchase. A good time for signing is when you see the client to explain the mortgage terms, and you can then act as the client's witness as well. There is no need for the lender to execute the deed unless, unusually, the lender is entering into new covenants. You will date the mortgage deed the same date as the purchase deed, although technically the mortgage is completed fractionally later (on the basis that the client cannot mortgage the property until he or she actually acquires it). You should check the lender's instructions at this stage as some lenders require to be advised as soon as completion takes place.

7.2.2.3 Reporting on title

Before the lender will be willing to release the mortgage advance it will insist on a written report on title from the solicitor. The report should confirm that the title is good and marketable, free from adverse incumbrances and can be safely accepted by the lender as security. If the solicitor considers that the title is not acceptable then this must be drawn specifically to the lender's attention.

Rule 6(3) of the Solicitors' Practice Rules 1990 contains a compulsory common-form report on title for all solicitors acting for both lender and borrower in an institutional mortgage of property to be used as a private residence only. The use of the report is not obligatory for mortgage advances secured on commercial property, or for so-called 'buy to let' mortgages of residential property where the owner does not occupy the property. As an alternative to printing the approved certificate for each transaction, you may use a short form certificate of title which incorporates the approved certificate by reference. You should note, however, that even the short form report should always include in the following order:

- The title 'Certificate of Title'
- The contents of the details box in the order set out below:
  TO: (Lender)
  Lender's Reference or Account No:
  The Borrower:
  Property:
  Title Number:
  Mortgage Advance:
  Price stated in transfer:
  Completion Date:
  Conveyancer's Name and Address:
  Conveyancer's Reference:
  Conveyancer's bank, sort code and account number:
  Date of instructions:
- The wording, 'We, the conveyancers named above, give the Certificate of Title set out in the Appendix to rule 6(3) of the Solicitors' Practice Rules 1990 as if the same were set out in full, subject to the limitations contained within it.'

If as a result of your investigation of title, searches and enquiries, you consider that the title is not acceptable, you must draw this specifically to the lender's attention.

For mortgages being secured on residential leasehold titles, remember to check the following:

(a) Ensure you have a clear receipt for the last ground rent.

(b) Ensure there is no provision for forfeiture on bankruptcy of the tenant or any superior tenant.

(c) Ensure there is a mutual enforceability covenant allowing the tenant to enforce other tenants' covenants in the block.

(d) Check that the lessor's covenants for repair and maintenance of the structure and common parts are adequate.

(e) Check that you have the current name and address of the lessor and any management company and that, if limited companies, neither have been struck off the register.

(f) Are you satisfied with the last three years' accounts of any management company? If not, send them to the lender for clearance.

(g) If the tenants control the Management Company you must keep with the deeds an up-to-date copy of the company's Memorandum and Articles of Association, the borrower's share certificate and a blank transfer signed by the borrower.

(h) Check that any management company has an interest in land and that the lessees are all members of it. If this is not the case, the lessor should be obliged to carry out the management company's obligations should it fail to do so.

(i) If required, check that the lessor's consent to the proposed lease assignment has been obtained.

Of course a practitioner who is in any doubt about whether a particular adverse matter will result in the mortgage offer being withdrawn should refer the matter to the mortgagee *before* contracts are exchanged. Indeed, to avoid delay, all queries should be referred to the lender as soon as they arise, which will normally be at the investigation of title stage, i.e. before exchange.

The report asks you to confirm that no breaches of planning condition or building regulation consent have occurred and further that you have complied with all the lender's instructions. Clearly these are matters that must be checked before exchange but it is not always possible for the practitioner to be absolutely clear about certain matters, such as compliance with planning conditions. If in any doubt, you would be wise to qualify your report by adding the words, 'as far as we are aware from our usual searches, enquiries and investigation of title'.

The report on title will include a request to the lender for the mortgage advance. As some lenders require several days' notice of draw-down of funds, the Form should be submitted to the lender in good time for completion. It is a breach of the Solicitors' Accounts Rules to draw against a lender's cheque before it has cleared, and at least three working days should be allowed for clearance. In urgent cases where time is short and for advances say in excess of £100,000 the lender will often agree to send the advance monies by telegraphic transfer, deducting the transfer fee from the advance. The advance monies are regarded as clients' money and as such must be paid into a client account.

Pending completion the practitioner holds the mortgage advance on trust for the lender and must comply with the lender's instructions. Non-compliance will constitute a breach of trust; see *Target Holdings Ltd v. Redferns* [1996] AC 421. In particular do not release funds and complete until the borrower has properly executed and you have received the mortgage deed (and any other security documentation). If there is any delay in completion, the lender's instructions may require the advance to be returned, with interest.

In all cases before the advance is drawn down the lender will require confirmation that the borrower is not bankrupt and that there are no insolvency proceedings. The practitioner for the lender should therefore conduct a bankruptcy search against each individual borrower's full name at the Land Charges Department (Form K16 is used for a 'bankruptcy only' search). If the borrower is a company, a company search should also be conducted to ensure that the company is not in liquidation and that there are no winding-up proceedings.

7.2.2.4 Perfecting the mortgage

The mortgage deed should of course be dated on the day of completion. Following completion, if the borrower is a company incorporated in, or with an established place of business in, England and Wales, the mortgage must be registered at the Companies Registry within twenty-one days of completion (Companies Act 1985, ss. 395 and 409). If it is not registered, the charge will be void against the company's creditors or a liquidator or administrator. It is important not to delay in registering the charge as an extension of time cannot be given without a court order and such orders are rarely made. You should also note that Land Registry's practice is not to raise a requisition requiring a charge to be so registered. The Registry will instead simply enter a note in the charges register referring to the relevant section of the Companies Act.

For registered land, remember to lodge your application to register the charge at Land Registry before the expiry of the priority protection period of your official search. If the land acquired is unregistered, you must apply for first registration (and registration of the mortgage) within two months of completion. If the mortgaged property is leasehold, check the notice requirements in the lease. It will usually be necessary to give notice to the lessor of any mortgage of the leasehold estate within a set time, and to pay a fee. The notice should be given in duplicate with a request that one copy be returned receipted. When the Title Information Document is returned by Land Registry, remember to check that the lender's mortgage duly appears in the charges register of the title and that the registered title is otherwise in order.

7.3 SUBJECT ASSESSMENTS

As in previous chapters there now follows some examples of assessment questions in the subject area. Commentary and a suggested answer accompany the standard assessment questions. These are then followed by multiple choice questions (with answers) and short answer questions with suggested answers.

7.3.1 STANDARD QUESTIONS, COMMENTARY AND SUGGESTED ANSWERS

Question 1

Your firm acts for David Hobbs and Stephen Christopher Ingles both of 7 Brookfield Lane, Basingstoke Hants BR1 7JK in their purchase as tenants in common in equal shares of land to the rear of 10 Ellesmere Close, Hereford for £70,000. The land they are buying forms part of a registered title number KM 74859 comprising the whole of 10 Ellesmere Close. The seller is Ingrid Kirsten Smits. Contracts were exchanged last week for completion three weeks today. The contract provides for the grant of easements to your clients and corresponding reservations in favour of Ms Smits. It also provides for the buyers to enter into restrictive covenants with the seller. The contract provides for a full title guarantee and incorporates the Standard Conditions of Sale. Your principal has asked you to deal with the post-contract conveyancing work and has passed you the file.

(a) Having regard to the standard conditions and other matters, explain what factors are relevant so far as the submission, approval and execution of the purchase deed are concerned. (5 Marks)

(b) Identify and explain the contents of the purchase deed that would be acceptable to both buyer and seller. (15 Marks)

Commentary

This question appears quite straightforward but you must read the facts carefully. You should always consider the terms of the contract, as these will govern the contents of the purchase deed. Moreover, a competent answer to part (a) will be impossible unless you grasp the significance of the reference to the Standard Conditions of Sale.

Once you have recognised that the transaction involves a sale of part of registered land, part (b) at least should be plain sailing. Note that part (b) is worth three times as many marks as part (a) so do not get carried away on part (a). Leave yourself enough time to give part (b) the attention it deserves. For part (b) you should identify the relevant transfer deed (in this case, Form TP1) and then explain concisely its contents, i.e. how you would fill it in. For ease of reference when considering the suggested answer we refer you to blank Form TP1 in Appendix 7.1

Many students get confused as to when an acknowledgement for production and undertaking for safe custody of deeds is required in a purchase deed. Such a clause is normally only appropriate on a sale of *part* of *un*registered land or, on a sale by personal representatives (PRs) of *un*registered land (whole or part) where the grant of representation is being retained by the PRs. As PRs are fiduciary owners, they can only give the acknowledgement, not the undertaking.

An acknowledgement and undertaking is not required on the transfer of part of registered land. This is because the transferor will not be retaining any title deeds. Accordingly, it is not necessary to include an acknowledgement and undertaking clause in the purchase deed under discussion in this question.

Suggested answer

(a)

The contractual completion date is three weeks today. As the contract incorporates the Standard Conditions of Sale regard must be had to standard condition 4.3.2. Where the period between exchange and completion is fifteen working days or more (see standard condition 4.3.4), as is the case here, the draft transfer should be sent to the seller at least twelve working days before the completion date. The seller then has four working days after delivery to approve or revise the draft and either return it or retain it for use as the engrossment. If the draft is returned, the buyer must send an engrossment to the seller at least five working days before the completion date.

The transferor must execute the deed in order to transfer the legal estate. Execution by both transferees is also necessary in this case because the transfer imposes fresh restrictive covenants and other obligations on the transferees.

When the transfer has been approved and the engrossment is ready for signature, the transferees should execute the transfer first. This is because the transferor will not wish to complete before the transferees have executed it bearing in mind that they are entering into new obligations. After execution by the transferees, the transfer deed will be delivered to the transferor in escrow (i.e. conditional upon the transferor also executing it) for execution by the transferor in readiness for completion.

(b)

The Law of Property Act 1925, s. 52(1) provides that in order to transfer the legal estate to the buyer the transfer document must be in the form of a deed. This deed must implement the terms of the contract and will mirror those terms.

As 10 Ellesmere Close has a registered title the relevant purchase deed is a Land Registry transfer, the form of which is prescribed by the Land Registration Rules 2003. The clients are buying part of the land within the registered title of 10 Ellesmere Close and so the appropriate form of transfer is a transfer of part of registered title, namely Land Registry Form TP1. I would complete the form as follows:

Box 1: This can be left blank as stamp duty on the deed has been replaced by stamp duty land tax on the transaction (1 December 2003).

Box 2: I would insert title number KM 74859 being the title number out of which the property is transferred.

Box 3: This is left blank as there are no other relevant title numbers.

Box 4: I would insert a description of the land being acquired. The description of the land given in the contract should be adequate for this purpose. I must attach a plan showing the land being acquired edged red and 'check' the first square box. The land retained by the seller should also be defined and identified on the plan, as reference to it will be made later in the document (see Box 13 below). The plan should be securely attached to the engrossed transfer.

Box 5: The date is left blank until completion.

Box 6: I would insert the full name of the transferor i.e. seller, Ingrid Kirsten Smits.

Box 7: I would insert the full names of my client purchasers, namely David Hobbs and Stephen Christopher Ingles.

Box 8: I would insert my clients' intended address for service for entry on the register. This should be their home address rather than the subject property address. I would therefore insert 7 Brookfield Lane, Basingstoke Hants BR1 7JK. An email address may also be given.

Box 9: This provides that the transferor transfers the subject property to the transferee i.e. my client purchasers.

Box 10: Checking the first square box I would insert the consideration of £70,000 in both words and figures.

Box 11: The question tells me that the contract provides for a full title guarantee and so I would check the full title guarantee box.

Box 12: In accordance with my instructions I would indicate that the transferees are to hold the property on trust for themselves as tenants in common in equal shares.

Box 13: The contract provides for the mutual grant and reservation of easements and these must be expressly repeated in the transfer deed. The same applies to the new restrictive covenants. Reference can be made to the subject property (edged red on the plan) and the retained land (edged blue on the plan) which should be defined. The contract incorporates the Standard Conditions of Sale. Standard condition 3.4 provides that where the seller is retaining land near the property, the buyer will have no right of light or air over the retained land. As this applies here, box 13 should include a declaration by the parties in these terms.

Box 14: The transfer will conclude with the attestation provisions, providing for execution by all parties in the presence of a witness. The reason why the transferees must execute the deed is because they are entering into new obligations. The attestation provisions will read 'signed as a deed' to make it clear on the face of the document that it is deed (The Law of Property (Miscellaneous Provisions) Act 1989 s. 1(2)).

Question 2

You will recall in Chapter 5, standard question 3 that you were acting for the buyers of The Corner House and were asked to raise requisitions on the abstract of the unregistered title.

Assume that contracts have been exchanged and you are required to draft the purchase deed. Your clients are Trevor Clarke and his wife Kathleen Clarke both currently residing at 2 Churchacre, Pitton, Cornshire. They are purchasing as joint tenants in equity and the price they are paying for the property is £90,000. The contract incorporates the Standard Conditions of Sale.

Consider the Abstract of The Corner House again (refer to Appendix 5.3). Draft the document that will vest the title in Mr and Mrs Clarke and explain fully its contents.

Commentary

The Law Society places much emphasis on the need for law students to acquire vital legal skills before they start their training contracts. The skill of drafting is an essential part of any property lawyer's armoury and you should therefore expect a drafting question to crop up from time to time in Property Law and Practice subject assessments.

As a drafting exercise, this question is very straightforward, especially if you choose the simpler form of purchase deed in unregistered conveyancing, the Land Registry transfer, instead of the more traditional conveyance. A transfer is entirely acceptable and appropriate in a situation where the whole of an unregistered title is being sold, as is the case here. You should appreciate however that the transfer does not necessarily lead to any greater simplicity in drafting where the transaction involves a sale of part of unregistered land and new easements and covenants are being created. For this you may prefer to use a traditional conveyance.

In this question you would not lose marks for electing to draft a conveyance but this would necessarily involve you in a lengthier drafting exercise and could leave you short on time for the other questions in the assessment.

Obviously there is more to the question than simply drafting a purchase deed. You have to explain fully its contents as well. Do not fall into the trap of making your explanation too general. You have been given specific information and are referred to a lengthy abstract of title, which you must read and assimilate before you begin your answer. In this way you can determine whether, for instance, a buyer's indemnity covenant is required.

Whereas in the previous question you were concerned with Form TP1 transferring part of a registered title, here you will use Form TR1 transferring the whole of an unregistered title.

Suggested answer

The suggested form of draft transfer (TR1) is set out in Appendix 7.2

Explanation

The freehold title to the property is unregistered. Since 1 December 1990 the whole of England and Wales has been in a compulsory registration area. Consequently the title to the property is compulsorily registrable following the sale to Mr and Mrs Clarke.

The document that will vest the title in Mr and Mrs Clarke is known as the purchase deed. Although it is customary to use a traditional conveyance as the purchase deed for unregistered titles, the Land Registration Rules 2003 provide that where the transaction, as here, gives rise to first registration, the deed may take the alternative form of a Land Registry transfer. It is submitted that a transfer is the more appropriate deed to vest the title in Mr and Mrs Clarke because it is shorter and simpler to prepare than a conveyance. For example, in a transfer deed there is no requirement for recitals. The relevant transfer deed for the purchase of the whole of an unregistered title is Form TR1.

The contents of the transfer on Form TR1 in this transaction are explained as follows:

Box 1: This can be left blank as stamp duty on the deed has been replaced by stamp duty land tax on the transaction (1 December 2003).

Box 2: The title number is left blank as the land being transferred has an unregistered title.

Box 3: Description of the property. The full extent of the land transferred should be precisely described. If a verbal description is not possible, a detailed plan must be attached to the transfer, or be identified by referring to the plan on a prior deed, which forms part of the title deduced. In this case, reference should be made to the plan in the conveyance of 18 January 1975 made between (1) Mark Ellins and (2) Charles Lane. As this conveyance is also mentioned later in box 12, it is defined here for the sake of clarity as 'the Conveyance'.

It is not necessary to refer to the right of way granted by the 1975 conveyance as this will pass automatically by virtue of the Law of Property Act 1925, s. 62. However it is often customary to mention existing easements introduced by the words 'Together with . . .' so that they are not overlooked by Land Registry on first registration. There could also be added a statement of any existing incumbrances—in this case the covenants and conditions in the 1975 conveyance—introduced by the words 'subject to . . .'. Again this is not compulsory but would draw Land Registry's attention to them. If the easements and covenants were to be referred to in the transfer one would run out of room in box 3 and it would be necessary to use a continuation sheet (form CS) and to staple it to the transfer form.

Box 4: The date of the transfer is entered on completion.

Box 5: The full names of the seller Flora Nicholson are entered here.

Box 6: The full names of the buyers for entry on the register are entered here.

Box 7: The buyers' full address(es) for service in the UK and for entry on the register is entered here. The correct address for these buyers is The Corner House, Chiltern Road, Pitton (where they will reside after completion) rather than their current one given in the question (2 Churchacre, Pitton). An e-mail address may also be given.

Box 8: These are known as the operative words in the transfer which show the seller's intention to pass the legal estate to the buyers.

Box 9: A statement of receipt follows the consideration. Although not conclusive evidence of payment, the receipt acts as sufficient discharge to the buyer (s. 67 of the Law of Property Act 1925). It also acts as authority to the buyer to pay the purchase money to the seller's solicitor (s. 69 of the Law of Property Act 1925).

Box 10: The extent of the seller's title guarantee will have been agreed in the contract. The significance of the title guarantee is that it implies the relevant covenants for title by the seller under the Law of Property (Miscellaneous Provisions) Act 1994. In this case, assuming the seller is the sole beneficial owner, a full title guarantee is appropriate.

Box 11: The declaration of trust is appropriate where there is more than one buyer (i.e. where a trust of land arises). We are told that the buyers will hold the equitable interest in the property as joint tenants. The declaration to this effect will of course mean that Land Registry will not enter a tenancy in common restriction in the proprietorship register when they create the new registered title.

Box 12: An indemnity covenant should be given by Mr and Mrs Clarke to the seller in respect of any future breach of the covenants and the conditions contained in the 1975 conveyance. An examination of the title reveals that a chain of indemnity covenants has been built up by successive owners right the way through to the seller. As the contract incorporates the Standard Conditions of Sale, standard condition 4.6.4. obliges the buyer to enter into an indemnity covenant if the seller will remain bound by any obligation affecting the property. Clearly the seller remains bound by her own indemnity covenant given to Elizabeth Campbell in the conveyance of 14 January 1994.

Box 13: A testimonium (i.e. 'In witness etc.') is not required in Land Registry transfers but the deed must contain proper attestation provisions. The Law of Property (Miscellaneous Provisions) Act 1989 s. 1(2) provides that an instrument shall not be a deed unless it makes it clear on its face that it is intended to be a deed. The attestation will therefore read, 'Signed as a deed by . . .'. The seller will execute the deed to transfer the legal estate and the buyers will also execute it as they are entering into an indemnity covenant.

Question 3

You are acting for Mr and Mrs Irving in their purchase of Coronation House in the small village of Hursey for £600,000. They are buying the house with the aid of a repayment mortgage from one of the well-known building societies. The mortgage deed is in the building society's standard printed form and incorporates the usual comprehensive general conditions found in a building society mortgage. The property has a registered title.

Your firm is on the society's panel of solicitors and accordingly the society has instructed the firm to complete and perfect the mortgage in accordance with the CML Lenders' Handbook. What steps will you take to achieve this in your dual role as solicitor for the buyer and solicitor for the mortgagee?

Commentary

This is a straightforward question provided you read it carefully and answer it methodically. You will notice that the mortgage is a repayment one so you will need to discuss the matters that are relevant to this type of mortgage. Do not be drawn into a discussion of other types of mortgage, such as endowment or pension mortgages.

You must also understand what is meant by 'perfect the mortgage'. Completing the mortgage is only part of the mortgagee's solicitor's job; the perfection of the security lies in the post completion work, in particular the registration of it. In this respect, notice how the question tells you that the property has a registered title.

There is no magic in acting for a mortgagee as well as a buyer. After all, the interests of the mortgagee will nearly always coincide with those of the purchaser (although be aware that conflicts of interest can arise). The purchaser will want to buy and the mortgagee will want security upon a property which is free from unusual incumbrances and has a good and marketable title. The question tells you that the CML Lenders' Handbook is being used so you should make reference to this in your answer.

If you have a sound knowledge of the conveyancing process and you adopt a systematic approach to your answer you are almost guaranteed to achieve high marks. Explain clearly, precisely and in chronological order each stage of the process, highlighting areas of particular importance. Do not be afraid to spell out, for instance, that the buyers must execute the mortgage deed before the funds are released on completion!

Suggested answer

The steps we would take to complete and perfect the mortgage on Coronation House can be summarised as set out below. At all times we would have regard to the detailed provisions of the CML Lenders' Handbook, both generally (part 1) and more specifically for this lender (part 2).

1. We would conduct all the usual pre-contract searches and enquiries for a registered property of this nature. For example, local search, commons search (as the property is in a small village) and standard enquiries of the seller's solicitors.

2. We would investigate title to the property in the normal way by examining official copies of the registered title.

3. We would approve the draft contract and, provided we and our clients are satisfied on all points (including the terms and conditions of the mortgage offer), we would then exchange contracts.

4. Following exchange we would check the mortgage offer/instructions again, in particular the special conditions, and make sure there are no outstanding matters which need to be covered.

5. We would check the precise amount available from the lender on completion. Will there be any retention in respect of works to the property? Will a mortgage guarantee indemnity premium be deducted from the gross advance?

6. By reference to our mortgage instructions, we would fill in the blanks in the mortgage deed in readiness for execution by our clients. For example, in the mortgage deed we would insert the property description (including the title number), names of borrowers and the initial rate of interest.

7. We would ask the clients to come into the office to sign the mortgage deed in the presence of a solicitor (the CML Lenders' Handbook considers this to be good practice). All requisite documentation would have to be executed *before* completion.

8. Before obtaining the borrowers'/buyers' signatures to the mortgage deed we would explain to them its contents and effect. For example, it will probably contain covenants by the borrower to keep the property in good repair, not to sublet without the mortgagee's consent and not to carry out structural alterations. We would check for any interest penalty on early redemption and advise our clients accordingly (we should already have checked and advised on this when we received the mortgage offer before exchange). Most importantly, the buyers must realise that their home is at risk if they default on the terms and conditions of the mortgage.

9. We would obtain the buyers' execution to all other necessary mortgage documents (e.g. bank mandate form). A solicitor should normally witness signatures. It is good practice to let the buyers have

copies of the documents they have signed. At the same time we would arrange for our clients to complete and sign Form SDLT1 in respect of Stamp Duty Land Tax (SDLT) payable immediately after completion.

10. We would undertake all necessary pre-completion searches including a bankruptcy search against the full names of the buyers/borrowers. The bankruptcy search is an essential requirement of all mortgagees.

11. Once we were satisfied on the title and the results of our searches, we would send our report on title and advance cheque request to the lender in good time for the advance monies to reach our office by the day of completion. If the results of any searches are outstanding, our report would be qualified to say that the report is 'subject to satisfactory results of searches'.

12. We would ask our clients to put us in funds for any balance due as set out in a financial statement that we would have prepared for them.

13. On the day of completion we would complete the purchase in the normal way and date the mortgage deed.

14. Following completion, we would perfect the mortgagee's security by attending to the crucial post completion formalities. These would be:

   • submitting Form SDLT1 to the Inland Revenue and paying the SDLT of £24,000 (calculated as 4% of the purchase price which exceeds £500,000)
   • obtaining prior to registration at Land Registry the SDLT Certificate of Payment from the Inland Revenue, and
   • applying to register the transfer and mortgage at Land Registry on Form AP1 accompanied by all necessary documentation.

15. Upon completion of the registration at Land Registry, we would check the Title Information Document to ensure that the entries are correct and then check the lender's requirements concerning the custody of documents relating to the subject property.

Question 4

RICHARDS ABBEY AND PARTNERS, SOLICITORS
INTERNAL MEMORANDUM

To   The Trainee Solicitor

From   The Training Partner

Re our client Sanjay Miandad: proposed mortgage

We act for Sanjay Miandad of 14 Willow Way, Drynoch who intends to lend £20,000 to his nephew Javed Khan to help him with his launderette business, which is running into financial difficulties.

Javed Khan and his wife live in a leasehold flat in Drynoch, which they bought with the aid of a mortgage from the local building society. Mr Miandad has told me that Mr Khan is happy to give our client a second charge on the flat to secure the loan.

Mr Khan does not wish to incur the expense of instructing his own solicitor and, in view of their close relationship, says he will gladly rely on our firm's expertise in this area to prepare the necessary paperwork.

He wants us to draw up a mortgage this afternoon, collect it on his way home from work and get his brother-in-law to sign it this evening before he flies to Pakistan tomorrow.

What matters should we consider before advising our client to proceed with these arrangements, if at all?

Commentary

These facts are typical of the kind of thing you will come across in practice, especially as far as commercial clients are concerned. Here, the client has already reached agreement and decided in his own mind what he wants from you. However, do not be brow-beaten by the client into doing what he wants without first considering carefully all the facts.

There are several areas of concern here, not least how you are going to react to the time-pressure of the client's request for a document to be drafted immediately. Never sacrifice carefully thought out advice in the interests of speed and expediency. The client is not a trained lawyer and is unlikely to have considered the full implications of his proposed course of action. That after all is your job, and you have a professional duty to ensure that vital issues are not overlooked.

Note the words in the question, 'if at all'. This should alert you to the possibility that the client may be best advised not to proceed in the first place.

You should recognise that a professional conduct issue has reared its head in the guise of Rule 6 of the Solicitors' Practice Rules 1990—acting for two parties in the same conveyancing transaction. Remember that conduct is a pervasive topic on the Legal Practice Course and is always likely to crop up in the context of a Property Law and Practice problem. Rule 6 is an obvious one and you should be looking out for it, even in a situation like this, which is not a buyer/seller type problem.

Always have regard to whether the subject property is freehold or leasehold. If it is the latter—as in this case—there is likely to be a good reason for it, and you should be addressing your mind to possible leasehold issues which may be relevant. Here, it is the question of whether the landlord's consent may be required to the proposed mortgage by the tenant.

Finally, a reminder that your answer should be given in the form of a concise memo in response to the partner's memo. Do not be tempted into writing an essay which will lose you marks for style.

Suggested answer

RICHARDS ABBEY AND PARTNERS, SOLICITORS
INTERNAL MEMORANDUM

To   The Training Partner

From   The Trainee Solicitor

Re our client Sanjay Miandad

I refer to your memo regarding the above. I recommend that the following points should be considered before the client can be advised to proceed.

1. Mr Khan must be advised to seek independent legal advice before signing the mortgage. Rule 6 of the Solicitors' Practice Rules 1990 prohibits a solicitor from acting for both lender and borrower in a private mortgage at arm's length. Although it could be argued that this transaction may not be at arm's length given the blood relationship between the borrower and lender, we must in any event be fully satisfied that there is no conflict of interest before we can act for both parties. On the facts of this case I take the view that a conflict would arise if the mortgagor were seen to be relying on our advice and expertise.

2. As this is a proposed second charge we should inspect the first charge to establish whether the consent of the first mortgagee is required to the creation of the second charge.

3. If consent is required this should be obtained in writing before completion of the loan. The first mortgagee may require Mr Miandad to enter into a separate deed of postponement.

4. Importantly, the first mortgagee should also be asked to confirm the current amount outstanding so it can be checked whether there is sufficient equity in the property to cover the proposed advance.

5. The property is leasehold. The lease should be inspected to see if landlord's consent is required to charge the property. If so, consent must be obtained before completion otherwise the charge will not bind the landlord. Following completion it may be necessary to give notice of the charge to the landlord, and this should also be checked in the lease.

6. We should investigate title and conduct searches and enquiries in the same way as if our client were buying the property. Before we can advise our client to proceed we must be satisfied that the title is good and marketable and free from any unusual incumbrances.

7. We must obtain clear results to pre-completion searches including a bankruptcy search against the full name of Mr Khan.

8. I note that Mr Khan lives in the flat with his wife. We must establish if she is a joint owner, in which case she will also have to join in the mortgage as joint mortgagor.

9. Even if Mr Khan is the sole legal owner, Mrs Khan may have an equitable interest in the property and will have statutory rights of occupation under the Family Law Act 1996. She must give her written consent to the proposed charge and agree to postpone all rights behind our client's charge. Reasonable steps must be taken to ensure that she understands the nature of the transaction and the postponement of her rights (if any). To this end, I recommend we insist that she receives separate independent advice. This should be sufficient to counter any assertion by her at a later date that her husband exerted duress or undue influence on her (see *Barclays Bank plc v. O'Brien* [1992] 4 All ER 987).

10. Does Mr Khan own the launderette premises? If so, have the parties considered the alternative possibility of Mr Miandad taking security on these premises? This avenue should be explored as it may prove less complicated.

11. Given the important issues which need to be addressed, we cannot sensibly comply with our client's instructions to draft the mortgage immediately. If Mr Miandad is coming into the office this afternoon I will be happy to see him and explain the position.

TIME ENGAGED 40 MINUTES

TRAINEE SOLICITOR

7.3.2 MULTIPLE CHOICE QUESTIONS AND ANSWERS

We set out below examples of ten multiple choice questions that you might encounter in a subject assessment. Answers to these then follow. Remember our initial guidance. Never leave multiple choice answers with a blank. If there are four possibilities and you are not sure of the answer select the one you think might be right; after all, you have a one in four chance of getting it right! Also look at the instructions on the paper. If it says select the right answer on the paper by circling the correct choice then do just that. Do not make a tick or underline your selection as the strict response would be to fail you even though the selection may be correct. Think carefully before selecting your answer and have correcting fluid to hand just in case you make a mistake or change your mind. To assist you, we have given brief explanations for the answers but generally this is not something you will be required to do (unless your exam paper says so!).

7.3.2.1 Multiple choice questions

Unless otherwise directed, select the right answer by circling it in each question. Should you think that none of the selections apply please explain why not in your answer book.

1. Acting for a purchaser in connection with the proposed assignment next month of a registered lease dated 30 January 1995, it will be necessary to include an express covenant of indemnity in the purchase deed as this is not implied by statute. Is this statement TRUE/FALSE? Please delete the incorrect choice.

2. The traditional form of purchase deed in relation to the acquisition of an unregistered freehold title is:

   (a) a transfer

   (b) an assignment

   (c) a conveyance

   (d) an assent

3. Under the Solicitors' Practice Rules 1990 which of the following is NOT required to be included in the solicitors' approved certificate on title to the lender (assuming that the subject property will be used as the borrower's private residence):

   (a) mortgage advance

   (b) price stated in transfer

   (c) completion date

   (d) property description

4. In registered land the form of mortgage that must be used is Form CH1, as prescribed by the Land Registration Rules 2003.

   Is this statement TRUE/FALSE? Please delete the incorrect choice.

5. A transfer of part of registered land contains new restrictive covenants on the part of the buyer and the grant and reservation of new easements in favour of the buyer and seller respectively. The transfer deed should be executed by:

   (a) the seller alone

   (b) the buyer alone

   (c) both the seller and buyer

   (d) the seller, the buyer and the buyer's mortgagee

6. Your client has decided to take a fixed rate mortgage with Cornshire Building Society. The interest rate is fixed for five years and there is an early redemption penalty. When advising your client on the contents of the mortgage deed, which of the following would you generally NOT include in your advice:

   (a) that the lender has the right to call in the loan and sell the property if the borrower defaults on the mortgage

   (b) that the initial rate of interest and monthly payments may be varied by the lender at any time

   (c) that if the client repays the mortgage within the first five years the lender can charge an interest penalty

   (d) that your client will be unable to let the premises without the lender's prior consent

7. In registered land, legal mortgages rank in priority according to their order of creation not their order of registration.

   Is this statement TRUE/FALSE? Please delete the incorrect choice.

8. When drafting the purchase deed the contents of the draft deed are governed primarily by:

   (a) the official copies of the seller's title

   (b) the buyer's instructions

   (c) the correspondence between the seller's and buyer's solicitors

   (d) the contract

9. The correct form of Land Registry transfer to use on a purchase of part of unregistered land from an estate owner is:

   (a) TR1

    (b) TP1

    (c) TR2

    (d) TP2

10. On a transfer of part of registered land the solicitor for the transferee may sign the transfer on behalf of the transferee.

    Is this statement TRUE/FALSE? Please delete the incorrect choice.

7.3.2.2 *Answers to multiple choice questions (with brief explanations)*

1. The statement is false. Crucially the lease is dated before 1 January 1996 (when the Landlord and Tenant (Covenants) Act 1995 came into force). The Land Registration Act 2002, Sch. 12 para. 20, replicates the effect of the old s. 24 of the Land Registration Act 1925 by providing for an implied indemnity to be given by the purchaser of the leasehold estate to the seller. Accordingly it is unnecessary to include an express covenant of indemnity in the purchase deed.

2. The correct answer is (c). There is very little to be said here—this is probably the easiest question in the whole book so no excuses for getting it wrong!

3. The correct answer is none. Under r. 6(3) of the Solicitors' Practice Rules 1990 *all* of these facts should be included in the solicitors' certificate on title to the lender.

4. The statement is false. The use of Form CH1 is only optional not compulsory (Land Registration Rules 2003, r. 103).

5. The correct answer is (c). The seller should always execute the deed in order to transfer the legal estate. The buyer should also execute the deed where he or she is entering into new obligations, which is the case here. The buyer's mortgagee does not execute the purchase deed.

6. The correct answer is (b). This is an example of where you should read the question carefully. When advising a client on a mortgage you would generally mention (b) but of course in this case you are told that it is a fixed rate mortgage. Accordingly the mortgagee cannot raise the interest rate during the first five years.

7. The statement is false. Section 48(1) of the Land Registration Act 2002 states that registered charges are 'to be taken to rank as between themselves in the order shown in the register'. Thus following completion, it is essential that the appropriate registration of the charge is made within the priority period of your pre-completion land registry search.

8. The correct answer is (d). The contract sets out the terms on which the sale will proceed whereas the purchase deed effectively implements them.

9. The correct answer is (b). A traditional conveyance may be used but of those forms listed only the TP1 may be used. This might appear a little odd given that Form TP1 refers in its body to a transfer of part of *registered* title. However the Land Registry are happy to accept a TP1 on a transfer of part of unregistered land as well, if the land comprises part of the land in the previous conveyance to the transferor. Forms TR2 and TP2 relate to transfers by mortgagees under a power of sale. Form TR1 is used on a transfer of whole (registered or unregistered land), not part.

10. The statement is false. Unless the solicitor has been duly appointed as attorney for the transferee, the transfer should be signed by the transferee personally.

7.3.3 SHORT ANSWER QUESTIONS

Question 1

Comment on the validity of the execution of the following purchase deeds (you may assume that the signatures are valid).

(a) *Conveyance of freehold land in 1989*:

SIGNED SEALED and	)	
DELIVERED by	)	James Hart
JAMES HART	)	
in the presence	)	
of:	)	

(b) *Transfer of freehold land in 2004*:

Signed as a deed by	)	
Kay Trew	)	Kay Trew
in the presence of:	)	
Signature of witness	)	William Jones

Name   W. JONES

Address   188 Langdale Road Norwich NT1 4EG

Question 2

You act for Behemoth Bank Plc in connection with a loan facility to a development company, which is acquiring a greenfield site (unregistered land) for development as a business park. Other solicitors are separately representing the developer. The drawdown of the initial advance for the acquisition of the land and completion of the fixed charge on the land has been completed. List the items you would now require from the developer's solicitors to enable to you proceed with the perfection of your client's security and outline the steps you would take to perfect that security. You may assume that the seller had a small mortgage on the land.

Question 3

You act for Mrs Sandra Dee the wife of a company director who has agreed in principle to allow their matrimonial home to be mortgaged to help secure the business debts of Mr Dee's company. The matrimonial home is registered in the joint names of Mr and Mrs Dee. Mrs Dee seeks your advice in connection with the proposed mortgage. Explain what matters you should have regard to before advising Mrs Dee.

7.3.3.1   *Suggested answers to short answer questions*

Question 1

I comment on the validity of the execution of these purchase deeds as follows.

(a) *Conveyance of freehold land in 1989*

The requirement for execution before 31 July 1990 was that a deed should be signed, sealed and delivered. The wording here indicates an intention that the deed is delivered and in the absence of any contrary indication, this can be assumed. We are told to assume that James Hart's signature is valid. Although there is no witness to his signature, a witness is not necessary for validity. The problem with this conveyance is that there is no evidence that it has been sealed. Accordingly the conveyance has been invalidly executed and the document is not a deed. The consequence of this is that the legal estate has not been transferred by this conveyance (s. 52(1), Law of Property Act 1925).

(b) *Transfer of freehold land in 2004*

The requirements for execution of a deed on or after 31 July 1990 are:

- that the document must make it clear on its face that it is a deed,
- it must be signed by the necessary parties in the presence of a witness, and
- it must be delivered by the person executing it (there is no requirement for a seal) (s. 1 of the Law of Property (Miscellaneous Provisions) Act 1989).

In this transfer, Kay Trew's signature has been witnessed and the document clearly indicates on the face of it that it is a deed. Although there is no reference to delivery, this can be assumed in the absence of any indication to the contrary. Accordingly, the transfer appears to be validly executed and will be accepted by Land Registry for registration. The legal estate will be transferred on registration.

Question 2

It is important to appreciate that this is a commercial lending transaction in which we act for the lender alone and that we are at the post completion stage. It is therefore not necessary to discuss such matters as title investigation, searches or verifying the company's memorandum and articles of association. We would already have considered these matters before reporting to our client, i.e. before completion.

The items we shall require from the developer's solicitors to enable us to proceed with the perfection of our client's security are listed below. Before completion we should receive an undertaking from the developer's solicitors to supply these documents.

- As this is unregistered land, the unregistered title deeds (originals or examined copies).
- Executed purchase deed (conveyance or, more likely, TR1).
- We are told that the seller has a mortgage so we shall require the seller's legal charge duly vacated (or an acceptable form of undertaking from the seller's solicitors).
- All appropriate security documentation duly executed, i.e. fixed charge, possibly floating charge, directors' guarantees, etc.
- Originals of all relevant planning permissions.
- Completed and signed Land Registry cover for first registration, i.e. Form FR1.
- Receipt for payment of any stamp duty land tax payable on the purchase.
- Completed company Form 395 for each new charge.
- If not already received, certified copy board minutes of the development company's resolution to accept the loan facility and execute the security documentation.

To perfect the security on behalf of our client lender we will:

- Register the newly created charge(s) at Companies Registry within twenty-one days of completion. Each charge is accompanied by completed Form 395.
- Apply to Land Registry for first registration of title within two months of completion. The application is made on Form FR1 accompanied by the unregistered title deeds, including the seller's vacated charge.
- Check the Title Information Document on receipt from Land Registry to ensure that our client's fixed charge has been registered as a first charge on the charges register, and that the newly registered title is otherwise in order.

Question 3

Before advising Mrs Dee I must have regard to the guidelines laid down by the House of Lords in *Royal Bank of Scotland v. Etridge (No. 2)* [2001] 4 All ER 449. These guidelines apply to any solicitor who is advising someone in a non-commercial relationship who has offered to guarantee the debts of another. The usual situation is the one we have here, which is where a wife is being asked to mortgage the family home to secure her husband's business debts. I would consider the following matters:

- I must be satisfied that I have the necessary expertise and time to interpret or advise on what may be very detailed financial information.

- I must be satisfied that I can properly act for Mrs Dee as well Mr Dee, i.e. that there is no conflict of interest.

- I must obtain full financial information concerning Mr Dee's business account. This will normally include information on the purpose for the new facility, the indebtedness, the amount and terms of the borrowing and a copy of any application form.

- I should meet Mrs Dee face to face in the absence of Mr Dee (telephone calls and letters are not sufficient).

- I must confirm what is Mrs Dee's understanding of the transaction and correct any misapprehension she may have.

- I must explain in non-technical language the nature of the documents and their practical consequences, e.g. if her husband's business fails, the risk of losing her home and being made bankrupt.

- I must emphasise the seriousness of the risks involved.

- I must explain the length of time the security will last.

- I must explain that Mrs Dee has a choice and that the decision to proceed is hers and hers alone.

- If Mrs Dee wishes to proceed I should get clear confirmation from her that this is the case, and she should authorise me to provide written confirmation of this to the lender.

I should also consider the following matters of good professional practice:

- Who will pay my firm's fee for advising Mrs Dee? If she decides not to guarantee the proposed loan, will my fees get paid at all?

- I should open a separate file and send Mrs Dee a retainer letter which clearly defines my firm's relationship with her.

- I should keep a clear record of my advice, especially if the transaction appears to be to Mrs Dee's disadvantage. I should consider asking her to counter-sign a copy of that advice.

- Mrs Dee's authority for my firm to provide a 'certificate' to the lender should be given in writing.

7.4 REFERENCES TO WIDER READING INCLUDING PRACTITIONER TEXTS

- *A Practical Approach to Conveyancing* by Abbey R. and Richards M. (6th edn, OUP)—Chapter 7 (The Purchase Deed and Mortgage).

- *The Law Society's Conveyancing Handbook 10th edition* by Silverman F—Section E dealing with Pre-completion including the purchase deed and the buyer's mortgage and Section H dealing with lenders generally.

- *Emmet on Title*: Chapters 13–15, 20 and 25.

- Ruoff and Roper Registered Conveyancing (Sweet and Maxwell).

- *Textbook on Land Law* by MacKenzie J.A. and Phillips M. (9th edn, OUP)—Chapter 19 (Mortgages).

7.5 **RELEVANT WEBSITES FOR MORE INFORMATION**

- Acts of Parliament, http://www.hmso.gov.uk/acts.htm
  Keep up to date with statutory developments.

- Council of Mortgage Lenders, http://www.cml.org.uk
  There is an on-line version of the CML Lenders'Handbook available at this site and should be referred to in cases of doubt about the requirements of the lender in relation to the subject transaction.

- Financial Services Authority, http://www.fsa.gov.uk

- House of Lords judgments, http://www.parliament.the-stationery-office.co.uk/pa/ld199697/ldjudgmt/ldjudgmt.htm
  Keep up to date with important new cases.

- Inland Revenue, http://www.inlandrevenue.gov.uk/home.htm

- Land Registry, http://www.landreg.gov.uk

- Land Registry Internet register access, http://www.landregistrydirect.gov.uk
  The location for on-line applications for official copies of registered title.

- Law Commission, http://www.lawcom.gov.uk
  Keep up to date on proposals for law reform.

- Law Society, http://www.lawsoc.org.uk

- Location statistics, http://www.upmystreet.com

- National Association of Estate Agents, http://www.naea.co.uk

- Ordnance Survey, http://www.ordnancesurvey.co.uk
  It might be useful to consult a detailed Ordnance Survey map when drafting descriptions of land in the purchase deed (e.g. sales of part).

- A street map anywhere in the UK, http://www.streetmap.co.uk

- Valuation Office, http://www.voa.gov.uk

APPENDIX 7.1 LAND REGISTRY FORM TP1

**Transfer of part
of registered title(s)**

Land Registry

TP1

If you need more room than is provided for in a panel, use continuation sheet CS and attach to this form.

1. Stamp Duty

Place "X" in the appropriate box or boxes and complete the appropriate certificate.

☐ It is certified that this instrument falls within category ☐ in the Schedule to the Stamp Duty (Exempt Instruments) Regulations 1987

☐ It is certified that the transaction effected does not form part of a larger transaction or of a series of transactions in respect of which the amount or value or the aggregate amount or value of the consideration exceeds the sum of £ _____

☐ It is certified that this is an instrument on which stamp duty is not chargeable by virtue of the provisions of section 92 of the Finance Act 2001

2. Title number(s) out of which the Property is transferred *Leave blank if not yet registered.*

3. Other title number(s) against which matters contained in this transfer are to be registered, if any

4. Property transferred *Insert address, including postcode, or other description of the property transferred. Any physical exclusions, e.g. mines and minerals, should be defined. Any attached plan must be signed by the transferor.*

The Property is defined: *Place "X" in the appropriate box.*

☐ on the attached plan and shown *State reference e.g. "edged red".*

☐ on the Transferor's title plan and shown *State reference e.g. "edged and numbered 1 in blue".*

5. Date

6. Transferor *Give full name(s) and company's registered number, if any.*

7. Transferee **for entry on the register** *Give full name(s) and company's registered number, if any. For Scottish companies use an SC prefix and for limited liability partnerships use an OC prefix before the registered number, if any. For foreign companies give territory in which incorporated.*

Unless otherwise arranged with Land Registry headquarters, a certified copy of the Transferee's constitution (in English or Welsh) will be required if it is a body corporate but is not a company registered in England and Wales or Scotland under the Companies Acts.

8. Transferee's intended **address(es) for service (including postcode) for entry on the register** *You may give up to three addresses for service **one** of which **must** be a postal address but does not have to be within the UK. The other addresses can be any combination of a postal address, a box number at a UK document exchange or an electronic address.*

9. **The Transferor transfers the Property to the Transferee**

10. Consideration *Place "X" in the appropriate box. State clearly the currency unit if other than sterling. If none of the boxes applies, insert an appropriate memorandum in the additional provisions panel.*

☐ The Transferor has received from the Transferee for the Property the sum of *In words and figures.*

☐ *Insert other receipt as appropriate.*

☐ The transfer is not for money or anything which has a monetary value

11. The Transferor transfers with *Place "X" in the appropriate box and add any modifications.*

☐ full title guarantee ☐ limited title guarantee

12. Declaration of trust *Where there is more than one Transferee, place "X" in the appropriate box.*

☐ The Transferees are to hold the Property on trust for themselves as joint tenants

☐ The Transferees are to hold the Property on trust for themselves as tenants in common in equal shares

☐ The Transferees are to hold the Property *Complete as necessary.*

13. Additional provisions
Use this panel for:
- *definitions of terms not defined above*
- *rights granted or reserved*
- *restrictive covenants*
- *other covenants*
- *agreements and declarations*
- *other agreed provisions.*

The prescribed subheadings may be added to, amended, repositioned or omitted.

Definitions

Rights granted for the benefit of the Property

Rights reserved for the benefit of other land *The land having the benefit should be defined, if necessary by reference to a plan.*

Restrictive covenants by the Transferee *Include words of covenant.*

Restrictive covenants by the Transferor *Include words of covenant.*

14. Execution *The Transferor must execute this transfer as a deed using the space below. If there is more than one Transferor, all must execute. Forms of execution are given in Schedule 9 to the Land Registration Rules 2003. If the transfer contains Transferee's covenants or declarations or contains an application by the Transferee (e.g. for a restriction), it must also be executed by the Transferee (all of them, if there is more than one).*

APPENDIX 7.2   LAND REGISTRY FORM TR1

Transfer of whole
of registered title(s)

Land Registry

If you need more room than is provided for in a panel, use continuation sheet CS and attach to this form.

1.	**Stamp Duty**

Place "X" in the appropriate box or boxes and complete the appropriate certificate.

☐ It is certified that this instrument falls within category ☐ in the Schedule to the Stamp Duty (Exempt Instruments) Regulations 1987

☐ It is certified that the transaction effected does not form part of a larger transaction or of a series of transactions in respect of which the amount or value or the aggregate amount or value of the consideration exceeds the sum of ☐ £

☐ It is certified that this is an instrument on which stamp duty is not chargeable by virtue of the provisions of section 92 of the Finance Act 2001

2. Title Number(s) of the Property *Leave blank if not yet registered.*

3. Property
The land fronting Chiltern Road Pitton Cornshire comprising 1.9 acres or thereabouts more particularly delineated and described on a plan annexed to a conveyance dated 18 January 1975 made between (1) Mark Ellins and (2) Charles Lane ("the Conveyance")

4. Date

5. Transferor *Give full names and company's registered number if any.*
Flora Nicholson

6. Transferee **for entry on the register** *Give full name(s) and company's registered number, if any. For Scottish companies use an SC prefix and for limited liability partnerships use an OC prefix before the registered number, if any. For foreign companies give territory in which incorporated.*
Trevor Clarke and Kathleen Clarke

Unless otherwise arranged with Land Registry headquarters, a certified copy of the Transferee's constitution (in English or Welsh) will be required if it is a body corporate but is not a company registered in England and Wales or Scotland under the Companies Acts.

7. Transferee's intended **address(es) for service (including postcode)** for entry on the register *You may give up to three addresses for service **one** of which **must** be a postal address but does not have to be within the UK. The other addresses can be any combination of a postal address, a box number at a UK document exchange or an electronic address.*
The Corner House Chiltern Road Pitton Cornshire CN4 7PT

8. **The Transferor transfers the Property to the Transferee**

9. Consideration *Place "X" in the appropriate box. State clearly the currency unit if other than sterling. If none of the boxes applies, insert an appropriate memorandum in the additional provisions panel.*

☑ The Transferor has received from the Transferee for the Property the sum of Ninety Thousand Pounds (£90,000.00)

☐

Insert other receipt as appropriate.

☐

The transfer is not for money or anything which has a monetary value

---

10. The Transferor transfers with *Place "X" in the appropriate box and add any modifications.*

☑ full title guarantee   ☐ limited title guarantee

---

11. Declaration of trust *Where there is more than one Transferee, place "X" in the appropriate box.*

☑ The Transferees are to hold the Property on trust for themselves as joint tenants

☐ The Transferees are to hold the Property on trust for themselves as tenants in common in equal shares

☐ The Transferees are to hold the Property *Complete as necessary.*

---

12. Additional provisions *Insert here any required or permitted statements, certificates or applications and any agreed covenants, declarations, etc.*

The Transferees hereby jointly and severally covenant with the Transferor by way of indemnity only that they and the persons deriving title under them will at all times hereafter observe and perform the covenants and conditions contained in the Conveyance so far as the same affect the land hereby transferred and are still subsisting and capable of being enforced

---

13. Execution *The Transferor must execute this transfer as a deed using the space below. If there is more than one Transferor, all must execute. Forms of execution are given in Schedule 9 to the Land Registration Rules 2003. If the transfer contains Transferee's covenants or declarations or contains an application by the Transferee (e.g. for a restriction), it must also be executed by the Transferee (all of them, if there is more than one).*

Signed as a deed by Flora Nicholson
in the presence of:

Signed as a deed by Trevor Clarke
and Kathleen Clarke
in the presence of:

8 PRE-COMPLETION PROCEDURES AND COMPLETION

8.1 INTRODUCTION

To understand this fascinating area of Property Law and Practice you will have to be fully conversant with all aspects of pre-completion searches as this is one topic that comes up in subject assessments time and time again. The reason for this is really quite obvious, pre-completion searches are a critical part of any property transaction. Indeed the choice of searches and understanding the results of them can be fraught with all sorts of pitfalls for the unwary practitioner. In the first place there is the obvious but well repeated point that with two land law systems, registered and unregistered, there will always be confusion for the ill prepared about which searches to make. Secondly, there is also the potential for confusion from the dual role of acting for the buyer and the lender at the same time. Thirdly, there is the variety of different but relevant searches that can confuse. The moral is to know your searches and when to use them. Then you should do well.

Although Property Law and Practice is about land law and its application (including the process of conveyancing), it is also about money and the transfer of valuable assets, both small and large. This is nowhere more clearly demonstrated than at completion. It is at this point in property transactions that large sums of money will change hands. It is for this reason that assessment questions in this area will require you to demonstrate an ability to handle uncomplicated mathematics. Some examination boards will specifically authorize you to take a calculator into the examination room. Always do so if permitted, as it will be the case that most if not all of us will find them faster at computing the figures required. Be prepared to work out Value Added Tax as of course this is payable on not just legal fees but also estate agent's charges. Indeed it is also important that you are aware of the prevailing rates for stamp duty land tax. (There will also be stamp duty land tax on rents on the grant of a lease but as this can be quite complicated it is unlikely that you will be required to calculate such an amount in an exam. However you should be aware of the principles involved.)

Another area of potential confusion arises from the use of the Law Society's National Conveyancing Protocol and the fact that some transactions will proceed within it and some will not. Those that do will, in the absence of agreement to the contrary, complete in accordance with the Law Society's Code for Completion, ('the Code'). Those that do not, will only complete within the terms of the Code if the parties' solicitors specifically agree to adopt the Code. What this means for you is that you will be required to know the difference between the two systems as far as completion is concerned. You will also need to identify the weaknesses of both and how these can be addressed. In this topic knowledge of case law will be relevant.

You will have realised by now that every area of property law and practice can be separately identified but will usually be examined in the context of allied topics. A clear example in this area is set out in the first question where you will need to consider from whom you have received instructions as well as the effect that a change of parties might bring to the overall transaction. Similarly matters of professional conduct will surface especially in the context of completion and the requirements of the Law Society's Code. Accordingly, throughout this whole area you should be continually aware of matters of professional conduct and whether or not they should be mentioned in your answer. Questions of conflict of interest will always need to be mentioned and particularly in relation to possible completion arrangements.

8.2 AN OVERVIEW OF THE SUBJECT AND A LOOK AT SOME PROBLEM AREAS

8.2.1 PRE-COMPLETION PROCEDURES

The first flowchart sets out the steps to be taken after exchange and before completion from the perspective of a practitioner acting for a buyer. The second flowchart sets out the steps to be taken after exchange and before completion from the perspective of a practitioner acting for a seller.

8.2.2 PRE-COMPLETION SEARCHES

Pre-completion searches are a key part of the overall conveyancing process. However, the results of these searches can be riddled with all sorts of pitfalls for the unwary practitioner. First, there is the obvious point that with two current land law systems, registered and unregistered, there will always be confusion for the ill-prepared about which searches to make. Secondly, there is also the potential for confusion arising from the dual role where a practitioner acts for the buyer and the lender at the same time. Thirdly, there is the variety of different but relevant searches that can confuse the ill-prepared.

The buyer's practitioner will be the person to carry out pre-completion searches. This is because the buyer (and the buyer's lender) will want to ensure that the title is in order and is free from undisclosed encumbrances and is therefore available to be a security for a loan without restraint. (Of course if the lender is separately represented then the lender's practitioner will carry out all searches on behalf of the lender. Sometimes a lender's practitioner will pass on this obligation to the borrower's practitioner.)

Pre-completion searches are made to ensure that the information about the title, given prior to exchange, remains the same up to completion. So, in the case of registered land,

Pre-completion procedures on behalf of a buyer

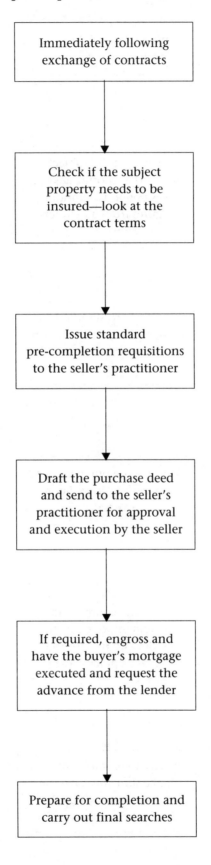

After exchange and before completion on behalf of a seller

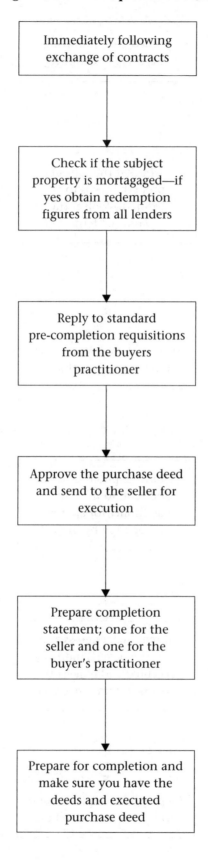

Immediately following exchange of contracts

Check if the subject property is mortagaged—if yes obtain redemption figures from all lenders

Reply to standard pre-completion requisitions from the buyers practitioner

Approve the purchase deed and send to the seller for execution

Prepare completion statement; one for the seller and one for the buyer's practitioner

Prepare for completion and make sure you have the deeds and executed purchase deed the search will refer to the date of the copy registers supplied by the seller, namely, the issue date of the official copies from the Registry, and will disclose any changes since that time. As to unregistered land, the search may disclose many different types of entry such as any mortgages not detailed in the abstract of title and which have been created as a second or subsequent charge since the seller purchased the property.

There is another purpose to these searches and that is to obtain a protective period during which completion and registration can take place and during which the buyer will have priority over anyone else seeking to register an entry against the subject property.

The choice of appropriate pre-completion searches can be resolved by reference to the following decision grid:

Q. 1 Is the seller a company?	
Yes Complete a search against the company name at Companies House	No Go to Q. 2
Q. 2 Is the property registered?	
Yes Complete the appropriate land registry search—Go to Q. 3	No Complete a Land Charges K15 search against all estate owners from at least the root of title and go to Q. 4
Q. 3 Is this a sale of the whole of the registered title?	
Yes Complete a land registry OS1 search	No It is a sale of part so complete a land registry OS2 search
Q. 4 Is this a residential purchase with a mortgage from a bank or building society?	
Yes Complete a K16 bankruptcy search against the borrowers	No Go to Q. 5
Q. 5 Have you advised your client to inspect the property prior to completion	
Yes Go and do something else!	No This should be done to check the state of the property, whether there any unlawful occupiers, etc.

8.2.3 COMPLETION STATEMENTS

Completion statements are prepared to show a client how much is required to complete or how much will be available on completion or how much is needed on completion. In detail they are as follows:

1. *A completion statement prepared by the seller's practitioner for the seller.* The purpose of this statement is to show the seller how much will be left over on completion by way of the net proceeds of sale, either to be applied towards an allied purchase or as the simple net proceeds of sale.

2. *A completion statement prepared by the seller's practitioner for the buyer's practitioner.* The purpose of this statement is to show to the buyer how much is required to be paid over at completion. Clearly if this is only the balance of the purchase price after taking into account the deposit then a full-scale statement is unnecessary. These statements can be quite complex and lengthy when the subject property is leasehold. In these circumstances the statement will have to include apportionments of monies paid in advance, or still outstanding and due to be paid. This could include ground rent, insurance payments and service charges.

3. *A completion statement prepared by the buyer's practitioner for the buyer.* The purpose of this statement is to show the buyer how much will be needed to complete the purchase of the subject property. This will normally be prepared and issued shortly after exchange so that the buyer can put his or her practitioner in funds in good time for completion. If the figures are to be fully comprehensive, a bill of costs should accompany this statement. Failure to use cleared funds is a breach of the Solicitors' Accounts Rules.

8.2.4 COMPLETION

Completion is the point when the buyer pays the balance of the purchase price to the seller in exchange for the deeds, executed purchase deed, keys and, if the contract so provides, vacant possession. In unregistered land the conveyance or assignment constitutes the passing of title of a legal estate and as such this is effectively completion of the transaction in all respects, see *Killner v. France* [1946] 2 All ER 83 (subject of course to the requirement to submit the title to the Land Registry for first registration).

This is not the exact position in registered land where the passing of title of a legal estate is only really completed with the registration of the buyer as the registered proprietor at the Land Registry. On a practical basis, as the buyer has the obligation to register, completion is, to all intents and purposes, at the time the money is handed over in exchange for the transfer (and any supporting deeds such as the original lease in registered leasehold titles). However, practitioners must always remember to proceed with registration without delay, and to do so within their search priority period.

8.2.5 PROBLEMS THAT CAN ARISE AT COMPLETION

Where there is a first mortgage and the seller has received instructions to deal with redemption for the lender, sale proceeds will be applied immediately after completion for the purposes of redemption. This being so, the vacating receipt for unregistered mortgages or Form DS1 for a registered charge will not be available on completion. In these circumstances, practitioners must rely upon professional (and enforceable) undertakings. Such undertakings must only be taken from solicitors or licensed conveyancers, and most certainly not from an unqualified person whose 'undertaking' will of course be unenforceable. The Law Society has issued a recommended form of undertaking and we endorse its use by practitioners wherever possible (see (1986) 83 LSG 3127). The wording is:

'In consideration of you today completing the purchase of [insert subject property postal address or description] we hereby undertake to pay over to [insert identity of the lender] the money required to discharge the mortgage/legal charge dated [insert date of mortgage/legal charge] and to forward the receipted mortgage/legal charge/Form DS1 to you as soon as it is received by us from [insert identity of lender].'

Until recently this arrangement for the supply of completed forms of mortgage discharge worked satisfactorily. However a problem arose out of the decision in *Patel v. Daybells* [2000] EGCS 98 (QBD, 19 July 2000). Gray J held that a solicitor could be held to be negligent in relying upon a solicitor's undertaking in the format generally used by the legal profession. On the face if it, this is an extraordinary decision and one, in theory that should cause practitioners all sorts of headaches when it is time for completion. Why then, one may reasonably ask, did the judge come to this conclusion that on the face of it is so problematic? In understanding the decision you have to consider three questions raised by the judge.

1. Does the acceptance of the undertaking involve foreseeable risk?
2. Could that risk have been avoided?
3. If so was there an act of negligence in failing to avoid that risk?

The judge considered that there was a risk in the industry standard practice of undertakings and that a different form of completion (probably based on attendance) can avoid the risk. Frankly the decision may be accurate but it is definitely not practical. Personal completions are a thing of the past and have no place in modern residential conveyancing practice. The decision would also seem to require practitioners to call for the availability of Form DS1 at completion. However, lenders of course will not provide the form at that time, as they have not yet been paid.

One way to address the difficulty is to ensure that the seller's practitioner is also the Agent of the seller's lender. If then the Agent fails to redeem by paying over an incorrect amount, the dispute will be between the Agent (the seller's practitioner) and Principal (the seller's lender) because with this procedure the lender will be bound to redeem. Express appointment as Agent by the lender is required and the buyer's practitioner should ask for a copy of the letter of appointment as confirmation. In practice this is unlikely to be forthcoming and the risks attendant upon industry standard completion undertakings will remain. If there is any doubt then we suggest you ascertain the amount required to redeem and on the day of completion send the redemption amount direct to the lender and the balance to the seller's solicitor.

It should be remembered that a crucial element of the Law Society's Code for Completion is that the buyer's solicitor appoints the seller's solicitor as his or her unpaid agent for completion. Furthermore, the seller's solicitor must confirm instructions from the seller to receive the sale monies and that he or she has been appointed the authorised agent of any lender authorising the receipt of monies required to redeem.

Mortgages and their repayment regularly feature at completion. Consequently, another problem might occur when the lender is not a member of the Council of Mortgage Lenders. This is because members of the Council will stand by redemption statements issued by them before completion and relied upon at completion but which may ultimately prove to be incorrect. In effect this means that a deed of discharge, forming the subject matter of an undertaking, will be issued even if the lender has issued incorrect figures (and therefore has received incorrect redemption monies).

This is not the case for non-members, who can agree or indeed disagree about the amount required to redeem even though completion may have already taken place and undertakings issued. If there is a lender that is not a Council member then it is recommended that actual redemption take place along with completion, probably at the offices of the lender or the offices of the lender's solicitor. Typical members of the Council include the Abbey National Plc., the Britannia Building Society, the Co-operative Insurance

Society Ltd and HSBC Bank Plc. These represent archetypal lenders that are former building societies, existing building societies, insurance companies and high street banks.

Additionally, a redemption statement should be read circumspectly to check assumptions made by the lender about payments to be made by the borrower. It might assume that the next instalment due before completion but after the date of the statement will be made. If it does, the seller must make that payment or a shortfall will arise.

How payment is made at completion can amount to another cause for concern. Standard condition 6.7 in the 4th Edition of the Standard Conditions stipulates that the buyer is to pay over the completion monies in one way:

'The buyer is to pay the money due on completion by credit transfer and, if appropriate, an unconditional release of a deposit held by a stakeholder.'

Accordingly, the only contractually approved method of payment is by direct electronic bank transfer. You should immediately appreciate the lack of any reference to payment by cheque. Of course this can always be agreed between the parties and the terms of the contract amended accordingly. However, in practice, payment at completion by cheque is quite rare. This is because a cheque can be stopped before payment, or perhaps even dishonoured at the bank. (The bank might take this action should there be insufficient funds to pay the amount on the face of the cheque). Building society cheques (i.e. cheques drawn on an account of the society itself, sometimes called a counter cheque) are rarely stopped, but there is still the potential problem of dishonesty affecting the validity and or acceptability of the cheque.

In all the circumstances practitioners are advised not to accept cheques on completion, even client account cheques, and to insist on standard condition 6.7 prevailing. (Moreover, if you did so without instructions from the client approving such a payment method, then there could be a claim for negligence, see *Pape v. Westacott* [1894] 1 QB 272.) Two further points are worth noting. First, in theory, where a practitioner as a stakeholder is holding a deposit, the buyer's practitioner should give the stakeholder a written release authorising payment of the deposit to the seller. Bearing in mind that in many cases the seller's solicitor or licensed conveyancer will be the stakeholder as well, it is rare for there to be such a written release, as it is simply implied. If, unusually, the deposit is with the selling agents, then a written release may be necessary.

Secondly, if the buyer offers to pay in legal tender (here meaning banknotes), you should immediately be concerned about the dangers of money laundering. This is an increasingly important area and a professional conduct matter that should always be uppermost in the minds of conveyancing practitioners. Where you act for that buyer you need to be sure that the client is not committing a money laundering offence. A practitioner is in danger of committing an offence by not reporting such circumstances. Efforts should therefore be made to investigate the source of these cash funds and indeed the identity of the client. Any cause for concern should be reported to the firm's money laundering officer with a view to reporting the matter to an external authority and in particular the National Criminal Intelligence Service.

8.3 SUBJECT ASSESSMENTS

It is inevitable that you will encounter some or all of the topics covered in this chapter in a subject assessment of Property Law and Practice or Conveyancing. Pre-completion searches and completion can be problems areas in practice and if for no other reason examiners will want to be sure that students have a thorough grounding in these often complex areas.

8.3.1 **SUBJECT ASSESSMENT QUESTIONS: A COMMENTARY UPON THE TYPE AND CONTENT OF SUBJECT ASSESSMENT QUESTION AND SUGGESTED ANSWERS**

Question 1

Your clients The Moorcroft Business Parks Company Limited and Derek Land are purchasing together as a joint venture from Wayne Colin Lime part of his new office and shop development being 1 to 16 (out of the whole development numbering 1 to 32) The Central Street in Brantwood for £975,000. They are buying with the aid of a proposed first mortgage of £750,000 from the Barchester Bank Plc. for whom you are also acting. The title number is AGP 362638. Contracts were exchanged two weeks ago and completion is due in two weeks' time.

(a) Please list the pre-completion searches you would arrange and explain your reasons for doing so.

(b) What would change if your client were purchasing an unregistered property and why?

(c) Would your answer be different if the seller was a limited company?

Commentary

This is a question in this area that could appear in subject assessment papers with predictable regularity. If there is one area of paramount importance within pre-completion procedures then this must be it. Searches at this stage of a conveyance are of critical significance and will therefore be central to the examination of your knowledge of the conveyancing process. As is always the case with subject assessment questions, information is contained within it for a reason. For example here you have been told that you also act for the Bank. This should immediately raise alarm bells in your mind that your set of double instructions will mean additional information required in your answer. Similarly the reference in the latter part of the question to changes consequent upon the property being unregistered will require you to highlight the alternate searches required for unregistered land. The question also talks about 'searches you would arrange'. This is because you should also arrange to have the property to be purchased inspected before completion. You should always refer to a pre-completion property inspection as a search in an answer of this kind. (Remember the effects of *Williams & Glyn's Bank Ltd v. Boland* [1981] AC 487 and the fact that commercial lessees can leave premises without warning.) Finally, you will also need to show the need for an extra search should the seller be a limited company.

Suggested answer

The searches required in the several situations contemplated by this question are as follows:

1. Registered land
   (a) land registry search—OS2
   (b) bankruptcy search against one of the buyers—K16
   (c) inspection of the property

2. Unregistered land
   (a) land charges search—K15
   (b) bankruptcy search against one of the buyers—K16
   (c) inspection of the property

3. Limited company seller
   (a) as above and also a full search in the Companies Register

1. <u>Registered land</u>

The buyers are purchasing part of a registered property and as a consequence the first pre-completion search that should be carried out is an official search of part of the register at the Land Registry. Buyers should only accept as proof of title official copy entries as searches should not be made against mere photo-copies. Indeed, best practice dictates that searches should only be made against official copy entries that are less than twelve months old. Accordingly the buyer will want to check that there are no additional entries on the register that have not been seen and made since the date of the issue of the official copies. As it would appear that the clients are buying a part of the seller's title the search is carried out on Form OS2 and the search will be from the date of the official copy entries and must be accompanied by a clear scale plan that plainly identifies the property to be sold. The search will reveal whether or not there are any adverse entries made since that date and the buyer is given a priority period of thirty days. This priority period gives the buyers time during which their registration of ownership at the Land Registry can take place with-out regard to any other application adverse or otherwise made during that period.

Apart from the buyer's instructions there are also instructions from the lenders and a bankruptcy search against one of the buyers, (Mr Land), is made on behalf of the Bank. The search is carried out at the Land Charges Registry on Form K16. The purpose is of course to check that this individual buyer is not an undis-charged bankrupt. Any adverse entry disclosed could very well mean that the mortgage offer is withdrawn and as a consequence any such entry has to be reported to the lender without delay.

Finally the subject property should be inspected prior to completion. The reason for this is primarily to check on exactly who is in occupation. The existence of a third party occupant might amount to an over-riding interest to which the purchase would be subject. (As was the case in *Williams & Glyn's Bank Ltd v. Boland* [1981] AC 487.)

2. Unregistered land

If the property is unregistered then two of the three searches mentioned above would still apply, and for the same reasons. Accordingly, the bankruptcy search would be carried out and the pre-completion inspection would still be necessary. However if the land is unregistered an official search of the register at the Land Register would be wholly inappropriate and should be replaced by a land charges search in the regis-ters maintained by the Central Land Charges Department in Plymouth. Section 198 of the Law of Property Act 1925 provides that registration is deemed to be actual notice of any registrable matter whether or not a search is carried out. It is therefore imperative to make such a search against all estate owners on Form K15. A period of years is required for each estate owner but when in doubt the period can be expressed to be from 1925 to the year the search is being made. Any adverse entries will be disclosed on the search result including a puisne mortgage, an estate contract such as an option to purchase or a restrictive covenant affecting the property. (In domestic transactions, registrations under the Family Law Act 1996 will also be disclosed.) The search result confers a priority period of fifteen working days upon the searcher/applicant. Accordingly, if completion takes place during this period, the searcher/applicant will take free of any entries placed on the register between the date of the search and the completion date, on the proviso that com-pletion did indeed take place within the priority period. (You should note that it is not necessary to apply for first registration of title within the search priority period; the time limit is simply two months from the completion date. See s. 6(4) of the Land Registration Act 2002.)

3. Limited company seller

If the seller is a limited company then there will be an alteration to the list of searches required and the additional search will apply to both registered and unregistered land. Where the seller is a company, a search of the Companies Register at Companies House should be carried out. This can either be done in person or through search agents. In the case of registered land a companies search will be necessary because a buyer may wish to be sure that the company still subsists and has not been struck off the register, perhaps for failing to file returns. Of course if the company were subject to winding up proceedings these too would be shown by this search and would be information that a buyer would need to be aware of in the context of the imminence of completion. If the land is registered then there is no need to carry out a company search to check on financial charges made by the company, as they will only bind a purchaser if they are registered at the land registry.

In the case of unregistered land the company search is very important. The search will reveal floating charges, specific charges created before 1 January 1970 and the commencement of winding up proceedings. All three items are of material importance to a buyer and any such registration would be clearly adverse. No purchaser should proceed until the seller has in the appropriate way shown how and when the adverse entry would be dealt with. Bearing in mind that any disposition by a company subject to winding up proceedings is void, (s. 127 Insolvency Act 1986), it will be appreciated just how important a company search can be. Finally it should be noted that there is no priority period of protection available for a company search. Consequently such a search should therefore be made immediately before completion.

Question 2

Your clients Mr and Mrs Gerry Zamora are buying a house and paddock at 1 Alma Terrace Hassocks with the aid of a Florian Building Society mortgage for whom you also act. The house is registered with title absolute, while the paddock is unregistered. The unregistered title is simple being just a conveyance made sixteen years ago between the original sellers Gesso Estates Plc. and the present seller Wayne Faience Limited. This serves as the root of title and there are no other deeds involved in the abstract of title.

You have just been passed the file by your supervising Partner who has pointed out that contracts were exchanged two months ago on the first of June and completion is due in two days time, on the third August next. The contract provides for vacant possession on completion. She has also said that everything has been done in readiness for completion, but would you please check the papers and in particular the searches. She added that the person who previously had the conduct of this matter has now left the firm. All requisitions have been raised and answered, the purchase deed settled and the firm is in funds in readiness for completion.

You have looked at the file and you have noted that there is a clear land charges search result against Wayne Faience for the proper sixteen-year period and this search was issued by the Land Charges Department on the first July. There is also a clear OS1 search disclosing no adverse entries that was issued by the Land Registry on the second July. There are no other searches. Please advise your supervising partner of the position on the file as far as searches are concerned.

Commentary

This question is of course about searches again but this time you are required to evaluate whether or not the position as shown in the question is acceptable. Clearly the position cannot be right otherwise there would be little or no point to the question! So your job is to highlight just what is wrong with the file. Frankly in the light of the several difficulties contained within the paperwork it is not surprising that the person who previously had the conduct of the file has now left the firm.

You should expect just this kind of question in a Property Law and Practice subject assessment and indeed you are likely to encounter similar problems in actual practice. Consequently, this style of question is one you should anticipate particularly where searches and time limits are concerned. Indeed time limits can amount to a property practitioner's nightmare and for this reason if nothing else an examiner will return to the topic time and time again. As to the format of the answer you should prepare a memorandum of advice for your supervising partner. It is best practice to show at the start of the answer the faults that you have identified so that the examiner's attention is seized from the very outset. After that you can go on to show why there are these faults and what should be done to remedy them. Finally, please be aware that the answer requires you to consider errors and omissions. As ever with almost any examination or subject assessment question in this area you will need to highlight what has been left out as much as correct what has been stated.

Suggested answer

RICHARDS ABBEY AND PARTNERS, SOLICITORS
OFFICE MEMORANDUM

To   The Supervising Partner

From   The Trainee Solicitor

Re 1 Alma Terrace Hassocks

I refer to this file that you passed to me concerning this proposed purchase by Mr and Mrs Zamora and set out below my report on the file as far as searches are concerned. To begin with I can confirm that I have identified the following areas of difficulty that I will explain subsequently:

1. The land charges search is unreliable for two reasons.

2. The Land Registry search is unreliable.

3. There is no company search.

4. There is no bankruptcy search, and,

5. there does not seem to have been any pre-completion reinspection of the property.

1. The land charges search

This must be resubmitted to the Land Charges Department, as the existing search is invalid. First, the search was made against the wrong name. The seller is Wayne Faience Limited while the search has been made against Wayne Faience. For the search to be valid the full and proper name of the estate owner must be quoted. (See *Oak Co-Operative Building Society v. Blackburn* [1986] Ch 730.) Secondly, the search is now out of date. An official search provides a priority period of protection for a buyer such that no registration made at the Registry after the date of the search result will be binding on the buyer if the completion of the relevant transaction takes place within fifteen working days of the result. On the facts contained within the file the search result is out of date and cannot be relied upon.

2. The Land Registry Search

This must be resubmitted to the Land Registry, as the existing search is out of date. An official search provides a priority period of protection for a buyer such that no application made at the Land Registry after the date of the search result will be binding on the buyer provided the buyer lodges his application for registration at the Land Registry within the priority period of thirty working days from the date of the result. From the facts within the file this cannot be done and the existing search cannot be relied upon.

3. Company search

A search of the file has failed to show a company search. The seller is Wayne Faience Limited, a limited company. This seller is selling both registered and unregistered land and in both cases a company search at Companies House is vital. In both cases a search will reveal if there are subsisting winding up proceedings or if the company has been struck off say for failing to file returns. In the case of the unregistered land the search will show many critical matters including floating charges registered only at Companies House and pre 1970 specific charges. I therefore recommend an immediate company search and shall I instruct our search agents to proceed?

4. Bankruptcy search

We are acting for the Building Society as well as the buyers. We have an obligation to them to check on the status of the proposed borrowers. To do this a K16 bankruptcy search at the Land Charges Department is required. It will reveal whether there are pending bankruptcy actions or whether either is an undischarged bankrupt. A search of the file has failed to show this vital search and one should be made immediately. If we did not carry out this search we would be in breach of our duty to the proposed lender. They require to know, before completion of the loan, that the proposed borrowers are persons to whom they may lend. Clearly any involvement in bankruptcy proceedings would need to be reported to the lenders.

5. Pre-completion inspection

There is no note on the file to show that anyone has carried out an inspection of the property. Similarly I cannot see any letter to the clients suggesting that they themselves carry out such an inspection. This is an oversight and I would recommend that either the clients or I go and inspect the property now. I make this suggestion as I see that the contract provides for vacant possession on completion. It will be necessary to check the subject to ensure that vacant possession will indeed be available and that there are no undis-closed third party occupants. If there are, their occupation could amount to an overriding interest. For this reason alone it is vital to reinspect and at the same time other checks can be made such as the continued existence of chattels to be left at the property at completion. Clearly if there is anything amiss then it would need to be resolved by the seller before completion. (Please see *Williams & Glyn's Bank v. Boland* [1980] 2 All ER 408 which highlights the possible dangers of third party occupants.)

   In all the circumstances I suggest the position is retrievable by repeating the two out of date searches, by making a company search and a bankruptcy search and by arranging an inspection of the property.

TIME TAKEN 45 MINUTES

TRAINEE SOLICITOR

Question 3

Your client is Susan Dawkins who is due to buy the freehold property being 6 Devon Rise Evesham on the completion date in five days' time. The purchase price is £99,000. Your client paid a deposit of £1,250 on exchange and a preliminary deposit of £250 was paid to the estate agents acting for the seller Nevis Browne. You have mortgage instructions from the Hampshire Building Society, for a proposed loan of £62,750, from which you have noted the following:

1. There is a mortgage commission deduction of £695.

2. There is a indemnity policy premium charged of £425.

3. There is a completion monies transfer fee charged of £26, and

4. there is a Society minimum membership fee of £15.

Your principal has advised you that the firm's fees will be £295 exclusive and that the Land Registry fees are £180. You have checked the accounts ledger for the client in the accounts department and have noted the following debit entries in the office account:

1. local search fee	£175
2. Coal search fee	£25.50
3. commons search	£10
4. land charges fee	£2
5. L.R. search fee	£5

Because completion is fast approaching your principal has asked you to immediately prepare a completion statement for the buyer. You have also been asked to write a letter to Susan Dawkins, enclosing the statement, to explain the contents and to explain how the shortfall is to be paid.

Your principal will prepare the actual bill of costs. Please provide a draft of the statement and accompanying letter.

Commentary

It is now common practice in modern Property Law and Practice subject assessments or exams to advise candidates to bring with them into the examination a calculator. This question shows why this is necessary! You may find just such a question in your Property Law and Practice subject assessment, as examiners are keen to ensure that you understand the financial mechanisms involved. In the final analysis Property Law and Practice is a practical subject where legal theory is applied to commonplace situations like buying a property. The most practical element of the whole process is completion when the purchase price is paid and the deeds handed over. However there are of course two sides to the transaction and a buyer will be involved in financial matters just as much as the seller. It is for this reason that a completion statement will be required for the buyer and will have to be prepared by the buyer's lawyer.

This question looks quite straightforward. Indeed in most respects that is indeed true. However, as you will have come to expect nothing in Property Law and Practice is as simple as it seems. First the legal fees are expressed to be exclusive. This should immediately make you appreciate that you must consider VAT. Secondly, the purchase price is £89,000 and this again should make you realise that not all the necessary facts and figures have been set out in the question. As the payment in question is the largest the buyer will have to make it is important that it is not overlooked!

Finally, as to the style of the answer all you need to do is provide a short introduction and then set out the draft completion statement followed by the draft letter. An essay would be quite inappropriate.

Suggested answer

There are set out below drafts of the completion statement and accompanying letter for Susan Dawkins. Two points were not mentioned and which have been incorporated in the drafts namely VAT on the legal costs and stamp duty land tax of 1% of the purchase price.

1. DRAFT COMPLETION STATEMENT

6 Devon Rise Evesham

Browne to Dawkins

Purchase price		£99,000.00
DEDUCT deposits paid		
On exchange	£1,250.00	
To Agents	£250.00	
	£1,500.00	£1,500.00
		£97,500.00
DEDUCT net mortgage		
Gross advance	£62,750.00	
Less retention	695.00	
Less indemnity fee	£425.00	
Less transfer fee	£26.00	
Less membership fee	£1.00	
NET advance	£61,603.00	£61,603.00
		£35,897.00

ADD stamp duty at 1%   £990.00
                                                          £36,887.00

ADD costs and other payments
         Legal fees   £295.00
         VAT thereon @ 17.5%   £51.63
         Local search fee   £175.00
         Coal search fee   £25.50
         Commons search fee   £10.00
         Land Charges fee   £2.00
         Land Registry fee   £180.00
         Land Reg. search fee   £5.00
                                     £744.13   £744.13
REQUIRED from you   £37,631.13

2. DRAFT LETTER TO THE CLIENT

Dear Ms Dawkins,

6 Devon Rise Evesham

I refer to your purchase of the above property and now write to let you have details of the amount required by this firm to enable us to complete the transaction. As you will recall completion is due in five days' time.

Please find enclosed a completion statement giving details of the amounts involved. The statement shows the purchase price from which you will see the deposits have been deducted as well as the net amount available from the Building Society. To explain the deductions from the advance you should first refer to your mortgage offer. However to clarify all these deductions have been made by the Society in accordance with their offer. The net advance is the amount that we will receive from the Society. The mortgage commission is a deduction by the Society for their commission that they have charged you for making this loan. The indemnity premium has been explained in the offer but if you require further information please let me know. The transfer fee is a bank charge made and deducted by the Society for the transfer of the net advance to our account.

I have shown stamp duty as a separate item as this will be your largest payment. This is a simple tax at 1% of the full purchase price and I will have to pay this to the Inland Revenue within 30 days of completion to avoid a penalty fee being levied for late payment.

As to this firm's costs please find enclosed a note of our charges [NB to be drafted by principal] which I trust meet with your approval and accord with the original estimate given to you at the start of the transaction. For the sake of clarity I have set out on the completion statement the legal fees and the VAT thereon together with all other payments being what lawyers term disbursements. In the main these are search fees to be paid on your behalf along with fees to the Land Registry for the registration of your ownership of the property at the government Land Registry. If any items are still unclear please do not hesitate to contact me and I will provide further detailed clarification.

In the end the amount required from you to enable us to complete is £37,631.13. Solicitors are required by the Law Society to be in possession of cleared funds to enable them to pay out monies from those funds. In effect this means that all cheques received must be fully cleared before payment is made. If you pay these monies by cheque then I will have to specially clear that cheque in view of the short period of time before completion. This will incur an additional disbursement being a bank special clearance fee. However I can only accept such a cheque within the next two days otherwise there will not be enough time to clear the cheque. Accordingly I would appreciate it if you could please let me have a payment of the sum concerned by a Banker's Draft that is tantamount to cash and does not need clearance. You can obtain this from your own bankers. However as the draft is in effect cash please deliver it by hand or special delivery post.

If there are any points you are not clear on please let me know and I will do my best to assist but in the meantime I await a banker's draft for the sum mentioned above to enable me to proceed.

Yours sincerely.

Question 4

You act for Robert Morrison who has contracted to sell his freehold shop and upper part being 88 Victoria Road Newcastle with vacant possession for £159,950 to Alison Tasker. The property is registered. Completion is due in four days' time. Your supervisor is just about to go on holiday and has asked you to help with the transaction. You have to prepare a completion statement for the other side and a draft completion statement for the client.

You have looked at the file and have noted the following details:

1. The selling agents hold a deposit of £100.

2. A deposit was paid to the firm on exchange of £8,000.

3. There is a first mortgage with Lloyds Bank where the redemption figure is £62,356.55.

4. There is a second charge with ABC Loans plc where the redemption figure is £19,955.32.

5. The Estate Agent's fees are £3758.83 inclusive.

6. Official copies cost £10.

7. Our legal fees were originally quoted at £575 exclusive.

8. The contract provides for the sale of chattels at a price of £975.

Please draft the statements required together with a letter to the client explaining the contents of his completion statement.

Commentary

This is another example of a Property Law and Practice question that requires a calculator but this time from the seller's perspective. If you are confident about your knowledge of the conveyancing process and also your mathematical ability then this is the question for you. Frankly, the question is perfectly straightforward and high marks can be obtained if you carefully structure the two statements. There is no mention of any allied purchase for your client and as this would seem to be a business rather than a domestic conveyance you could ask the client if the net proceeds of the sale are to be issued direct to the client or whether they can be placed on deposit.

Suggested answer

There are set out below drafts of the completion statements and accompanying letter for Robert Morrison. It is assumed that a bill of costs will be prepared in addition to the documents set out below.

1. Completion statement for the buyer

COMPLETION STATEMENT

88 Victoria Road Newcastle

Morrison to Tasker

Purchase price	£159,950.00

DEDUCT deposits paid

On exchange	£800.00	
To agents	£100.00	
	£8,100.00	£8,100.00
		£151,850.00

ADD amount payable for chattels £975.00

TOTAL payable on completion £152,825.00

2. Completion statement for the seller

COMPLETION STATEMENT

88 Victoria Road Newcastle

Morrison to Tasker

Sale price		£159,950.00
ADD amount payable for chattels		£975.00
		£160,925.00

DEDUCT mortgage redemption monies

Lloyds Bank	£62,356.55	
ABC Loans plc	£19,955.32	
	£82,311.87	£82,311.87
		£78,613.13

| DEDUCT estate agents charges | £3,758.83 |
| | £74,854.30 |

| DEDUCT Land Registry copy deeds fee | £10.00 |
| | £74,844.30 |

DEDUCT Legal fees

Agreed costs	£575.00	
ADD VAT (17.5%)	£100.63	
	£675.63	£675.63

BALANCE DUE TO YOU, see letter attached, £74,168.67

3. DRAFT LETTER TO THE SELLER

Dear Mr Morrison,

<u>88 Victoria Road Newcastle</u>

I refer to your sale of the above property where completion is due in four days' time and now write to provide you with financial details. Please find enclosed a completion statement giving details of all monies received, paid out and to be paid out. A formal account for our fees has been sent to you in a separate letter today. You will see that the sale price of the chattels has been added to the sale price of the property as of course both amounts will be paid on completion. The first deductions after that are the repayments of the two mortgages to the bank and to the loan company. These have been calculated by the lenders and checked by us and include all interest payable up to and including the date of sale.

The estate agent's charges will be paid by us, in accordance with your letter of instructions received last week confirming that we should proceed so to do. I can confirm that their account will be paid on the basis of their fees at 3% of the sale price with value added tax thereon. I will seek a receipted invoice from the agents and send it to you when I receive it as I imagine that you will require this for your accountants for tax purposes.

The only other deductions are the Land Registry copy deeds fee and this firm's costs. The Land Registry copy deeds fee is the amount they levy for official copies of your deeds that we are required to send to the buyers to prove your title to this property. As to our costs these were originally quoted to you at the level of £575 being the amount you subsequently agreed and they remain at this agreed level. As you will appreciate, these fees attract VAT at 17.5% amounting to £100.63. For the sake of clarity I have shown these separately and then on a combined basis for the costs and VAT. If you have any queries on this or any other points arising from the details supplied please do not hesitate to contact me and I will do all that I can to clarify matters.

In the end I have shown the net proceeds of sale and due to you on completion. I can either send this amount to you immediately on completion or I can if you wish place the monies on deposit until you have made a further decision as to the ultimate destination for the monies. If you require the monies to be sent to you I can do this by cheque or by bank transfer. The latter is quicker but I would have to deduct the bank charges of about £26 for sending the money in this way. If I am to send the money by transfer I will require your full bank details. I await your kind instructions.

Yours sincerely

8.3.2 MULTIPLE CHOICE QUESTIONS AND ANSWERS TO MULTIPLE CHOICE QUESTIONS

We set out below examples of ten multiple choice questions that you might encounter in a subject assessment. Thereafter you will find some typical short answer questions that can also feature in a subject assessment and which cover pre-completion and completion matters. Answers to both are also set out below. Remember our initial guidance. Never leave multiple choice answers with a blank multiple choice. If there are four possibilities and you are not sure of the answer select the one you think might be right, you have a one in four chance of getting it right! Also look at the instructions on the paper. If it says select the right answer on the paper by circling the correct choice then do just that. Do not make a tick or underline your selection, as the strict response would be to fail you even though the selection may be correct. Also none of the answers given might be right. In these circumstances follow the rubric in the question paper and explain why none of the listed answers apply.

8.3.2.1 Multiple choice questions

Unless otherwise directed, select the right answer by circling it in each question. Should you think that none of the selections apply please explain why not in your answer book.

1. You are buying for a client a commercial unit in Hackney in the centre of London. It is registered and your client is a company that is a cash buyer. Which of the following searches will you make before completion?:
   (a) local land charge search
   (b) land charges search
   (c) Land Registry search
   (d) bankruptcy search

2. You client has instructed you to complete a purchase of a new residential flat in a newly erected block in the centre of Liverpool. You have exchanged and completion is next week. The title to the whole block is registered under title number LPL 362638 and our client is a cash buyer. Which of the following searches will you make before completion?:

   (a) OS1
   (b) K15
   (c) OS2
   (d) K16

3. You act for the buyer of an unregistered title in North Yorkshire. You have just completed your final land charges search and this reveals a C(i) entry affecting the title. Which of the following should you do?:

   (a) identify this as a limited owner's charge and ask the seller to make arrangements to pay off the outstanding tax
   (b) recognise this as a general equitable charge and ask the seller to clarify the nature of the charge
   (c) identify this as an estate contract and ask the seller to explain how the entry relates and how it will be removed
   (d) recognise this as a puisne mortgage (a second charge) and ask the seller to confirm that it will be discharged on completion

4. If a lease is granted, containing restrictive covenants for the lessee to perform, and the lease is unregistered then you should register them as a D(ii) land charge to ensure their enforceability.

   Is this statement TRUE/FALSE? Please delete the incorrect choice.

5. The priority period for a land registry search result is thirty days.

   Is this statement TRUE/FALSE? Please delete the incorrect choice.

6. Section 47(9) of the Law of Property Act 1925 authorises a seller to retain deeds and documents of title when that seller retains any part of the land comprised within that title. Consequently, at completion where there has been a sale of part of an unregistered title the seller will:

   (a) give the buyer only one of the several original conveyances forming part of the seller's title
   (b) give the buyer all but the last conveyance (the one to the seller) from the seller's title deeds
   (c) ensure that a full set of photocopies of all the deeds will be handed over at completion
   (d) ensure that examined photocopies of the deeds or an examined abstract are handed over at completion.

7. At completion the seller's practitioner confirms that an END will deal with the seller's mortgage. This means that:

   (a) when the lender is satisfied that their charge has been redeemed in full an END is sent to the Land Registry over the Land Registry Direct System
   (b) when the buyer is satisfied that the charge has been redeemed in full an END is sent to the Land Registry over the Land Registry Direct System
   (c) when the borrower is satisfied that the charge has been redeemed in full an END is sent to the Land Registry over the Land Registry Direct System
   (d) When the Land Registry is satisfied that the charge has been redeemed in full an END is issued by the Land Registry via the Land Registry Direct System

8. The Law Society's code for completion by post includes the crucial element that the buyer's solicitor appoints the seller's solicitor as his or her unpaid agent for completion.

   Is this statement TRUE/FALSE? Please delete the incorrect choice.

9. A contract not relying on the Standard Conditions stipulates that the buyer is to pay over the completion monies in one or more of the following ways:

   (a) legal tender

   (b) a banker's draft

   (c) a direct credit to a bank account nominated by the seller's solicitor

   (d) a solicitor's client account cheque

   Please select the choice that would otherwise be within the Standard Conditions.

10. Acting for a buyer at completion of the purchase of a registered freehold subject to a first charge, which of the following might you expect to receive in exchange for the purchase monies:

    (a) the transfer duly signed and dated

    (b) the charge certificate

    (c) Form DS1

    (d) the keys

    Please select the choice NOT available at completion.

8.3.2.2 *Answers to multiple choice questions*

1. The correct selection is (c). As the property is registered and your client is a company the only pre-completion search listed that will apply is a Land Registry search. A local search is carried out before exchange, a land charges search is only necessary for unregistered land and your client is a company so the bankruptcy search is inappropriate.

2. The correct selection is (c). As the property is registered and your client is buying a new flat forming part of the seller's title, the only pre-completion search listed that will apply is an OS2 being a search of part. The remaining searches are inappropriate because an OS1 is a search of whole, (and your client is only buying part), a K16 is only relevant to unregistered land and a K16 is a bankruptcy search (used by lenders to ensure a borrower is solvent) that is not required as your client is a cash buyer.

3. The correct answer is (d). A C(i) entry relates to unregistered title second mortgages that cannot be protected by the deposit of title deeds, the first lender being in possession of them.

4. The statement is false. This registration covers restrictive covenants created after 1925, other than restrictive covenants in a lease (or a pre-1926 restrictive covenant). Lease covenants are not registrable as D(ii)'s because their enforceability depends upon landlord and tenant law and the enforcement of covenants between such parties.

5. This statement is false. The priority period for a registered land search is 30 *working* days. Weekends and bank holidays are therefore excluded from the days counted for priority purposes.

6. The correct answer is (d). If within the title there has been a sale of part then some original deeds may not be available. (s. 47(9) of the Law of Property Act 1925 authorises a seller to retain deeds and documents of title when that seller retains any part of the land comprised within that title.) If this is the case then a careful check must be made to ensure that examined copies or an examined abstract is handed over at completion and not mere photocopies

7. The correct answer is (a). The Land Registry has been developing a scheme with lenders that will make DS1 forms a rarity. It has been using an Electronic Notification of Discharge (END) to replace the DS1.

When the lender is satisfied that their charge has been redeemed in full an END is sent to the Land Registry by the lender computer over the Land Registry Direct System.

8. The statement is true. The crucial element of the Code is that the buyer's solicitor appoints the seller's solicitor as his or her unpaid agent for completion. The buyer's solicitor must provide full instructions for the 'agent' relating to the buyer's requirements. These instructions should clearly set out for the seller's solicitor what the buyer's solicitor requires him or her to do and what is to be sent on from the seller to the buyer, after completion has been effected. The seller's solicitor must confirm instructions from the seller to receive the sale monies and that he or she has been appointed the authorised agent of any lender authorising the receipt of monies required to redeem.

9. The choice covered by the standard conditions is (c). Completion monies can only be paid pursuant to standard conditions 6.7 by a direct electronic bank transfer with a release of any deposit held by a stakeholder.

10. The correct answer is none can be selected as they could all be available at completion! Therefore as none of the selections apply you should explain why not in your answer book. Since 13 October 2003 the land or charge certificate is no longer required when submitting a transfer for registration and need not be handed over at completion. However, best practice dictates that the seller should hand over the certificate especially if it contains other documents such a conveyance containing restrictive covenants. The transfer duly signed and dated must be handed over at completion along with Form DS1. Finally the keys can be available at completion.

8.3.3 SHORT ANSWER QUESTIONS WITH ANSWERS

Question 1

You are acting for Brian Deepdale on a purchase of registered land and you are due to complete next Thursday. You have completed your Land Registry OS1 search and the result has just arrived. The search result is attached. Is it acceptable? If not please say why not and what should be done, if anything.

Question 2

You are acting on a purchase of unregistered land being The High Street Wimble Worcestershire DY41 5XH and you are due to complete next Thursday. You have completed your Land Charges K15 search and the result has just arrived. The search result is attached. Is it acceptable? If not please say why not and what should be done, if anything.

Question 3

You are acting on the sale of a commercial property. Completion is due tomorrow. The title is in two parts, both registered freehold, but one part is a part of title sale while the other is a sale of the whole title. The latter title is subject to one mortgage but the former is not subject to any encumbrance other than an occupational fifteen-year lease with eleven years still unexpired. The buyer is aware of the lease as it was disclosed in the contract and is to take over the receipt of the rent at completion. Your Principal has asked you to list the documents to be handed over at completion. Please list the relevant items.

8.3.4 *Suggested answers to short answer questions*

Question 1

There are two entries disclosed in the search result. The first is really procedural in that a new edition of the register has been opened and a new set of official copies of the title showing the entries subsisting has been disclosed. The result is subject to such entries. An immediate comparison of the new entries should be made of the old set originally supplied by the seller. If they are the same then nothing more needs to be done. If there are any changes these must be referred to the seller for clarification and if necessary for removal at the seller's expense. The second entry is more problematic. This appears to be a unilateral or non-consensual notice probably registered by a claimant against the seller as a protective entry possibly for monies due to the claimant from the seller. The entry should be immediately referred to the seller for clarification and for the immediate removal of the entry at the seller's expense

Question 2

The result discloses four estate owners. The first two A.J. and C.M. Wilberforce show no subsisting entries and as such my be safely ignored as being of no consequence. However the following three estate owners disclose entries. A. Ponsonby-Smythe has a D(ii) restrictive covenants entry affecting the subject property. This registration covers restrictive covenants created after 1925, and not restrictive covenants in a lease or pre-1926 restrictive covenants. You need to check if the entry relates to covenants disclosed in the title on or around 2 June 1988. If the entry ties up with disclosed covenants there is nothing more to do. If not you need to require the seller to disclose details and to check that they are not onerous. Immediate reference to the seller of the land charge entry is imperative. The final two entries relate to a C(i) entry, and you need to recognise this as a puisne mortgage (a second charge of unregistered land). This is a legal charge that does not have protection by the deposit of the title deeds. You will have to ask the seller to confirm that it will be discharged on completion.

Question 3

The documents to be handed over are:

1. Transfer (covering both titles but with a scale plan for the transfer of part).
2. Counterpart Lease and any supporting deeds such as licences to assign, etc.
3. Authority from the seller to the lessee for the payment of future rents to the buyer.
4. Any old land or charge certificates to be kept with pre-registration deeds and documents.
5. Form DS1 for the mortgage or an undertaking in the Law Society format. If an END is to be employed then an END undertaking is required.
6. Releases for keys and or deposits paid to the agents and or at the time of exchange.

8.4 REFERENCES TO WIDER READING INCLUDING PRACTITIONER TEXTS

- *A Practical Approach to Conveyancing* by Abbey R. and Richards M. (6th edn, OUP)— Chapter 8.
- *The Law Society's Conveyancing Handbook 10th edn* by Silverman F.—Sections E and F dealing with pre-completion and completion matters.
- *Emmet on Title*:
  —Searches before completion generally—Chapter 8, Part 1
  —Position Pending Completion—Chapter 6
- For more detail on the changes introduced by the Land Registration Act 2002 see *Blackstone's Guide to The Land Registration Act 2002* by Abbey R. and Richards M. (OUP).
- *Textbook on Land Law* by MacKenzie J.-A. and Phillips M. (9th edn OUP)—Chapter 2 (buying a house); Chapter 4 (unregistered land); Chapter 5 (registered land).

8.5 RELEVANT WEBSITES FOR MORE INFORMATION

- Association of British Insurers, http://www.abi.org.uk
  Remember insurance may be required from the time of exchange. Look at the contract terms to check.

- Bank of England, http://www.bankofengland.co.uk

- Companies House, http://www.companieshouse.gov.uk
  You can make on-line pre-completion searches at Companies House. They will be vital in unregistered transactions when the seller is a corporation.

- Council of Mortgage Lenders, http://www.cml.org.uk
  There is an on-line version of the Handbook available at this address and should be referred to in cases of doubt about the requirements of the lender at this stage of the transaction.

- Inland Revenue, http://www.inlandrevenue.gov.uk/home.htm
  The site for information on any problems about the possible payment of stamp duty.

- Land Registry, http://www.landreg.gov.uk
  The location for pre-completion registered land searches.

- Land Registry internet access, http://www.landregistrydirect.gov.uk
  The location for on-line pre-completion registered land searches.

- Location statistics, http://www.upmystreet.com

- National House Building Council, http://www.nhbc.co.uk

- National Land Information Service, http://www.nlis.org.uk
  Almost all pre-completion searches can be made on-line through one of the service providers authorised by the NLIS.

- A street map anywhere in the UK, http://www.streetmap.co.uk

APPENDIX 8.1
LAND REGISTRY SEARCH RESULT

Official Certificate of the Result of Search of Whole	HM Land Registry	Form OS1R

Official search no. 097 - A4-FF	Certificate date [yesterday] Priority Period began at 16:24:45	Priority Period expires on [30 working days time] at midnight but see the note below

Particulars of search as Supplied

Title Number	WCS 1425778
Applicant(s)	Brian Deepdale

Result

It is certified that the official search applied for has been made with the following result:

Since 5 August 2004 a new edition of the register has been opened and an official copy dated 12 August 2004 and timed at 15:04:22 showing the entries subsisting then is enclosed. The result is subject to such entries. If further official search applications are made the "search from" date to be quoted must be the date of the official copy.

UNILATERAL NOTICE registered on the [seven days ago] in favour of Secondary Glazing and Wind- Proofing Plc C/O Maggins & Co 45 Brown Lane Wimble Worcestershire DY44 5CF

******

END OF RESULT

Note: To be sure to obtain priority for your application you should deliver it to the proper office by 12.00 (noon) on the date when priority expires.

Your reference: RM505428	Key Number 1028864	Any enquiries concerning this certificate to be addressed to
RICHARDS ABBEY &CO DX1212 CHANCERY LANE/LONDON		BIRKENHEAD ROSEBRAE DLR ROSEBRAE COURT WOODSIDE FERRY APPROACH BIRKENHEAD MERSEYSIDE CH41 6 DU Tel No: (0151) 472 6666

APPENDIX 8.2
LAND REGISTRY FORM K18

LAND CHARGES ACT, 1972   FORM K18
CERTIFICATE OF THE RESULT OF SEARCH
CERTIFICATE DATE   PROTECTION ENDS ON

PARTICULARS SEARCHED	
COUNTY	WORCESTERSHIRE, HEREFORD AND WORCESTER

[yesterday]   [15 working days ahead]

NAME(S)	PERIOD	Fees £
Particulars of charge		
ALAN JOHN * WILBERFORCE *	1977 - 1988	1.00
NO SUBSISTING ENTRY		
CHRISTINE MARY * WILBERFORCE *	1977 - 1988	1.00
NO SUBSISTING ENTRY		
ANNE * PONSONBY-SMYTHE *	1988 - 1989	1.00
(1) D(ii) NO 10582 DATED 2 JUNE 1988		
(2) 1 THE HIGH STREET DY41 5XH		
(3) WIMBLE		
WORCESTERSHIRE		
THOMAS ANTHONY * BROWN *	1989 - 2003	1.00
(4) C(i) NO 10452 DATED 7 MAY 2000		
(5) 1 THE HIGH STREET DY41 5XH		
(6) WIMBLE		
WORCESTERSHIRE		
PAULENE ANN * BROWN *	1989 - 2003	1.00
(1) C(1) NO 10452 DATED 7 MAY 2000		
(2) 1 THE HIGH STREET DY41 5XH		
(3) WIMBLE		
WORCESTERSHIRE		

----------- END OF SEARCH -----------

APPLICANTS REFERENCE	KEY NUMBER	
RMA505447	107552 AMOUNT DEBITED	£ 5.00

RICHARDS ABBEY & CO. DX1212 CHANCERYLANE/LONDON	Please address any enquiries to HM LAND REGISTRY Land Charges Department Plumer House Crownhill Plymouth PL6 5HY DX no 8249 Plymouth (3) TEL 01752 636666 or 636601 FAX 01752 636699

9 | POST COMPLETION PROCEDURES: DELAYS AND REMEDIES

9.1 INTRODUCTION

Just when the practitioner thinks a sigh of relief is in order now that completion has taken place it is suddenly realised that there is still more to do! Just because completion has successfully passed by does not mean that you can down tools and turn to something else. Stamping, registration and allied topics beckon.

This chapter deals with two areas that provide some of the more direct forms of question that you might encounter in a Property Law and Practice examination. You will be concerned with time limits, with 'what if' scenarios and with the mechanics of stamping and registration. In particular, delays and remedies are a fertile source for assessment questions.

Apart from knowledge of the work that is directly within the conveyancing process and which deals with the closing steps you will also need a basic knowledge of the law of damages. You will need this knowledge in relation to breaches of the terms of conveyancing contracts. There will inevitably be questions centred around a 'what if' scenario arising from one party to the agreement failing to honour their contractual obligations. In these circumstances you will need to show your knowledge and understanding of what claims can arise and what damages can be awarded.

This is an area where lists come into play, for example lists of actions to be taken, documents to be supplied and payments to be made. As a result do not be surprised if your answer must be written as a list. Indeed for many practitioners lists are the way they make sure that they have done all that they need to do on any particular file. Checklists can assist even the most assiduous of conveyancers and should not be looked down upon. If a checklist saves you from acting negligently then it will have done its job, and probably saved yours. Having said that never be a slave to your checklist. Always have regard to the individual matters that require attention in a particular file.

In practice it is usually the buyer that fails to complete, usually because the purchase monies are not available. In any event if the completion date has passed by and a party to the contract has failed to complete standard condition 6.8 will come into consideration. So far as completion is concerned, you are well advised to be fully aware of the terms of standard condition 6. You should be able to commit to memory the basic terms required in a notice to complete and you should be able to confirm when it can be served and how long the period of notice will run and from when the period is to start. As to compensation standard condition 7.3 is also of consequence. As to case law this is one particular area in the conveyancing process where you may be required to demonstrate your knowledge of various recent decisions. You will see this more clearly expressed in the section for question two below. However, statute remains pre-eminent throughout. (This is really the position for conveyancing generally.) In the final analysis you will score high marks if you can show a strong grip upon the practical procedures involved in this end of the conveyancing process.

One factor to be considered at the beginning of this chapter is just what is the effect of completion? In essence, at common law, the contract is considered to be at an end as it is deemed to have merged with the purchase deed. The result of this is that the buyer can only sue the seller under the covenants for title through title guarantee, contained or referred to in the purchase deed; there is no right to sue under the contractual terms. (Merger takes effect only where the contract and purchase deed cover the same subject matter. If the contract contains ancillary matters then merger will not affect these.) However, standard condition 7.4 provides that 'completion does not cancel liability to perform any outstanding obligation under this contract'. This has the effect of negativing the doctrine of merger. Accordingly, if you want merger to apply then an express special condition must be incorporated excluding from the agreement the effect of standard condition 7.4. In the absence of such an exclusion the buyer will still be able to sue the seller for breach of contract once completion has occurred. In practice standard condition 7.4 is rarely excluded.

9.2 AN OVERVIEW OF THE SUBJECT AND A DETAILED LOOK AT SOME PROBLEM AREAS

9.2.1 POST-COMPLETION PROCEDURES

The first flowchart sets out the steps to be taken after completion from the perspective of a practitioner acting for a buyer.

The second flowchart sets out the steps to be taken after completion from the perspective of a practitioner acting for a seller.

9.2.1.1 Company mortgages

When you are acting for a buyer or a lender and in the case of a new mortgage by a company borrower, the mortgage must be lodged and accepted for registration by the Registrar of Companies within twenty-one days of completion. (This must be accompanied by Form 395, particulars of mortgage or charge, and is required by Pt XII of the Companies Act 1985.) If you fail to comply with this very strict time limit, you cannot register the mortgage without an order of the court, and such orders are given only in very exceptional circumstances. (Failure to register is an unanswerable case of professional negligence that would have to be referred to your indemnity insurers.) There is a fee payable for the registration of a charge at Companies House. The papers and fee should be sent to Companies House in Cardiff immediately after completion has occurred.

Acting for a buyer after completion

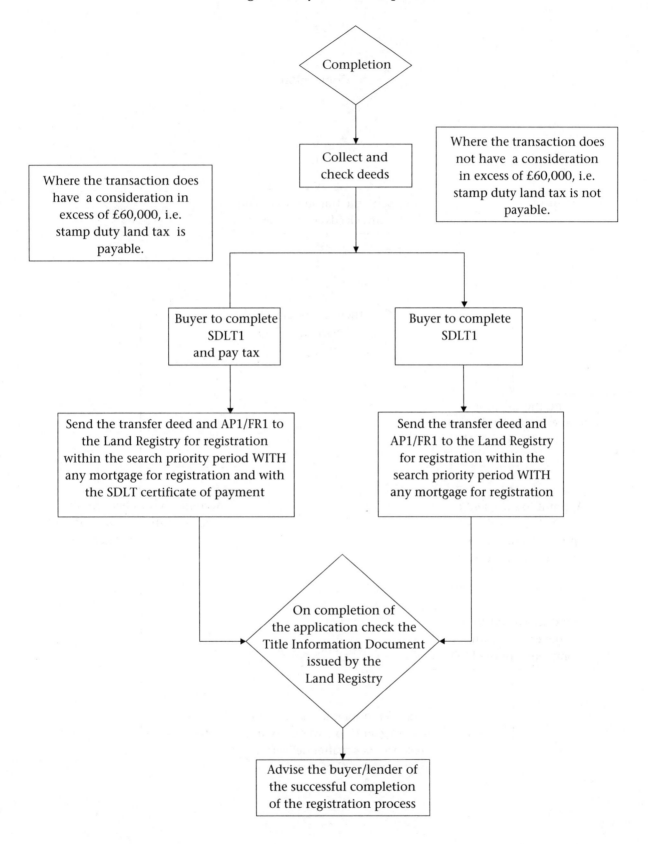

Acting for a seller after completion

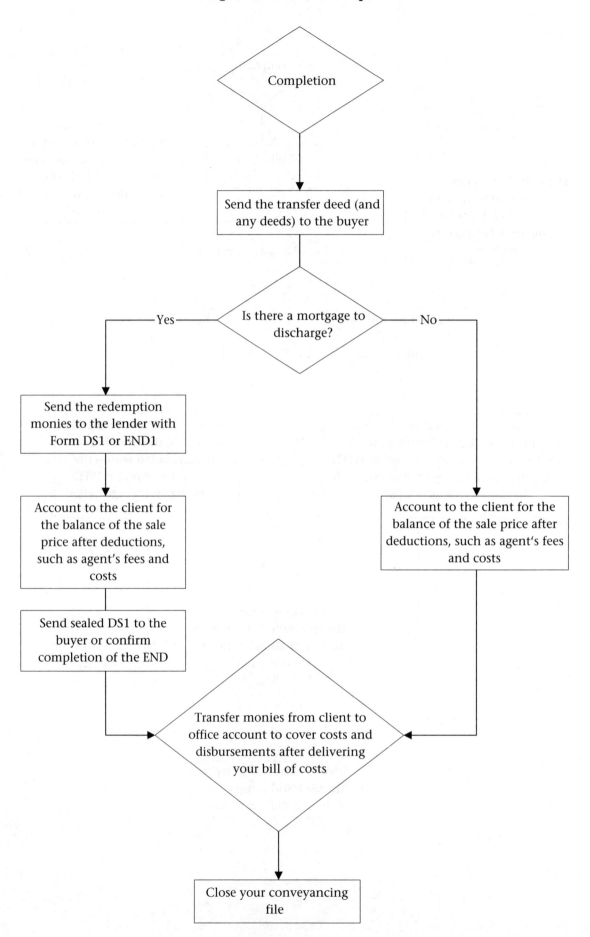

9.2.1.2 **Stamp Duty Land Tax**

Stamp Duty Land Tax is a new tax based on the taxation of transactions in place of deeds or documents which was the case for the old stamp duty regime. It is assessed directly against the buyer rather than the property being purchased. The 2003 Budget set out the details of this reform to the taxation of residential and commercial property transactions. Those details created a new tax, called Stamp Duty Land Tax ('Land Tax'). It would seem that the new tax was introduced for three reasons. First, to further the present governments desire to modernise, secondly, to anticipate the needs of e-conveyancing and thirdly, to try to limit tax avoidance.

The new regime came into force on 1 December 2003. Section 43 of the Finance Act 2003 defines land transactions as the focus for Stamp Duty Land Tax and is an extremely wide definition covering dealings in estates and interests including those that are equitable. The starting threshold for the payment of Land Tax is £60,000 for residential property, but £150,000 for non-residential or commercial properties. To assist in the need to distinguish between residential and non-residential practitioners should note that there is guidance on the Revenue website at http://www.inlandrevenue.gov.uk/so. A selection of simple questions should lead to the Inland Revenue's view of the status of a subject property. Practitioners also need to be aware that transactions under either threshold (£60,000 or £150,000), will be taxed at 0% but will still require a land transaction return to be completed for these transactions. Details of the land transaction returns are set out below. Land Tax will be at 1% on a consideration above £60,000 or £150,000 up to the value of £250,000, 3% for £250,001 to £500,000 and 4% from £500,001. The Revenue will be implementing a regime of random checks to verify that the correct land tax has been paid.

In many disadvantaged areas across England and Wales Land Tax will not be payable on residential transactions where the consideration does not exceed £150,000 and will not be payable at all on non-residential land or commercial transactions. This disadvantaged area relief is also available on new non-residential leases. Similarly, the relief is available on residential leases where the premium does not exceed £150,000 and the average annual rent does not exceed £15,000.

The areas attracting the relief can be identified from a list available on the Inland Revenue website. The website http://www.inlandrevenue.gov.uk/so also contains a search engine, which, if you enter the subject property's postcode, will tell you whether it is in a disadvantaged area. You can also phone the Revenue's enquiry line 08456030135 for assistance. The Land Tax return (see below) contains a box that is completed to show the relief is being claimed. Nothing else is required to make the claim for relief and in particular no certificate is needed in any deed or document other than the Land Tax return.

For transactions in land and buildings in the UK, completed on or after 1 December 2003, practitioners do not need to arrange for documents to be physically stamped. Instead the Revenue will require the completion and submission of a land transaction return to their data capture centre in Merseyside within 30 days of the completion of the transaction. The centre address is Inland Revenue (Stamp/Taxes MSD) Comben House Farriers Way Netherton Merseyside L30 4RN. If a return is filed late the buyer will be liable to a fixed penalty of £100, or if more than three months late, £200. The buyer may also be liable to a tax-related penalty, not to exceed the tax payable.

The land transaction return should be submitted to notify:

1. any transfer of a freehold or assignment or assignation of a lease for consideration, whether or not giving rise to a charge

2. any transaction for which relief is being claimed

3. the grant of a lease for a contractual term of seven years or more or which gives rise to a charge

4. any other transaction giving rise to a charge.

The following transactions are not notifiable and as such no Land Tax return is required. However, a self-certificate will be required to enable the transaction to be registered at the Land Registry:

- The acquisition of a freehold or leasehold interest in land for no chargeable consideration. (Note that there will normally be chargeable consideration where there is a gift of property subject to an existing debt such as a mortgage.)

- Transactions made in connection with the ending of a marriage.

- Transactions varying the dispositions made, whether effected by will or laws of intestacy, within two years after the person's death not involving any consideration in money or money's worth, and

- A transaction which effects something other than a major interest in land chargeable with tax at 0%. An example of such a transaction would be an interest, which is not a major interest in land, such as the grant of an easement where the consideration does not exceed £60,000. This would attract Land Tax at 0%, provided it is not linked to any other transaction that would bring the total consideration to more than £60,000.

The land transaction return, form SDLT1 (supplemented by SDLT2 and 3 and 4) replaces the existing 'Stamps L(A)451' (the 'Particulars Delivered' Form). The effect of this is to abolish the need for and the use of the PD form. Furthermore the Land Tax system means that certificates of value are now redundant and can be excluded from all conveyances and transfers.

For most transactions, the submission of the land transaction return and the correct payment will be all that is required. Payment may be made by cheque, enclosed with the return or electronic payment (BACS, CHAPS, etc.) or at a bank, Post Office or by Alliance and Leicester/Giro account using the payslip included in the return.

The changes to stamp duty also usher in a new regime for the rental element of commercial leases. The new charge will be at a rate of 1% on the net present value (NPV) of the total rent payable over the term of the lease. Future rents will be discounted at 3.5% per annum in order to arrive at the NPV. Leases where the NPV of the rent over the term of the lease does not exceed £150,000 will be exempt. The Revenue have suggested that change in the regime could mean that some 60% of all commercial leases could avoid any Stamp Duty Land Tax on the rental element.

Once the Revenue have received and processed a proper Land Tax return and payment they will issue a certificate of payment. The certificate is issued under s. 79 of the Finance Act 2003 and evidences that Land Tax has been accounted on the particular transaction notified to the Revenue. This must be sent to the Land Registry to enable an application to register to proceed. Finally the rule that deeds were inadmissible in court if they were not stamped will no longer apply. Unstamped deeds and documents can therefore be relied upon in court should reference to them be required.

9.2.1.3 Registration

Section 4 of the Land Registration Act 2002 ('LRA 2002') specifies the events that trigger compulsory registration. Section 4 (1) of the Act calls this the 'requirement of registration'. If you are in any doubt about whether an event induces registration on a compulsory basis, then only the courts can give a definitive interpretation of the section. Registration requirements are dealt with elsewhere, see Chapter 1. Remember that voluntary first registration is possible. The application must be made on Form FR1. Land Registry Form DL, in duplicate, must always accompany Form FR1. On Form DL you must list, in order, all the documents lodged in support of the application for first registration.

You must apply for first registration within two months of the date of completion of the transaction concerned (s. 6(4), LRA 2002). If you do not do so, the transaction becomes void as regards the transfer, grant or creation of a legal estate under s. 7(1), LRA 2002. The effect of this is:

(a) if the transaction was a transfer, conveyance or assent, the legal estate reverts to the transferor, who will hold it on a bare trust for the transferee;

(b) if the transaction was a lease or mortgage, it takes effect as if it were a contract for valuable consideration to grant the lease or mortgage concerned (see s. 7(2), LRA 2002).

As to what deed or document is used to induce first registration, there is a choice. A conveyance of unregistered land must be made by deed, but the form of deed is not required to be in a particular format, so long as it is clear and contains all the provisions that are necessary to give effect to what the parties have agreed. Thus, a conveyance that will lead to compulsory first registration can be made either in the traditional form, i.e. a deed of conveyance or by using the appropriate Land Registry form of transfer, the TR1 or TP1. Accordingly, you may use any form of conveyance that complies with the Law of Property Act 1925, instead of a transfer form. However, transfers are easier to prepare and lend themselves to electronic completion.

9.2.2 DELAYS AND REMEDIES

In an agreement for the sale and purchase of a legal estate in land that is regulated by the standard conditions the completion date will either be specified on the front page of the contract within the particulars or, more rarely, by standard condition 6.1. This states that completion will be twenty working days after the date of the contract. In this way the normal arrangements for completion are straightforward. However, practitioners need to be aware of what is the position should completion be delayed.

9.2.2.1 Late completion

If a contract for the sale and purchase of land states a completion date without qualification, that date is not a strict and binding date that would allow an innocent party to withdraw from the contract on the occasion of a breach, i.e. late completion. On the other hand if it is expressly stated in the agreement that time is of the essence then a strict interpretation arises. Therefore, if there is a failure to complete on the stipulated date then there will be a breach of contract of such magnitude that the innocent party will be free to pursue all remedies, which can include immediate termination or rescission of the contract.

In a contract regulated by the standard conditions, standard condition 6.1 specifically states that time is not of the essence unless a notice to complete is served. The parties to the contract can vary this term to make time of the essence but of course this cannot be achieved unilaterally. To make time of the essence the standard conditions should be varied to delete the word 'not' from standard condition 6.1, and the words 'unless a notice to complete has been served' should be replaced with 'without the necessity for the service of a notice to complete'. In addition the words 'time shall be of the essence of the contract' should be inserted next to the stated completion date. Although this second element is not essential it nevertheless will remind all parties of this critical element of the agreement.

Standard condition 6.8 states that at any time on or after the date fixed for completion, either party who is ready, able and willing to complete may give the other a notice to complete. Standard condition 1.1.3 defines when a party is ready, able and willing, i.e. he or she would have been in a position and ready to complete but for the default of the other party. (If the party concerned is the seller then standard condition 1.1.3(b) states that the seller is so ready even though the property remains subject to a mortgage if the amount to be paid at completion will be enough to pay off that mortgage.) Standard condition 6.8.2 states that the parties are to complete the agreement within ten working days of giving the notice to complete. The ten-day period excludes the day on which the notice is given. The condition goes on to state the essential wording, namely, 'for this purpose, time is of the essence of the contract'.

If you need to serve a notice to complete in connection with a contract incorporating the standard conditions, the following is a suitable precedent. It will be addressed to the defaulting party:

'On behalf of [insert your client seller/buyer and address] we hereby give you NOTICE that with reference to the contract dated [insert the date of the agreement] and made between [insert the seller's full names and the buyer's full names] for the sale and purchase of [insert the property address or description in the contract] we place on record the fact that the sale/purchase of the property has not been completed on the date fixed in the contract for completion. We further give you NOTICE that the seller/buyer [delete the party not ready] is ready able and willing to complete. We therefore give you NOTICE pursuant to condition 6.8 of the Standard Conditions of Sale (4th Edition) and require you to complete the contract in compliance with that condition.'

This can be given by letter or a separate form, but either way it should be sent to the defaulting party in such a way that you would be able to prove delivery, i.e. service of the notice.

9.3 SUBJECT ASSESSMENTS

9.3.1 SUBJECT ASSESSMENT QUESTIONS: A COMMENTARY UPON THE TYPE AND CONTENT OF SUBJECT ASSESSMENT QUESTION AND SUGGESTED ANSWERS

Question 1

RICHARDS ABBEY AND PARTNERS, SOLICITORS
OFFICE MEMORANDUM

From   The Training Partner

To   The Trainee Solicitor

URGENT

Re our client Derek Hunt; sale of 6 Dorset Way Cardiff and purchase of 10 Bentley Street Cardiff

We have a problem here that I would like you to look at urgently. Derek Hunt has exchanged contracts for the sale and purchase of the above properties and completion on both is set for next Friday. The contracts include the Standard Conditions of Sale, (4th Edition). The client rang me this morning in a bit of a state to say that the owner of 10 Bentley Street was tragically killed last night in a sudden boating accident on Lake Coniston in the Lake District. The client went on to say that the deceased's wife understandably wants to call the whole deal off. Derek Hunt has said he will help in any way he can, but he's obviously worried about his own position, given that his buyers are expecting to move in on Friday, and there is a long chain above them. Derek Hunt is coming in this afternoon. Please consider the advice we should give him and prepare for the meeting later today.

Commentary

This is the classic kind of question you should always anticipate in this area, namely what can be done if a party to the transaction drops dead before completion. In effect you have to be sure whether the benefit or burden of the contract passes to the deceased's personal representatives or whether it dies with the deceased. The question is going to be a favourite with examiners because it is an easy and relevant 'what if' problem that can be set in property law and practice exams. In this question the problem has been put forward in the form of an urgent office memorandum from the Training Partner to you the Trainee Solicitor. This being the case you should construct your reply as an urgent memorandum in reply just in case the partner wants to see your notes before the meeting with the client. Please note that, as ever, one important bit of information has been left out of the question that means that your answer must provide alternate advice.

Suggested answer

RICHARDS ABBEY and PARTNERS, SOLICITORS

OFFICE MEMORANDUM

To   The Training Partner

From   The Trainee Solicitor

<u>URGENT</u>

<u>Re our client Derek Hunt; s/o 6 Dorset Way Cardiff and p/o 10 Bentley Street Cardiff</u>

I refer to your urgent memorandum received this morning and set out below my notes that you may find of assistance for the meeting later today with our client. The principal in all cases of this nature is that the death of a party to the contract after exchange and before completion does not invalidate the contract. The benefit or burden of that agreement passes to the deceased's personal representatives who are then bound to complete according to the terms of the contract. The position is different if the deceased was a joint tenant and I refer to this in the following notes:

1. Is the deceased's wife a co-owner? If the answer is no (that is to say the deceased was the sole owner), then the position in law will be as follows:

    (a) The contract for the sale of 6 Dorset Way Cardiff is not discharged by the death of the seller. The personal representatives of the seller are bound to complete on Friday otherwise there will be a breach of contract. They step into the shoes of the deceased seller and must perform all the obligations of the agreement entered into by the deceased.

    (b) In order to complete the title, the personal representatives will need to obtain a grant of representation. Although they can apply for an expedited grant it is still unlikely to be issued by Friday. (It should be noted that normally the Probate Registry will not issue a grant of probate within seven days of the date of death or fourteen days in the case of an administration. Exceptions can be made in emergencies with the leave of two registrars and it is understood that these circumstances would normally be accepted as an emergency.) If there is a will the executor's authority arises on death as it is derived from the will. If there is no will the administrator's authority will only arise from the grant. However in either case a buyer will still require a certified copy of the grant without which their ownership will not be registerable.

(c) Delay therefore seems inevitable unless all parties in the chain can agree to postpone the contractual completion date for all the transactions in that chain.

(d) Although the deceased's wife has asked Derek Hunt to call off his purchase, we cannot advise him to do so, unless he is willing and able to move into temporary accommodation. The reason for this is of course that he is bound to complete his sale and give vacant possession on Friday, failing which he will be in breach of his sale contract.

(e) Derek Hunt could try to contact all the sellers and buyers in the chain of transactions to see if they are willing to call off their transactions, but frankly I am of the view that this an impractical suggestion.

(f) The personal representatives will be advised by their own solicitors to complete as soon as possible to try to mitigate any liability for the deceased's estate. Delay will result in a claim by Derek Hunt for interest under standard condition 7.3. or damages. His claim will include any compensation he has had to pay to his purchaser. This could be avoided by the personal representatives allowing Derek Hunt into possession of Bentley Street before completion of his purchase, thus enabling him to complete his sale on time. The rights of Derek Hunt and the personal representatives will then be governed by standard condition 5.2. where the buyer will occupy the property as a licensee and not a tenant. The detailed terms of the occupancy are set out in standard condition 5.2.2 (a-h). However the buyer may be reluctant to go into early possession as to do so would give rise to a stamp duty land tax liability even though the full consideration has not been paid. (See s. 44(5)(a) of the Finance Act 2003.)

(g) If the widow has a related purchase due to complete on the same day she will be in breach twice over if she fails to complete on Friday. If our client is forced to complete his sale and cannot complete on the purchase any loss he suffers can be claimed against the personal representatives including the cost of temporary accommodation for our client.

(h) If necessary we should consider the possibility of applying for an Order for specific performance against the personal representatives if they insist they won't complete in any event. Furthermore, it is unlikely that time was of the essence in the purchase contract but you can serve a notice to complete to make it so. Under 6.8 of the standard conditions the notice will cause time to be of the essence and the notice can be served upon the executors or if none on the Treasury Solicitor on behalf of the President of the Family Division. (Until a grant of administration is issued the property vests in the President of the Family Division.) Of course this tactic is only of help if our client wishes to bring the contract to and end because without a grant the personal representatives cannot complete. It will serve to reinforce the buyer's concern by putting further pressure, in terms of time, on the other side in the hope that this will urge them on to obtain the grant of representation and complete.

2. If the wife *is* a co-owner:

(a) Is she a joint tenant or tenant in common? If a joint tenant, she can convey as beneficial owner, acquiring her late husband's equitable interest by survivorship. To complete the title all she has to do is produce and hand over a certified copy death certificate at completion. Of course the transfer will need to be redrawn. Just to make sure that there is no question of any severance of the joint tenancy, another check of the office copies and the final Land Registry search is recommended.

(b) If the title is unregistered you will again need to consider whether the joint tenancy has been severed. In view of the provisions of the Law of Property (Joint Tenants) Act 1964, you can assume that there has been no severance if the widow sells as beneficial owner or the conveyance says she is solely and beneficially entitled. Further there should of course be no memorandum of severance endorsed on the conveyance to the deceased and the wife (see s. 1(1)(a) of the Law of Property (Joint Tenants) Act 1964.)

(c) As a final check a land charge search should be repeated against the deceased and the wife to make sure that there are no bankruptcy matters registered as bankruptcy will sever the joint tenancy.

(d) If the deceased was a tenant in common with the wife, another trustee must be appointed to enable her to properly convey the property. The purchase deed will have to be changed to reflect any changes but delay in completion should hopefully be avoided.

Finally, in view of the circumstances and the possibility of delay, you should consider registering the contract either as a C(iv) land charge if the title is unregistered, or as a notice if the title is registered.

Question 2

RICHARDS ABBEY AND PARTNERS, SOLICITORS

OFFICE MEMORANDUM

From   The Training Partner

To   The Trainee Solicitor

<u>Re our client the Rutland Building Society and their sale of 27 Raith Row Skipton</u>

We act for the above local building society who are selling as mortgagee in possession. Contracts were exchanged a month ago and completion was due yesterday. As you will know the society are important clients of ours and we must do our utmost to protect their interests at all times. Unfortunately, notwithstanding the contractual date for completion was yesterday, the buyer has failed to complete. I rang the other side's solicitors who told me they were not in funds and were having difficulty getting instructions from their client purchaser who seems to have suddenly become somewhat elusive. The sale price for this freehold cottage is £57,000. We have a stakeholder deposit of £5,500 in our client deposit account and the contract incorporates the Standard Conditions of Sale, 4th Edition.

Sally Rubin, the Rutland's local manager, has been on the telephone to me this morning saying she has another buyer interested who can proceed to exchange immediately, albeit at a lower price of £56,000. She believes that the offer is genuine and that the buyer could indeed exchange very swiftly. What are our options for advice for the clients in the light of these circumstances? Can I please hear from you today in view of the buyer's default.

Commentary

This is another question that you could almost predict might appear in a Property Law and Practice examination when there is to be a question about one party to the contract failing to complete and what the other party can do about it. Failure to complete is a fairly common occurrence in practice and as such examiners will want to be sure that you know how to deal with these circumstances. You will need to know the relevant conditions in the second edition of the standard conditions and you should be able to draft a simple notice to complete if that is what the question requires. This should not present you with a difficulty as the operative words in such a notice simply repeat the appropriate part of standard condition 6.8.

This is also an area where case law will come into consideration particularly concerning the question of damages. You will need to know the basic law about the measure of damages for breach of contract so far as it relates to contracts for the sale and purchase of land. You may also need to demonstrate when and if a party to the contract is entitled to seek an order for specific performance. Finally, you should by now appreciate that if the question is set in the form of an office memorandum that your reply should be couched in the same terms.

Suggested answer

RICHARDS ABBEY AND PARTNERS, SOLICITORS

OFFICE MEMORANDUM

To   The Training Partner

From   The Trainee Solicitor

Re our client the Rutland Building Society and their sale of 27 Raith Row Skipton

I refer to your memorandum received earlier today and now write to respond as more particularly set out in the following points. However to assist I can confirm that, should your time be limited, the essence of my advice is contained in the final point.

1. The purchaser is in breach of contract because he has not completed on the contractual completion date. It should be noted that late completion is a breach on the part of the defaulting party that will enable the injured party to claim damages for any loss suffered as a consequence of that delay. (See *Raineri v. Miles; Wijeski (Third Party)* [1981] AC 1050.)

2. However, you have not said whether or not time is of the essence of the contract, but I will assume that time is not of the essence so the client has no grounds for treating it as discharged by breach. In effect when time is not of the essence the agreement on its own does not entitle the injured party to terminate the agreement.

3. To remedy this problem, we can make time of the essence by serving a notice to complete upon the purchaser's solicitors. (I can confirm that standard condition 1.3.2 states that giving a notice or delivering a document to a party's solicitor has the same effect as giving or delivering it to that party.)

4. May I please refer you to standard condition 6.8. If we are 'ready able and willing to complete' we can serve notice to complete, making it a term of the contract that completion must take place within ten working days of the giving of the notice, excluding the day of service. A party is ready able and willing if that party could be but for the default of the other party (standard condition 1.1.3). As the amount to be paid on completion would enable the property to be transferred freed of all mortgages it is clear that the seller must be deemed to be ready able and willing to complete (see standard condition 1.1.3 (b)). Standard condition 6.8.3 (b) provides that on receipt of a notice to complete if the buyer paid a deposit of less than 10%, the buyer is forthwith to pay a further deposit equal to the balance of that 10%. I have noted from your memorandum that the buyer was £200 short of a 10% deposit and in theory we can demand of the other side the additional deposit. Of course if they have no funds this demand may be somewhat worthless. The amount will still form part of our claim for damages.

5. If the purchaser does not comply with the notice that is to say by completing within the time limits prescribed by the completion notice, our client can treat the contract as discharged. If this happens then the building society can forfeit the buyer's deposit. Thereafter they can also seek to sell to the other interested party. Such sale must of course proceed on the basis that the price and other terms still acquit our clients of their obligations on a sale as a mortgagee. (Please see *Cuckmere Brick Co. Ltd v. Mutual Finance Ltd* [1971] Ch 949 and *Palk v. Mortgage Services Funding plc* [1993] 2 WLR 415, CA.)

6. I have noted that the sale price in the present contract is £1,000 more than that offered by the new buyers. It may help you to know that any loss incurred on the resale can be recovered as damages under *Hadley v. Baxendale* principles that is to say loss arising naturally from the breach. (*Hadley v. Baxendale* (1854) 9 Exch 341). However, any claim must be reduced by the amount of the forfeited deposit. See also standard condition 7.5.2. Having said that the effect of s. 49(2) of the Law of Property Act 1925

should be noted. This provision allows the court a wide discretion to order repayment of the deposit and will do so dependant upon various factors like the conduct of the parties, the size of the deposit or the significance of other matters in question.

7. Actual financial loss can also be claimed provided that the loss was as a result of the breach. Under this heading our client could claim our costs incurred in the abortive transaction up to the time of sale.

8. The client also has the option of seeking a decree of specific performance from the court against the defaulting purchaser. However, this is an equitable remedy that will only come into play if damages may prove to be insufficient compensation for the breach. Accordingly this remedy would normally only be used as a last resort, say, where the seller has no reasonable prospect of selling the property in the fore-seeable future. It should be noted that as this is an equitable remedy the other maxims apply. This being the case a decision to go for specific performance should be made reasonably promptly otherwise 'delay will defeat equity'. Bearing in mind that there is already another interested party the option of specific performance would not seem appropriate. Indeed it is the client's duty to mitigate their loss by trying to re-sell without any delay. This being the case the society are probably under an obligation to accept such an offer bearing in mind it is so close to the original sale price. (You should bear in mind that if the client is not seen to be attempting to mitigate the loss the award for damages could be reduced for failure to mitigate.)

9. In conclusion, my recommendation is for the immediate service of a notice to complete pursuant to standard condition 6.8 upon the buyer's solicitors bearing in mind the buyer has become somewhat elu-sive. If the purchaser still fails to complete, we should rescind the contract, forfeit the deposit, proceed with the sale to the other purchaser and seek additional compensation, if appropriate. If I can assist you further please let me know.

TIME ENGAGED 55 MINUTES

TRAINEE SOLICITOR

Question 3

(a) The sale of the freehold at 'Mon Repos' 27 Deepdale Drive Bradford for £55,000 has today been completed by a transfer. The purchaser has simultaneously mortgaged the property to secure a loan of £35,000. How will you deal with Stamp Duty Land Tax considerations for a transaction of this type? (5 Marks)

(b) Your client Jim Smith has today completed his purchase of two residential properties from the same seller Jock Stein. The sale contract was at £80,000 but the two transfers were prepared so as to show one at £50,000 and the other at £30,000. What is the stamp duty land tax liabil-ity, if any, for your client bearing in mind the figure of £60,000 as the starting threshold for the payment of this tax? (5 Marks)

(c) You have just been instructed by Milly Sorensen who has passed to you the deeds of her home at 629 Wildwood Street Brighton West Sussex. When she bought the property, she conducted her own conveyancing and paid £70,000 for this freehold residential property. She has given you all her deeds saying it was an unregistered title but there should be no problem because she only completed the purchase this year; in fact just four months ago. You have checked and the title appears to be in order up to the conveyance to the client. Ms Sorensen did not pay any stamp duty land tax at the time of the purchase because she said it was not a registered title. She now wants to sell quickly as she has a very keen buyer at £85,000. She has an offer of an excellent job in Sweden and wants to move abroad with all expedition. This is the main rea-son for the proposed quick sale. Please advise her. (10 Marks)

Commentary

Practitioners, as well as being lawyers must also be unpaid tax collectors! In fact the involvement of stamp duty land tax in many transactions is the reason that this kind of question could well appear. Indeed it could be said that Stamp Duty Land Tax occurs in all transactions even if it is just a question of submitting a return where there is no Stamp Duty Land Tax payable, i.e. where the consideration does not exceed £60,000. The importance of this question is that if you know the area of the law concerned you can earn high marks without having to spread the knowledge in your answer too widely. In this case the amount of marks, out of 20 are shown in the body of the question. Accordingly apportion your time in the same proportions so that the section that earns the most marks enjoys the main thrust of your time and effort.

Apart from indicating in your answer the need for the prompt payment of stamp duty land tax and registration it is important to also highlight what the position is if a client fails to pay the Stamp Duty Land Tax (and as a result fails to register a purchase deed. You will see that this is certainly needed in section (c) if high marks are to be obtained. Always consider the ramifications of oversights, as the examiner will want you to show an understanding of all the sides to the scenario set out in the question.

This question also contains another example of a problem requiring you to comment on what has not been highlighted in the question as well the obvious matters for you to consider in your answer. The question seems to be about just Stamp Duty Land Tax but there is more to the third section as will be shown from the answer set out below. You will need to address more than just the tax angle to score well.

Finally, this is an example of a question that can be answered in the form of an essay. Clearly, you will need to construct your answer in three parts thereby addressing the individual units in the body of the question. You will also need to advance evidence on your behalf to back up your assertions particularly when dealing with information that has not necessarily been mentioned or referred to in the question.

Suggested answer

(a) Stamp Duty Land Tax (SDLT) is a compulsory tax that is payable on the value of a transaction. For transactions up to £60,000 the tax rate is at zero for residential property and £150,000 for commercial or non-residential property. It is assumed that this property, judging from the address, is residential. Even if it is not the answer will be the same namely that no stamp duty land tax is payable but an SDLT1 (the Stamp Duty Land Tax return) must be completed and signed by the taxpayer (the buyer) and then sent to the Revenue. Returns must be filed even where the value of the transaction falls below the £60,000/£150,000 threshold. If a transaction is chargeable to tax then the tax at the correct rate must be paid, (s. 42 Finance Act 2003).

(b) It is true to say that the threshold figure for the payment of Stamp Duty Land Tax in residential cases is at present £60,000. However that does not mean that if you apportion a purchase price between properties so as to allocate an amount to each property of less than £60,000 that there will not be a stamp duty payable. If the transaction effected forms part of a larger transaction or series of transactions in respect of which the amount or value or aggregate amount or value of the consideration exceeds £60,000 then tax is payable on the aggregate amount or value. As each transfer forms part of a larger transaction each transfer would attract Stamp Duty Land Tax at 1% of the stated consideration. The buyer must complete a Stamp Duty Land Tax return. The return includes a question about allied transactions and the buyer must certify the truthfulness of the return. (Question 13 on the form asks, 'Is this transaction linked to any other?'. If it is the buyer must give the total consideration for all linked transactions). Consequently it would not help to make each property the subject of a separate contract between the parties, as this would be considered to be a series of transactions that would again be caught by Stamp Duty Land Tax.

(c) Milly Sorensen has two major difficulties facing her that will inhibit her wish to sell the property quickly and move abroad. First, no Stamp Duty Land Tax has been paid in respect of the purchase transaction, and secondly the title has not been sent to the Land Registry for first registration. Until both these processes have been completed she will be unable to prove title and consequently will not be able to sell.

Dealing first with the failure to pay Stamp Duty Land Tax, she completed the purchase recently at a price of £70,000. Stamp Duty Land Tax should have been paid within 30 days of the completion of the transaction in the sum of £700. Until the duty is properly paid she cannot obtain from the Revenue a certificate of payment. This certificate of payment is vital because without it the Land Registry will not register any registration application. Ms Sorensen needs to immediately complete an SDLT1 form, the Stamp Duty Land Tax return and sign it and send it to the Inland Revenue (Stamp/Taxes MSD) Comben House Farriers Way Netherton Merseyside L30 4RN. If a return is filed late the buyer will be liable to a fixed penalty of £100, or if more than three months late, £200. The buyer may also be liable to a tax-related penalty, not to exceed the tax payable. She is plainly over the time limit for stamping purposes and as such until the duty is paid the freehold title will be unacceptable to a buyer.

Turning now to the question of registration, the property is in Brighton and is thus in an area of compulsory registration, as all of England has been compulsorily registrable since 1990. We have checked the title and it is in order and we must therefore assume that there are no other dispositions prior to the conveyance to the client that might have induced first registration. This conveyance will certainly induce first registration being a transfer for value of the freehold estate. Obviously the client will need to pay the Stamp Duty Land Tax. Thereafter the title documents will have to be sent to the Land Registry with the necessary registration fee. If an application for first registration is not made with in two months of the date of the deed in theory the buyer loses his or her right to that legal estate. However, a late application can be made and if the Land Registry accepts it, as mostly they are, then the applicant will eventually receive a title information document confirming their ownership of their legal estate. Again it is clear from the facts that the client is out of time for the submission of the registration application and as such has no title to sell. Section 6 of the Land Registration Act 2002 imposes a requirement upon an estate owner to register within two months of the date of the conveyance or transfer to the new estate owner. Should an estate owner fail to comply with s. 6, s. 7 provides that a transfer will become void. Should this occur then the transferor would hold the legal estate on a bare trust on behalf of the transferee. In this case our client wants to sell quickly and move abroad. Accordingly once the Stamp Duty Land Tax has been paid the registration application should be made using Form FR1. A letter explaining the reasons for the late application could be sent with the other deeds and documents. Once the application has been successfully concluded title can be proved and the sale can proceed and the client can then successfully move abroad.

Question 4

Re sale of 4 First Way Manchester and purchase of 8 End Way Manchester

Your clients are Mr Mohammed Rashid and Ms Janet West. They are selling the freehold at 4 First Way for £65,000. It is registered under title number MN 142536. There are two mortgages on this property the first being an endowment mortgage with the Rutland Building Society and the second with Barclays Bank. The redemption amounts are £30,045.60 and £16,255.98 respectively. They are contemporaneously buying the leasehold property at 8 End Way for £75,000 with the aid of a repayment mortgage of £50,000 from the Rutland. It is also registered under title number MN 152637. They are buying and selling as tenants in common. Completion has now taken place in both the sale and the purchase.

Please list the steps you will take following completion in respect of both transactions. Please draft a letter to the clients reporting completion and advising them of the steps you will be taking to finalise matters. Please also advise them as to the way they will be holding the property. Within what period should the registration application be made?

Commentary

This is a straightforward question that simply requires you to show that you know what steps are taken in both a sale and a purchase once completion has taken place. It is often mistakenly thought that once completion has been effected that there is nothing more to be done. Clearly you need to show to the examiner that you appreciate that there a several critical steps to be taken to protect your client's interests on both a sale as well as a purchase. You will be aware of the more obvious and pressing needs, such as stamping and registration, but you will also need to show you are aware of other important points like re-assignment of life policies previously part of an endowment mortgage. Indeed you will also need to show that you are aware that ultimately a practitioner is there to make money in the form of costs and that it is after completion that these monies can be yours. It is of course a cardinal sin not to remember this element of the process!

Remember the question asks for lists and that is exactly what the examiner will want to see as your answer. This being the case do not write an essay but actually provide two separate lists as requested setting out all the steps concerned. The question contains no tricks, no missing elements and no ambiguities. All you need to do therefore, is to marshall your information and make sure you include all the detail required and you will score high marks. In effect the question requires you to demonstrate your ability to apply your knowledge in an orderly and efficient manner, something you will need to show just as well in practice.

Finally, remember that there are two additional points at the end of the question that should not be overlooked. First, you need to consider what the examiner wants you to highlight about the fact that the clients are tenants in common and second you must indicate when the registration application must be made.

Suggested answer

Re sale of 4 First Way Manchester and purchase of 8 End Way Manchester

A. Specimen steps to be taken following completion

1. Telephone the clients to report the successful completion of both transactions. Advise both clients that you will be writing to confirm.

2. 4 First Way Manchester

(i)   Write to the first mortgagees the Rutland Building Society enclosing a cheque for redemption monies, £30,045.60, Form DS1 (the Land Registry discharge of mortgage form) for sealing together with the life policy mortgage or assignment for release and re-assignment. Usually the first mortgagees will have allowed for redemption to be by cheque but there will be exceptions where the redemption monies should then be sent by bank telegraphic transfer.

(ii)   Telegraphically transfer to Barclays Bank the redemption monies required to redeem their loan in the sum of £16,255.98.

(iii)   Write to Barclays Bank confirming the above method of payment and the amount sent and enclose Form DS1 for their second charge for execution and return. Ask for their written confirmation that your undertaking to the Bank is now fully discharged.

(iv)   Pay the estate agent's commission account if instructed to do so by client. (Browning and Associates of Manchester.)

(v)   Transfer payment of your professional costs from clients to office account.

(vi)   Write to the local water authority advising them of the sale and purchase details, stating that no apportionment of water rates was made, and requesting any refund due or demand to be sent to clients at their new address.

(vii)   Give notice of re-assignment of the life policy to the Life Company at their head office. Send the original policy to client for safekeeping with all assignments and re-assignments and receipted notices concerning the same. (The life office will require all these documents should a claim arise under the terms of the policy.)

3. 8 End Way Manchester

(i)   Report the completion of new mortgage to the mortgagees, the Rutland Building Society using their standard report form, if supplied, with the mortgage instructions.

(ii) Within thirty days of the day of completion arrange the completion and signature of an SDLT1 (Stamp Duty Land Tax return). Within that period arrange for the filing of the SDLT1 with the Revenue and for the payment of stamp duty land tax to be paid on the purchase in the sum of £750 being 1% of the purchase price, (£75,000.)

(iii) Within the priority period, (thirty days), disclosed on your Land Registry search, (OS1), apply to the Land Registry on Form AP1 for registration of the clients as proprietors of this title. If there was a mortgage on the seller's title, there is no need to wait for the discharge of the seller's mortgage (Form DS1) to be received from the seller's solicitors. This can follow later if the priority period is about to expire although a further Registry search to extend the period is possible before completion only.

(iv) If not already done, draft and obtain clients' execution of a trust deed recording their beneficial interests in the property in view of their ownership as tenants in common.

(v) If required by the terms of the lease give notice of assignment and charge to the Lessor's solicitors and pay the registration fee prescribed by the lease.

(vi) Transfer your costs from clients to office account.

4. Draft letter to clients on completion

RICHARDS ABBEY AND PARTNERS, SOLICITORS

4 Red Lion Square London WC1

Partners

M. Richards

R. M. Abbey

Mr M Rashid and Ms J West
8 End Way
Manchester
MC1 2TV

Dear Mr Rashid and Ms West,

Your sale of 4 First Way and purchase of 8 End Way Manchester

I refer to my telephone conversation with you today and I am pleased to formally confirm completion today of your sale and purchase of the above properties. I trust that the move went smoothly but of course if there are any points outstanding that I can assist with please do not hesitate to contact me.

Concerning your sale, I have paid off both your mortgages on the sale and the amounts so paid were as previously indicated by me in correspondence. In accordance with your written instructions I have paid the commission account of your estate agents, Browning and Associates of Manchester. I have written to the local water authority advising them of the sale and purchase and requesting a refund of water rates or a demand to be sent to you at your new address. I will arrange for your life policy to be re-assigned and will give notice of re-assignment to the life company. I enclose the original policy for safekeeping. When the completed re-assignment and receipted notice are to hand I will send these on to you. Please keep all these deeds and documents and the policy itself in a safe place as they will all be required should a claim on the policy arise.

Turning to your purchase, the stamp duty land tax return that you approved and signed is being sent with the requisite amount of stamp duty land tax to the Revenue and thereafter the deeds will be sent to the Land Registry for the registration of your ownership along with your new mortgage. I shall attend to the registration procedure. The application for registration of title at the Land Registry should take about one or two weeks. When it is completed I shall send you a copy of the title showing you both as registered owners.

Finally, can I remind you of my previous advice that you both need to consider the preparation of a formal document that will clearly evidence the basis of your joint ownership of the property. You will both also need to consider making wills, as there is no automatic transfer of a deceased's share in the house to the survivor. This must be covered by wills that match each other in their contents. Can I suggest that you consider this and contact me to arrange an appointment to discuss the documents further?

I should like to once again take this opportunity of thanking you for your kind instructions and to wish you all the very best in your new home.

Yours sincerely,

Question 5

You are a firm's training partner. You have decided that more explicit documentation is required for the guidance of trainees in your residential conveyancing department. To that end, please prepare post-completion checklists for the guidance of your trainees for when your firm are acting for sellers and also for buyers. You will need to cover all post-completion matters including those required in connection with registration and stamping. You will be covering aspects of the conveyancing process from completion right through to the physical dispatch of the deeds to the lender or the client or into the partnership strong room. You are also required to set out a checklist covering delays and remedies to encompass the basic details of these subjects.

Commentary

Much of what is done in conveyancing is repetitive. This being so this is yet another good example of a question where an essay type answer will not be acceptable. The question specifically calls for the preparation of checklists, first, a seller's post-completion list, secondly, a buyer's pre-completion list, and lastly, a delays and remedies checklist. This is what the examiner will want to see you produce. Anything else within your answer is irrelevant and will lose you precious marks. It is also an illustration of the type of question where a wide display of procedural knowledge will be necessary, and in particular your knowledge of the practical processes of conveyancing after completion as well as stamping and registration.

This question straddles both registered and unregistered land and also covers property subject to a mortgage. Moreover, you will need to prepare your answer from two perspectives, one for the buyer and the other for the seller. Neither should be overlooked nor should you devote more time to one to the detriment of the other. You should therefore appreciate that this kind of examination question requires an answer that is broadly based and almost exclusively concerned with your knowledge of conveyancing procedure. When dealing with delays and remedies remember the question only asks for basic details. Limit your answer accordingly.

Suggested answer

A post-completion checklist when you are acting for the seller:

1. If completion is by post inform all parties by phone of completion, i.e. the seller, the practitioner acting for the buyer and if any, the selling agents, so that the keys for the subject property can be released.

2. Commit to the post on the day of completion the deeds and documents of title with the executed and dated purchase deed and keep a dated file copy of the deed.

3. If the subject property is subject to a mortgage send, on the day of completion, sufficient redemption monies to the lender along with Form DS1 for registered land and the mortgage deed for receipting in unregistered land.

4. If the mortgage is an endowment one remember to also send to the lender all the mortgages of life policies for release, and also give notice of reassignment to the life companies.

5. When the receipted document(s) are returned to you from the lenders remember to check the details and if all is well send Form DS1 or vacated mortgage to the buyer's practitioner with a request that you be released from your undertaking given at completion.

6. On receipt of the released mortgage of life policy and receipted notice or reassignment from the life office send to the client the original policy and all released mortgages of life policies and notices as these will be required by the client should a policy claim arise.

7. Pay to the client the net proceeds of sale and supply full accounts, including a note of your own charges, if you have not already done so or alternatively apply the net proceeds towards an allied purchase if these are your instructions.

8. Make sure you have transferred monies to your office account for all costs and pre-paid disbursements.

9. If you have instructions to do so, pay the estate agents their commission charges and request a receipted account from them.

10. Remind the client to cancel all standing orders to the lender, any buildings insurance and payments to the local authority in the nature of council tax.

11. If there is a sale of part and the deeds are in your possession ensure you have instructions as to their custody and if they are to remain with you, place them all within a fireproof safe.

A post completion checklist when you are acting for the buyer:

1. Advise the buyer, and the buyer's lender, that completion has been effected by you in accordance with the contract terms.

2. Ensure the seller's practitioner has or will later on the day of completion send all the deeds and documents to you in the post.

3. On receipt of the purchase deed deal with the Stamp Duty Land Tax requirements being Stamp Duty Land Tax for purchases currently exceeding £60,000. Ensure the Stamp Duty Land Tax return (SDLT1) is sent to the Revenue (along with a payment for the duty where the consideration exceeds £60,000) within thirty days of completion to avoid any penalty fee for late submission.

4. If the title is unregistered submit the deeds for first registration within two months of completion and if the title is registered submit the dealing for registration within your search priority period.

5. Make sure you use the correct cover for your Land Registry application and include certified copy documents where you want the originals returned. Remember to include the appropriate Land Registry fee.

6. If there is a mortgage created by a limited company make sure the mortgage is registered at Companies House within 21 days of the completion date, and remember this is an unequivocal deadline incapable of extension without recourse to the court.

7. Give notice of assignment to life offices of any life policies forming part of the security for the lender.

8. If the subject property is leasehold and if the lease terms require it, give notice of assignment or transfer to the lessor's practitioner and pay any requisite fee and request a receipted copy of the notice to be placed with the deeds.

9. If the subject property is subject to a tenancy, give notice to the tenant of the change of ownership and indicate to whom all future rent should be paid.

10. When the title information document is back from the Registry check the new entries carefully and return it to them if there any errors in need of correction.

11. Make sure you have transferred monies to your office account for all costs and pre-paid disbursements.

12. If there are any deeds are in your possession ensure you have instructions as to their custody and if they are to remain with you, place them all within a fireproof safe.

A delays and remedies checklist:

1. Has the time for completion set out in the contract elapsed or expired?

2. If it has does the client want you to serve a notice to complete, i.e. have you taken instructions for approval for this step?

3. If you have instructions have you served a notice using the appropriate wording and in such a way so as to enable you to prove service of the notice?

4. Has the period set out in the notice expired and if so does the client want to rescind the agreement sell the property elsewhere and sue for damages?

5. Is there some other form of breach of contract? If so have you obtained a full history of the conveyancing transaction with all supporting papers and what remedy does the innocent party select?

6. Are you able to quantify the client's loss arising from the breach? If so how much is that loss?

7. In the light of 6. above, is it economic sense to commence proceedings bearing in mind the costs that will be incurred?

8. Apart from the other party to the contract might there be a claim elsewhere, e.g. against a conveyancing practitioner or surveyor in negligence?

9.3.2 MULTIPLE CHOICE QUESTIONS AND ANSWERS TO MULTIPLE CHOICE QUESTIONS

We set out below examples of ten multiple choice questions that you might encounter in a subject assessment. Thereafter you will find some typical short answer questions that can also feature in a subject assessment and which cover pre-completion and completion matters. Answers to both are also set out below. Remember our initial guidance. Never leave multiple choice answers with a blank multiple choice. If there are four possibilities and you are not sure of the answer select the one you think might be right, you have a one in four chance of getting it right! Also look at the instructions on the paper. If it says select the right answer on the paper by circling the correct choice then do just that. Do not make a tick or underline your selection, as the strict response would be to fail you even though the selection may be correct. Also none of the answers given might be right. In these circumstances follow the rubric in the question paper and explain why none of the listed answers apply.

9.3.2.1 Multiple choice questions

Unless otherwise directed, select the right answer by circling it in each question. Should you think that none of the selections apply please explain why not in your answer book.

1. After completion a mortgage discharge will be dealt with by the following:
   (a) Form DS1
   (b) END1
   (c) mortgage vacating receipt
   (d) promissory note release
   Please select the choice that cannot apply.

2. Your client has completed a freehold purchase for £60,000. What is the stamp duty land tax liability? Is it:
   (a) £6,000
   (b) £600
   (c) £12,000
   (d) nil

3. The Land Registry has introduced a new method of lodging applications. Practitioners who use Land Registry Direct can now lodge applications to change the register electronically. The service is called 'e-lodgement' Which of the following cannot be applied for as an e-lodgements:

   (a) severance of a joint tenancy by notice
   (b) change of property description
   (c) change of proprietor's address
   (d) change of proprietor's name (by deed poll/marriage).

4. On completion of a registration application from 13 October 2003, which of the following will be issued?:

   (a) a Title Information Document
   (b) a land certificate
   (c) a charge certificate
   (d) a land charges certificate

5. First registration applications must be made within eight weeks of completion, failing which the legal title will not vest in the buyer until the Registry has completed an application.

   Is this statement TRUE/FALSE? Please delete the incorrect choice.

6. If a binding land contract states a completion date without qualification, that date is not a strict and binding date that would allow an innocent party to withdraw from such a contract on the occasion of a failure to complete on the contractual completion date.

   Is this statement TRUE/FALSE? Please delete the incorrect choice.

7. A notice to complete can be served in respect of a contract containing the standard conditions:

   (a) at any time on or after the date fixed for completion, either party who is ready, able and willing to complete may give the other a notice to complete
   (b) at any time on the date fixed for completion, either party who is ready, able and willing to complete may give the other a notice to complete
   (c) at any time on or after the date fixed for completion, only the seller who is ready, able and willing to complete may give the buyer a notice to complete
   (d) at any time before the date fixed for completion, either party who is ready, able and willing to complete may give the other a notice to complete

8. In respect of a contract containing the standard conditions, how long should the notice to complete period be?:

   (a) the period within which it would be reasonable to allow completion to take place, when all the outstanding steps are taken into consideration
   (b) ten working days of giving the notice to complete
   (c) ten days of giving the notice to complete
   (d) 14 days of giving the notice to complete

9. Where a contract has not been completed, and where a cause of action has arisen, an innocent party to that contract can consider all available remedies. These remedies are:

   (a) specific performance
   (b) a claim for compensation by way of damages
   (c) rescission
   (d) A summons for possession

   Please select the choice that cannot apply.

10. A seller will be entitled to claim a lien (i.e. a right to retain possession of another's property pending discharge of a debt) over the subject property in relation to any unpaid element of the purchase price.

Is this statement TRUE/FALSE? Please delete the incorrect choice.

9.3.2.2 *Answers to multiple choice questions*

1. The incorrect selection is (d). A mortgage will be dealt with in registered land either by a form DS1 or if there is an electronic discharge an END1. If the mortgage affects unregistered land then a mortgage vacating receipt will be used. A promissory note release has nothing to do with the redemption of mortgages of land.

2. The correct answer is (d). If the consideration for the subject property is at or under the Stamp Duty Land Tax base threshold, currently £60,000, then no Stamp Duty Land Tax is payable. Land tax is payable, currently at 1%, up to £250,000 above that other tiers of tax apply.

3. You should appreciate that all of these events can be the subject of e-lodgement. You can also register the death of a joint proprietor of land by the same method. As none of the answers given are right then follow the rubric in the question paper and explain why none of the listed answers apply.

4. The correct answer is (a). After 13 October 2003 a title information document will be issued, in effect a certificate of title registration completion. The title information document will comprise a copy of the register and, where the application has resulted in the preparation of a new or amended title plan, a copy of that title plan. The title information document will not be a document of title as it is issued for information purposes only. There is no requirement to lodge this with any subsequent application affecting the same property.

5. The statement is FALSE. Applications must be made *within two months* of completion, failing which the legal title will not vest in the buyer until an application has been completed by the Registry. Section 6.(4) of the Land Registration Act 2002 states that 'The period for registration is 2 months' beginning with the date on which the relevant event occurs, i.e. the dispositions giving rise to first registration.

6. The statement is TRUE. What can be done if one of the parties delays completion? It is plain that such a delay will be a breach of contract. Can an injured party, immediately upon the happening of the breach, terminate the contract? It would seem not, because this remedy is only available to the innocent party if time was of the essence in relation to the completion date. When time is of the essence, there is no leeway for delay; completion must be on the date specified, failing which all remedies will be available to the aggrieved party.

7. The correct selection is (a). Standard condition 6.8 states that at any time on or after the date fixed for completion, either party who is ready, able and willing to complete may give the other a notice to complete.

8. The correct selection is (b). Standard condition 6.8.2 states that the parties are to complete the agreement within ten working days of giving the notice to complete. The ten-day period excludes the day on which the notice is given.

9. The correct selection is (d). Where a contract has not been completed, and where a cause of action has arisen, an innocent party to that contract party can consider four available and different remedies. These remedies are (a) specific performance, (b) a claim for compensation by way of damages, (c) rescission, and (d) a vendor and purchaser summons. Accordingly a summons for possession cannot apply as this will be the order required where a landlord is seeking possession of premises from a defaulting tenant.

10. This statement is TRUE. A seller will be entitled to claim a lien (i.e. a right to retain possession of another's property pending discharge of a debt) over the subject property in relation to any unpaid part of the purchase price. The lien is an equitable charge enforceable by the court by an order for the sale of the property or for the setting aside of the contract. The lien should be protected by a notice in registered land and as a C(iii) registration for unregistered land.

9.3.3 SHORT ANSWER QUESTIONS WITH ANSWERS

1. You work for Land and Partners of 1 The High Street Lime Dorset. You act for Jack Brown who has bought for £145,000 the whole of the freehold registered property at 1 The Park Lime Dorset DS1 2QP currently registered with title number DST 132435. He was a cash buyer who has already paid your costs and disbursements. Stamp Duty Land Tax for the transfer inducing his registration as proprietor has been paid. The property was bought from his mother Jean who sold the unencumbered property with a simple clean title as she has retired to Spain and Jack has moved in some tenants. Please complete the attached Land Registry Form to deal with the transaction on behalf of your client. The Land Registry fees are £150. Please note your client still lives next door to the subject property at 2 The Park.

2. You work for Land and Partners of 1 The High Street Lime Dorset. You act for Alice Gowen who has bought for £95,000 the whole of the freehold unregistered property at 5 High Street Lime Dorset DS1 4QP. Stamp Duty Land Tax for the transfer inducing first registration has been paid. She was a cash buyer who has already paid your costs and disbursements. The property was bought from her father Daniel who sold the unencumbered property with a simple clean title as he has retired to Italy. Alice will use the property for her retail fancy goods business. Please complete the attached Land Registry Form to deal with the transaction on behalf of your client. The Land Registry fees are £100. Please note your client will live above the shop.

3. You work for Land and Partners of 1 The High Street Lime Dorset. You act for Mustafa Hadji of 22 The Drive Wembley Middlesex who has contracted to buy the freehold registered property at 11 The Wash Lime Dorset DS1 7QP. He is a cash buyer who has already put you in funds. The transaction was due to complete yesterday pursuant to the terms of a contract exchanged on the 2nd of this month. The seller Bazlur Rashid of 6 The Cut Bethnal Green London E2R 5TY would not complete because there was a delay on his allied purchase. His solicitors are S. States & Co. of 69 The High Street Lime Dorset. Please draft a notice to complete.

Suggested answers

1. The facts cover a straightforward registered land registration application on Form AP1. You should be able to complete such a form with little or no difficulty given the relevant information set out for you in the question. The answer is shown below on the completed Form AP1. This is an uncomplicated question that should enable you to earn good marks quickly and simply.

2. Again, the facts cover a straightforward unregistered land first registration application on Form FR1. You should be able to complete such a form with little or no difficulty given the relevant information set out for you in the question. The answer is shown below on the completed Form FR1. Similarly, this too is an uncomplicated question that should enable you to earn good marks quickly and simply.

3. This is a simple matter of applying the facts to standard condition 6.8. As such the notice should be in

the following format:

LAND AND PARTNERS

1 The High Street Lime Dorset

Partners

A. Land

C. Berners

S. States & Co.
69 The High Street
Lime
Dorset.

Dear Sirs,

<u>11 The Wash Lime Dorset DS1 7QP</u>

On behalf of Mustafa Hadji of 22 The Drive Wembley Middlesex we hereby give you NOTICE that with reference to the contract dated 2nd of this month and made between Bazlur Rashid of the one part and Mustafa Hadji of the other part for the sale and purchase of 11 The Wash Lime Dorset DS1 7QP we place on record the fact that the purchase of the property has not been completed on the date fixed in the contract for completion. We further give you NOTICE that the buyer is ready able and willing to complete. We therefore give you NOTICE pursuant to condition 6.8 of the Standard Conditions of Sale (4th Edition) and require you to complete the contract in compliance with that condition.

Yours faithfully

Land and Partners

9.4 REFERENCES TO WIDER READING INCLUDING PRACTITIONER TEXTS

- *A Practical Approach to Conveyancing* by Abbey R. and Richards M. (6th edn, OUP)—Chapter 9.
- *The Law Society's Conveyancing Handbook 10th edn* by Silverman F.—Sections G and M dealing with post-completion and delays and remedies.
- *Emmet on Title*:

    —Chapter 7, Remedies for Breach of Contract

    —Chapters 8 to 10, Completion and Registration.
- For more detail on the changes introduced by the Land Registration Act 2002 see *Blackstone's Guide to The Land Registration Act 2002* by Abbey R. and Richards M. (OUP).
- *Textbook on Land Law* by MacKenzie J.-A. and Phillips M. (9th edn, OUP)—chapter 2 (buying a house); chapter 4 (unregistered land); chapter 5 (registered land).

9.5 **RELEVANT WEBSITES FOR MORE INFORMATION**

- Council of Mortgage Lenders, http://www.cml.org.uk
  This site will set out post completion requirements of lenders within their CML handbook

- Inland Revenue, http://www.inlandrevenue.gov.uk/home.htm
  This is the site for all stamp duty enquiries as well as any other taxation matters that might arise post-completion.

- Land Registry, http://www.landreg.gov.uk
  For all post-completion matters relating to registered land.

- Land Registry internet register access, http://www.landregistrydirect.gov.uk

- National Association of Estate Agents, http://www.naea.co.uk
  Of benefit should a dispute arise over the payment of the estate agent's account

- The Royal Institute of British Architects, http://www.riba.org
  After completion the client might want to carry out alterations additions or a complete reconstruction. If so an architect will be needed.

APPENDIX 9.1 LAND REGISTRY FORM AP1

Application to
change the register

Land Registry

AP1

If you need more room than is provided for in a panel, use continuation sheet CS and attach to this form.

1.	**Administrative area and postcode** if known - Lime Dorset

2.   Title number(s)
DST 132435

3. If you have already made this application by **outline application**, insert reference number:

4.   This application affects *Place "X" in the appropriate box.*

    ☑   the **whole** of the title(s) *Go to panel 5.*

    ☐   **part** of the title(s) *Give a brief description of the property affected.*

---

5.   Application, priority and fees *A fee calculator for all types of applications can be found on Land Registry's website at www.landregistry.gov.uk/fees*

Nature of applications numbered in priority order	Value £	Fees paid £
1.	145,000	150

TOTAL £ 150

Fee payment method: *Place "X" in the appropriate box.*
I wish to pay the appropriate fee payable under the current Land Registration Fee Order:

☑ by cheque or postal order, amount £150———————— made payable to "Land Registry".

☐ by Direct Debit under an authorised agreement with Land Registry.

FOR OFFICIAL USE ONLY
Record of fees paid

Particulars of under/over payments

Fees debited £

Reference number

---

6.   Documents lodged with this form *Number the documents in sequence; copies should also be numbered and listed as separate documents. Alternatively you may prefer to use Form DL. If you supply the original document and a certified copy, we shall assume that you request the return of the original; if a certified copy is not supplied, we may retain the original document and it may be destroyed.*
Transfer, (TR1)

7. **The applicant is:** *Please provide the full name(s) of the person(s) applying to change the register.* Jack Brown **The application has been lodged by:** Land Registry Key No. (if appropriate) Name (if different from the applicant) Land and Partners Address/DX No. 1The High Street Lime Dorset Reference rma E-mail rma@land.co.uk	FOR OFFICIAL USE ONLY Codes Dealing Status
Telephone No. 0693 512512	Fax No.	

8. **Where you would like us to deal with someone else** *We shall deal only with the applicant, or the person lodging the application if different, unless you place "X" against one or more of the statements below and give the necessary details.*

☐ *Send title information document to the person shown below*

☐ *Raise any requisitions or queries with the person shown below*

☐ *Return original documents lodged with this form (see note in panel 6) to the person shown below*

If this applies only to certain documents, please specify.

Name

Address/DX No.

Reference

E-mail

Telephone No.	Fax No.

9. **Address(es) for service of the proprietor(s) of the registered estate(s). The address(es) will be entered in the register and used for correspondence and the service of notice.** *Place "X" in the appropriate box(es). You may give up to three addresses for service **one** of which **must** be a postal address but does not have to be within the UK. The other addresses can be any combination of a postal address, a box number at a UK document exchange or an electronic address.*

☐ Enter the address(es) from the transfer/assent/lease

☑ Enter the address(es), including postcode, as follows:
2 The Park Lime Dorset DS1 2QP

☐ Retain the address(es) currently in the register for the title(s)

10. Disclosable overriding interests *Place "X" in the appropriate box.*

☑ This is not an application to register a registrable disposition or it is but no disclosable overriding interests affect the registered estate(s) *Section 27 of the Land Registration Act 2002 lists the registrable dispositions. Rule 57 of the Land Registration Rules 2003 sets out the disclosable overriding interests. Use Form DI to tell us about any disclosable overriding interests that affect the registered estate(s) identified in panel 2.*

☐ Form DI accompanies this application

The registrar may enter a notice of a disclosed interest in the register of title.

11. Information in respect of any new charge *Do not give this information if a Land Registry MD reference is printed on the charge, unless the charge has been transferred.*

Full name and address (including postcode) for service of notices and correspondence of the person to be registered as proprietor of each charge. *You may give up to three addresses for service **one** of which **must** be a postal address but does not have to be within the UK. The other addresses can be any combination of a postal address, a box number at a UK document exchange or an electronic address. For a company include company's registered number, if any. For Scottish companies use an SC prefix and for limited liability partnerships use an OC prefix before the registered number, if any. For foreign companies give territory in which incorporated.*

Unless otherwise arranged with Land Registry headquarters, we require a certified copy of the chargee's constitution (in English or Welsh) if it is a body corporate but is not a company registered in England and Wales or Scotland under the Companies Acts.

12. Signature of applicant
or their conveyancer _____ **Date** _____

APPENDIX 9.2 LAND REGISTRY FORM FR1

First registration application

Land Registry **FR1**

If you need more room than is provided for in a panel, use continuation sheet CS and attach to this form.

1.	**Administrative area and postcode** if known - Lime Dorset

2. **Address or other description of the estate to be registered**

5 High Street Lime Dorset DS1 4QP

On registering a rentcharge, profit a prendre in gross, or franchise, show the address as follows:- "Rentcharge, franchise etc, over 2 The Grove, Anytown, Northshire NE2 9OO".

3. **Extent to be registered** *Place "X" in the appropriate box and complete as necessary.*

☐ The land is clearly identified on the plan to the _____
Enter nature and date of deed.

☐ The land is clearly identified on the attached plan and shown _____
Enter reference e.g. "edged red".

☑ e description in panel 2 is sufficient to enable the land to be clearly identified on the Ordnance Survey map

When registering a rentcharge, profit a prendre in gross or franchise, the land to be identified is the land affected by that estate, or to which it relates.

4. **Application, priority and fees** *A fee calculator for all types of applications can be found on Land Registry's website at www.landregistry.gov.uk/fees*

Nature of applications

in priority order	Value/premium £	Fees paid £
1. **First registration of the estate**	£95,000	£100
2.		
3.		
4.		
	TOTAL £100	

Fee payment method: **Place "X" in the appropriate box.**

I wish to pay the appropriate fee payable under the current Land Registration Fee Order:

b☑ heque or postal order, amount £100 _____ made payable to "Land Registry".

☐ by Direct Debit under an authorised agreement with Land Registry.

FOR OFFICIAL USE ONLY
Record of fees paid

Particulars of under/over payments

Fees debited £

Reference number

5. **The title applied for is** *Place "X" in the appropriate box.*

☑ absolute freehold ☐ absolute leasehold ☐ good leasehold ☐ possessory freehold

☐ possessory leasehold

6. *Documents lodged with this form* List the documents on Form DL. We shall assume that you request the return of these documents. But we shall only assume that you request the return of a statutory declaration, subsisting lease, subsisting charge or the latest document of title (for example, any conveyance to the applicant) if you supply a certified copy of the document. If certified copies of such documents are not supplied, we may retain the originals of such documents and they may be destroyed.

7. **The applicant is:** *Please provide the full name of the person applying to be registered as the proprietor.*	FOR OFFICIAL USE ONLY
Alice Gowen	Status codes
Application lodged by:	
Land Registry Key No.(if appropriate)	
Name (if different from the applicant) Land and Partners	
Address/DX No. 1 The High Street Lime Dorset	
Reference rma	
E-mail rma@land.co.uk	

Telephone No. 0693 512512	Fax No.

8. **Where you would like us to deal with someone else** *We shall deal only with the applicant, or the person lodging the application if different, unless you place "X" against one or more of the statements below and give the necessary details.*

☐ **Send title information document to the person shown below**

☐ **Raise any requisitions or queries with the person shown below**

☐ **Return original documents lodged with this form (see note in panel 6) to the person shown below**

If this applies only to certain documents, please specify.

Name

Address/DX No.

Reference

E-mail

Telephone No.	Fax No.

9. **Address(es) for service of every owner of the estate. The address(es) will be entered in the register and used for correspondence and the service of notice.** *In this and panel 10, you may give up to three addresses for service **one** of which **must** be a postal address but does not have to be within the UK. The other addresses can be any combination of a postal address, a box number at a UK document exchange or an electronic address. For a company include the company's registered number, if any. For Scottish companies, use an SC prefix, and for limited liability partnerships, use an OC prefix before the registered number if any. For foreign companies give territory in which incorporated.*

5 High Street Lime Dorset DS1 4QP

Unless otherwise arranged with Land Registry headquarters, we require a certified copy of the owner's constitution (in English or Welsh) if it is a body corporate but is not a company registered in England or Wales or Scotland under the Companies Acts.

10. Information in respect of a chargee or mortgagee *Do not give this information if a Land Registry MD reference is printed* *on the charge, unless the charge has been transferred.*

Full name and address (including postcode) for service of notices and correspondence of the person entitled to be registered as proprietor of each charge. *You may give up to three addresses for service; see panel 9 as to the details you should include.*

Unless otherwise arranged with Land Registry headquarters, we require a certified copy of the chargee's constitution (in English or Welsh) if it is a body corporate but is not a company registered in England and Wales or Scotland under the Companies Acts.

11. Where the applicants are joint proprietors *Place "X" in the appropriate box*

☐ The applicants are holding the property on trust for themselves as joint tenants

☐ The applicants are holding the property on trust for themselves as tenants in common in equal shares

☐ The applicants are holding the property *(complete as necessary)*

12. Disclosable overriding interests *Place "X" in the appropriate box.*

☑ **No disclosable overriding interests affect the estate**

☐ **Form DI accompanies this application**

Rule 28 of the Land Registration Rules 2003 sets out the disclosable overriding interests that you must tell us about. You must use Form DI to tell us about any disclosable overriding interests that affect the estate.

The registrar may enter a notice of a disclosed interest in the register of title.

13. The title is based on the title documents listed in Form DL which are all those that are in the possession or control of the applicant.

Place "X" in the appropriate box. If applicable complete the second statement; include any interests disclosed only by searches other than local land charges. Any interests disclosed by searches which do not affect the estate being registered should be certified.

☐ All rights, interests and claims affecting the estate known to the applicant are disclosed in the title documents and Form DI if accompanying this application. There is no-one in adverse possession of the property or any part of it.

In addition to the rights, interests and claims affecting the estate disclosed in the title documents or Form DI if accompanying this application, the applicant only knows of the following:

14. *Place "X" in this box if you are NOT able to give this certificate.* ☐

We have fully examined the applicant's title to the estate, including any appurtenant rights, or are satisfied that it has been fully examined by a conveyancer in the usual way prior to this application.

15. We have authority to lodge this application and request the registrar to complete the registration.

16. Signature of applicant or their conveyancer _____ **Date** _____

Note: Failure to complete the form with proper care may deprive the applicant of protection under the Land Registration Act if, as a result, a mistake is made in the register.

© Crown copyright (ref: LR/HQ/CD-ROM) 6/03

10 | LEASEHOLDS AND COMMONHOLD

10.1   INTRODUCTION

This chapter covers leaseholds and the new topic of Commonhold. Leases are a very long-established contractual relationship that offers tenants a legal estate in land. The use of leaseholds has really taken off in urban environments with the conversion of large houses into several flats and the development of business leases for commercial properties. However, the relationship between the lessor and lessee can be a troublesome one and the interface is strewn with litigation. In recent years there has been an up swelling of demand for the reform of this relationship. This has given rise to several recent statutory attempts at reform.

The present Government has introduced a statute that may make substantial changes to leasehold property law and conveyancing. It is called the Commonhold and Leasehold Reform Act 2002. It is intended that there will be a new form of holding a freehold estate. It will be called Commonhold land. It is actually a freehold but held by Commonhold across several estate owners in combination. The purpose of the new form of holding is to address the current deficiencies in relation to the enforceability between lessees of covenants and other lease provisions. (For the same reason it also addresses the related problems with freehold flats, i.e. flying freeholds.)

As a consequence we will consider in this chapter some of the more important aspects of recent attempts at reform along with some of the major areas of concerns in leases.

10.2   AN OVERVIEW OF THE SUBJECT AND A LOOK AT SOME PROBLEM AREAS

10.2.1   LEASEHOLDS

A lease is an agreement whereby an estate in land or property is created, but only for a finite term. Different types of leases with differing contents are required to deal with different types of property. No one lease is exactly the same as another. A lessor will require the lease to include clauses and/or covenants that adequately protect the reversionary interest. To that end the lessor will include a long list of obligations of covenants requiring the lessee to do and not to do various things. However, above all else the lease must contain the most important protection for the lessor, which is a right of re-entry or forfeiture. A lessee will also require essential clauses or covenants, but these are in many cases entirely opposite to those favoured by the lessor. A lessee will seek to limit the number and extent of the lease covenants. Moreover a prudent lessee will also seek covenants from the lessor to perform the obligations resting with the lessor, for example, to keep the main structure of the property of which the subject property forms part insured and in good repair.

10.2.1.2 **Typical lease covenants and other provisions**

To pay rent and other outgoings including service charges. A covenant to pay rent is fundamental and should appear in all leases that include a rental obligation. The lessee will want to introduce another clause that suspends the payment of rent if the property is destroyed or damaged by an insured risk. The lessor should agree this provided the lessor can control the insurance of the whole property and thus include loss of rent as an insurable risk. This leads on to the consideration of the payment of other outgoings such as insurance. This can be by way of an additional rent. Similarly any service charge payable can be made a rent. This benefits the lessor because if there are arrears these can be recovered as a rent, rather than as a result of a breach of covenant. The lease can also include a rent review provision allowing the rent to be increased (and/or decreased) at regular intervals. Rent reviews are rare in residential leases, which tend to include fixed increases at regular intervals but are common in commercial leases. The lease will also require the lessee to pay all outgoings applicable to the subject property such as council tax and water rates.

To keep the property in good repair. Where the lease is of a whole house or of one of two maisonettes, then it would be sensible to expect the lessee to keep the house or maisonette fully repaired. However, where there is a building in multiple occupation, the converse should apply and the lessor should maintain the whole property. This is to ensure that there is an appropriate level of consistent repair instead of a patchwork of different levels of repair that would occur if all the lessees dealt with repairs separately. Where there is a property in multiple occupation the usual repairing arrangement is for the lessee to be required to keep in good repair the inner skin of the demised property. This would require the lessee to keep properly maintained the plaster, the ceiling and flooring materials, but not much else. All structural elements of the property, including the floor and ceiling joists, the load-bearing walls, the roof and foundations, should all be repairable by the lessor with all the lessees paying a service charge to reimburse the lessor for this expense.

User. It is possible for the lease to include a covenant imposing an absolute restriction on the lessee against changing the use from any user precisely stated in the lease. In the case of a residential lease it is indeed desirable that the user clause be such that there can be only one permitted use that cannot be changed. The reason for this is that this form of extremely restrictive covenant will ensure conformity of use amongst all the lessees and ensure that there is no breach of planning law.

The covenant can be qualified requiring the lessor's consent before the use can be changed, and this is more commonly seen in commercial leases. (In such commercial leases an absolute user covenant will mean that the rent on review could be subject to a reduction in valuation. This is because a restriction on the user makes the lease less attractive to lessees and will therefore command less as a rental. However, a qualified covenant may avoid this limitation on the rent review.) There is no statutory provision that implies that the lessor's consent to change of use cannot be unreasonably withheld, as is the case with alienation covenants.

Alienation. In this context, the term 'alienation' covers covenants against assignments, underlettings, mortgages and other material dealings with the legal estate. There is no such restriction against alienation unless there is express provision to that effect within the lease. Many leases include a covenant whereby the lessee cannot assign the lease without the prior written consent of the lessor, such consent usually not to be unreasonably withheld. Some leases extend this provision to include sub-lettings as well as assignments. If the lease states that the lessor's consent is required but does not refer to reasonableness then statute adds this qualification (Landlord and Tenant Act 1927, s. 19(1)(a)). The Landlord and Tenant Act 1988 requires the lessor to deal with applications for consent to an assignment within a reasonable time of the making of the application. Should the lessor fail to do so, the lessee can, if the lessee has suffered loss as a consequence of the lessor's delay, sue the lessor for damages for breach of statutory duty.

The alienation covenant is of great concern for business leases. It is now considered inappropriate to fetter a lessee's right to deal freely with a long leasehold legal estate. The lessee of such an estate should be able to deal with it unhindered, just as any absolute owner would in relation to a fee simple. Therefore the question for a practitioner should be: Is there any restriction against alienation; and if so, should there be such a provision in the lease of the subject property? Frankly the answer is in the negative where the lease is a long lease of residential property. However, there can be exceptions. For example, the lease may require an incoming lessee, before being registered with the lessor as the new leaseholder, to enter into a direct covenant with the lessor to observe all the terms and especially the covenants in the lease. The same arrangement could be predicated upon the incoming lessee applying for licence to assign. The licence would then incorporate an observance covenant in the same format.

Alterations, additions and/or improvements. This is a topic of concern in both residential and business leases. Clearly the reversioner will want to ensure that unauthorised alterations do not take place. Furthermore the reversioner will want to be sure that the alterations that do take place will be such that the integrity of the structure will not be adversely affected. This will also be the case for additions and improvements. Of course lessees of long residential leases will argue that they should be free to do what they like with their property. Certainly this would seem to be a tenable argument where the lease is of a house. However, it is less tenable where the lease is of a flat or maisonette. Clearly in these circumstances, alterations, additions and improvements could very well affect adjacent or adjoining property, and the lessor may therefore feel that there should be controls over what may be done by the lessee in the way of alterations. An absolute bar on alterations or additions must be considered unacceptable in a long lease.

Quiet enjoyment. This is a covenant given by the lessor and appears in almost all leases. Indeed, if an express covenant is absent, an implied covenant will apply. The nature of the covenant is to confirm that the lessee can physically enjoy the complete benefit of the property without the lessor adversely affecting that enjoyment.

10.2.1.3 Liability on covenants in leases; enforcement

Until recently, it was the position that the original lessor and original lessee were liable to each other under the covenants in their lease for the full term granted by the lease. As a consequence of the effects of privity of contract this liability remained enforceable in the courts even if the lessee had subsequently assigned the residue of the term of the lease. The practical effect of this used to be that a lessee could be sued for arrears of rent, even though that lessee had not been the tenant in occupation for many years and, indeed, even where there had been many other subsequent lessees liable to pay rent under the terms of the original lease.

A measure of reform was made by the provisions of the Landlord and Tenant (Covenants) Act 1995. These provisions apply only to new leases created on or after 1 January 1996. In essence a lessee who assigns such a lease automatically enjoys a release through statute of any continuing liability under the lease covenants. However, a lessor can require the outgoing lessee to enter into a form of guarantee stipulated by the statute and known as an authorised guarantee agreement (AGA). This statute made a major change to the law affecting leasehold covenants. It means that the benefit and burden of lease covenants pass on assignment automatically without any question of whether or not they touch and concern the land. The successor in title, the assignee, will take the benefit and burden of the lease covenants by reason of statute and the assignor, the original lessee, will be released from liability (unless he or she is required to enter into an AGA).

Where a buyer is purchasing a flat in a block containing many other similar flats and where all are on long leases, the doctrine of privity of contract can cause major problems where one lessee is involved in a dispute with another about the enforcement of lease covenants. To enable enforcement to take place, and for all lessees in the block to know the extent of the lease terms for all the occupants of the block, the lease should state that all the leases granted for the block will or do contain the same terms as that for the subject property. Coupled with this there should be a covenant by the lessor on request by one lessee (and with that lessee agreeing to indemnify the lessor's costs) to enforce lease covenants against another lessee. Without this provision one lessee has no legal right to enforce covenants against another lessee as the covenant is not with the other lessee but with the lessor. However, the lease can be drawn up to include a covenant between the lessor, lessee and all the other lessees in the block. If this appears, each lessee can take action against any other lessee.

Since 11 May 2000, when the Contracts (Rights of Third Parties) Act 1999 came into force, the direct enforcement of covenants between lessees may be possible, but only in relation to leases granted on or after that date and where the lease does not exclude the Act.

10.2.2 COMMONHOLD

It has been the law for many years that positive obligations cannot be enforced in freehold land. In essence a burden of a positive covenant does not run with the land, see *Auterberry v. Oldham Corporation* (1885) 29 Ch D 750. This was re-iterated in the more recent case of *Rhone v. Stephens* [1994] 2 AC 310. In that case the court made it very clear that the only way the law was to change was if Parliament took steps towards reform. Their response was the concept of Commonhold land. This is defined in the Commonhold and Leasehold Reform Act 2002 (CLRA) as the land specified in the memorandum of association in relation to which a Commonhold association exercises functions (see s. 1(1)). It is in effect the name for the special way freehold land will be held by a community of freeholders entitled to participate in the association. Each separate property in a Commonhold development will be termed a unit. A unit can be either residential or commercial and the owner will be the unit-holder. There will be a Commonhold association that will own and manage the common parts. It will be a company limited by guarantee where all the members will be the unit-holders. Thus unit owners will have a duality of ownership. First, they will own their units and, secondly, they will own a share of the Commonhold association and thus indirectly the common parts.

All Commonhold will be registrable at the Land Registry that will require on registration a Commonhold Community Statement (CCS) and the memorandum and articles of association. The CCS will contain the rules and regulations for the Commonhold. It will be possible for owners of existing non-Commonhold property to seek to convert their title to a Commonhold arrangement, but 100% of all owners will have to agree to the conversion. The freeholder must consent to the conversion, without which conversion cannot proceed.

In summary the unit-holder will in effect own, freehold-style, his or her flat or property instead of being a leaseholder. The unit-holder will share in the running of the Commonhold held common parts and be required to pay a management or service charge. Unlike leaseholds, the units will not be wasting assets; neither will they be at the whim of a freeholder and/or the freeholder's management policies.

10.3 **SUBJECT ASSESSMENTS**

10.3.1 SUBJECT ASSESSMENT QUESTIONS: A COMMENTARY UPON THE TYPE AND CONTENT OF SUBJECT ASSESSMENT QUESTION AND SUGGESTED ANSWERS

Question 1

Your firm is acting for Sammy Hung who is proposing to take the grant of a new lease at a price of £75,000 of a flat in Gateshead for a term of one hundred and twenty five years from the first of January this year with an annual rent of £75.00 increasing to £112 after fifty years. You have received a draft Lease for approval, containing inter alia the following clauses:

'2. The Lessee hereby covenants with the Lessor as follows:

(a) <u>Alienation</u>

not to assign transfer underlet charge mortgage or part with or share the possession of or grant licence over the demised premises or any part thereof.

(b) <u>Alterations</u>

not to make any alterations or additions to the demised premises.'

Your Index Map Search result shows that the freehold is registered under Title No. GH 418527.

(i) Consider and explain any amendments you would make to these clauses in order to protect your client.

(ii) What are the essential actions you will need to take following completion in order to perfect the Lease?

(iii) Explain whether or not you will be entitled to investigate the lessor's freehold title. If the title is not investigated what are the risks to which the lessee is thereby subjected?

Commentary

This is a typical, straightforward subject assessment question that requires a point-by-point well-structured answer. It would be possible to answer the question by way of an essay although you must make sure that the structure of your answer is clear, highlighting the necessary points for the examiner. The answer below adopts a structured approach with headings and in point form. You have been given enough information to appreciate that there are three sections to the answer and you should ensure that you provide detailed answers to all three to earn high marks. It is bad examination practice to concentrate on one section of a multi-section question. Unless the marks for each section are shown on the paper and it is clear from those marks that a concentration of effort is required in one section then you should balance your efforts between the several sections concerned. In this particular question there is no such marking guidance and in its absence you should therefore spread your efforts more or less equally between the three sections without giving any preference to any of them.

The areas concerned are leasehold covenants, post-completion requirements and your entitlement to inspect the superior title. You will therefore appreciate that the spread of information required is wide and you should only answer a question of this nature if your knowledge is sufficiently detailed in all three areas to enable you to answer the question with confidence.

Suggested answer

There are three elements to this question, first a consideration of the amendments to the draft lease concerning tenant's covenants, secondly post completion requirements and thirdly an examination of the buyer's entitlement to inspect the superior or freehold title. Each section will be considered separately as follows:

(i) <u>Amendments to draft lease</u>

Clause 2(a)

This covenant is an absolute bar on assignments mortgages underlettings and other aspects of alienation. This is an unacceptable restriction in a ninety-nine year lease of a residential flat. A tenant will almost always have to make a payment to obtain the lease and will therefore want to be able to dispose of it and recover the premium perhaps with a profit. Indeed the tenant may wish to mortgage the property and will probably need to finance the acquisition itself by way of a loan from a bank or building society. The lease should be amended to allow assignments, etc. of the whole premises subject to lessor's written consent (although an absolute bar in connection with part only of premises would be acceptable). Section 19(1)(a) of Landlord and Tenant Act 1927 will then apply so that consent cannot unreasonably be withheld. The lessor will be able to demand payment of reasonable legal expenses incurred in giving consent.

Clause 2(b)

Again, this is an absolute bar on alterations or additions and must therefore be considered unacceptable in a lease of this length. The lease should be amended to allow alterations with the lessor's written consent. To the extent that proposed alterations amount to improvements s. fig. 19 of Landlord and Tenant Act 1927 will then apply so that consent cannot be unreasonably withheld, and the lessor cannot demand any payment beyond his or her reasonable legal and other expenses incurred in granting consent. However to avoid any argument about whether an alteration is or is not an improvement the clause should be amended to allow alterations or additions with the lessor's consent, such consent not to be unreasonably withheld. In this way the lessor will be required to justify any refusal of permission, ultimately in court, and would therefore not be an avenue the landlord would go down without real justification. It should be noted that the statute does not stop the lessor from seeking a reasonable sum should the proposed amendments diminish the value of the premises or indeed any adjacent premises in the ownership of the same lessor. Similarly if the alteration or addition does not add to the letting value of the premises the statute does not prevent the lessor from obtaining from the tenant a covenant to reinstate the premises to their former condition at the end or sooner determination of the lease.

(ii) <u>Action following completion</u>

To avoid a penalty fee for late payment being made by the Inland Revenue a buyer must send a signed Stamp Duty Land Tax return (SDLT1) to the Stamp Office within thirty days of completion and:

(1) Submit payment at the same time for the full Stamp Duty Land Tax. This will be on the full price at the relevant rate being in this case £750, i.e., 1% of the consideration. There is also SDLT to be paid on

the rent. The SDLT charge will be at a rate of 1% on the net present value (NPV) of the total rent payable over the term of the lease. Future rents will be discounted at 3.5% per annum in order to arrive at the NPV. Leases where the NPV of the rent over the term of the lease does not exceed £150,000 will be exempt. This being the case it would appear that there will be no SDLT payable on this rental as it will clearly be below the tax threshold. After payment of SDLT the buyer needs a Revenue certificate of payment without which no application to the Land Registry can proceed.

(2) A buyer's solicitor must then apply for first registration of the lease with a new and separate registered title. This is because the new lease is being granted out of a registered title for more than seven years. In these circumstances s. 4 of the Land Registration Act 2002 requires such a deed to be submitted to the Land Registry for first registration within two months of the date of completion. On completion of the process of first registration the lease will then also be noted within the charges register of the Lessor's Title. It should be noted that the new legal estate is only created on registration and that the effect of failure to apply for first registration is that the transaction stalls and the effect is that there is a contract made for valuable consideration to grant the legal estate concerned (see s.7 Land Registration Act 2002). If this happens then in theory the title has not been perfected and all the buyer can claim is a mere contractual right! (If this is the case then it could be that the seller will be a bare trustee for the buyer until such time as the first registration of the lease is finally completed.)

(iii) Entitlement to inspect the superior or freehold title

On the grant of a lease, the tenant has no automatic right to investigate the lessor's freehold title unless the lessor agrees otherwise. If this is the case the purchase contract should contain a provision requiring the seller to deduce the freehold title. Please see standard condition 8.2.4 that requires the seller to deduce a title that will enable the buyer to register the lease at Land Registry with an absolute title. Of course in these circumstances the freehold title will have to be deduced to ensure the grant of an absolute title. Accordingly the purchase contract must be checked, first, to ensure it is drawn up on the basis of the fourth edition of the standard conditions and secondly that no attempt has been made in the special conditions of that contract to limit or exclude condition 8.2.4.

If title is not investigated the tenant runs the risk that the lease may not have been validly granted or may not bind a mortgagee of the freehold. For example, the freehold may be in mortgage and the mortgage may specifically preclude the borrower or seller from granting any leases. There is also the risk of being bound by unknown third party interests affecting the freehold, being either overriding interests or other interests protected by entry on the registers of the freehold title when the lease was granted. These risks are of course unacceptable to the tenant.

Question 2

Standard Grand Estates Plc through their manging director Samuel MacSweeney has consulted you about their intended development in Battersea. They have purchased a mansion block of flats and intend to sell all seventy flats once they have been fully refurbished. They want to know from you how to deal with the question of subsequent repairs or redecoration required to the block. They wish to know this in the light of their clear requirement to be completely released from any such involvement. Their instructions are that once the leases have been granted they simply want to collect the rents and do nothing else. They have asked you to write to them to indicate how this might be accomplished. In your letter of advice please indicate the appropriate method of complying with their instructions and how it might work in practice.

The company have also indicated that once all the flats have been sold they may well want to sell their freehold reversion by auction. However they believe there maybe a problem about this and have asked you for your advice. Please indicate what this problem might be and how it could affect your client.

Commentary

This is a two-part question that covers, first, how to deal with repairing obligations that avoid any liability on the lessor's part and secondly the effect of the Part I of the Landlord and Tenant Act 1987. The answer required is in the form of a letter of advice. In these circumstances the structure of the letter must be clear and direct and must provide the advice required by your clients. The advice must be directed to the particular areas concerned. If you know the law the second part of the question is simple, all you need to do to obtain high marks is to show how the statute will affect the proposed sale. The first part of the question is more demanding. You will need to be aware of at least two distinct ways in which the requirements of the client can be accommodated and then you will need to recommend one against the other. Good advice examines the possibilities available to the client and then puts forward a choice for the client to consider. Because, in the main, law is a set of boundaries showing what people cannot do rather than what they can, lawyers can easily fall into the trap of simply being negative in their advice. A good lawyer will help the client by showing what the client can do and not what the client cannot do.

Suggested answer

Dear Mr MacSweeney,

Advice required by Standard Grand Estates Plc ('the company')

This letter is written in two parts, the first concerning future maintenance of the block and the second in relation to a statutory provision that could upset their auction plans, namely Part I of the Landlord and Tenant Act 1987.

Future maintenance arrangements

The company wishes to grant seventy leases on the basis that they are not involved in the subsequent upkeep of the block. This is an area of real concern for you because potential lenders will only lend on the security of the leases if they are satisfied with the repairing arrangements for the entire block. They will take the view that the leases must contain terms that ensure that the block is well maintained so that the value of their security is upheld.

The company have a choice, they can either go for the simple option and impose on all their lessees repairing covenants or they can create a more complicated situation of a third party to all the leases namely a management company assigned the responsibility of the repair and upkeep of the block. There is the alternative of the lessor providing these services but this is of course exactly what the company wishes to avoid. Each option will be considered in turn, with a recommendation for the company after that.

The simple option of the imposition of repairing covenants is, the easiest to arrange but does have considerable practical disadvantages that may outweigh the attraction of simplicity. It is true to say that in a long lease the tenant is normally expected to be responsible under lease covenants for the maintenance and upkeep of the demised premises. However there are inherent problems with this arrangement in the case of flat leases in a block where there are lots of flats such as in this mansion block in Brixton. It is not difficult to imagine the piecemeal or patchwork effect that might arise if the tenants were each individually responsible for repairs. Some leaseholders may well be diligent and comply in full with their obligations. However, undoubtedly there will be others who will not and consequently the block will suffer from uneven care and attention. Indeed when considering the main structure unless there are very detailed and lengthy definitions within the leases it may not be clear just who will be expected to repair what. For example should those flat owners on the top floor be the only ones responsible for repairing the roof? If so they are unlikely to sell as of course most buyers would be very reluctant to proceed with a purchase that could involve such an onerous obligation. As can be seen this patchwork approach is fraught with difficulty and has the major disadvantage for you of making the flats harder to sell. This alone may be enough to persuade you to consider the other option, that of the management company.

The leases could be drafted so that there were three parties to the lease being the lessor, the lessee and a management company. The lessor would grant the leases to the lessees on the basis that in future they simply collect the ground rent whilst the management company is charged with the responsibility of the future repairs to the block. All tenants will be under an obligation to them to pay service charges either in advance or on demand. The best element is however that each individual lessee will have a say in how the maintenance company acts as the leases will provide for each of them to be a member of the maintenance company. This can be by individual shares or by being simple members if the company is one limited by guarantee. (Such a company is suggested as it does away with the necessity of share certificates, etc.) The lease will further say that no lease transfer registration can take place without there being a prior transfer of membership, such as a transfer of the management company share from the seller to the buyer. The attraction to the company of this arrangement is that mortgagees prefer it and this will in turn lead to the flats being readily saleable. Further there will be an element of democratic control available to all tenants as far as repairs are concerned and this in itself could be a strong selling point. Accordingly the best advice for the company must be for you to set up a management company to look after future repairs.

Auction plans and Part I of the Landlord and Tenant Act 1987

The company may wish to sell their freehold reversion at auction once all the leases are sold and you have enquired about whether this could be a problem. Unfortunately there could be a difficulty caused by the effects of the statute mentioned above ('the Act'). The Act gives tenants in a block such as this a right of pre-emption where the lessor intends to dispose of the freehold. The lessor must give notice of the proposed disposal to the tenants, (s. 5 of the Act) and the notice will give them the right to buy the lessor's interest. At least 50% of the flats must be held by qualifying tenants (in effect long leaseholders) and the block must contain two or more flats. It is clear that both these pre-conditions apply in this case and the Act will therefore apply to any such sale by the company. An auction is clearly a disposal contemplated by the Act (see s. 4 of the Act) and the company will be obliged to offer the reversion to the tenants before the auction. If at least half of the qualifying tenants take up the offer the lessor will be obliged to sell on the same terms as those that gave rise to the notice. It is presumed that the price will therefore be not less than the auction reserve price.

The Act contains clear provisions should the lessor sell without serving the necessary notices. Section 11 provides for a notice to be served by the tenants on the purchaser requiring information about the sale and s. 12 then contains a provision to force the buyer to transfer the freehold to the tenants on the same terms as were made for the disposal to that purchaser. However, any dispute about the terms, including the price can be referred to and decided by Tribunal. A further practical problem is that the time constraints contemplated by the Act are lengthy. For example the period during which the tenants must respond to the notice is in effect two months with further time delays possible. Accordingly the timing of the disposal may be greatly delayed by the effect of the Act.

I do hope the above is of assistance but if I can help further please do not hesitate to contact me.

Yours sincerely

Question 3

RICHARDS ABBEY AND PARTNERS, SOLICITORS
OFFICE MEMORANDUM

To   The Trainee Solicitor

From   The Senior Partner

Re our client The Megalopolis Bank Plc

The Bank have offered financial assistance by way of a proposed advance in the form of a first mortgage of £175,000 to Mr and Mrs Charles Chatterway in their proposed purchase of the leasehold dwellinghouse, number 102 Seaview Road, Whitegates Lancashire for the residue of a term of ninety-nine years from 1 January 1954 at a yearly rent of £25. The purchase price is £200,000 for this detached four-bedroom house in one of the more select areas of Whitegates.

The Bank has instructed us to look after their interests in taking a first charge over the property. Mr and Mrs Chatterway are separately represented by Ottershaw Eager & Co. You will be aware that the Bank will require a report on title with particular reference to the lease. The bank manager has seen a copy of the purchase contract and is a little worried because it refers to the lease being registered with good leasehold title. He thinks that there might be a problem bearing in mind that the Chatterways came to the Bank for the loan only after exchanging contracts. Consequently, we should bear in mind that it could be that Mr and Mrs Chatterway have had problems raising a loan. We therefore need to exercise some discretion in this case. However, completion is next week, so we shall need to work quickly on the preparation and submission of the report on title.

Please let me have a list of the documents we shall need to inspect before we are able to give a satisfactory report on title to the bank. Could you in particular let me have your thoughts about the nature of a good leasehold title and the term of the lease?

Commentary

This is an interesting question in that while it is about a lease it is from the perspective of a lender proposing to make a loan secured on the leasehold title. You will need to consider what constitutes an acceptable title for a mortgagee and what does not. In these circumstances, where a lease is involved, you will need to show why a particular leasehold may not be acceptable. Accordingly there are two elements to this question, first, whether or not the title offered as a security is acceptable, and secondly, what you as a solicitor for the lender will need to see to enable you to check and report on the title for the bank. The particular point that will need detailed consideration is of course on the question of a good leasehold title. You will only be able to score high marks if you can demonstrate a clear appreciation of the nature of such a title and its limitations. Now that all of England and Wales is subject to compulsory first registration this kind of question is going to remain popular with examiners particularly as the question of good leasehold titles remains an area of continuing concern. Finally, please note that the question asks you to list the documents requires. Accordingly you should make sure that in your answer you do exactly that and list the documents. Of course each part of the list will include your reasons for the inclusion of that particular document.

Suggested answer

RICHARDS ABBEY AND PARTNERS, SOLICITORS
OFFICE MEMORANDUM

To   The Senior Partner

From   The Trainee solicitor

Re our client Meglopolis Bank Plc 102 Seaview Road Whitegates Lancashire

I refer to your recent memo concerning the above property. I set out below a list of the documents the firm will require together with my comments on the good leasehold title and other pertinent factors that will be of concern to the clients.

Dealing first with the good leasehold title, as you will know this title is issued by Land Registry when the superior or freehold title has not been deduced. Because the freehold has not been deduced it cannot be proved to the Registry who therefore issue a good leasehold title instead of an absolute title. In these circumstances we shall need to inspect official copies of the leasehold title to confirm that the title is in fact only good leasehold. Assuming this to be the case, then there is no guarantee that the lease has been validly granted and also, if the freehold title contains a defect the fact that the lease has been registered with a good leasehold title does not release the leasehold from any knock-on effect of the freehold title defect (see s. 10 Land Registration Act 2002). This could mean that the landlord might not have the right to grant the lease in the first place but as the title was not deduced no one has checked on this threatening possibility. It is therefore clear that we cannot report to the clients that the leasehold title is good and marketable without also having investigated the freehold title.

Accordingly, we shall need to inspect the following documents:

1. Official copies of leasehold title including the title plan

This of course constitutes the registered element of the title to the lease.

2. On the assumption that the freehold title is unregistered, evidence of such freehold title from a point at least fifteen years ago and down to the date the lease was granted will be required

This is necessary to get around the problems with the good leasehold title.

3. Land charges search or land registry search in respect of freehold title, depending on whether freehold is registered or unregistered.

We will need to check whether any adverse entries existed at the time of the grant of the lease.

4. Contract

This is required to confirm the terms of the transaction and also to see if the contract allows the buyer to investigate the superior title. It probably does not whereupon the buyer is likely to be in difficulties in satisfying our requirement on behalf of the bank.

5. Copy of lease

This will need to be seen to make sure that none of the covenants are particularly onerous or unusual and in particular that there is not a prohibition in the lease against creating mortgages. It would also be prudent to check on whether the lease requires the lessor's consent to the creation of a legal charge over the leasehold title. We must also make sure that the lease does not allow forfeiture on bankruptcy.

6. Replies to requisitions on title

These should be seen to check on the questions raised by the buyer to avoid duplication by us in our own requisitions of the buyer's solicitors. It is also appropriate to check that the necessary arrangements have been proposed for the redemption of all existing mortgages to ensure that there will be no obstacles to our client bank's mortgage being a first charge.

7. Result of land registry search of leasehold title

This is required to check on any adverse entries and to ensure that if there are any that they are dealt with to our entire satisfaction on or before completion.

8. Replies to pre-contract enquiries made of the seller's solicitors (or Property Information Forms)

To check on the answers to see if any matters have been disclosed that could be disadvantageous to our clients or its proposed mortgage.

9. Local authority search

To check on any adverse entries or replies made by the local authority.

10. Water search

To check on the nature of the water supply and drainage facilities for the subject property.

11. Other searches

We should consider whether other searches are required such as a coal mining or commons registration search. This will depend on the location of the property and I can give further assistance once the copy title details are to hand. We will also need to see the result of the buyer's environmental report.

It should be mentioned that s. 62(2) of the Land Registration Act 2002 allows for the upgrade of a good leasehold title to an absolute title if the Registrar is satisfied as to the freehold title and indeed any intermediate title. In effect this necessitates the production to the Registry of the superior title or titles and for the Registry's acceptance. This will require the Registrar to be satisfied that the original lessor had the power to grant the lease in the first place and that if there any incumbrances that affect the lease that they are disclosed.

One further item should be mentioned to the bank and that concerns the residue of the term granted by the lease. I believe we should highlight the fact that this lease was granted in 1954. I am aware that some lenders are reluctant to lend on lease with less than 60 years to go bearing in mind that a lease is in effect a 'wasting asset' in that as each year passes the term is correspondingly shorter and of less value. However I have also noted that the property in question is described as a leasehold dwellinghouse and it may well be that the current owner of the property could qualify as a tenant capable of enfranchising, of demanding the freehold, pursuant to the provisions of the Leasehold Reform Act 1967. If the freehold can be acquired in this manner then of course it could remove both difficulties namely the problem with the good leasehold title and the difficulty over the residue of the term of the lease.

TIME ENGAGED 45 MINUTES

TRAINEE SOLICITOR

Question 3

Your client Paulene Keane inherited two adjoining semi-detached homes and moved into the one on the right looking at the properties from the road. Both are freehold. The other house was originally tenanted by an elderly single woman who has recently died so that this property is now vacant. Dorothy has decided she does not want the hassle of being a lessor and therefore intends to sell. However your client wants to continue to exert a measure of control over the next-door property even after it has been sold. Her motivation is to ensure that the adjacent property does not adversely affect the value of her own. In particular she has written a letter to you asking you how this can be achieved for the following:

1. that the house will remain a residential property,

2. that it will always be well maintained,

3. that it will not be altered or extended without her prior approval, and

4. all fences between the two houses will be maintained by the next door owner.

You consider and suggest to Ms Keane that the best way of achieving these objectives is by a new long lease. Please list with explanations the main provisions you would incorporate in such a lease. Is there a complication that you need to refer to the client concerning your suggestion?

Commentary

If any question on leases might be predicted, this could be it. This is a decidedly broad question but particular in its requirement for you to demonstrate a good working knowledge of what should be in a lease. However, the lease contents must be in accordance with the client's requirements. Accordingly, what is required is a list of the main provisions with a specific analysis of the four particular items set out in the body of the question. Of course the difficulty in answering a question of this nature is selecting what should go in and what you can safely leave out. Many residential leases of this kind can stretch to over fifty pages and may contain more than sixty covenants for the tenant to perform. It is therefore not difficult to see why you must discipline yourself by adhering to what are the main lease provisions with specific reference to the four items in the question.

In the light of the demands of this type of question you should keep a careful eye on the clock to make sure that you do not exceed the time allotted to the writing of this answer. The best way of doing this is to plan your answer carefully before starting and then make sure you stick to the plan even if, with the pressure of time, you end up with numbered points at the conclusion of your answer rather than full paragraphs. At least this way you will be able to show to the examiner the extent of your knowledge and still be able to devote enough time to your other answers. As to format you could answer the question by way of an essay or you could adopt a letter form in reply to the letter mentioned and written by the client. Finally, you must consider what the examiner might want to see in your answer as a complication and here you will need to show an understanding of the effect of the Leasehold Reform Act 1967.

Suggested answer

The following are the main provisions that I consider should be in the lease of Ms Keane's adjacent property:

1. After setting out the parties to the deed the lease must commence with a clear and precise description of the property together with a scale plan. The main reason for this is to ensure certainty as to the extent of the property comprised in the lease.

2. This should be followed by a statement of the rights accruing to the property along with the rights to which it is subject. This again is to ensure certainty particularly as to rights of access or parking, etc.

3. There should be a clear statement as to the term of the lease and the annual rent to be paid and whether or not the rent is fixed or subject to upward only review. All leases should contain such critical components.

4. After these provisions there should then be listed the tenant's covenants including a covenant to pay the rent. One particularly important provision is a covenant restricting the tenant's use of the property. This is of special concern for Ms Keane and can be addressed by a covenant by the tenant restricting his or her use of the property to only residential use for the occupation of the family of the tenant solely. The covenant can be absolute or qualified by reference to the lessor's consent and if it is so qualified it is not implied that consent may not be unreasonably withheld. However for the sake of certainty the advice to Ms Keane should be to insert in the lease an absolute covenant by the tenant not to use the property other than a private dwellinghouse for the occupation of the tenant and the tenant's family.

5. Ms Keane requires the house to be well maintained and to accomplish this she can insert in the lease a covenant on the part of the tenant to put and keep the premises in good and substantial repair and condition. This places an extremely heavy burden upon the tenant such that the tenant will have to put the property in good repair even if it was not in such good repair at the start of the lease. The clause could be further amplified to extend the tenant's liability to replace worn and damaged parts of the property including brick stonework roofing materials and ironwork.

6. To further ensure proper maintenance the lease should also contain two further clauses, one requiring the tenant to redecorate the interior at least every five years and the other requiring the tenant to redecorate the exterior every three years. These clauses would operate on a rolling cyclical basis, thus ensuring continued maintenance throughout the lease term.

7. Ms Keane requires the tenant to seek her permission for any proposed alterations or additions. This can again be ensured by a tenant's covenant not to alter or add to the property without the prior written permission of the lessor. The covenant is qualified and as such statute implies that consent cannot be unreasonably withheld in the case of improvements (s. 19(2) Landlord and Tenant Act 1927). It is

suggested that to avoid any difficulty in this respect that the covenant be made absolute. The reason for this kind of covenant is to stop unwelcome, unsightly or unbalanced alterations that could affect the lessor's next-door property.

8. To ensure that the boundary fences are maintained there should be inserted in the lease a covenant on the part of the tenant not to allow the boundary fences to fall into disrepair but to maintain all of them, which ever they are, in good and weatherproof condition. This will put an obligation on the tenant to repair all the fences in accordance with the client's requirements.

9. The lease should also require the tenant to insure the property to the full reinstatement value and to use all insurance monies received in reinstating the property. This is to ensure that the property is repaired after being damaged by any insurable risk.

10. The lease should also contain a forfeiture clause to the intent that should the tenant be in breach of any covenant the lessor can forfeit the lease. This is of course the reason for making all the restrictive covenants in that the forfeiture clause enables the lessor to exert a sanction against the tenant of the ultimate loss of the residue of the lease term. So far as any covenants by the lessor there should only be one being the covenant by the lessor allowing the tenant quiet enjoyment of the premises. This is best made an express covenant, as the lessor may want to limit the possible effects of such a clause.

11. Finally there should be a covenant by the tenant to repair as a party structure equally with the adjoining owner any walls, foundations, roofs or roof timbers used in common with that adjoining owner. This must be included as the properties are semi-detached.

12. There is one complication that should be mentioned to the client and that is the effect of the Leasehold Reform Act 1967. This statute applies to long leases such as this (s. 3 Leasehold Reform Act 1967 as amended) and in particular where there is a lease of a house. If the tenant has held the lease to the property for at least two years then the tenant will be allowed to demand the freehold from Ms Keane. On paying the open market value the tenant may enfranchise. If the lease is in its early stages the value will be low and on acquisition the lessee can merge the lease into the freehold. The Act does set out what terms are to be in the freehold transfer. The statute contemplates the inclusion of such terms as are required to put the parties in the same position as they were in under the lease. It may therefore be possible to include some additional covenants that bind the freeholder in the manner required by the client. However, this will be subject to negotiation between the parties at the time of enfranchisement.

10.3.2 MULTIPLE CHOICE QUESTIONS AND ANSWERS TO MULTIPLE CHOICE QUESTIONS

We set out below examples of ten multiple choice questions that you might encounter in a subject assessment. Thereafter you will find some typical short answer questions that can also feature in a subject assessment and which cover pre-completion and completion matters. Answers to both are also set out below. Remember our initial guidance. Never leave multiple choice answers with a blank multiple choice. If there are four possibilities and you are not sure of the answer select the one you think might be right, you have a one in four chance of getting it right! Also look at the instructions on the paper. If it says select the right answer on the paper by circling the correct choice then do just that. Do not make a tick or underline your selection, as the strict response would be to fail you even though the selection may be correct. Also none of the answers given might be right. In these circumstances follow the rubric in the question paper and explain why none of the listed answers apply.

10.3.2.1 **Multiple choice questions**

Unless otherwise directed, select the right answer by circling it in each question. Should you think that none of the selections apply please explain why not in your answer book.

1. If a lease states that the lessor's consent is required for an assignment of the residue of the term but does not refer to reasonableness then statute adds this qualification. Is it :

    (a) Landlord and Tenant Act 1954, s. 40

    (b) Landlord and Tenant Act 1927, s. 19(1)(a)

    (c) Law of Property (Miscellaneous Provisions) Act 1989, s. 2

    (d) Landlord and Tenant Act 1987, s. 4

2. Commonhold is a new legal estate.

    Is this statement TRUE/FALSE? Please delete the incorrect choice.

3. Which of the following legal leases does not need to be made by deed?

    (a) lease for five years at a market rent

    (b) sub-lease for nine years (less ten days)

    (c) lease for ninety-nine years at a premium of £10,000 but at a nominal rent

    (d) lease for three years at a market rent

4. Alienation covenants are governed by LTA 1927 s. 19(1)(a) that says:

    (a) if there is a qualified covenant, the lessor cannot unreasonably withhold his or her consent

    (b) if there is a qualified covenant the lessor can unreasonably withhold his or her consent

    (c) if there is a qualified covenant the lessor can ignore alienation applications

    (d) if there is a qualified covenant the lessee can avoid making alienation applications

5. If a lease states that the lessor's consent is required for a change of use but does not refer to reasonableness then statute adds this qualification. Is it :

    (a) Landlord and Tenant Act 1927, s. 19(1)(a)

    (b) Landlord and Tenant Act 1954, s. 40

    (c) Landlord and Tenant Act 1987, s. 4

    (d) Law of Property (Miscellaneous Provisions) Act 1989, s. 2

6. A lender will not, in any circumstances, accept as security for a loan, a residential long lease that contains forfeiture on bankruptcy of the lessee.

    Is this statement TRUE/FALSE? Please delete the incorrect choice.

7. Which of the following does not apply to a Commonhold:

    (a) commonhold association being a company limited by guarantee

    (b) a Commonhold Community Statement

    (c) the memorandum and articles of association

    (d) an Authorised Guarantee Agreement

8. Under the Landlord and Tenant (Covenants) Act 1995 unless the lessee has entered into an 'authorised guarantee agreement', the lessee will not on assignment be automatically released from any liability in the future on lease covenants.

    Is this statement TRUE/FALSE? Please delete the incorrect choice.

9. The Leasehold Reform Act 1967 allows lessees to claim the freehold of which of the following premises:

    (a) maisonette

    (b) office

    (c) flat

    (d) house

10. If a lessee of a flat wishes to extend their lease term under the provisions of the Leasehold Reform, Housing And Urban Development Act 1993, which of the following applies as a qualifying condition for the claim:

(a) the lessee must have held the lease for at least two years

(b) the lessee must have lived in the flat for at least three years

(c) the lessee must have at least four other lessees making the same claim against the same lessor

(d) the lessee must have a registered lease

10.3.2.2 *Answers to multiple choice questions*

1. The correct answer is (b). If the lease states that the lessor's consent is required but does not refer to reasonableness then statute adds this qualification (Landlord and Tenant Act 1927, s. 19(1)(a)).

2. Commonhold is a not a new legal estate. This statement is therefore false. Commonhold is a freehold community. It is in effect a new way of holding a freehold amongst a community of freeholders that can be set up by the Commonhold and Leasehold Reform Act 2002.

3. The correct answer is (d). Because the lease term is for three years it does not need to be made by deed and can by in the form of a tenancy agreement, i.e. a contract not sealed or even granted orally.

4. The correct answer is (a). Alienation covenants are governed by LTA 1927 s. 19(1)(a) that says that if there is a qualified covenant, the lessor cannot unreasonably withhold his or her consent.

5. None of these apply. There is no statutory provision that implies that the lessor's consent cannot be unreasonably withheld. However, s. 19(3) of the Landlord and Tenant Act 1927 does provide that if a consent for a change of use is required, then the lessor is not allowed to demand a premium or extra rent for giving that consent.

6. This statement is true. If a lease allows a right of re-entry on the bankruptcy of the lessee, the lease will not be mortgageable. The reasoning is of course that if the lessee did indeed become bankrupt and the lessor forfeited the lease then the lender's security would evaporate.

7. The correct answer is (d). Authorised Guarantee agreements relate to leases and specifically the enforcement of leases for post 31 December 1995 leases.

8. This statement is false. The Landlord and Tenant (Covenants) Act 1995 applies to all leases granted on or after 1 January 1996 and under the terms of the Act unless the lessee has entered into an 'authorised guarantee agreement', the lessee will, on assignment, be automatically released from any liability in the future on lease covenants. If there is an 'authorised guarantee agreement' then the outgoing lessee acts as guarantor for the first successor in title only.

9. The correct answer is (d). This statute applies to long leases, i.e. those for a term exceeding twenty-one years (Leasehold Reform Act 1967, s. 3 as amended), of houses.

10. The correct answer is (a). Because of changes made by the Commonhold and Leasehold Reform Act 2002 all that the lessee claimant must show is that the lessee has held the lease for at least two years. This requirement replaces the previous condition that was three years residence.

10.3.3 **SHORT ANSWER QUESTIONS WITH ANSWERS**

1. Your firm acts for Erica Bridge who wishes to buy a residential ninety-nine-year lease for £125,000. The draft documents have just arrived from the seller's solicitor and you have been asked by your Principal to check the draft lease to make sure it is acceptable. Please compile

a checklist of the main points of concern about the draft lease and the contract terms that should be considered and checked for this purpose.

2. Your firm acts for developers who have recently built a new small estate of eight light industrial workshop units on the edge of town. They want to dispose of them by sales to individual workshop owners in such a way that ensures that the maintenance of the common areas (the estate roads and pavements and surrounding garden areas) are kept to a high standard but they do not want to get involved in making sure that this is what is done. Please advise the developers of their options.

3. Your Training Partner is concerned that the fee earners handling residential long leasehold purchases are aware of items in a residential lease that would be unacceptable to a buyer/mortgagee. She has asked you to prepare a list of items that you consider could be considered defects meriting concern. Please draft such a list.

Suggested answers

1. The following constitutes an appropriate checklist that covers some of the major points of concern.
   (a) The description of the subject property in the lease. Are all the walls, floors and ceilings included or excluded?
   (b) Is there a garden at the front or rear, and if so does either or both form part of the property to be purchased?
   (c) Are there adequate rights of access to and from the subject property over the parts leading to the premises?
   (d) Are there mutual rights of support, protection and entry for repairs?
   (e) Is the buyer aware of rental at the levels shown in the draft?
   (f) Are the lessee's covenants reasonable and in particular is there any restriction on alienation and if so is that restriction fair to a long leaseholder?
   (g) Does the lease allow forfeiture on bankruptcy? If so, take steps immediately to remove this provision.
   (h) Is there a covenant requiring the lessor to enforce covenants against other lessees in the block? This must be included.
   (i) Does the contract make proper and exact reference to the estate and term to be sold to your client?
   (j) Are there any lease-specific special conditions and if so are they acceptable in the context of your instructions for the buyer?
   (k) If the buyer intends to purchase with the assistance of a mortgage, we must make sure that the lease terms accord with the lender's requirements. We must therefore check the details of the mortgage offer and the CML Handbook together with any particular requirements the lender may list with the client's offer of mortgage.

2. The developers wish to sell off their development to individual workshop owners while ensuring that there is a mechanism in place to maintain the common areas of the development. This can be achieved in one of two ways. First, by granting leases and then vesting the freehold in a management company where the shareholders are the eight lessees. Secondly, by creating a Commonhold that governs this estate.

(1) Leasehold solution

The developers will grant leases with three parties. The first will be themselves as lessors. The second will be the lessee/purchaser and the third will be a management company given the title to the common parts by a lease with the developers and with whom the lessee must covenant to pay a service charge levied by the company. They will control that company, as each owner will have a share in the company. In this way the management company will be obliged to maintain the common parts and the lessees will be obliged to pay for it.

(2) <u>Commonhold solution</u>

Alternatively the developers can sell off Commonhold units. Each separate property in a Commonhold development will be termed a unit. A unit can be either residential or commercial and the owner will be the unit-holder. There will be a Commonhold association that will own and manage the common parts. It will be a company limited by guarantee where all the members will be the unit-holders. Thus unit owners will have a duality of ownership. First they will own their units and, secondly, they will own a share of the Commonhold association and thus indirectly the common parts. The unit-holder will share in the running of the Commonhold held common parts and be required to pay a management or service charge.

3. A residential long lease will be considered defective if any of the following appear in the lease we are considering for our client buyer:

   (a) If the lease contains a forfeiture on bankruptcy provision.

   (b) If the lease fails to include proper repairing covenants that ensure the ongoing maintenance and renewal of the main structure, roof, foundations and common parts. This will require the involvement of the lessor or a management company.

   (c) If the property is in a newly constructed block of flats where the developer is not offering an NHBC guarantee. Although not strictly a lease defect, many lenders will not lend in the absence of this protection.

   (d) If the lease does not include a covenant by the lessor to take action against another lessee for breach of covenant at the request of a lessee who agrees to indemnify the lessor for that action.

   (e) If the lease has inadequate insurance provisions, or the lessor is under no obligation to look after unlet or unsold property in a large block.

10.4 REFERENCES TO WIDER READING INCLUDING PRACTITIONER TEXTS

- *A Practical Approach to Conveyancing* by Abbey R. and Richards M. (6th edn, OUP)—Chapter 10.

- *A Practical Approach to Commercial Conveyancing and Property* by Abbey R. and Richards M. (2nd edn, OUP).

- *The Law Society's Conveyancing Handbook 10th edn* by Silverman F.—Sections K and L dealing with Leaseholds and Tenanted Property.

- *Emmet on Title*—Chapters 26 to 28, Leases.

- For more detail on the changes introduced by the Land Registration Act 2002 see *Blackstone's Guide to The Land Registration Act 2002* by Abbey R. and Richards M. (OUP).

- *Textbook on Land Law* by MacKenzie J. A. and Phillips M. (9th edn, OUP)—Chapter 8 (the leasehold estate); chapter 9 (Obligations of landlord and tenant); chapter 10 (Commonhold).

- *Commonhold The New Law* by Clarke D. N. (Jordans Publishing Ltd).

10.5 RELEVANT WEBSITES FOR MORE INFORMATION

- Housing Corporation, http://www.housingcorp.gov.uk
  The Housing Corporation is a Non-Departmental Public Body, sponsored by the Office of the Deputy Prime Minister. Their role is to fund and regulate housing associations in England.

- Housing Forum, http://www.thehousingforum.org.uk
  The Housing Forum has established itself as the only housing organisation whose membership spans all sectors of housing construction.

- Inland Revenue, http://www.inlandrevenue.gov.uk/home.htm
  This site will help you ascertain how Revenue concerns may affect leases, especially relating to Stamp Duty Land Tax.

- Land Registry, http://www.landreg.gov.uk
  The registration of leases now affects all leases granted for a term of more than seven years.

- Land Registry internet register access, http://www.landregistrydirect.gov.uk
  This site deals with the Registry online.

- Landmark Information group, http://www.landmark-information.co.uk
  For searches and reports on leasehold properties.

- Lands Tribunals http://www.landstribunal.gov.uk
  The Lands Tribunal was established by the Lands Tribunal Act 1949 to determine questions of disputed compensation arising out of the compulsory acquisition of land; to decide rating appeals; to exercise jurisdiction under s. 84 of the Law of Property Act 1925 (discharge and modification of restrictive covenants); and to act as arbitrator under references by consent.

- Law Society, http://www.lawsoc.org.uk
  Law Society information that may relate to leases.

- Law Society's Gazette, http://www.lawgazette.co.uk
  The weekly publication from the Law Society that contains much relevant information concerning leases.

- Licensed Conveyancers, http://www.conveyancer.org.uk
  The other profession that can deal with leases.

- Location statistics, http://www.upmystreet.com
  A detailed neighbourhood guide.

- National Land Information Service, http://www.nlis.org.uk
  Online searches for leasehold properties.

- Office for National Statistics, http://www.ons.gov.uk
  National statistics as they may relate to leases or leaseholders.

- Office of the Deputy Prime Minister, http://www.odpm.gov.uk
  Visit this site to consider the effect of government policies and proposals as they affect leases.

- Ordnance Survey, http://www.ordsvy.gov.uk/home/index.html
  For lease plans.

- Royal Institution of Chartered Surveyors, http://www.rics.org
  Information about Chartered Surveyors.

- Street maps of the UK, http://www.streetmap.co.uk
  Street maps anywhere in England.

- UK Parliament, http://www.parliament.uk
  Details of Parliamentary business.

11 | COMMERCIAL CONVEYANCING AND PROPERTY

11.1 INTRODUCTION

This chapter covers the substantial part of Property Law and Practice that deals with commercial Conveyancing and Property. The topics considered cover aspects of Revenue Law, Commercial Conveyancing and business leases including the granting of such leases as well as their renewal. The phrase 'Commercial Conveyancing' covers the granting and renewal of business leases as well as the buying and selling of properties that are let or are being built to be let. It could also include the sale and purchase of businesses as going concerns and commercial lending transactions.

11.2 AN OVERVIEW OF THE SUBJECT AND A LOOK AT SOME PROBLEM AREAS

11.2.1 COMMERCIAL CONVEYANCING

Property Law and Practice covers both commercial and domestic property transactions. This means that a well-rounded Property lawyer will need to be aware of the requirements for both areas of practice although a specialist will concentrate on one or other. While many areas of Commercial Conveyancing may resemble similar practices and procedures utilised in residential Conveyancing, the nature of the subject matter has in many aspects of the process dictated a different approach. Commercial Conveyancing services and supports the market in and for commercial property. As a result, this chapter will concentrate on several different topics that all relate to commercial property and which all involve specialist knowledge of Commercial Conveyancing. However, for most property lawyers concerned with Commercial Conveyancing the subject will be seen to be synonymous with commercial leases. As students you can expect to be examined in all aspects of a commercial lease. That will include the formation and negotiation of new leases as well as the renewal of existing leases.

11.2.2 VAT ON COMMERCIAL PROPERTY

Value added tax is a complication that can affect commercial rents paid on commercial properties. It is an area of concern for both lessors and lessees and can quite possibly appear in a Property Law and Practice assessment. This is because VAT being part of Revenue Law is deemed to be a pervasive topic that can arise anywhere within the subjects taught on the LPC. If a commercial lease is granted, the rule is that it is generally exempt from value added tax but it is nevertheless subject to the option to tax, i.e. to make the letting vatable. The option to tax arises when the lessor decides voluntarily to give up the normal exemption and to opt for a VAT liability at the standard rate (s. 89 of the Value Added Tax Act 1994). It is in effect an option to waive the standard exemption. For these purposes then the lessor must be registered for VAT and, if there is such a registration, written notice must be given to the Revenue within thirty days of the election having been made. Because the lessees will have to pay the VAT on their rent it is vital that at the same time they are advised of the VAT election. This election is personal to the elector. This means that if there are sub-lessees the sub-lessor must also elect if there is to be VAT payable on the rents payable by the sub-lessees.

Electing to charge VAT will only suit a lessor who wishes to recover input tax. However, careful consideration should be given to the effect of charging VAT on the rent, as many prospective lessees will be put off where they are not registered for VAT and therefore cannot recover the VAT themselves. Consequently the election can be seen very much as a double-edged sword and one that needs to be handled with care. Indeed, where the lessee is registered for VAT there is in effect a cash flow problem. The lessee will have to pay VAT on the rent and service charge (if any), and therefore seek to recover the VAT.

On the assumption that there is an existing lease and it is silent as to the payment of VAT, the lessee will nevertheless have to pay VAT on the rent should the lessor decide to opt to tax. However, there is one vital point to note where you are acting for a lessor who intends to grant a new lease and also intends to opt to tax. You must advise the lessor not to make the election *before* the grant of the new lease. If the election precedes the grant, the Revenue will deem the new rent to be *inclusive* of VAT (and thereby diminishing to actual amount of rent the lessor will keep). This pitfall can be avoided by electing immediately after the grant of the lease by including in the lease a covenant requiring the lessee to pay any VAT on all the rents. In practice this would be very unpopular with the tenant. The Revenue view any rent-free period or periods that are granted as an inducement to a new lessee, as vatable. Consequently VAT will be payable on the unpaid rent.

11.2.3 RENT REVIEWS

Because lessors make a profit from the rents charged on their commercial leases perhaps of greatest concern to the lessor is the nature and extent of the rent review provision. Rent review clauses allow the lessor to vary the rent stated in the lease so as to increase the income from the subject property. Lessors will therefore include in leases a provision allowing the rent to be reviewed at fixed intervals, usually only in an upward direction.

(If the review mechanism permits downward reviews, as well as upward, the rent could actually be reduced on review, something that occurred in the property slump of the late 1980s and early 1990s.) Some leases simply link the annual rent to inflation, e.g. the Index of Retail Prices (see *Blumenthal v. Gallery Five Ltd* (1971) 220 EG 31). Others state the amount to be paid in the future by way of fixed increases. However, most do not state the amount of the increase but try to define in the lease how the lease rental should be revalued on review. However, this gives rise to the all-important question of what that market value is and how it will be ascertained. Therefore the procedure for triggering and handling the review is critical.

The new lease should contain a procedure by which the reviewed rent should be ascertained. If the lease terms say the intention is to fix a 'rack rent' then this is the full rent for the property (see *Corporation of London v. Cusack-Smith* [1955] AC 337). Thus such a rental would reflect the changes in the property market as assessed by a valuer or surveyor. Alternatively, if the lease required the rent to be reviewed as a 'market rent' then this will be the same as for a new lease granted under the terms of the Landlord and Tenant Act 1954, but including the factors that the Act contemplates being ignored.

There is nothing to stop the lease incorporating detailed assumptions upon which the review is to be based. If the lease stipulates assumptions to be made on a rent review then they will be central to the valuation process for the subject property. Typical assumptions are that the rent is to be reviewed at the renewal date, assuming the property is vacant for a term equal to that either originally granted or the residue of the term and for the permitted user stated in the lease. Modern rent review clauses will also allow the valuer to ignore any diminution in the value of the rental as a result of the lessee having failed properly to repair the subject property. Some review clauses also import assumptions with regard to improvements made by the lessee. If the lease is silent on the point, the rent review will be based on the nature of the premises at the time of review, including any improvements made by the lessee even though they were made at the lessee's cost (see *Ponsford v. HMS Aerosols Ltd* [1979] AC 63).

Modern rent review clauses trigger the process by requiring the lessor to serve a notice upon the lessee calling for a review of the rent at the rent review date. Some trigger notices will be required by the review procedure to state what the lessor requires as a new rent. Others may simply call for the review process to be commenced. If an amount is specified, some clauses require the lessee to agree or disagree with the stated amount within a specified period. A trap exists here for the unwary. If time is of the essence for the lessee's response then, should that time limit not be complied with, the rental stated by the lessor, no matter how exaggerated it may be, will prevail as the rent for review.

Lessors can also be late calling for review by not complying with a time scale stated in the lease rent review provisions. In *United Scientific Holdings Ltd v. Burnley Borough Council* [1978] AC 904 it was held that unless the clause makes it so, time is *not* of the essence for a rent review clause. If the clause makes time of the essence of part or all of the procedure then the time limits are absolute and incapable of extension. In the absence of express provision, though, delay will not defeat a lessor's claim for a rent review. Time can be of the essence even if the rent review provision does not include that actual wording. If the words of the rent review clause are such that it is possible to show that there was an intention to make time limits absolute, then the courts will infer time of the essence (see *Henry Smith's Charity Trustees v. AWADA Trading and Promotion Services Ltd* (1984) 47 P & CR 607). Time of the essence can also arise if other wording in the lease supports this possibility. Accordingly, if the lessee can, by notice, terminate the tenancy at the review date, it has been held that this means that time is of the essence for the review (see *Al Saloom v. Shirley James Travel Services Ltd* (1981) 42 P & CR 181). Sensible rent review clauses will also have one further provision. This will be the possibility of referring the rent to an arbitrator for a final decision should the lessor and lessee be unable to agree the level of the new rent. If arbitration is contemplated, it will involve provisions within the Arbitration Act 1996. Should the appointment of the arbitrator be in dispute the lease can provide that the appointment be by the President for the time being of the Royal Institute of Chartered Surveyors.

11.2.4 ALIENATION RESTRICTIONS

If there is one covenant in business leases that gives rise to the most litigation, then the alienation covenant must be it. Alienation covers covenants against assignments, under letting, mortgages and other material dealings with the legal estate. This covenant is of great concern for business leases. The reason for this is that a business lessor will want to know who is in occupation of the property and in particular that the financial strength of the person or company in occupation is such that the rents required by the lease will be paid. As a consequence the lessor will seek to validate intending lessees to try to be sure that they will be able to pay the lease rentals. If the lessor has approved the status of the incoming lessee, then the lessor will normally require the proposed assignee to enter into a deed of licence. This will incorporate direct covenants between the lessor and assignee requiring the assignee to comply with the lease terms for the residue of the term of the lease. This is now subject to the terms of the Landlord and Tenant (Covenants) Act 1995. There is no restriction against alienation unless there is express provision to that effect within the lease (see *Keeves v. Dean* [1924] 1 KB 685 and *Leith Properties Ltd v. Byrne* [1983] QB 433). Many commercial leases include a covenant whereby the lessee cannot assign the lease without the prior written consent of the lessor, such consent usually not to be unreasonably withheld. This is known as a fully qualified covenant. Some leases extend this provision to include sub-lettings as well as assignments. If the lease states that the lessor's consent is required but does not refer to reasonableness then statute adds this qualification (Landlord and Tenant Act 1927, s. 19(1)(a)). (What amounts to reasonableness in the context of s. 19 is stated in *International Drilling Fluids Ltd v. Louisville Investments (Uxbridge) Ltd* [1986] Ch 513.) However, if the lease includes an absolute prohibition then the lessee simply cannot assign the lease and must remain in the premises for the residue of the term. Section 19(1A) of the Landlord and Tenant Act 1927 (introduced by s. 22 of the Landlord and Tenant (Covenants) Act 1995) allows the parties to a lease to agree conditions or circumstances which must be satisfied before the lessor will give consent. Section 19(1A) only relates to qualified covenants against assigning, i.e. not sub-letting or charging.

Many modern business leases will include an absolute covenant against dealing with part of the subject premises. There are really two good reasons for including such a provision. First, good estate management dictates that the fewer lessees there are in a block the easier it is to manage the building as a whole. Secondly, under the Landlord and Tenant Act 1954 business lessees in occupation at the end of a business lease are entitled by statute to renew their lease. If there have been sub-lettings of parts, the lessor is required by statute to issue new leases to all the sub-lessees in occupation and not to the original lessee who became the sub-lessor but did not remain in occupation. In this way the superior lessor could end up accidentally with several lessees where originally there was just one.

The Landlord and Tenant Act 1988, s. 1(3), requires the lessor to deal with applications for consent to an assignment within a reasonable time of the making of the application. Should the lessor fail to do so, the lessee can, if the lessee has suffered loss as a consequence of the lessor's delay, sue the lessor for damages. The lessor can attach conditions to any consent but those conditions themselves must be reasonable (see s. 1(4) of the 1988 Act). Even mere delay in dealing with the application for consent could amount to unreasonableness (see *Lewis and Allenby (1909) Ltd v. Pegge* [1914] 1 Ch 782). The burden of proof is upon the lessor to show that the lessor has acted reasonably. This applies as to the reasonableness of conditions to consent or refusal of consent. The lessee must make a court application seeking a declaration that the lessor has acted unreasonably. If successful, the lessee can seek an award for costs and the lessor may also be liable for damages where the claimant has suffered loss (s. 4 of the Landlord and Tenant Act 1988).

11.2.5 LEASE RENEWALS AND THE LANDLORD AND TENANT ACT 1954

Part II of the Landlord and Tenant Act 1954 provides security of tenure for the majority of business lessees by giving to those lessees a statutory right to renew their lease or tenancy. The court will order a new lease but will require the tenant to pay a market rent prevailing at the time of renewal. In general terms provided the lessee occupies the subject property for business purposes, that lessee can remain in the property at the end of the contractual lease and can seek to renew the letting, and the lessor is obliged by statute to agree a renewal.

11.2.5.1 Lease termination

If the provisions of the 1954 Act protect a tenancy, there will be no automatic termination of the lease at the end of the lease term. Once the contractual tenancy ends the lessee is entitled to remain at the subject property on the same terms and conditions as existed prior to the date of the expiry of the term. The lessee is said to be 'holding over' on the same terms and conditions. As a consequence of s. 24(1) any protected tenancy does not come to an end unless the tenancy is terminated in accordance with the terms of the Act. This will apply to tenancies that have expired through effluxion of time or prematurely, say, where the lessor has exercised a break clause in a lease. (Where there is a break clause the notice terminating should comply with the lease terms *and* the Act (*Keith Bayley Rogers and Co. v. Cubes Ltd* (1975) 31 P & CR 412).)

11.2.5.2 Lessor's notice under s. 25

A lessor may terminate a tenancy by giving notice in writing in a prescribed form, which must be made not more than twelve months before the end of the lease term (s. 25(2)). (In practice this notice is commonly called a s. 25 notice.) As the period of notice cannot be less than six months, the notice should be served with at least six months of the term left to run so that the notice expires with the expiry of the term of the lease. There is a prescribed form of notice. The form of notice requires an expiry date to be specified within it. If the lessor is late this does not mean a s. 25 notice cannot be issued. In these circumstances the lessee will hold over on the same terms until a notice is served and the six months have expired. The notice must also specify whether or not the lessor intends to oppose an application to the court by the lessee; and if so, on what grounds. Section 30 lists the grounds for opposition and these are (in general terms):

The grounds for opposition

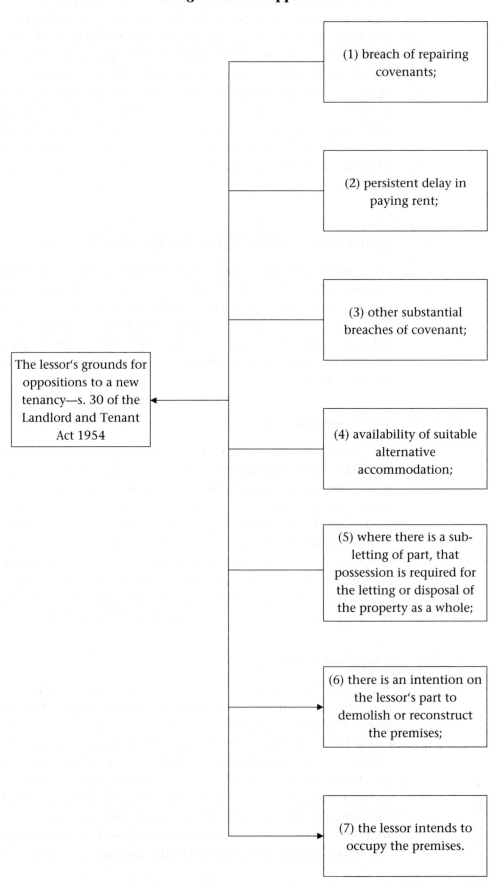

The lessor's grounds for oppositions to a new tenancy—s. 30 of the Landlord and Tenant Act 1954

(1) breach of repairing covenants;

(2) persistent delay in paying rent;

(3) other substantial breaches of covenant;

(4) availability of suitable alternative accommodation;

(5) where there is a sub-letting of part, that possession is required for the letting or disposal of the property as a whole;

(6) there is an intention on the lessor's part to demolish or reconstruct the premises;

(7) the lessor intends to occupy the premises.

No other grounds are allowed, and if the lessor intends to oppose the lessee's court application, the grounds for opposition must fall within the above categories. The notice should be served upon the lessee in occupation, and this could mean a sub-lessee where the whole property has been sub-let, thereby cutting out the intermediate non-occupying head tenant. Where part of the subject premises has been sub-let, the lessor can either serve notice on the lessor's tenant and require that lessee to take a lease of the whole of the premises (s. 32(2)), or the lessor can give notice to the immediate and sub-tenants. In this second case each lessee will be entitled to renew while in the first case the new lease will be granted to the lessor's direct lessee, subject to the sub-letting of part.

Because there are time limits set out by this statute, it is vital to appreciate the timing and sequence of events when there is a landlord's notice. It is as follows:

When there is a landlord's notice

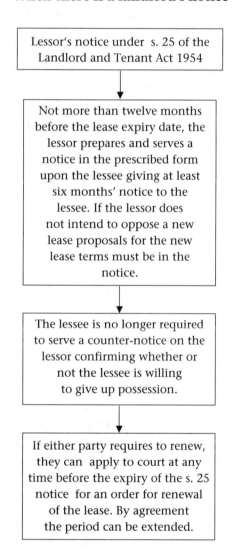

Lessor's notice under s. 25 of the Landlord and Tenant Act 1954

Not more than twelve months before the lease expiry date, the lessor prepares and serves a notice in the prescribed form upon the lessee giving at least six months' notice to the lessee. If the lessor does not intend to oppose a new lease proposals for the new lease terms must be in the notice.

The lessee is no longer required to serve a counter-notice on the lessor confirming whether or not the lessee is willing to give up possession.

If either party requires to renew, they can apply to court at any time before the expiry of the s. 25 notice for an order for renewal of the lease. By agreement the period can be extended.

At this point the lessor needs to consider the necessary response, i.e. dependant on whether the lessor intends to seek possession or not. The lessor also needs to consider whether an interim rent application is advisable, without which no rent increase can be claimed during these proceedings.

11.2.5.3 **Lessee's request for a new tenancy under s. 26**

A lessee is entitled to call upon the lessor to grant a new lease or tenancy by way of renewal pursuant to s. 26 of the Act. (The lessee must have had the benefit of an original lease where the term exceeded one year to be able to call for a new tenancy.)

The request form must be in a prescribed format and must include the date the lessee requires the new tenancy to commence. It must be served not more than twelve months before the end of the lease term. As the period of notice cannot be less than six months the request should be served with at least six months left to run so that the notice expires with the expiry of the term of the old lease The lessee must set out in the request what is to be the subject property for the new lease, the desired new rent and other provisions, including the term of the new lease.

The lessor must, if there is an intention to oppose the request for a new tenancy, within two months of the receipt of the request serve upon the lessee the lessor's counter-notice in which the lessor must state the grounds for the intended opposition. The grounds are the same as those set out above. Failure to serve a counter-notice or to do so within the time limit will mean that the lessor loses the right to oppose the request.

Because there are time limits set out by this statute, it is vital to appreciate the timing and sequence of events when there is a tenant's request for a new tenancy. It is as follows:

Tenant's request for a new tenancy

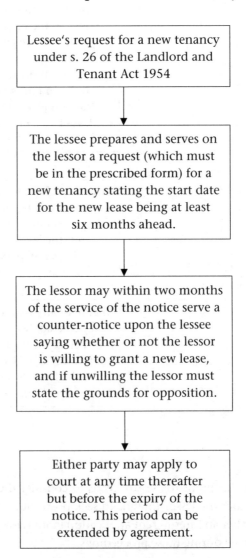

Lessee's request for a new tenancy under s. 26 of the Landlord and Tenant Act 1954

The lessee prepares and serves on the lessor a request (which must be in the prescribed form) for a new tenancy stating the start date for the new lease being at least six months ahead.

The lessor may within two months of the service of the notice serve a counter-notice upon the lessee saying whether or not the lessor is willing to grant a new lease, and if unwilling the lessor must state the grounds for opposition.

Either party may apply to court at any time thereafter but before the expiry of the notice. This period can be extended by agreement.

At this point the lessor needs to consider the necessary response, i.e. dependant on whether the lessor intends to seek possession or not. The lessor also must consider the need for an interim rent application, without which no increase in rent can be claimed during these proceedings.

11.2.5.4 **The court application**

At any time before the expiry of either the s. 25 notice or s. 26 request, either party can make an application to the court for an order for lease renewal. As we have seen, if the lessor wishes to oppose the grant of a new lease there are only seven possible statutory grounds. Of these grounds, three, (d), (f) and (g), if proved, allow the court no discretion and the lessee's application for a new tenancy must be denied. The remaining grounds are such that if proved the court still has a discretion as to whether or not to grant an order for a new tenancy. The last two have given rise to a great deal of litigation and the following details are therefore relevant to them:

'(f) There is an intention on the lessor's part to demolish or reconstruct the subject premises'.

This is a ground that has provoked much litigation as it is one that is clearly open to interpretation. This ground for opposition means that the lessor must show at the time of the hearing that the lessor intends to demolish or reconstruct the whole or a substantial part of the subject property, or carry out some considerable work of construction, *and* that the lessor cannot reasonably carry out these proposed works with the lessee still in possession. The lessor therefore needs to show the relevant intention along with the need for possession of the property. The intention need only exist at the time of the hearing and not necessarily when the ground for opposition is first raised (*Betty's Cafés Ltd v. Phillips Furnishing Stores Ltd* [1959] AC 20). The lessor must be in a position actually to carry out the proposed works. Thus the lessor will need to show that any necessary planning matters have been or will be resolved and that the lessor has the financial resources to carry through the proposed works.

What constitutes sufficient works of demolition, or reconstruction or construction is a matter of fact for the court to decide. As to what might be accepted as works deemed to be sufficient to prove the ground, or not, court decisions have shown that the demolition of a wooden garage and a wall were sufficient (*Housleys Ltd v. Bloomer-Holt Ltd* [1966] 1 WLR 1244) but the landscaping of a field was not (*Botterill v. Bedfordshire County Council* [1985] 1 EGLR 82). Each case will be decided on the merits of the lessor's evidence. However, the lessor's case will be greatly strengthened if, at the date of the hearing, the lessor can show the necessary planning consents, architect's plans, that the required finance is in place and that other appropriate consents and professional advisers are available. Section 31A allows the lessee to request a new lease that incorporates rights for the lessor that would enable the lessor to carry out the desired works, or a new lease of premises that are separate, thereby enabling the lessor to carry out the desired works.

'(g) The lessor intends to occupy the premises'.

To rely upon this ground the lessor must show that the lessor intends to occupy the premises either for business purposes, or as a residence. This ground is not available to a lessor who has acquired the reversionary interest within five years of the termination of the old tenancy (s. 30(2)). The lessor's intention to occupy must be capable of being put into effect within a reasonable time after the full court hearing. So, if the occupation would require a prior planning application and consent, the court would need to be shown that the application had been made and be convinced that there was a reasonable chance that consent would be forthcoming (*Gregson v. Cyril Lord Ltd* [1963] 1 WLR 41, CA).

11.3 **SUBJECT ASSESSMENTS**

11.3.1 **SUBJECT ASSESSMENT QUESTIONS: A COMMENTARY UPON THE TYPE AND CONTENT OF SUBJECT ASSESSMENT QUESTION AND SUGGESTED ANSWERS**

Question 1

RICHARDS ABBEY AND PARTNERS, SOLICITORS
INTERNAL MEMO

To   Trainee Solicitor

From   Commercial Property Partner

Re Foxton Investments Ltd

We act for Foxton Investments Ltd, a property investment company. Our client purchased the freehold of 30 Red House Lane Oxford in January 2001. The property is subject to an occupational lease in favour of an architect, Mr Richard Sykulu. Mr Sykulu has always paid his rent on time and is not in breach of any lease covenants. The lease expires on 29 September 2005 and our client is keen to secure vacant possession of the property as soon as possible to carry out various improvements and alterations prior to using the premises as its own local office. Mr Sykulu has indicated informally to the client that he does not wish to give up possession.

   Please prepare a memorandum of the legal advice we should give our client and the procedure for recovering possession.

Commentary

This is a relatively straightforward question that can be anticipated in relation to contested lease renewals. What a good answer will cover is the renewal procedures under Part II of the Landlord and Tenant Act 1954. Accordingly, it is vital that you have a detailed working knowledge of the Act and how it works in practice before you attempt to answer this type of question. From a perspective of style the question is posed in a memorandum and so you need to answer it in the same format. You also need to carefully reflect upon the structure of your answer. Because you are replying in a memo does not mean that you can simply write a thinly disguised essay. A good answer could in fact be written using numbered or bullet points. In essence your answer should be direct and to the point, offering the legal advice required and the procedure necessary for recovering possession.

Suggested answer

RICHARDS ABBEY AND PARTNERS, SOLICITORS
INTERNAL MEMO

From   Trainee Solicitor

To   Commercial Property Partner

Foxton Investments Ltd

You have asked me for a memorandum of the legal advice we should give our above mentioned client and the procedure for recovering possession of 30 Red House Lane Oxford from the tenant Mr Richard Sykulu when the current lease expires on 29 September 2005. I therefore set out below the relevant points of law and advice required by the client as follows:

Legal Advice

1. The tenant Mr Sykulu appears to be a protected tenant by reason of the terms of Part II of the Landlord and Tenant Act 1954. This is because he would seem to be occupying premises for the purpose of a business. Consequently our client can only terminate the lease occupancy by one of the ways prescribed by the 1954 Act.

2. On the facts presented to me it would seem that there is no question of forfeiture or even of a negotiated surrender. As a result we will need to serve a s. 25 notice and in that notice we will have to establish one or more of the grounds for possession under s. 30 (1) of the Act.

3. The fault grounds, e.g., breach of repairing covenants or persistent delay in paying rent or other substantial breaches of covenant do not, on the facts, appear to apply. Indeed, nor does ground (e)—where there is a sub-letting of part, that possession is required for the letting or disposal of the property as a whole. In these circumstances the lessor must consider other grounds such as the (i) the possibility of alternative accommodation, (ii) redevelopment or (iii) own-use grounds.

4. I appreciate that our client is keen to secure vacant possession of the property as soon as possible to carry out various improvements and alterations prior to using the premises as its own local office. However, the own-use ground cannot be used at present because the client purchased the reversion only three years ago and as a result the five-year rule applies. To rely upon the own-use ground the lessor must show that it intends to occupy the premises for business purposes. This ground is not available to a lessor who has acquired the reversionary interest within five years of the termination of the old tenancy (s. 30(2)). The lessor's intention to occupy must be capable of being put into effect within a reasonable time after the full court hearing. So, if the occupation would require a prior planning application and consent, the court would need to be shown that the application had been made and be convinced that there was a reasonable chance that consent would be forthcoming (*Gregson v. Cyril Lord Ltd* [1963] 1 WLR 41, CA).

5. Bearing in mind the time limits set out above it would be possible to allow Mr Sykulu to hold over and then serve the s. 25 notice in January 2006. This would satisfy the five-year rule for ground (g). However, it would also mean that the lessee would pay rent at the current level for an extended period and this rent might be well below the market value. Furthermore the tenant might pre-empt us and serve a s. 26 request for a new tenancy earlier. The effect of this would be to deny us the ability to use ground (g).

6. There is one final alternative ground that of possible redevelopment. However, on the facts this ground is only a mere possibility. The courts will need to see redevelopment that amounts to substantial reconstruction, etc. The lessor must show at the time of the hearing that the lessor intends to demolish or reconstruct the whole or a substantial part of the subject property, or carry out some considerable work of construction, *and* that the lessor cannot reasonably carry out these proposed works with the lessee still in possession. This would seem unlikely on the facts although we would need to get further details of the proposed works from the client.

Procedure

7. The correct procedure is that we should on behalf of the lessor serve a s. 25 notice on on the lessee on the 29 September 2004 specifying a termination date between six and twelve months hence. A prescribed form of notice is required and having checked I can confirm that there is a precedent for one on

our computer system. It should be noted that the termination date cannot be earlier than 29 September 2005 being the contractual expiry date.

8. Immediately thereafter the lessor can apply without delay for an order that the old lease terminate and that there be no new tenancy for the reason(s) set out in the termination notice. If the ground(s) for possession can be proved the court will not order a tenancy renewal. If the lessor fails in this application the court can make an order for a new lease without the lessee making a fresh application.

9. If no such application to deny a new tenancy is made then at any time before the expiry of the termination notice either party can apply to court to renew. This period can be extended by agreement.

Question 2

Your firm acts for Charlotte Enterprises Ltd ('Charlotte'), a public relations company, that occupies 20a Broad Street Oxford ('the Premises'), a suite of offices on the first and second floors of 20 Broad Street, a three-storey building in the centre of Oxford. Charlotte has a lease of the Premises from the present landlord Stiletto Shoes Ltd ('Stiletto'). The lease expires in six months' time.

Stiletto has a lease of the whole of 20 Broad Street from the present freehold reversioner, Aragon Investments Ltd ('Aragon'). This lease was granted for a term of twenty-five years and expires in six months and ten days. Stiletto occupies and trades from the ground floor shop premises.

(i) Your training partner has asked you to prepare a memo that provides advice for Charlotte.

(ii) Would your advice be different if Charlotte's lease was for the whole of 20 Broad Street?

Commentary

This is another straightforward question that can be anticipated in relation to lease renewals. This time the question centres upon the problems for a party to a commercial lease where there are sub-lettings involved and where the sub-lettings are either of the whole or of part of the lease premises. What a good answer will cover is the renewal procedures under Part II of the Landlord and Tenant Act 1954 as they relate to this specific topic. Accordingly, it is vital that you have a detailed working knowledge of the Act and how it works in practice before you attempt to answer this type of question. From a perspective of style the question is not posed in a memorandum but you still need to answer it in the appropriate format. If you look again at the question it asks you to prepare a memo. You therefore need to carefully reflect upon the structure of your answer. Once again a good answer could in fact be written using numbered or bullet points. In essence your answer should be direct and to the point, offering the legal advice required. However, remember that there are two parts to the question so make sure your answer deals with both elements.

Suggested answer

RICHARDS ABBEY AND PARTNERS, SOLICITORS

INTER-OFFICE MEMO

From   Trainee Solicitor

To   Training Partner

<u>Charlotte Enterprises Ltd and 20/20a Broad Street Oxford</u>

(i) My advice for Charlotte Enterprises Limited ('Charlotte') is set out below. To clarify, the parties involved in this matter are Aragon Investments Limited ('Aragon'), the freeholder, Stiletto Shoes Limited ('Stiletto'), the head tenant and Charlotte, the sub-tenant and our client.

1. Making the first move—The tenant could consider making the first move on the lease renewal procedure. However, the lessee should only do so if certain conditions prevail in the local lettings market. If it is apparent that market rents in the locality of the subject property have risen then the lessee could make an application to the lessor for a new tenancy as a pre-emptive strike stating twelve months hence as end date. If the lessee does so then that way the lessee will get six months at the existing or old rent but for a period extending beyond and after the contractual lease expiry date. Indeed if market rents have actually fallen Charlotte will want the new lease in place as soon as possible to take advantage of a lower rent. In the circumstances our advice to Charlotte is to serve a s. 26 Request stating six months hence as the lease end date.

2. Who is the competent Landlord?—Stiletto's lease has less than fourteen months to run but Stiletto is 'in occupation' and so Stiletto's lease continues under the Act until terminated in accordance with the Act (e.g. Aragon serves on Stiletto a s. 25 Notice or Stiletto serves on Aragon a s. 26 Request, in either case terminating Stiletto's lease within fourteen months). Charlotte can find out whether Stiletto's lease has been terminated in accordance with the Act by serving on Stiletto a s. 40 Notice. The identity of the competent landlord can change more than once during the course of any litigation and renewal procedure. To request information about superior leases, sub-leases and whether notices or requests have been given, landlords and tenants can serve on each other a notice under s. 40 of the Act. Ideally, the s. 40 notice should be served before or simultaneously with the notices or requests under ss. 25, 26 and 27. When acting for a tenant serving a s. 40 notice on a landlord, we should request in the covering letter a copy of any s. 25 notice received by the landlord terminating its tenancy. We can then serve s. 40 notices and similar covering letters on the superior landlord(s) until we reach the competent landlord for our anticipated renewal period.

(ii) My advice will be different if Charlotte's lease was for the whole of 20 Broad Street. Stiletto would then not occupy the premises and thus would have no security of tenure under the Act. Stiletto's lease would therefore come to an end within fourteen months and Charlotte's competent Landlord would be Aragon (assuming Aragon is the freeholder). Charlotte's s. 26 Request should therefore be served on Aragon.

Question 3

Your firm acts for a property investment company Solid Investments Limited. It has instructed the firm to act on the purchase of a mixed-use property in Sunderland. There is a business occupant on a ten-year lease in the ground floor and a residential tenant in the upper two floors. You have recently joined the Property Department in the firm for your second six-month department secondment. Your new training partner has asked you to assist him in this work and has sent you the following inter-office memo.

RICHARDS ABBEY AND PARTNERS, SOLICITORS
INTER-OFFICE MEMO

To   Trainee Solicitor

From   Training Partner

Solid Investments Ltd and 205/205a Petershead Road Sunderland

Welcome to the department. As a first exercise I would like you to assist me on the purchase. The company intend to buy this unit for £120,000. There are two lettings that we know about and as such the property is fully let. A contract has just come in and the freehold title is registered. I have yet to see full details of the two tenancies but the basic details are on the file.

Please let me know what you think we should do about making preliminary enquiries. I appreciate we will be issuing the usual standard enquiries but I am really thinking of additional requirements to the normal questions. Please also suggest anything new that might assist. Many thanks.

Commentary

There is a considerable commercial market in the purchase and sale of properties that are subject to the occupation of lessees with some form of statutory security of tenure. This is particularly so in relation to property occupied by business tenants, but many of the special factors required in transactions involving commercial property will apply as well to properties sold with residential tenants. In essence, in addition to the matters of importance to a domestic seller or buyer, the terms of the letting will be of material importance in relation to the title, contract enquiries and requisitions. You have been asked to make suggestions about what extra enquiries are required and so you must concentrate on that area. You have received a memo and so you should reply in the same style. Try to show a structure to your answer by using headings and structured paragraphs. Keep to relevant information only. An answer of this type could fool the weaker candidate into writing all they know about enquiries before contract. This is not going to do anything other than annoy the marker. Try to remain relevant to the details of the question at all times. So do not write about enquiries of the local authority as they form part of the local authority search and you are not being asked to discuss searches.

Suggested answer

RICHARDS ABBEY AND PARTNERS, SOLICITORS
INTER-OFFICE MEMO

From   Trainee Solicitor

To   Training Partner

<u>Solid Investments Ltd and 205/205a Petershead Road Sunderland</u>

I refer to your recent memo and set out below my suggestions and comments about additional enquiries regarding the above property. I also comment on new enquiry forms recently issued that relate specifically to commercial properties.

1. <u>Additional enquiries generally</u>

In addition to the standard enquiries that need to be made in this conveyancing transaction, it is critical that enquiries are made with regard to the two lessees in occupation. We also need to enquire about whether their rents are paid in advance or in arrears. It is therefore appropriate to request details of previous rent reviews along with copies of rent review memoranda recording the previous changes in rent. Service charge accounts should be requested for the last three years, with details of sinking funds and arrears that may exist in respect of these payments. Details should be requested of any permitted changes of use as these too could materially affect the future, or indeed current, rental potential. If the property is Vatable, details of the VAT position will need to be investigated along with accounts of VAT payments made by lessees or details of arrears. Insurance details need to be investigated, particularly if the lessor insures the building and either or both lessees repay part of the premium. The seller should also be asked to consider detailed environmental and contamination enquiries about the property and the locality.

2. Additional enquiries—commercial

In addition to the standard enquiries that are always raised, it is appropriate to make further enquiries in relation to commercial lettings in so far as they may be affected or regulated by legislation. In essence the buyer will want to know how far, if at all, the ground lease is influenced by Pt II of the Landlord and Tenant Act 1954. The buyer will want to know if there has been a court application and if so will want to see what order the court made. If the lease has been recently renewed under the terms of the Act, the buyer will want details to ascertain how the length of the term eventually granted was settled along with the other terms of the lease. Perhaps of more consequence would be to see the basis upon which the rental was finally settled. Valuers' reports would be of use and copies should be requested. The buyer will also want to know if the lessor originally sought to oppose the grant of the lease and why. The ground for possession would be of material interest to the buyer, especially if it related to a breach of covenant or for arrears of rent. In the circumstances detailed enquiries should be directed to the seller's practitioner seeking as much information as possible about the circumstances of any recent statutory renewal. Finally, if the lease was granted after 1 January 1996 on assignment an Authorised Guarantee Agreement may be involved. Enquiries should be made of the terms of this agreement.

3. New enquiries

There are now some standard enquiries for commercial properties. The Commercial Property Standard Enquiries (CPSEs) are a set of documents that have been drafted by members of the London Property Support Lawyers Group under the sponsorship of the British Property Federation (BPF). We can use these documents quite freely and without charge, subject to us identifying them as being part of the suite of documents comprising the CPSEs. CPSE.1 is designed to cover all commercial property transactions and will (together with any additional enquiries relevant to the particular transaction) be sufficient if the transaction deals only with a freehold sold with vacant possession. Consequently the next form will be of more relevance to our client. It is CPSE.2 and should be used where the property to be purchased is to be sold subject to existing tenancies.

4. Additional enquiries—residential

In addition to the standard enquiries it is appropriate to make further enquiries in relation to residential lettings in so far as they may be affected or regulated by legislation. The buyer will want to enquire as to the status of the tenant in occupation of the first and second floors, and in particular whether the tenant can claim any form of statutory protection providing any element of security of tenure. After 28 February 1997, s. 96 of the Housing Act 1996 makes all subsequent residential tenancies assured shorthold tenancies, and they are so without the need to comply with any particular formalities such as formal notices, etc. This is not retrospective and only applies to new tenancies granted after this date. Accordingly, the date of creation of the tenancy is a crucial item of information which needs to be disclosed to the buyer and should be elicited through a specific preliminary enquiry. This is all the more so as different forms of security of tenure will apply to tenancies depending upon when they were created. If the tenancy arose prior to 28 November 1980 the tenancy will be covered by the Rent Acts and will be a protected tenancy with full security of tenure. If the tenancy commenced after this date but before 15 January 1989, it could either be a protected tenancy under the Rent Acts, or it might also be a protected shorthold where there is limited security with the lessor being entitled to a mandatory ground for possession. If the tenancy arose after 15 January 1989 the Housing Act 1988 applies, and the tenancy will usually be an assured tenancy with full security or an assured tenancy again with limited security. This is not a complete listing as this is an area of great complexity. Please let me know if you require anything further on this particular point.

Finally further enquiries should be made as to the statutory control of the rents payable by the residential tenant. Tenancies granted after 28 February 1997 will have minimal control as a consequence of the

Housing Act 1996. Tenants in these circumstances can merely, and only during the first six months of their tenancy, refer the rent to a rent assessment committee for scrutiny. Tenancies created previously will have differing elements of statutory control of rents depending on when the tenancy was first created. Please let me know if there is anything more I can do to assist you with this transaction.

TIME ENGAGED 45 MINS

TRAINEE SOLICITOR

Question 4

You are instructed by Camera Ring Limited, a company that intends to take the grant of a new lease from local freeholders, Ross Developers (Edgware) Limited. Your client will be taking a short five-year lease of a stand-alone light industrial unit for the warehousing of camera equipment and accessories. The unit is a fairly old one having been built in the 1950s. You have been instructed to approve the form of draft lease issued by the lessor. However your client has asked you to take particular care with the repairing and alterations clauses. This is because once before the client had been the lessee of a different lease that had cost them a great deal at the end of the term when they had to pay a large bill for repairs. The company has therefore asked you to make what you think are reasonable changes to the proposed clauses to protect their position. The relevant clauses are set out below. Please make such amendments as you think necessary to comply with your instructions and explain why you have made these changes.

At all times during the term fair wear and tear excepted:

1. to well and substantially cleanse repair and renovate to the reasonable satisfaction of the lessor's chartered surveyor

    1.1 all present and future structures or buildings forming all or any part of the demised premises and

    1.2 all fixtures additions and improvements which may at any time be attached placed or made upon the demised premises and

    1.3 to clean and repair the external stone and brickwork.

2. to repair:

    2.1 the exterior and interior of the demised premises and all additions thereto including any machinery and fixtures boundary walls and fences drains soil and other pipes and sanitary water gas electrical central heating telephony and computer apparatus within the demised premises

    2.2 doors and windows floors ceilings walls stairways landings lifts roofs guttering and foundations in good and substantial repair throughout the term.

    2.3 But nothing in this lease will require the lessee to put the demised premises in any better condition than that set out in the Schedule of Condition completed immediately prior to the grant of this lease and forming Appendix 1 of this lease.

3. To decorate all of the outside of the demised premises every third year of the term and to decorate the inside of the demised premises every fifth year and in both cases in the last year of the term using good quality paint and materials in colours first approved by the lessor's chartered surveyor (such approval not be unreasonably withheld) but the lessee will not be required to redecorate in the last year of the term if the lessee has redecorated within the previous twelve months.

4. Not to alter cut harm or remove any of the principal or load bearing walls floors or other structures of or enclosing the demised premises nor to make any other alterations improvements or additions of a structural nature.

5. Not to make any alterations or additions of a non-structural nature to the demised premises without having first obtained the prior written consent of the lessor such consent not to be unreasonably withheld except that the lessee may install alter and remove demountable partitioning without such consent.

Commentary

On the face of it this is a straightforward question on the detailed contents of a business commercial lease. It raises concerns that can be anticipated in relation to the specific approval of lease terms. A good answer will cover the actual amendments you consider necessary along with clear reasons for the proposed changes. Commercial conveyancers will spend much of their time in just such a task, i.e., the approval of leases and it is therefore highly likely that you could encounter just such a task both in the office as well as in a Property Law and Practice subject assessment. In essence your answer should be direct and to the point, offering the explanations required and the actual amendments required to the specimen clauses.

Suggested answer

(a) Amendments

I would make the following changes and my amendments by deletions are shown as struck through while my additions are underlined.

At all times during the term <u>fair wear and tear excepted</u>:

1. to well and substantially cleanse repair ~~renew~~ and renovate ~~and when necessary replace and rebuild~~ to the <u>reasonable</u> satisfaction of the lessor's <u>chartered</u> surveyor

   1.1 all present and future structures or buildings forming all or any part of the demised premises and

   1.2 all fixtures additions and improvements which may at any time be attached placed or made upon the demised premises and

   1.3 to clean and repair the external stone and brickwork ~~replacing such stone and brickwork as required~~

2. to repair ~~and to put and keep~~:

   2.1 the exterior and interior of the demised premises and all additions thereto including any machinery and fixtures boundary walls and fences drains soil and other pipes and sanitary water gas electrical central heating telephony and computer apparatus within the demised premises

   2.2 doors and windows floors ceilings walls stairways landings lifts roofs guttering and foundations in good and substantial repair ~~including any arising from inherent defects~~ throughout the term.

   2.3 <u>But nothing in this lease will require the lessee to put the demised premises in any better condition than that set out in the Schedule of Condition completed immediately prior to the grant of this lease and forming Appendix 1 of this lease</u>

3. To decorate all of the outside of the demised premises every third year of the term and to decorate the inside of the demised premises every fifth year and in both cases in the last year of the term using good quality paint and materials in colours first approved by the lessor<u>'s chartered surveyor (such approval not to be unreasonably withheld) but the lessee will not be required to redecorate in the last year of the term if the lessee has redecorated within the previous twelve months</u>

4. Not to alter cut harm or remove any of the principal or load bearing walls floors or other structures of or enclosing the demised premises nor to make any other alterations improvements or additions of a structural nature

5. Not to make any alterations or additions of a non-structural nature to the demised premises <u>without having first obtained the prior written consent of the lessor such consent not to be unreasonably withheld</u> except that the lessee may install alter and remove demountable partitioning without such consent

6. ~~The lessor may as a condition of giving consent require the lessee to enter into any covenants as the lessor shall require regarding the implementation of any such works and the reinstatement of the demised premises at the end or sooner determination of the term of this lease~~

(b) <u>Reasons</u>

Following the numbering of the lease clauses the reasons for the changes are as follows:

1. The insertion of the reference to fair wear and tear is to try to reduce the repairing liability. The other changes are made with the intention of making it clear that with a short five-year term the lessee should not be under an obligation to renew or rebuild the property especially when it is noted that the property is over fifty years old and may not been in a very good condition. The surveyor should be professionally qualified.

    1.1 No changes

    1.2 No changes

    1.3 This change is made with the intention of making it clear that with the short term the lessee should not be under an obligation to renew parts of the property especially when it is noted that the property is over fifty years old and may not been in a very good condition.

2. This is another attempt to limit the repairing liability. It should also be remembered that a covenant requiring the lessee 'to put and keep the property in good and substantial repair' is a covenant that can be construed in the courts as being particularly substantial in its effect. (see *Elite Investments Limited v. T.I. Bainbridge Silencers Limited* [1986] 2 EGLR 43). Where the covenant contains the obligation 'to keep' the premises in repair then the courts have decided that this means that the premises must be kept in repair at all times throughout the term of the lease. If a defect arises then there is an immediate breach of covenant (see *British Telecommunications plc v. Sun Life Assurance Society plc* [1995] 3 WLR 622).

    2.1 No changes

    2.2 With a building of this age a lessee should not assume liability for inherent defects

    2.3 This shows that the lessee has prepared a schedule of the condition of the property at the commencement of the lease and is seeking to ensure that the lessee will not be required to improve upon that condition as a result of the repairing obligations in the lease.

3. These items should be approved by the lessor's chartered surveyor and not the lessor and that approval should not be unreasonably withheld. As the lease is only for five years the lessee should not be required to redecorate in the last year of the term if the lessee has redecorated within the previous twelve months

4. No changes.

5. Alterations should be allowed having first obtained the prior written consent of the lessor such consent not to be unreasonably withheld. The unit is self-contained and as such no other neighbouring tenant is concerned. The limited consent is made subject to the test of reasonableness.

6. This clause might be more acceptable if the lease was longer. However, as it is only a five-year term the provisions are far too onerous to accept. The lessee will want to try to delete all of clause 6 as this gives an extremely wide discretion to the lessor to impose virtually any condition it chooses on the giving of permission for alterations.

11.3.2 **MULTIPLE CHOICE QUESTIONS AND ANSWERS TO MULTIPLE CHOICE QUESTIONS**

We set out below examples of ten multiple choice questions that you might encounter in a subject assessment. Thereafter you will find some typical short answer questions that can also feature in a subject assessment and which cover pre-completion and completion matters. Answers to both are also set out below. Remember our initial guidance. Never leave multiple choice answers with a blank multiple choice. If there are four possibilities and you are not sure of the answer select the one you think might be right, you have a one in four chance of getting it right! Also look at the instructions on the paper. If it says select the right answer on the paper by circling the correct choice then do just that. Do not make a tick or underline your selection, as the strict response would be to fail you even though the selection may be correct. Also none of the answers given might be right. In these circumstances follow the rubric in the question paper and explain why none of the listed answers apply.

11.3.2.1 **Multiple choice questions**

Unless otherwise directed, select the right answer by circling it in each question. Should you think that none of the selections apply please explain why not in your answer book.

1. If you act for a limited company client, any mortgage that it takes out, i.e. where the company is borrowing the money, *must* be registered at Companies House within how many days of the completion date pursuant to s. 395 of the Companies Act 1985).

    Is it:

    (a) 14 days
    (b) 28 days
    (c) 21 days
    (d) 30 days

2. Where you a granting a commercial lease and the client requires it to be an 'F.R.I.' lease, does this mean:

    (a) full rates involved
    (b) fully repaired internally
    (c) full repairing and insuring
    (d) fully but reasonably insured

3. Your client is the tenant of a twelve-year lease of a lock-up shop used as a newsagent. The lease term expired last Monday. Your client wishes to continue trading in the property. Your advice is:

    (a) to leave the premises as the lease term has ended
    (b) to remain and to continue to pay rent and await a notice to quit
    (c) to write to the court immediately asking to renew the lease
    (d) to write to the Local Authority claiming the property

4. You are acting for a lessee taking a new seven-year lease of offices with an option to renew. You should remember to register a lease option by a notice or restriction on the lessor's unregistered title.

    Is this statement TRUE/FALSE? Please delete the incorrect choice.

5. Your client is a tenant taking a new lease where you are instructed to agree an alienation clause that gives the lessee the widest possible rights. Which of the following is to be preferred:

   (a) not to assign without the lessor's consent which cannot be unreasonably withheld or delayed

   (b) not to assign without the lessor's consent and without offering to enter into a authorised guarantee agreement

   (c) not to assign without first offering a surrender to the lessor

   (d) not to assign the residue of the term granted by the lease

6. A lessee can claim the benefits of Part II of the Landlord and Tenant Act 1954 only if three conditions can be fulfilled, which of the following does NOT apply:

   (a) there is a lease or tenancy within the terms of the Act

   (b) the lessee must be a limited company only

   (c) the lessee is in occupation of the property

   (d) the lessee so occupies the property for the purposes of the lessee's business

7. All commercial leases should include a clause enabling the lessor to re-enter the subject property and terminate the lease term as a result of a breach of covenant by the lessee or as a consequence of the happening of a specified occurrence.

   Is this statement TRUE/FALSE? Please delete the incorrect choice.

8. Which of the following will benefit from the provisions of Part II of the Landlord and Tenant Act 1954:

   (a) a tenancy at will of a shop

   (b) a mere licence of a workshop

   (c) a letting for a fixed term of one year of a member's tennis club

   (d) a letting of a factory for a fixed term of six months

9. If a lessor wishes to serve a termination notice under the 1954 Act and wishes to oppose the grant of a new tenancy, which of the following is NOT one of the grounds for opposition under s. 30(1):

   (a) a permitted sub-lessee is in occupation of the whole of the property

   (b) availability of suitable alternative accommodation

   (c) persistent delay in paying rent

   (d) breach of repairing covenants

10. In a lease forfeiture clause which of the following would not normally give rise to the right to forfeiture:

    (a) non-payment of rent

    (b) breach of a lease covenant

    (c) the lessee's liquidation or bankruptcy

    (d) a change of use with the landlords licence

11.3.2.2   *Answers to multiple choice questions*

1. The correct answer is (c). If you act for a limited company client, any mortgage that it takes out, i.e. where the company is borrowing the money, *must* be registered at Companies House within twenty-one days of the completion date (see s. 395 of the Companies Act 1985).

2. The correct answer is (c). In many cases the lease may be referred to as an 'F.R.I.' lease, i.e. a full repairing and insuring lease. The phrase has come to signify a lease that makes the tenant wholly responsible for maintaining the structure of the subject property.

3. The correct answer is (b). The tenant should remain in the premises and must continue to pay rent and await a notice to quit. This is because Part II of the Landlord and Tenant Act 1954 gives the tenant of business premises security of tenure.

4. This statement is false. Although the option needs to be protected the lessor's title is unregistered. Therefore the option needs to registered as a Class C(iv) land charge as the lessor's title is unregistered. If the option is not protected in this way, the lessee could have difficulty in exercising the option against a purchaser of the reversionary interest.

5. The correct answer is (a). The tenant has the widest rights from this clause that enables the lessee to deal with assignments in the knowledge that the lessor cannot withhold consent to a change of tenant unreasonably. All the other clauses have potential problems or conditions that provide more restrictive terms than the first one in (a).

6. The correct answer is (b). A lessee can claim the benefits of this statute if there is a lease or tenancy within the terms of the Act, the lessee is in occupation of the property, and the lessee occupies the property for the purposes of the lessee's business. The lessee can be a company or an individual and provided the previous three conditions apply then the Act will come into play.

7. This statement is true. The reason for this is that without such an express provision there is no right of forfeiture available to the lessor. The usual reasons stipulated in such a clause, giving rise to the right to forfeiture, include non-payment of rent, breach of another lease covenant and the lessee's liquidation or bankruptcy.

8. The correct answer is (c). Business purposes include a trade, profession or employment, and any activity carried out by a body of persons whether corporate or not. The courts have been fairly liberal in their interpretation of this requirement and have therefore included a members' tennis club (*Addiscombe Garden Estates Ltd v. Crabbe* [1958] 1 QB 513). The term must exceed six months. The Act does not apply to mere licences or true tenancies at will.

9. The correct answer is (a). All the other choices listed come with s. 30. The first one is not a reason to oppose renewal, as the occupant is a permitted sub-lessee in occupation of the whole of the property with consent. The sub-lessee will be the person upon whom the notice will be served.

10. The correct answer is (d). The first three are usual forfeiture provisions in a commercial lease. The last is not a reason to forfeit. Indeed if the change of use is with the licence of the lessor then there is written consent confirming the change and no breach has arisen.

11.3.3 SHORT ANSWER QUESTIONS WITH ANSWERS

1. XYZ Services Ltd ('XYZ') was granted a fifteen-year business lease in January 1998 and Mr Trevor White, a director of XYZ, guaranteed the tenant's liabilities under the lease. Explain whether or not Mr White is liable for the liabilities of the current tenant, Moondance Training Ltd, to whom XYZ assigned the residue of the lease last month.

2. On a lease renewal explain with authority whether an institutional landlord is likely to succeed in persuading a court to include terms that are more onerous on the tenant than those contained in the original lease that was granted prior to 1996.

3. On a lease renewal a lessor has succeeded in opposing your client's application to renew its five-year business tenancy of an office because the lessor wishes to occupy the premises. The lessee must move out next week even though it has been in occupation for the full five-year period. What other advice can you give your client in relation to its failed claim?

Answers

1. This is a 'new' lease. Under the Landlord and Tenant (Covenants) Act 1995, s. 24(2): where a tenant is released from liability on an assignment, so is his guarantor. Any attempt to extend the liability of the guarantor beyond this is void (s. 25) unless the original guarantee extended to any Authorised Guarantee Agreement given by XYZ. So, what needs to be ascertained is whether or not this is the case and whether or not XYZ has given an Authorised Guarantee Agreement.

2. Any change must be fair and reasonable taking into account the comparatively weak negotiating position of a sitting tenant requiring renewal (In the case of *O'May v. City of London Real Property Co. Ltd* [1983] 2 AC 726 it was held that the new lease would be on the same terms as the old lease unless one of the parties to the proceedings could show that a desired variation was fair and reasonable. Moreover, the court must have regard to the comparatively weak bargaining position of the lessee on renewal.) However a 'new' lease means that the tenant will no longer be liable for the whole term if he or she assigns so the terms of an alienation covenant may be modernised to reflect this.

3. Compensation may be payable as a result of the lessor succeeding at court in opposing the renewal application. Compensation may be payable if the lessor is successful in opposing the grant of a new tenancy on the ground that the lessor intends to actually occupy the subject property. The appropriate level of compensation is related to the rateable value for the property and is dictated by the Landlord and Tenant Act 1954 (Appropriate Multiplier) Order 1990 (SI 1990/363) and in this case the appropriate multiplier is one times the rateable value. (The multiplier can be two times the rateable value when the lessee or the lessee and the lessee's predecessors in title for the same business have been in occupation of the subject premises for at least fourteen years prior to the date of termination.) See also the recent changes made by The Regulatory Reform (Business Tenancies) (England and Wales) Order 2003 (SI 2003/3096).

11.4 REFERENCES TO WIDER READING INCLUDING PRACTITIONER TEXTS

- *A Practical Approach to Commercial Conveyancing and Property* by Abbey R. and Richards M. (2nd edn, OUP).
- *A Practical Approach to Conveyancing* by Abbey R. and Richards M. (6th edn, OUP)—chapters 12 and 13.
- *The Law Society's Conveyancing Handbook 10th edn* by Silverman F.—Sections K and L dealing with Leaseholds and Tenanted Property.
- *Emmet on Title*—Chapters 26 to 28, Leases.
- For more detail on the changes introduced by the Land Registration Act 2002 see *Blackstone's Guide to The Land Registration Act 2002* by Abbey R. and Richards M. (OUP).
- *Textbook on Land Law* by MacKenzie J. A. and Phillips M. (9th edn, OUP)—chapter 8 (the leasehold estate); chapter 9 (Obligations of landlord and tenant).

11.5 **RELEVANT WEBSITES FOR MORE INFORMATION**

This list is broken down into separate section to cover specific areas covered by this chapter.

1. **The following websites may assist in the process of Commercial Conveyancing**

- British Property Federation, http//www.bpf.org.uk
- Companies House, http://www.companieshouse.gov.uk
- Confederation of British Industry, http://www.cbi.org.uk
- Department of the Environment, Transport and the Regions, http://www.detr.gov.uk
- HM Stationery Office, http://www.hmso.gov.uk/ (locate official documents)
- Health and Safety Executive, http://www.hse.gov.uk
- Highways Agency, http://www.highways.gov.uk
- Land Registry, http://www.landreg.gov.uk
- Land Registry internet register access, http://www.landregistrydirect.gov.uk
- Inland Revenue, http://www.inlandrevenue.gov.uk/home.htm
- Landmark Information Group, http://www.landmark-information.co.uk
- Lands Tribunal On-Line, http://www.courtservice.gov.uk/tribunals/lands
- National Association of Estate Agents, http://www.naea.co.uk
- National House Building Council, http://www.nhbc.co.uk
- National Housing Federation, http://www.housing.org.uk
- National Land Information Service, http://www.nlis.org.uk
- Office for National Statistics, http://www.ons.gov.uk
- Ordnance Survey, http://www.ordsvy.gov.uk/home/index.html
- Public Record Office, http://www.pro.gov.uk

2. **The following websites may assist in the process of granting or renewing business leases**

- Chartered Institute of Arbitrators, http://www.arbitrators.org/Index.htm
- Estates Gazette, http://www.egi.co.uk
- Royal Institute of British Architects, http://www.riba.org.uk
- Royal Institution of Chartered Surveyors, http://www.rics.org
- Law Society, http://www.lawsoc.org.uk
- Law Society's Gazette, http://www.lawgazette.co.uk
- Street maps of the UK, http://www.streetmap.co.uk
- UK Parliament, http://www.parliament.uk
- Valuation Office, http://www.voa.gov.uk

3. **The following websites may assist with Commercial Property generally and in particular with their funding**

- Association of British Insurers, http://www.abi.org.uk
- Bank of England, http://www.bankofengland.co.uk
- British Bankers Association, http://www.bba.org.uk
- Chartered Institute of Bankers, http://www.cib.org.uk

- Council of Mortgage Lenders, http://www.cml.org.uk
- Financial Services Authority, http://www.fsa.gov.uk
- HM Treasury, http://www.hm-treasury.gov.uk
- Housing Corporation, http://www.housingcorp.gov.uk
- Housing Forum, http://www.thehousingforum.org.uk
- Law Commission, http://www.lawcom.gov.uk
- Licensed Conveyancers, http://www.conveyancer.org.uk
- Location statistics, http://www.upmystreet.com
- Lord Chancellor's Department, www.gtnet.gov.uk
- Royal Town Planning Institute, http://rtpi.org.uk
- Society of Construction Law, http://www.scl.org.uk

12 | NEW PROPERTIES

12.1 INTRODUCTION

You will appreciate from your studies that the sale of a new property is a more complicated transaction than the sale of an existing one and as a result it commends itself to the examiner. There are several reasons for the added complexity. First, a new property on an estate will comprise part of the developer's title to the whole estate, and a property lawyer must therefore think about 'sale of part' considerations such as the grant and reservation of new easements and the imposition of new covenants. There is a clear overlap here with the general topic of the draft contract, which we considered in Chapter 3 and standard question 1 in this chapter provides a typical example of a question concerning a new property.

There is also some overlap here with the topics of leasehold and commonhold, as the new property could of course be the grant of a lease or a new commonhold unit. You are therefore referred to Chapter 10 concerning leasehold and commonhold.

The National Protocol is not normally used by a developer's solicitor, but the spirit of it is usually invoked as the solicitor will invariably be required to send out a comprehensive package of documents at the beginning of the transaction to assist the buyer's solicitor. As you will see from the suggested answer to standard question 2, you will need to appreciate the items that are relevant, and why.

Where the property is in the course of construction there will also be a complication over the timing of completion because the builder/developer will not know precisely the date when the building will be physically completed. Accordingly, the builder cannot agree a fixed completion date and this can have a knock-on effect where the buyer of the new property has a related sale. This is one of the points raised in standard question 4.

There are obvious planning considerations where a property is newly constructed and it must be remembered that as well as the dwelling itself, you must consider estate roads, drains and sewers and their future maintenance and adoption by the local authorities.

In this respect, you will appreciate the overlap with the material you covered earlier in the course when you considered town and country planning, searches and enquiries. Remember that enquiries over and above the standard pre-contract enquiries will be appropriate where your client is buying a new property. This aspect is also dealt with as part of standard question 4.

12.2 AN OVERVIEW OF THE SUBJECT AND A LOOK AT SOME PROBLEM AREAS

In this section we shall consider briefly the important issues when acting for a developer or buyer, road and sewer agreements, structural defects insurance and synchronising completion of a related sale when acting for the buyer of new property.

12.2.1 ACTING FOR DEVELOPER

Acting for the developer, the trainee solicitor is likely to become involved in the day-to-day running of the conveyancing files for the individual plots. Typically a partner or senior assistant will first prepare the initial documentation, e.g. standard form contract, replies to standard enquiries, relevant search results, copies of the relevant planning consents and evidence of title. Once the legal paperwork has been set up, the trainee solicitor may handle the plot sale files. This will involve sending out to the individual buyer's solicitors the standard documentation with a covering letter or information pack, responding to any additional enquires and dealing with any suggested amendments to the contract and purchase deed. This will be of course be followed by exchange and completion.

Assuming title is registered, deduction of title on the plot sales is achieved by supplying official copies and a title plan. However, very often the title plan of an estate is large and unwieldy, and in this case the seller's practitioner may apply to Land Registry on Form OC1 for a certificate of official inspection of the title plan. This certificate on Form CI will certify that the subject property (i.e. the individual plot) to which it relates is within the seller's title. It will also indicate the entries on the title that affect the plot in question. Form CI will also assist the buyer's practitioner when carrying out the pre-completion official search; instead of having to attach a plan to Form OS2, the practitioner will simply quote the plot number specified on the Form CI.

Acting for the developer, some of the essential components of the draft contract are as follows:

- Include a full and accurate description of the property being sold by reference to a scaled plan.
- Negate any implied grant of easements in favour of the buyer under s. 62 of the Law of Property Act 1925 and the rule in *Wheeldon v. Burrows* (1879) 12 Ch D 31 whilst making provision for the grant and reservation of new easements and the imposition of new covenants.
- Annex to the contract the standard form of purchase deed for the plots. The purchase deed will include all relevant terms such as new restrictive covenants, easements, etc.
- Provide for legal completion to take place within a certain specified period after the seller's practitioner has notified the buyer's practitioner that the property has been completed and is fit for occupation.

- Specify that the builder will provide NHBC (or similar) protection and that the NHBC documentation will be supplied to the buyer before completion.

- If the buyer is paying an additional price for 'extras' (e.g. specially designed kitchen or bathroom fittings), the contract should itemise the extras and state the additional sums being paid.

- A full 10% deposit paid on exchange to be held as agent (so that it can be released to the developer client).

- The developer may wish to reserve the right to vary the method of construction or the materials used in the construction of the new properties.

In addition, do not forget other important issues of a more general nature, such as:

- If unusually the developer's title is unregistered, consider applying for voluntary first registration. It is easier to dispose of registered plots.

- Contact the developer's lender, if any, to make arrangements for the release of the individual plots from the lender's charge as and when they are sold.

- In conjunction with the developer client, arrange for a site inspection by a qualified surveyor and preparation of an estate layout plan for approval by Land Registry.

- Draft the standard form of purchase deed and arrange for it to be approved by Land Registry at the same time as the estate layout plan.

- Ensure that road and sewer agreements with supporting bonds are, or will be, in place (see below for further commentary on this).

- Check that the developer is registered with NHBC, or an alternative provider, and that all appropriate documentation is available.

- Carry out all necessary searches, copies of which are to be made available to the buyer's practitioner.

- Prepare information pack and/or covering letter.

12.2.2 ACTING FOR BUYER

It is common for the seller to refuse to negotiate any amendments on the standardised documentation. However the buyer's practitioner should as a matter of course always consider the draft documentation carefully and seek to make amendments which properly protect the buyer's (and any lender client's) interests. Here is a reminder of the principal concerns for the buyer when approving the draft contract for the sale of a new property:

- Ensure that the buyer has all necessary easements, e.g. for access, services and rights of entry onto adjoining plots.

- Ensure that the proposed covenants will not adversely affect the buyer's use and enjoyment of the property or the future sale or marketability of it; consider your mortgagee's instructions.

- Allow for the buyer/mortgagee's surveyor to inspect the property both before and after physical completion.

- Insist on a long stop date for completion after which your client can rescind the contract.

- Seller should be obliged to build in a good and workmanlike manner with good and substantial materials.

- Provide for the seller to rectify any snagging items, to remove all builder's rubbish before completion, to erect boundary fences and to landscape the garden and adjoining areas.

- If the seller reserves the right to vary the methods of construction or building materials this should be qualified by a proviso that neither the value of the property nor the accommodation shall be materially diminished.

- If property still in course of construction on exchange of contracts the risk of insurance should remain with the seller until physical and legal completion has occurred.

- Deposit to be held as stakeholder.

- Provide for NHBC protection; all relevant documentation to be supplied to the buyer on or before completion.

12.2.3 ROAD AND SEWER AGREEMENTS

One problem area for students is understanding the requirement for road and sewer agreements. As for estate roads, do remember that the roads and street lighting on a new estate will only become adopted by the local authority (and thus maintainable at the public expense) after the estate has been physically completed. The local authority is empowered to make up the roads and charge the house buyers for the cost of doing so and it is for this reason that buyers require the developer to enter into an agreement with the local authority under s. 38 of the Highways Act 1980. In this agreement the developer agrees to make up the roads and street lighting to an adoptable standard (i.e. to a standard acceptable to the authority) and the authority agrees to adopt them subsequently. As additional protection for the buyers in case of the developer's insolvency, the s. 38 agreement should be supported by a bond or guarantee from the developer's bank or insurer which provides for the buyers to be indemnified for any costs paid to the local authority should the developer default. The developer should complete a similar agreement and supporting bond in respect of the making up and adoption of the drains and sewers on the estate. This agreement is made with the local water authority under s. 104 of the Water Industry Act 1991.

Importantly, it is a standard requirement of mortgagees of properties on new large estates that s. 38 and s. 104 agreements with supporting bonds are in place before completion of the mortgage. This is confirmed in the CML Lenders' Handbook (para. 6.7). If they are not in place the lender will usually wish to make a retention from the advance, which will be released to the borrower only as and when the agreements come into force.

12.2.4 STRUCTURAL DEFECTS INSURANCE

All new dwellings and conversions should be insured against structural defects, and it is a standard requirement of lending institutions that new residential properties are protected in this way. Without such insurance the property will become unmortgageable and its future marketability adversely affected. The most popular current scheme which is now in use almost universally is the NHBC Buildmark scheme. An alternative scheme known as Newbuild is offered by Zurich Municipal. The insurance cover under both schemes lasts for ten years from completion of the construction of the property, although with Newbuild there is an option to extend cover for a further five years.

In some cases a lender may be willing to accept an architect's certificate of completion of the building in lieu of an NHBC or Newbuild scheme. This may apply, for instance, where the architect has supervised the construction of the building under a JCT contract (i.e. an agreement incorporating a standard set of conditions for a building contract). The insurance cover is effectively provided by the architect's professional indemnity insurers in the event of professional negligence on the part of the architect. The Lender may be willing to accept the monitoring of the development by a professional consultant employed by the borrower alone or by the borrower and the builder jointly. If so, and the Lenders' Handbook is being used, the professional consultant must complete a Professional Consultant's Certificate in the required form (see para. 6.6.1.5 of the Lenders' Handbook).

The NHBC Buildmark scheme is in two parts, comprising separate agreements in the form of warranties given by the builder and the NHBC respectively. In the first part, the builder agrees that the new dwelling will be constructed in a good and workmanlike manner and in line with the requirements of the NHBC. The builder also agrees to put right any defects in the property, notified to the builder in writing, which occur during the first two years (known as the initial guarantee period) and which occur as a result of the builder's failure to comply with the NHBC requirements. In the second part, the NHBC give separate warranties (i.e. the insurance), that will compensate the buyer against loss suffered as a result of:

(a) the builder becoming insolvent before the dwelling is finished (limited to 10% of the contract sum or £10,000, whichever is the greater),

(b) the builder failing to fulfil its own warranty to correct defects arising in the initial guarantee period, and

(c) any repair works to the property the cost of which exceeds £500 which occur during the eight years following the initial guarantee period. This eight-year period is known as the structural guarantee period. Cover includes double or multiple glazing and the costs of clearing up contamination as a result of action taken by a local authority or the Environment Agency.

12.2.5 SYNCHRONISING COMPLETION OF A RELATED SALE

Another problem area is the situation where a client is buying a new property and also selling an existing property at the same time. How do you synchronise completion dates when the developer/seller won't agree a fixed completion date on the new property? One way round this is to seek a condition in the sale contract regarding completion similar to that in the purchase contract, i.e., that completion shall occur a specified number of days after the seller's practitioner notifies the buyer's practitioner that the client is ready to complete. However if your client's buyer insists on a fixed completion date (e.g. because there is a chain behind), you would have to advise the client that it will not be possible to synchronise the two completions. If the client still wished to proceed, you would canvass two options. The client could either seek bridging finance to complete the purchase first (the consent of the existing lender may be required) or, more usually, complete the sale first and move into temporary accommodation until completion of the new property occurs. Whichever option the client decides upon, you must as a matter of great importance still ensure that the *act of exchange of contracts* is synchronised, so as to prevent the client ending up with two properties or none at all (see Chapter 6 generally regarding synchronisation of exchange on related sale and purchase transactions).

12.3 SUBJECT ASSESSMENTS

As in previous chapters there now follows some examples of assessment questions in the subject area. Commentary and a suggested answer accompany the standard assessment questions. These are then followed by multiple choice questions (with answers) and short answer questions with suggested answers.

12.3.1 STANDARD QUESTIONS, COMMENTARY AND SUGGESTED ANSWERS

Question 1

Explain what particular matters you would include in a contract for the sale of a residential free-hold property in the course of construction on a new housing estate. You may assume that the estate is being developed by a well-known and reputable builder. You should confine your answer to matters relevant only to new properties and make reference to matters which both parties would wish to see dealt with in the contract.

Commentary

When you come across a question like this it is important not to be panicked into writing everything you know about contracts for the sale of land. You will appreciate reading this chapter that the question concerns new properties but in the pressure cooker atmosphere of the exam room, crucial matters can get overlooked. The question asks specifically for matters which are peculiar to the sale of a *new property in the course of construction* and you should concentrate your mind on this, not contractual matters of a more general nature. Notice also that the house has not yet been built, which is a crucial factor in the form the contract will take.

The question invites a wide discussion of the contract from both the seller's and buyer's perspective. Do not be afraid to put each side's case—you will be given credit for explaining why the seller wants something included but the buyer does not, or vice versa. You have not received a memorandum so you can simply write your answer in a conventional format.

Suggested answer

This transaction is a sale of part of the seller's title and so the usual sale of part considerations apply. The seller will want to negate any implied grant of easements in favour of the buyer under the Law of Property Act, s. 62 and the rule in *Wheeldon v. Burrows* (1879) 12 Ch D 31. The contract should make appropriate provision for the grant and reservation of new easements and the imposition of new covenants. The easements will cover such matters as rights of way and the right to run services over the remainder of the estate, and the right to enter to inspect, maintain and repair accessways and services. The buyer must be satisfied that the new covenants do not unduly restrict the buyer's intended use and enjoyment of the property. Typical covenants include: restricting the use to residential only, not making any alterations without the seller's consent (the buyer should be advised to limit this in time to say, three years) and to maintain one or more fences around the plot. It should be noted that the easements and covenants will be actually created in the purchase deed, not the contract, but the contract will govern the contents of the purchase deed, so the contract will normally stipulate the exact wording of the easements and covenants.

Another important consideration on a sale of part is to ensure that the contract contains a full and accurate description of the property being sold. This should be done by reference to a scaled plan attached to the contract showing the individual plot edged red. The description will be short with the added words, 'more particularly described on the plan', thereby indicating that the plan is to prevail in the case of conflict or uncertainty (*Neilson v. Poole* (1969) 20 P & CR 909).

The builder cannot be absolutely sure when the house will be physically completed and ready for the buyer to move in. A fixed completion date therefore cannot be agreed on exchange of contracts. The contract should provide instead for legal completion to take place within a certain period after the seller's solicitors have notified the buyer's solicitor that the property has been completed and is fit for occupation. The period in question must be sufficient to allow time for the buyer to carry out the pre-completion searches, to request the drawdown of any mortgage advance and for the buyer's (and probably mortgagee's) surveyor to carry out a final inspection of the property. Fourteen days should be sufficient and is normally acceptable to both builder and buyer.

One point to note where the buyer is purchasing with the aid of a mortgage is that the mortgagee will not release the mortgage advance until the property has been completed to the satisfaction of the mortgagee's surveyor. The buyer's solicitor should therefore consider a provision in the contract whereby the buyer cannot be forced to complete until the mortgagee's surveyor is satisfied in this respect.

The buyer will also require a 'long stop date' for completion being a date, say six or nine months hence, after which the buyer may withdraw from the contract. Without this provision, if the property was never physically completed or the seller's notice was not served, the contract would remain open indefinitely, a state of affairs which ultimately would be unsatisfactory for both parties.

The builder/seller will want to ensure that the buyer carries out the investigation of title before exchange and that no requisitions may be raised on the title after exchange. This will be covered by a special condition. The buyer should be happy with this provided he has enough time to carry out the title investigation.

Assuming that the property will not be finished by the time contracts are exchanged, the seller should be responsible for it between exchange and completion. However standard condition 5.1 is not appropriate as the seller will not be transferring the property in the same physical state as it was at the date of the contract. This condition should therefore be excluded or amended, although the special condition doing so must make it clear that the risk remains with the seller until legal completion. Otherwise, the open contract position would apply and the buyer would assume the risk from exchange.

The builder is described in the question as 'well-known and reputable' so presumably the company is registered with the National House Building Council (NHBC). The new property will therefore have the benefit of the NHBC Buildmark scheme which provides a ten-year insurance for structural defects. The contract should specify that the builder will provide NHBC protection and that the NHBC documentation will be supplied to the buyer before completion.

The property is in the course of construction and the buyer would prefer to see a contractual obligation on the builder/seller to build the property and the rest of the estate in a good and workmanlike manner in accordance with the planning permission and the agreed plans and specifications. The buyer would also want the right (together with the buyer's mortgagee) to inspect the property during its construction and again finally when it is finished. Associated with this will be a provision requiring the seller to rectify any minor defects (known as 'snagging items') either before legal completion or within a specified time thereafter. A snagging list is normally prepared by the buyer's surveyor on final inspection. A prudent buyer would also insist on a clause in the contract whereby the seller agrees to remove all builder's rubbish before completion, to erect boundary fences and to landscape the garden and adjoining areas. The builder may prefer to confirm these points in its solicitors' replies to pre-contract enquiries rather than amend its standard form of contract.

Whilst it may be the intention of the builder to build the property in accordance with the agreed plans and specifications, the builder may wish to reserve a right to vary the method of construction or the materials used in the construction. The buyer will be reluctant to accept such a clause unless it is qualified to provide that such variation will not diminish the value of the property or the accommodation to be provided.

Like anyone in business the builder will be keeping a watchful eye on cash-flow and will therefore normally expect to receive a full 10% deposit from the buyer on exchange of contracts. Normally, the builder will want the deposit to be held by its solicitor as agent for the seller rather than as stakeholder, so that the deposit can be released to the builder as soon as the contracts are exchanged. The seller's solicitor should therefore cover the point and amend the standard conditions by a special condition to this effect. Conversely, the buyer would prefer the deposit to be held by the seller's solicitor as stakeholder, so that it remains secure in the solicitor's client account until completion! The argument can be put forward on behalf of the buyer that it may be several months before the transaction is completed and if the deposit is released to the seller and the seller later defaults (for example, because of insolvency), the buyer as unsecured creditor may never recover the deposit.

Finally, if the buyer is paying an additional price for 'extras' (e.g. specially designed kitchen or bathroom fittings) then, having regard to s. 2 of the Law of Property Act (Miscellaneous Provisions) Act 1989, the contract should specifically deal with this by itemising the extras and clearly stating the additional sum.

Question 2

RICHARDS ABBEY AND PARTNERS, SOLICITORS
INTERNAL MEMORANDUM

To   The Trainee Solicitor

From   The Property Partner

Re Newbuild Ltd

Several years ago we acted on the acquisition of a greenfield site by Newbuild Ltd, a major player in the UK building industry. The acquisition was financed by Acto Finance Ltd who took a first fixed charge on the site together with a floating charge over the company's assets. Newbuild Ltd has recently begun developing the site and is in the course of constructing thirty freehold detached houses. It has instructed us to act on the sale of the individual plots.

Please prepare a memo listing and explaining the items we should send to each buyer's solicitors.

Commentary

This question is in the form of a memo and asks for a memo in reply so do not write an essay on the subject! As you have to list *and explain* the items, it may be worth spending a few minutes first, jotting down on a piece of rough paper the items that you feel are relevant. That way you can calculate how long you will spend on each explanation. It would be frustrating to find near the end of the allotted time for this question that you have spent practically the whole time discussing at some length the contract and purchase deed, but left yourself no time to explain the other items. You may appreciate their significance but unless you can actually put it down on paper, sadly you will fail the question and this is something that regrettably happens all too often.

With the reference to fixed and floating charges, you may think that a comprehensive knowledge of secured lending is required in order to achieve high marks on this question. It is not—all you need do is stick to basic conveyancing principles. Every Property Law and Practice student, whether specialising in commercial property or not, should appreciate the requirements for the release or discharge of a mortgage on completion of sale of land.

Once again, ensure that your answer is germane to the question. You are told that the properties are freehold so you will get no marks for discussing leasehold issues; nor will you get any credit for writing about mutual rights of support because the properties are detached! Note also that the builder is a 'major player in the UK building industry', a clear pointer to registration with NHBC. Don't make the mistake though of saying that the NHBC documents will be included in the pre-contract package—these are not released to the buyer until after exchange.

Suggested answer

RICHARDS ABBEY AND PARTNERS, SOLICITORS
INTERNAL MEMORANDUM

To   The Property Partner

From   The Trainee Solicitor

Re Newbuild Ltd

I refer to your memo and report that in my opinion the following items should be prepared by us (or obtained) and sent to each buyer's solicitors as and when sales are agreed subject to contract:

1. The draft contract with a copy for the buyer's solicitor's use. On the sale of a new property the form of purchase deed is usually stipulated in the contract and this is permitted by the LPA 1925 s. 48. To comply

with s. 2 of The Law of Property (Miscellaneous Provisions) Act 1989 the contract must incorporate all the terms agreed by the parties.

2. The draft purchase deed will be prepared by us at the same time as the draft contract and annexed to it. The draft contract and purchase deed together will be sent in duplicate to each buyer's solicitors. We will inform the other side that no amendments to the documentation of substance will be accepted. This is prudent policy for a seller of multiple plots on a building estate who will prefer to have uniformity and standardisation of its legal documentation. The purchase deed will set out expressly all necessary grants and reservations of easements together with the new covenants being created.

   We are not told whether the title is registered or unregistered. If the title is registered a Land Registry transfer (TP1) will be the appropriate purchase deed. We can ask Land Registry for prior approval of the form of transfer. If the title is unregistered a draft conveyance will be appropriate (or if we prefer, a Land Registry transfer (TP1) as the plots will be compulsorily registrable).

3. The buyers will require evidence of our client's title to the site so that the title can be investigated in the normal way. If the land is registered we will supply official copies of the title and the title plan. The title plan may be too large and unwieldy in which case it will easier for us to send Land Registry a plan showing the layout of the estate and ask them to issue a Form C1 for each plot shown on the plan. The Form C1 will certify that the property to which it relates is within our client's title. It will also indicate those entries on the title plan that affect the plot in question. Form C1 will help the buyer's solicitors when they do their pre-completion Land Registry search because they can simply quote the plot number on the Form C1 when the search application is made.

   If the land is unregistered we should prepare an abstract of our client's title or alternatively an epitome of title with copy documents attached. It may be worth considering applying for voluntary first registration of our client's title as deducing title to registered land is likely to be simpler. We should especially consider voluntary registration if the unregistered title is complex.

4. Replies to buyer's enquiries before contract. We should prepare our own which we can gear specifically to the purchase of a new dwelling on a housing estate. In this event we shall be diverting from the standard forms under the National Protocol and so we must advise the buyers' solicitors that the Protocol is not being used. This can be done in our initial letter (see 8 below).

5. Replies to standard pre-completion enquiries and requisitions on title. As our client has mortgaged the site each prospective buyer will require confirmation that on completion the mortgage will be released by Acto Finance over that plot. Each buyer will also require a letter of non-crystallisation from Acto Finance in respect of the floating charge. Other matters that can be dealt with in these replies are the arrangements for collection of keys on completion and the furnishing of our bank details for transmission of funds by the buyer's solicitors on completion.

6. Copies of the planning permissions for the development and any building regulation approvals (although the latter are unlikely to be available yet). The buyers will want to be satisfied that the local planning authority has authorised the construction of the estate and that the builder has complied or will comply with all conditions of the planning permissions. We could advise the buyer's solicitors of any reserved planning matters in our initial letter (see 8 below).

7. Copies of agreements and supporting bonds under the Highways Act 1980 s. 38 and the Water Industry Act 1991 s. 104.

   The roads and street lighting on a new estate will only become adopted by the local authority (and thus maintainable at the public expense) after the estate has been physically completed. The local authority is empowered to make up the roads and charge the house buyers for the cost of doing so. The buyers will therefore require our client builder to enter into an agreement with the local authority under s. 38 of the Highways Act 1980, in which the builder agrees to make up the roads and street lighting to an adoptable standard and the authority agrees to adopt them subsequently. The buyers will be concerned that the builder may default in making up the roads (e.g. because of liquidation) resulting in the local authority making them up and charging the cost to the buyers. To protect against this, the s. 38 agreement is supported by a bond or guarantee from the builder's bank or insurers which provides for the buyers to be indemnified for any costs paid to the local authority should the builder default.

Our client should complete a similar agreement and supporting bond in respect of the making up and adoption of the drains and sewers on the estate. This agreement is made with the local water authority under s. 104 of the Water Industry Act 1991.

8. A standard letter for each buyer's solicitor enclosing the package of documents. The letter can confirm that we do not intend to use the Protocol. It can also provide useful general information about the new estate covering such matters as the anticipated dates for physical completion of the houses and details of where plans and specifications can be inspected. A general information pack could also be provided. We can make it clear at this early stage that no material amendments to the draft documentation will be accepted.

As a large reputable building company, Newbuild will of course be registered with the National House Building Council (NHBC). Accordingly our letter will confirm that our client is so registered and that we shall forward the appropriate NHBC documentation to the buyers' solicitors following exchange of contracts.

TIME ENGAGED 45 MINUTES

TRAINEE SOLICITOR

Question 3

RICHARDS ABBEY AND PARTNERS, SOLICITORS
INTERNAL MEMORANDUM

To   The Trainee Solicitor

From   The Property Partner

<u>Re Mr and Mrs C. Langley buying plot 71, The Saltings, Hythe</u>

As you know we are acting for Mr and Mrs Langley in their purchase of the above new freehold property from Forster Sidwell Ltd who are registered with NHBC. Ceridig Langley has just rung to say that he does not understand the defects insurance position on the property and would like a letter from us explaining the NHBC Buildmark scheme. Please would you write to Mr Langley today at 2 Bugs Bottom Cottages, Abbey Road, Blakey, explaining to him how the Buildmark scheme works.

Commentary

This is a straightforward question requiring you to explain how the NHBC defects insurance scheme operates, but it is important to appreciate that your answer will take the form of a letter of advice to your clients, not a memorandum or essay. As always, keep the letter clear and to the point. Remember that you are writing to a client not a lawyer so avoid convoluted or highly technical language.

Suggested answer

RICHARDS ABBEY AND PARTNERS, SOLICITORS

4 Little Titchfield Street London W1

Partners

M.B.Richards

R.M.Abbey

C Langley Esq.,

2 Bugs Bottom Cottages,

Abbey Road,

Blakey

Our ref: MR/TS/PP

[Date]

Dear Mr Langley

<u>Plot 71 The Saltings Hythe</u>

I refer to your recent telephone conversation with our Mr Richards in which you asked for some general guidance concerning the operation of the NHBC Buildmark scheme. I am pleased to advise you as follows.

The Buildmark scheme is used where a builder registered with the National House Building Council (NHBC) sells a newly constructed house or flat which the builder has built or converted. I confirm that the builder of your house, Forster Sidwell Ltd, is registered with the NHBC and you will therefore receive the benefit of the scheme.

In essence the Buildmark scheme will offer you protection in the form of an insurance policy against structural defects in the property which may arise during the first ten years. The scheme is in two parts, comprising separate agreements in the form of warranties given by the builder and the NHBC respectively. I will advise you on each part of the scheme in turn.

First, the builder agrees that the new dwelling will be constructed in a good and workmanlike manner and in line with the requirements of the NHBC. The builder also agrees to put right any defects in the property, notified to the builder in writing, which occur during the first two years (known as the initial guarantee period) and which occur as a result of the builder's failure to comply with the NHBC requirements.

Secondly, the NHBC give separate warranties which will compensate you against any loss you may suffer as a result of: (a) the builder becoming insolvent before the dwelling is finished, (b) the builder failing to fulfil its own warranty to correct defects arising in the initial guarantee period, and (c) any defects or major structural damage to the property which occur during the eight years following the initial guarantee period. This eight-year period is known as the structural guarantee period.

In the contract for the sale of the new house we will ensure that there is an obligation on the part of Forster Sidwell Ltd to provide you with full NHBC insurance cover without any extra cost to you or Mrs Langley. The builder will also agree to supply us with all the relevant NHBC documentation before completion.

The procedure is as follows. Once contracts are exchanged (which is when the terms of the contract become binding) the builder's solicitors will send us the following papers supplied by NHBC:

1. offer of cover form (BM1),

2. acceptance form (BM2) and

3. the Buildmark booklet (BM3) which sets out the terms of the scheme.

The acceptance form is signed by you (or by us on your behalf) and returned to NHBC. As soon as the NHBC receive the signed acceptance form, the cover will begin in respect of the builder's warranties and for any loss which is caused as a result of the builder becoming insolvent.

Once the NHBC have approved the completed dwelling on its final inspection, it will issue a notice of protection of cover for the full ten-year period (BM4). This is issued in duplicate. We place one copy with the deeds of the property (which will be held by your building society), and the other is given to you together with the offer of cover form and the Buildmark booklet.

If in the unfortunate event you have to make a claim under the scheme, this will be dealt with by the NHBC regional office where a Freephone service is provided. If there are defects which are the responsibility of the builder having arisen during the initial guarantee period, the regional office will normally arrange a conciliation meeting with the builder at the property. Where a claim is made during the structural guarantee period, the regional office will carry out an inspection to confirm the validity of the claim, and, the work to be carried out by the NHBC.

I trust this letter has helped to clarify how the NHBC Buildmark scheme works, but if you have any queries or wish to raise any further questions, please do not hesitate to contact me.

Yours sincerely

Question 4

RICHARDS ABBEY AND PARTNERS, SOLICITORS
INTERNAL MEMORANDUM

To   The Trainee Solicitor

From   The Training Partner

Re 36 Highfields, Barton St Mary

The firm has been instructed by Mr and Mrs Lavery to act for them in their purchase of the above freehold dwellinghouse which is in the course of construction by the seller/builder, Buildwell Ltd.

(a) The seller's solicitors are not using the National Protocol so please consider what relevant precontract enquiries we should raise of Buildwell Ltd's solicitors. (10 Marks)

(b) Mr and Mrs Lavery have a property to sell, the net proceeds of which they are utilising to help finance the purchase of 36 Highfields. Do you foresee any problem regarding synchronisation of completion of their sale and purchase and, if so, how can this be overcome? (8 Marks)

Commentary

In part (a) you are told that the builder's solicitors are not using the National Protocol and this is quite normal on the sale of a property on a new estate. As mentioned earlier, the builder's solicitors will often still adopt the spirit of the Protocol by supplying a package of documents including replies to standard enquiries. However, in this question you should start from the premise that no replies to enquiries have been given at all.

You will note the word 'relevant' and it is important to confine your enquiries (especially those of a general nature) to those that are pertinent to this type of property, i.e. one that is not yet built. Otherwise, you will risk wasting valuable time and marks. Two examples of general enquiries to avoid would be to ask the builder what fixtures and fittings are not included in the sale, and to ask for details of who is in occupation! You will see how the suggested answer deals first with the general enquiries and then the additional ones.

Note the slightly greater marks allocation for part (a) and structure your reply memo accordingly. Part (b) concerns the perennial problem of synchronisation where the client has a related sale and should present no problems to those of you who have revised this topic well.

Suggested answer

RICHARDS ABBEY AND PARTNERS, SOLICITORS
INTERNAL MEMORANDUM

To   The Training Partner

From   The Trainee Solicitor

Re 36 Highfields, Barton St Mary

In response to your memo concerning the above, I will deal with each point in turn.

(a) We must have regard to the fact that this a new property in the course of construction. Consequently, as well as raising some general pre-contract enquiries, we must also consider some additional enquiries which will be relevant on the purchase of a new property. I have given some thought to this and set out below my explanation of some general enquiries followed by some more specialised additional enquiries.

General enquiries

1. We should ask the seller whether it is aware of any past or current disputes regarding the land or its use, and if so, to provide details.

2. Is the seller aware of any rights or informal arrangements affecting the property, other than those disclosed in the draft contract? If so, we would require details and copies of any supporting documents.

3. Following on from this, if the title is registered, we would want confirmation that the seller is not aware of any unregistered interests which would override a registered dispositions (Land Registration Act 2002, Sch. 3). If the title is unregistered, we would want confirmation that the seller is not aware of any unregistered interests which would override a first registration (Land Registration Act 2002, Sch. 1).

4. We would ask the seller to confirm that all restrictions affecting the property or its use have been observed and performed, for example, restrictive covenants apparent from the title. If any person's consent or approval has in the past been required, we would want to see written evidence of that consent.

5. The seller must supply copies of all planning consents and building regulation approvals relating to the development. Linked to this we would seek confirmation that the builder/seller has complied with (or will prior to completion comply with) all conditions attached to the planning consents and building regulation approval and generally all the requirements of the local planning authority.

6. We would ask for particulars of any other notices (that is, apart from planning) relating to the property, or its use or enjoyment, of which the seller is aware.

Additional enquiries

1. Perhaps the first additional enquiry could be a simple request for confirmation of how many houses/units will be constructed on the estate and how many of these have been sold to date.

2. As this is a new development, it is unlikely that our clients' house will abut a public highway, but instead be served by a private unmade road leading to a public road. Accordingly we must be satisfied that the seller has entered into an agreement with the local authority under s. 38 of the Highways Act 1980 to

make up the estate roads to an adoptable standard, and that a supporting bond is in place. We would ask the seller to supply copies of these documents.

3. Whilst mentioning the estate roads, we might care to raise the practical question of when the seller expects to lay the final wearing surface to the roads.

4. In conjunction with additional enquiry 2 above, the position regarding the estate drains and sewers must also be investigated. The property is unlikely to be drained directly into the mains yet and, if this is the case, we would require copies of the seller's agreement with the local water authority under s. 104 of the Water Industry Act 1991 to make up the drains and sewers to an adoptable standard. We would also want to see a copy of the supporting bond.

5. We would ask the seller to confirm that it will pay for all charges for construction and connection of the drainage and sewage systems and all other services of which the property will have the benefit, e.g. electricity, gas, telephone. The developer may also be able to supply a plan showing the proposed route of all services to and from the property, and this could be requested.

6. We would seek confirmation that the property is to have the benefit of the NHBC 'Buildmark' scheme providing insurance protection against structural defects for up to ten years, and that the seller will supply us with all the necessary documentation.

7. The draft contract will normally provide for legal completion to take place only after the new property has been physically completed. If the seller will not agree any material amendments to the draft contract, we should ask the seller to confirm that our client buyer will not be called upon to complete until not only the property but also all services are finished and reasonable access to the property has been provided.

8. If the contract permits the seller the right to vary the construction or dimensions of the property but, as above, the seller will not agree to qualify that right in the contract, we must seek to protect our client's position by raising an enquiry along the following lines. Does the seller have any plans to vary the construction or dimensions of the property and can the seller confirm that any such variation will not diminish the accommodation to be provided or the value of the property?

9. Finally to end on a practical note, the plot number of the property will invariably not be the same as the postal address. We could therefore ask the seller to supply the postal address of the property.

(b) As Mr and Mrs Lavery's purchase is dependent upon completion of their sale, we must ensure that each transaction is completed on the same day. In this way, the sale proceeds will be readily available to apply towards the purchase price of the clients' new property, and Mr and Mrs Lavery will be able to move out of one property and into the other on the day of completion.

As their new property is in the course of construction, the builder/seller will be unable to agree in the contract a fixed completion date. Instead, the contract will contain a provision whereby completion will take place a given number of days after the seller's solicitors have notified us that physical completion of the new property has taken place.

The property our clients are selling is not of course a new property but an existing one, and it would be customary in a contract of this nature to agree a fixed completion date. However, if that were to occur here, Mr and Mrs Lavery would have no guarantee that the completion dates on their sale and purchase would be the same.

I would therefore recommend that we do not agree a fixed completion date on the sale, but seek to agree a condition in the sale contract regarding completion similar to that in the purchase contract. That is to say, completion shall take place a specified number of days after we, as the seller's solicitors, notify the buyer's solicitors in writing that our clients are ready to complete. We would want to serve this notice once we receive the completion notice on our clients' purchase. In order to give ourselves some leeway, the notice period in the sale contract should be say, one day less than the notice period in the purchase contract. As an example: if the purchase contract specified 14 days' notice of completion then upon receipt of the same we would prepare the sale contract notice and the following day serve it on the buyer's solicitors notifying them that completion will take place in thirteen days' time, i.e. the same completion day as the purchase.

If our clients' buyer insists on a fixed completion date (for instance because there is a chain behind), we must advise Mr and Mrs Lavery that they will be unable to synchronise the two completions. If they still wanted to proceed, I would advise them that they have two options. Either to seek bridging finance to complete the purchase first or, more usually, to complete the sale first and move into temporary accommodation until completion of the new property. Whatever they decide, we must still in any event make sure that the *act of exchange of contracts* is synchronised, so as to prevent Mr and Mrs Lavery ending up with two properties or none at all.

TIME ENGAGED 1 HOUR

TRAINEE SOLICITOR

12.3.2 MULTIPLE CHOICE QUESTIONS AND ANSWERS

We set out below examples of ten multiple choice questions that you might encounter in a subject assessment. Answers to these then follow. Remember our initial guidance. Never leave multiple choice answers with a blank. If there are four possibilities and you are not sure of the answer select the one you think might be right; after all, you have a one in four chance of getting it right! Also look at the instructions on the paper. If it says select the right answer on the paper by circling the correct choice then do just that. Do not make a tick or underline your selection as the strict response would be to fail you even though the selection may be correct. Think carefully before selecting your answer and have correcting fluid to hand just in case you make a mistake or change your mind. To assist you, we have given brief explanations for the answers although generally this is not something you will be required to do (unless your exam paper requires it).

12.3.2.1 Multiple choice questions

Unless otherwise directed, select the right answer by circling it in each question. Should you think that none of the selections apply please explain why not in your answer book.

1. A Land Registry certificate on Form C1 will certify that:
   (a) the individual plot to which it relates is within the developer's title
   (b) the developer has an absolute title
   (c) the new property has been completed in accordance with the plans and specifications for the development
   (d) the developer's title is unregistered and is not subject to a caution against first registration

2. The NHBC Buildmark scheme provides insurance protection for up to ten years against structural defects in new residential properties.

   Is this statement TRUE/FALSE? Please delete the incorrect choice.

3. Which of the following is NOT a requirement of the CML Lenders' Handbook:

   (a) the new home warranty must be in place on or before completion

   (b) the new property must receive a satisfactory final inspection before completion

   (c) the roads and sewers immediately serving the new property must be adopted and maintained at public expense

   (d) the monitoring of a newly built property by a professional consultant may be acceptable to a lender in certain circumstances

4. Which of the following would a buyer's solicitor NOT normally expect to receive from the solicitor acting for the developer/seller of a new property on a large estate:

   (a) draft contract

   (b) evidence of the seller's title

   (c) draft purchase deed

   (d) replies to standard enquiries before contract

5. A contract for sale of a new property in the course of construction will normally provide for legal completion to take place:

   (a) ten working days after exchange of contracts

   (b) 20 working days after exchange of contracts

   (c) on a fixed date agreed by the parties

   (d) within a specified period after the seller's solicitor has notified the buyer's solicitor that the property has been physically completed and is fit for occupation

6. The seller/developer of a new property in the course of construction should be responsible for insurance between exchange and completion and accordingly the buyer should ensure that standard condition 5.1 is not excluded from the contract.

   Is this statement TRUE/FALSE? Please delete the incorrect choice.

7. Your client is buying a new freehold house on an estate of 150 houses recently developed by Wimpole Homes Limited, who acquired the development site three years ago. The form of purchase deed that will be used to transfer the property into your client's name will be:

   (a) Form TR1

   (b) Form TP1

   (c) a conveyance

   (d) an assignment

8. If, in the draft contract, the seller reserves the right to vary the methods of construction or building materials the buyer would be wise to qualify this by a proviso that neither the value of the property nor the accommodation shall be materially diminished.

   Is this statement TRUE/FALSE? Please delete the incorrect choice.

9. Acting for a developer on the sale of a new property you will normally draft the contract to provide for the deposit paid on exchange to be held by your firm as:

   (a) agent for the seller

   (b) agent for the buyer

   (c) stakeholder

   (d) mediator

10. In respect of any estate which is registered or about to be registered, Land Registry will, free of charge, approve the plan prepared by the developer's surveyor showing the proposed

lay-out of the development and the individual plots (this is known as the estate lay-out plan).

Is this statement TRUE/FALSE? Please delete the incorrect choice.

12.3.2.2 *Answers to multiple choice questions (with brief explanations)*

1. The correct answer is (a). The title plan for a registered development is often large and unwieldy so the developer can apply for a certificate on Form CI. This certificate will assist the buyers' practitioner when carrying out the pre-completion official search; instead of having to attach a plan to Form OS2, the practitioner will simply quote the plot number specified on Form CI.

2. The statement is true. This question is quite straightforward and tests your basic knowledge of the NHBC structural defects insurance scheme.

3. The correct answer is (c). It is commonly the case that the estate roads and sewers are not yet adopted at the time of first occupation. In this case the lender will require suitable road and sewer agreements to be in place together with supporting bonds. If they are not in place the lender will usually wish to make a retention from the advance which will only be released to the borrower as and when the agreements come into force.

4. The correct answer is none as the seller should supply all of them. Remember that in estate conveyancing the seller's solicitor will want to standardise all legal documentation and this includes the form of purchase deed (which will be attached to the draft contract). Do not fall into the trap of choosing answer (c). Yes, the buyer prepares the draft purchase deed in most property transactions but not this one!

5. The correct answer is (d). As the property is in the course of construction the developer cannot commit itself to a fixed completion date. It serves notice on the buyer once physical completion of the new property has taken place.

6. The statement is false. This is a tricky question and should be read carefully. It is true that the seller should be responsible for insurance but standard condition 5.1 is simply not appropriate for a property in the course of construction. This is because the seller will not be transferring the property in the same physical state as it was at the date of the contract. Standard condition 5.1 should therefore be excluded or amended, although the special condition doing so must make it clear that the risk remains with the seller until legal completion.

7. The correct answer is (b). The developer's land will have a registered title because you are told that the developer acquired the site three years ago. Even if the land had previously been unregistered, compulsory first registration would have ensued following the developer's acquisition. Thus the current transfer of the house on the estate is a transfer of part of a registered title and Land Registry Form TP1 is the appropriate purchase deed in this case.

8. The statement is true. If the seller includes this clause in the draft contract this is a sensible amendment to make on behalf of the buyer.

9. The correct answer is (a). To assist its cash flow the seller/developer will require the deposit to be released to it as soon as possible, i.e. on exchange of contracts. Thus when acting for the seller/developer, draft the contract to provide that the deposit be held as agent for the seller (the buyer may of course try to resist this!).

10. The statement is true. Land Registry will be happy to approve the estate lay-out plan as a matter of course. Such approval will assist in avoiding boundary disputes, aid the deduction of title and help the buyer when carrying out the pre-completion official search at Land Registry.

12.3.3 **SHORT ANSWER QUESTIONS**

Question 1

Your firm is acting on the proposed acquisition of a leasehold industrial warehouse unit in the course of construction on a new business park on the outskirts of Reading. The proposed lease will be at a rack rent for a term of fifteen years. You have received a comprehensive pre-contract package from the developer's solicitors. This includes the draft contract with draft lease annexed, official copies of the registered freehold title (which reveals a legal charge in favour of Barclays Bank plc), Form CI, copy planning consents, copy road and sewer agreements (with supporting bonds) and replies to standard pre-contract enquires. Assuming that these documents are all in order, what additional enquiries might you wish to raise of the seller's solicitors?

Question 2

Assume that you are employed by the firm acting for the developer of the estate in the previous question. The estate is Reading Business Park, Wolsey Road Tilehurst Reading RG6 6EG. The title number for the estate is BK240327. An estate layout plan has been approved and the plot number for the subject warehouse unit is plot 5. The Gloucester Land Registry office deals with the administrative area of Reading. Your firm is Plant Page and Age of 10 Wilmott Street Reading RG1 4EY (telephone and fax number 01189 456244). It has a credit account with Land Registry. Your reference is 144/TS and your email address is plant@aul.com.

Apply for a certificate of official inspection of the title plan on Form OC1.

12.3.3.1 *Suggested answers to short answer questions*

Question 1

You should note that this is a new commercial property. It will therefore be inappropriate to raise issues regarding the NHBC Buildmark scheme. This scheme only applies to residential property and indeed structural defects insurance is rarely used in relation to commercial property. Do remember that in commercial property VAT may be chargeable and this should be clarified.

   The following additional enquiries might be considered in a transaction of this nature:

- As the grant of a commercial lease is exempt from VAT but there is an option to waive the exemption, please confirm whether the seller has elected or will elect to waive the exemption for VAT in respect of the subject property.

- Please confirm that the developer will pay for all charges for construction and connection of the drainage and sewage systems and all other services of which the property will have the benefit, e.g. electricity, gas, telephone and Internet connection.

- If available, please also supply a plan showing the proposed route of all services to and from the property.

- Please confirm that the buyer will not be called upon to complete until not only the property but also all services are finished and reasonable access to the property has been provided.

- When does the seller intend to lay the final wearing surface to the estate roads?

- Does the seller have any plans to vary the construction or dimensions of the property and can the seller confirm that any such variation will not materially diminish the accommodation to be provided or the value of the property?

- If known, please supply the postal address of the property.

- Please confirm how many industrial units will be constructed on the estate and how many of these have been let to date.

- We note that the freehold title is mortgaged. Please forward the consent of Barclays Bank to the grant of the lease.

Question 2

See completed Form OC1 in Appendix 12.1.

12.4 REFERENCES TO WIDER READING INCLUDING PRACTITIONER TEXTS

- *A Practical Approach to Conveyancing* by Abbey R. and Richards M. (6th edn, OUP)—chapter 11 (New Properties).
- *The Law Society's Conveyancing Handbook 10th edn,* by Silverman F.—Section I dealing with new properties and Appendix X.
- Ruoff and Roper Registered Conveyancing (Sweet and Maxwell)
- *Textbook on Land Law* by MacKenzie J. A. and Phillips M. (9th edn, OUP)—chapter 20 (easements).
- Emmet on Title: Chapter 1, part 5.

12.5 RELEVANT WEBSITES FOR MORE INFORMATION

- Council of Mortgage Lenders, http://www.cml.org.uk
  There is an on-line version of the CML Lenders' Handbook available at this site and should be referred to in cases of doubt about the requirements of the lender in relation to title matters.
- House of Lords judgments, http://www.parliament.the-stationery-office.co.uk/pa/ld199697/ldjudgmt/ldjudgmt.htm
  Keep up to date with important new cases.
- Land Registry, http://www.landreg.gov.uk
- Land Registry Internet register access, http://www.landregistrydirect.gov.uk
  The location for on-line pre-completion registered land searches.
- Landmark Information group, property and environmental risk information, http://www.landmark-information.co.uk
  Environmental searches can be obtained from the Landmark Information Group. These might shed light on former uses of the land perhaps revealed by covenants in the deeds.
- Law Commission, http://www.lawcom.gov.uk
  Keep up to date on proposals for law reform.
- Law Society, http://www.lawsoc.org.uk
- Location statistics, http://www.upmystreet.com
- NHBC, http://www.nhbc.co.uk
  Full information concerning NHBC structural defects insurance
- Ordnance Survey, http://www.ordnancesurvey.co.uk
  It might be useful to consult a detailed Ordnance Survey map when considering boundary problems and to compare with title deed plans.
- A street map anywhere in the UK, http://www.streetmap.co.uk

APPENDIX 12.1 LAND REGISTRY FORM OC1

**Application for official
copies of register/plan or
certificate in Form CI**

Land Registry

OC1

Land Registry Gloucester _____ Office

Use one form per title. *If you need more room than is provided for in a panel, use continuation sheet CS and attach to this form.*

1.	**Administrative area** if known Reading
2.	**Title number** if known BK240327
3.	**Property** Postal number or description Reading Business Park
	Name of road Wolsey Road
	Name of locality Tilehurst
	Town Reading
	Postcode RG6 6EG
	Ordnance Survey map reference (if known)

4.   **Payment of fee** *Place "X" in the appropriate box.*
 	
  ☐ The Land Registry fee of £ [____] accompanies this application.
 	
  ☑ Debit the Credit Account mentioned in panel 5 with the appropriate fee payable under the current Land Registration Fee Order.
	For official use only
	Impression of fees

5.   **The application has been lodged by:** Land Registry Key No. (if appropriate) Name Plant Page and Age Address/DX No. 10 Wilmott Street Reading RG1 4EY Reference 144/TS E-mail plant@aul.com

Telephone No. 01189 456244	Fax No. 01189 456244

6.   If the official copies are to be sent to anyone other than the applicant in panel 5, please supply the name and address of the person to whom they should be sent.   Reference

7.	Where the title number is **not** quoted in panel 2, place "X" in the appropriate box(es). As regards this property, my application relates to:

☐ freehold estate ☐ caution against first registration ☐ franchise ☐ manor

☐ leasehold estate ☐ rentcharge ☐ profit a prendre in gross

8.	In case there is an application for registration pending against the title, place "X" in the appropriate box:

☑ I require an official copy back-dated to the day prior to the receipt of that application **or**

☐ I require an official copy on completion of that application

9.	**I apply for:** *Place "X" in the appropriate box(es) and indicate how many copies are required.*

☐ ____ official copy(ies) of the **register** of the above mentioned property

☐ ____ official copy(ies) of the **title plan or caution plan** of the above mentioned property

☑ ____ a certificate in Form CI, in which case **either**:

   ☑ an estate plan has been approved and the plot number is [5]

   or

   ☐ no estate plan has been approved and a certificate is to be issued in respect of the land shown _____ on the attached plan and copy

10. Signature of applicant _____ **Date** _____

13 | PUTTING IT ALL TOGETHER, THE PROCESS AS A WHOLE

13.1   INTRODUCTION AND OVERVIEW

13.1.1   INTRODUCTION

We hope by now, at the final stage of this book, that you will immediately appreciate the significance of this chapter and in particular the questions within it. Property Law and Practice that includes Conveyancing is not just about the transfer of title, it is of course the process as a whole that enables that transfer to take place. We have, in the preceding chapters considered each part of that process. We have if you like deconstructed the process to reveal it constituent parts. We must now put all those parts together to see the whole picture. You should therefore understand the importance of the following questions because an examiner will want to be sure that you have fully grasped the complete process rather than understood parts of it in the hope that you will thereby be able to answer discrete questions. It is undoubtedly the case that in this subject your examiner will want to be sure that you can make the whole process work by being familiar with those constituent parts, so that you can complete the whole jigsaw. After all, this is what a Property Law practitioner must do and it is for this reason, if for none other, that the type of questions that follow are most likely to arise in your subject assessments. To do this your examiner will devise questions that either stretch across the whole subject or bring together several disparate elements. Either way, it will be your task to show an understanding of the subject that will enables you to cope with both types of questions. To help you we will consider both types of questions in this concluding chapter.

Dealing first with the kind of question that brings together several distinct elements, the best piece of advice we can give you is to read the question carefully. The point is that the question might start out to be the kind you want but because there are several sections, that last section might just be on a topic that you were not expecting. There is always the temptation to see a friendly topic in the first paragraph of a question and to think that this is to be your selection. There is then nothing more destabilising for you to launch into the answer and find two-thirds of the way in that you cannot actually give an answer to the final part. The moral is do not let initial relief and overconfidence inhibit the necessity for you to read all of the question all the way through just to make absolutely sure that it really is one for you.

Examiners know that these kinds of questions can be unpopular but then they are not there to be popular; they are there to test your knowledge and how you apply it, and these questions do just that! In these circumstances you can almost predict one of them in most Property Law and Practice subject assessment papers. If you find yourself in the unenviable position of not being able to find a last question to answer that you know that you can answer then think about attempting a multi-section question where you believe you can properly answer at least 75% of the sections. It is normally poor examination technique to do this but clearly when you have no choice there is little else you can do. Simply do your best in the sections that you can answer and make at least a structured attempt for the part that troubles you even if this means you will score perhaps only style marks. A few additional marks obtained in this way are better than just leaving the section unanswered.

Questions that seek to stretch over the whole subject are perhaps just as awkward to answer for a set of different and sometimes similar reasons. However, you must always expect this type of question in almost every type of Property Law and Practice subject assessment there is. Indeed, where assessment papers contain one compulsory question it is a strong probability that if there is an element of compulsion it will apply to just such a question. The reason for this is perfectly clear; these questions inevitably test your overall knowledge of Property Law and Practice and how you can apply it generally. For this reason it is again of considerable importance that you always read the whole question very carefully, including any deeds and documents annexed to it. It is good practice while you are going through the body of the question, and any deeds and documents, simply to note down any immediate thoughts that might occur to you. For example, you may see that there is a time limit that has been exceeded or that there is an inconsistency in the chronology of the question. Wherever you can always make a note of it so that you do not later overlook what could turn out to be of material importance.

This task will end up being very much what you will encounter in the office should you decide to become a Property Law practitioner. You will need to understand and analyse overlapping subjects in an assessment situation in just the same way as you will in the office. The process is the same, you will need to identify the problem areas and address them with solutions of your own. These solutions will be your advice to the client or in an examination situation your answer to the question. In both cases what you are trying to do is to achieve your client's goals, be that the sale or purchase, or leasing, or whatever of real property in England and Wales. In providing your answer our advice to you must be that you should try to avoid superficiality and try to structure your answer in such a way so as to be seen to be able to be incisive when giving an in depth reply. The risk with questions of this type is that they can entice you into thinking that you should simply write down all you know about what you think might be the subject of the question. This is a recipe for disaster. You need to be able to show an ability to be clear yet concise, structured, thorough and focused. Do not allow yourself to go on a ramble through your knowledge of Property Law, however extensive that may be. Your examiner will want to see your direct route to the correct answer.

Finally these questions have answers that are longer than many of the others in this book. This is deliberate as in many subject assessments longer answers will be expected, as more marks covering the assorted subjects are likely to be on offer for these questions. Furthermore, many subject assessments will be of the single question variety and will require all candidates to attempt this particular question. It may well have several sub-sections to it but essentially it will call upon the same fact pattern. The reasoning for this being that it will present a common instrument of assessment for the examiners to measure the full cohort of students. It will therefore enable the examiner to measure the achievement of students in the context of each other.

13.1.2 **OVERVIEW**

Putting it all together inevitably brings you to consider an overview of the process, of Property Law and Practice. It requires you to mentally stitch together all the little segments you have made so that you can see the complete patchwork quilt that makes up the subject. For example, you could accept the following as an overview of the Conveyancing process that applies in most residential cases and a lot of commercial cases—

(General Conveyancing—Outline of a simple Conveyancing transaction)

SELLER	BUYER
Take instructions	Take instructions
Prepare and issue draft contract	Make pre-contract searches and enquiries
Deduce title	Investigate title
	Approve draft contract
Exchange contracts	Exchange contracts
	Prepare purchase deed
Approve purchase deed	Make pre-completion searches
Prepare for completion	Prepare for completion
Completion	Completion
Post-completion procedures	Post-completion procedures

Of course this chart or table makes several assumptions, the most important of which will be readily obvious and that is that there may not be any borrowings involved for either party. However, the principles are sound and state a clear overview. In the same vein you could prepare an overview of the differences in the process between registered and unregistered titles. It could look something like this:

(Outline of main differences between registered
and unregistered Conveyancing)

STEPS TAKEN	UNREGISTERED	REGISTERED
Taking instructions	No real difference	No real difference
Draft contract	No real difference	No real difference
Pre-contract searches	Preliminary Enquiries of seller Local Land Charges Search Inspection of the property Search of Public Index Map Search in Central Land Charges Department	Same Same Same Not needed Not needed

Deduce title	By abstract or copies of title deeds, and production of originals at or shortly before completion	By official copies of the registered title
Investigate title	By perusing abstract or copies of title deeds and checking them against the originals	By checking official copies and overriding interests
Exchange of contracts	No basic difference	No basic difference
Preparation and approval of purchase deed	To be drafted by buyer's solicitor	To be prepared by buyer's solicitor on basis of prescribed forms of transfer
Pre-completion search	Central Land Charges Department	Land Registry Office
Prepare for completion	No difference	No difference
Complete	Title deeds and transfer handed to buyer. Legal estate passes	Only the transfer handed to buyer. Legal estate does not pass
Post-completion matters	Buyer registered as proprietor on first registration	Buyer registered as proprietor. Legal estate passes

In this way you can start to appreciate the way that an overview can provide you with insights into the way the processes operate in Property Law and Practice and how you might be able to better understand them.

In both cases what these charts show you is that you need to have an holistic approach to your understanding of Property Law and Practice. By this we mean that you need to see the complete picture before you can successfully deconstruct the process. In this way you will understand the mechanics of the conveyancing process more clearly by understanding the way they all come together to make Property Law and Practice.

Such an approach will also assist in your understanding of the process of lease renewals when a court application is required following the terms of Part II of the Landlord and Tenant Act 1954. The chart below sets out details of the steps in the process from the perspective of both the parties to the lease and also includes the cul-de-sac that arises when no renewal order is made.

The process of lease renewal

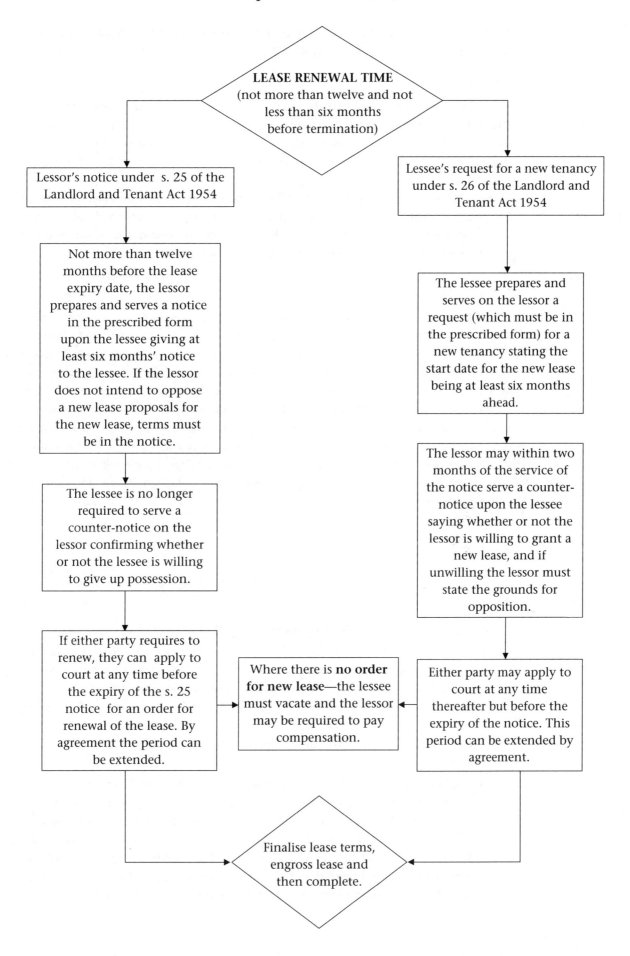

13.2 **SUBJECT ASSESSMENTS**

13.2.1 SUBJECT ASSESSMENT QUESTIONS: A COMMENTARY UPON THE TYPE AND CONTENT OF SUBJECT ASSESSMENT QUESTION AND SUGGESTED ANSWERS

Question 1

You have received instructions from Patricia Quinn in connection with her proposed purchase. She has told you that she will be buying a brand new house presently being built by Research Site Developers (Keele) Plc. in Newcastle-Under-Lyme Staffordshire. She believes that the present description is Plot 38 The Horwood Estate Hawthorns Newcastle-Under-Lyme and that the property is freehold.

You have had a preliminary letter from the developer's solicitors confirming that they will not be using the National Protocol and telling you that the property is registered and that the documentation will follow shortly. Please list, with reasons, what documents you expect to receive from the seller's solicitors and when, throughout the whole conveyancing process.

Commentary

This is a demanding question that highlights how an examiner can, in two short paragraphs, require you to show not only the main steps in a standard conveyance but also how these steps will vary when there is a sale by the developer of a new property. As you will see from the following answer the suggested approach that will earn high marks is to once again set out the answer in list form with explanations contained in the list. Do not misread the question by thinking that the Protocol applies. In many cases in practice developers do not use the Protocol as this could put them to extra expense. However it is also the case that they do supply a copious package of documents at the outset. This does not mean that you should overlook the fact that there will be other documents available throughout the course of the transaction and also of course at completion. Remember the question does refer to 'the whole conveyancing process' and you should therefore list all the documents you think are relevant from start to finish. Because of the number of documents involved do not be overzealous in your explanations; you only have a finite amount of time to answer the question.

Suggested answer

Please find set out below, with reason for their inclusion, the documents to be received on behalf of Ms Quinn and when:

1. At the very outset of the transaction the developer will send the following items:

   (a) The draft contract in duplicate. This is of course fundamental to the whole transaction and there is unlikely to be any developer willing to proceed straight to completion, without a sale contract. This will usually be in a standard form common to all the plots in the development. In view of s. 2 of the Law of Property (Miscellaneous Provisions) Act 1989 the agreement must be in writing signed by all the parties and contain all the terms agreed. This being the case a developer will insist upon a contract so that all the terms can appear within it to ensure the complete validity of the transaction.

   (b) Details of the developer's title. The developer's solicitors have confirmed that the title is registered and as a consequence the evidence of the developer's title will comprise official copy entries and an official copy of the title plan. It is important that official copies are supplied that are not more than twelve months old as best practice dictates that the copies should not be older than this. It is possible that if the estate is large the Land Registry will issue and the developer will therefore supply in lieu of the title plan, Form C1. This will be confirmation by the Land Registry that the plot is within the seller's registered title and it will also say which if any of the entries on the title affect this particular plot.

(c) Copy Planning Consents. This being a new property it is vital that a buyer's solicitor makes sure that the new house is being erected lawfully, that is to say with the consent of the local planning authority. Furthermore the planning consents may include conditions affecting the property and the buyer's solicitor will want to check these to make sure that they are being fully complied with, and to seek the seller's written confirmation that this is indeed the case.

(d) Copy building regulations approval. The same is true for these approvals and the situation is much the same as for (c) above. In some cases these documents may be issued by other approved authorities rather than the local authority. An example of an alternative authority able to be involved in this way is the National House Building Council ('NHBC').

(e) Form of draft transfer of part. Because this sale is one of many on the estate the seller will want to impose upon all the buyers similar covenants and conditions and this is a compelling reason for requiring the transfer to be in the seller's format. It will be the case that if such a transfer is required it will have to be incorporated in the contract as a document annexed thereto, in view of s. 2 of the Law of Property (Miscellaneous Provisions) Act 1989. For this reason the draft transfer will be issued at this early stage along with the draft contract.

(f) Replies to enquiries before contract. Most developers will, to save time, have standard answers ready to a standard set of preliminary enquiries. Indeed once these have been issued many will try to avoid answering any specific enquiries! Many of the answers will of course be apparent from the documents supplied in this package. Some have taken to using replies to the Protocol Property Information Forms while others still refer to pre-printed enquiry forms such as those issued by popular law stationers.

(g) Replies to requisitions on title. If it saves time to reply to standard enquiries it must be true of replies to standard requisitions on title. As the title is registered it should be possible to issue replies at this stage that are really perfectly straightforward. The requisitions should be fairly simple bearing in mind the need to issue reasonably up to date official copies for the purposes of the buyer's Land Registry search.

(h) Copy s. 38 Road making agreement and bond. Where there is to be a new road on the estate the developer will enter into an agreement with the local authority whereby the developer will make up the road and the authority will adopt it thereafter as a public highway (s. 38 Highways Act 1980). The bond is a guarantee that there will be sufficient funds to complete the road. Without this arrangement the road will be a private roadway with all the attendant problems about rights of way. There could also be a potential road-making financial liability for frontagers should the road be adopted by the authority some time in the future.

(i) Copy Drainage agreement. Following the terms of s. 104 of the Water Industry Act 1991 the developer will have entered into an agreement with the local water authority whereby the developer will build the new drainage system and the authority will adopt that system thereafter. Again it is important to the buyer to ensure that there will not be an extensive private drainage system serving the property that could incur in the future large maintenance bills for the owner.

2. On exchange of contracts the seller's solicitor will issue the seller's signed contract. This is of course the documentary evidence of the binding agreement between the parties and the terms thereof. By the same token the seller will hold the buyer's signed part of the agreement.

3. On exchange the seller's solicitors will also supply the NHBC documentation. Most builders will be in the NHBC Buildmark scheme that provides insurance protection against structural defects affecting the property during the first ten years of its life. (Some offer other similar arrangements with other companies but the NHBC scheme is the most used in practice.) Without this most mortgagees will not normally lend on a new property. Because this is the case it vital for all solicitors acting for a buyer to ensure that this documentation will be forthcoming and a condition in the contract to that effect is appropriate. The seller will

provide an offer form, an acceptance form and a Buildmark scheme booklet. The buyer must complete and send the acceptance form to the NHBC for the insurance cover to be ready on or after completion.

4. On completion the following will be required:

   (a) The transfer of part, duly sealed by the seller company. This is of course the crucial document to the whole process and without which the seller cannot be registered at the Land Registry as the registered proprietor of this particular freehold plot. The transfer will in most cases include a plan showing the extent of the property being transferred and this should also be sealed by the seller.

   (b) Consent of the seller's mortgagee. The official copies of the seller's title will show if there is a registered mortgage. If there is then a Form DS1 (the release form relevant to registered land), as to the part being sold will be required so as to release the plot from the effect of the seller's mortgage. A plan will be attached to Form DS1 showing the full area of the plot to be sold and will therefore also be required to be handed over at completion with Form DS1. An undertaking to supply Form DS1 and the plan is acceptable from a solicitor for the developer in the Law Society form of wording.

   (c) A prudent purchaser will make a precautionary company search and if this discloses a floating charge that was not disclosed on the Land Registry search then the seller's solicitors must hand over a certificate of non-crystallisation to confirm that the charge has not become fixed. (This search will also show if there are problems about impending insolvency and if this is the case then the seller must resolve this difficulty before completion.)

Question 2

You are instructed on behalf of Susan Yates in relation to her proposed purchase of a bungalow at 13 Cockfosters Way Southgate in North London, presently owned by Bazlur Ahmed. The property is leasehold under a lease for 125 years from 25 December 1959 at an annual rent of a peppercorn, if demanded. The property is registered with an absolute title under title number NGL 362638. It has the benefit of a ten-year timber treatment guarantee from Abel Timbers (Acton) Limited. Ms Yates is purchasing the property for £95,000 and will be doing so with the aid of a mortgage from the National Building Society for £45,000 who will be instructing you along with Ms Yates. The seller's solicitors have sent to you simple photocopies of their client's registered title from which you have seen that there is a first mortgage with a building society followed by a second mortgage with a bank. There is also a notice registered on the title under the provisions of the Family Law Act 1996 as well as a covenant not to use the property as a retail shop.

1. Please indicate with reasons the papers you will look for when title is deduced.

2. What will you do about the notice and the covenant? Please show the essence of your proposed advice to your client.

3. Please set down all the searches you will make before completion and say for whom they are being made and for how long they will remain in force.

4. Please set down the documents you require on completion.

Commentary

This is a typical example of the 'sweeping up' kind of question where from one set of facts you must answer several different sections all on different points. You must start with what is required as evidence of title. You must then deal with a restrictive covenant as well as a Family Law Act notice. You are then required to jump to final searches followed by completion! As you can see in one question you are being asked, in effect, to jump from the beginning of a transaction when you will inspect the title right down to the end and the completion process. Moreover, in the operation you are also required to consider notices and covenants along the way together with searches. You will therefore appreciate that the is a classic example of the kind of question considered at length in the introduction to this chapter and will pose all the problems highlighted by us. We therefore suggest you look again at that introduction to further appreciate what can be done in the circumstances of such a broadly based examination question. In particular, this is a clear example of where you must read the question carefully and where you should carefully note down as you are reading all the salient facts. Then pause and think, (P.A.T.), and sketch out your answers to each section so that you can feel sure that you will be able to complete the entire question. Only after you have gone through this important process should you actually embark upon your written answer.

On a matter of style, the answers required are as mixed as the topics in the question. The first section is in effect looking for a list with reasons. The second section should be answered on the basis of advice to the client either as a file memorandum or a letter. The third section requires a list with further information while the last section is really just a list of deeds and documents. Your answer should reflect these differences and should not be in the form of a unified essay. The structure of your answer is important and should not be overlooked as it could enable you to receive additional marks for style and answer structure.

Suggested answer

<u>Section 1</u>

Please find listed below, with reasons the deeds, documents and other papers I would require as evidence of the seller's title:

1. First and foremost, I will require a full set of official copies of the title and title plan that have been properly issued by the Land Registry. The sellers have at present simply submitted mere photocopies presumably of the seller's title information documentation and these are not acceptable. The reason for this is that best practice dictates that official copies used to deduce title should be less than twelve months old calculated from the date of issue by the Land Registry. Because s. 67 of the Land Registration Act 2002 confirms that official copies are guaranteed as to their accuracy by the State mere photocopies are not acceptable.

2. I will also require an official copy of the title plan to ensure that the extent of the property is shown correctly and in full.

3. I will also need to see and check any documents referred to on the registers of title number NGL 362638. I need to do this as these documents could contain onerous or unusual covenants or conditions that might adversely affect this property.

4. I will require a full and complete copy of the lease showing all Inland Revenue stampings and the execution of the deed by the original lessor. I need to check all the contents of the lease and in particular the lessee's covenants so that I can give Ms Yates full details. It should be remembered that the lease could contain a covenant requiring the lessor's licence to assign which would have to be obtained before completion could take place

5. I will also require any subsequent deeds that have affected the original lease such as deeds of variation or supplemental deeds that may have in any way affected or altered the original terms and covenants.

<u>Section 2</u>

INTER-OFFICE FILE MEMORANDUM

<u>Re Ms S. Yates and her purchase of 13 Cockfosters Way Southgate</u>

I set out below as a file record the essence of my proposed advice for the client in connection with two matters of concern affecting her proposed purchase, being a restrictive covenant and a Family Law Act 1996 notice.

(a) The Restrictive Covenant

Ms Yates will need to be advised of the existence of this covenant and the fact that it will be binding on her, to the effect that she will not be able to use the property as a retail shop. If she has that intention in mind she should be advised to withdraw from the transaction and seek another property elsewhere. It may be of use to explain that to try to have the covenant removed could prove to be a costly, lengthy and ultimately fruitless task.

(b) The Family Law Act 1996 notice ('the notice')

It is assumed that the notice has been registered by the seller's spouse, Mrs Ahmed under the terms of the Family Law Act 1996 ('the FLA') and which protects the spouse's rights of occupation in the property even though she is not shown as a registered proprietor. Because the notice has been registered our client is deemed to have good notice of the spouse's rights and cannot buy free of her interest. However, the FLA implies in circumstances such as prevail in this case that the seller will before completion discharge the notice. To do this the seller must complete Form MH4 and must support the application with sufficient evidence that the registration should be cancelled. Typically this will be a signed form of release by the spouse, a decree absolute or a court order for the release.

It is assumed that contracts have not yet been exchanged. In these circumstances the contract should be altered to require the seller to provide on completion:

(i) Form MH4 duly completed, and

(ii) sufficient evidence for cancellation.

There should be an additional condition in the contract requiring the spouse to release her interest in the bungalow obtained by the provisions of the FLA, to consent to the sale and to release any equitable interest she may have. If the spouse will not sign the contract incorporating such a release then our client must be advised not to proceed as it would be unsafe to do so.

Section 3

I set out below the searches required and for whom they are obtained and for how long they last:

1. Property inspection. The bungalow must be physically inspected just before completion to ensure that there are no undisclosed third party occupants. This will be for both the buyer and the mortgagee. This search is just before completion as of course it is not a time constrained search.

2. Land Registry search. A search must be made at the Land Registry on Form OS1 for both the buyer and the mortgagee. We are acting for both these parties and the search should accordingly be in the name of the mortgagee. In this way the buyer will have the protection of the search result as well and two OS1 searches will not be necessary. The priority period for this search is thirty working days from the date of the search certificate.

3. Bankruptcy search. Because we act for the mortgagee a bankruptcy search is required for the lender against the buyer. This is made on Form K16 and the result speaks from the date of the issue of the search.

Section 4

Please find set out below the documents required on completion:

1. Form DS1 for the first charge or undertaking in Law Society form of wording.

2. Form DS1 for the second charge or undertaking in Law Society form of wording.

3. Transfer duly signed and witnessed.

4.   Form MH4 duly completed.

5.   Form of evidence supporting release of the FLA notice.

6.   Original lease.

7.   Any other deeds and documents relating to the lease such as licences variations, etc.

8.   The original timber guarantee and if possible the original report and estimate.

9.   Pre-registration deeds, if any.

10. The keys, if available.

Question 3

You have been instructed by the National Equitable Building Society in connection with a proposed loan to Winston Douglas that is to be secured on his proposed purchase at 69 Bridge Street Selby Yorkshire. The property is a pretty cottage located at the edge of town. Mr Douglas recently applied for a mortgage on the property having started negotiations himself and having conducted his own conveyancing. You are not instructed by him and are simply looking after the interests of your Building Society client.

Completion is due in exactly one month's time. You wrote to the buyer confirming instructions with a request that he tell you if he is still doing his own conveyancing. He has now replied saying that he is and has sent to you the documents he believes you require. They are:

1.   The contract showing the title is an unregistered freehold free from incumbrances.

2.   The root of title being a conveyance between Jane Smith (1) and Paul Jones (2) dated 5 May sixteen years ago.

3.   the only other deed in the title being a conveyance on sale dated six months ago between Paul Jones (1) and the seller (2).

4.   A clear local authority search result disclosing nothing of an onerous or unusual nature.

5.   Standard pre-printed pre-contract enquiries with acceptable answers.

6.   A copy of the standard requisitions on title that he has sent to the sellers along with a form of draft conveyance that closely follows the format of the most recent deed to the seller.

Please comment on the sufficiency of the documents supplied and list with reasons any other documents you will request. Please also list the subsequent steps you will take to perfect your client's security.

Commentary

This is a complex question that covers many different aspects of conveyancing and from a different angle, namely that of a mortgagee, a lender. But do not be deceived into thinking that is all that this question is about. The facts in the question contain several hidden problems as well as pieces of information that are there but do not need further consideration. For example, you do not need to comment further on the contents of the local search in view of the statement in the question that there are no adverse entries in it. However, how old is it? If it is more than six months old at completion it will not be acceptable by the time completion takes place. Similarly there are acceptable replies to standard enquiries before contract, but are there further specific enquiries that need to be asked?

Beyond these two examples there are further topics that a good answer will have to address. As you will have seen before, in more demanding questions, the crucial elements are those that are not stated in the body of the question rather than those that are. This question is certainly demanding and is no exception. Remember there are three parts to your answer, your comments on the documents listed, a list with reasons of any further documents required and finally a list of subsequent steps to be taken to perfect your client's security.

Suggested answer

At the outset it is appropriate to say that at the moment the papers supplied are insufficient and that there are substantial problems with the paperwork and the title such that at the moment a clear report to the lender would not be possible. I set out below the reasons for this detrimental overview. Accordingly I will start with my view of the documents supplied, this will be followed by further documents required and I will finish with a list of steps to be taken to perfect the security.

1. The documents supplied

Regrettably the documents supplied are not as straightforward as might have been hoped and my comments on their sufficiency are as follows:

(a) The contract. This would seem to be acceptable except that there are severe problems with the title and as such the contract may not be acceptable in its present form. Please see my comments further on in relation to the conveyance to the seller.

(b) The root of title. This would seem sufficient although it is not clear if the conveyance is for value which would be preferred to a voluntary conveyance. It is at least over fifteen years old and is therefore potentially a good root. (See s. 44(1) of the Law of Property Act 1935 as amended by the Law of Property Act 1969.)

(c) The major problem with the title stems from the conveyance to the seller that was completed six months ago. The deed itself may well be properly constructed but the problem is that it was a conveyance on sale, for valuable consideration, and as such should have induced first registration of this title. Since 1 December 1990 the whole of England and Wales is an area for compulsory first registration. (Please see the Registration of Title Order 1989, SI 1989/1347.) In these circumstances where there is a conveyance on sale since that date the legal estate comprised in that conveyance must be submitted to the Land Registry for first registration. (See s. 4 of the Land Registration Act 2002.) Section 6 goes on to say the estate owner, or his successor in title, must, before the end of the period for registration, apply to the registrar to be registered as the proprietor of the registrable estate. The period for registration is two months beginning with the date on which the relevant event occurs, in this case the date of the transfer. If the requirement of registration is not complied with, the transfer becomes void as regards the transfer, and the title to the legal estate reverts to the transferor who holds it on a bare trust for the transferee (s. 7). Accordingly the seller at this time has no legal estate to sell and the buyer will have no legal estate to mortgage in favour of the Society! (see *Pinekerry v. Needs* (1992) 64 P & CR 245).

(d) The contents of the local authority search result appear satisfactory but how old is the search? If it is more than say five months old it will be out of date by the time completion is due. At completion it may be about six months old and really should not be relied upon when that old. Indeed, if it is that old it will not comply with the requirements of the CML handbook that imposes such a time limit.

(e) The replies to enquiries seem acceptable but have all necessary enquiries been made? It would seem that there are special and specific enquiries that could be made pertinent to this particular property and transaction. One example of this kind of extra enquiry could be 'is the seller aware of any mining operations within the locality of the property either currently or in the recent past?'

(f) Standard requisitions are acceptable, but there must now be additional requisitions that will relate to the title and the fact that the seller has no title to sell and must immediately apply for late first registration. The draft conveyance could be sufficient but in the circumstances it would probably be better to adopt the form of transfer stated in Rule 58 of the Land Registration Rules 2003 (SI 2003/1417) that could be used in first registration cases.

2. <u>Further documents required</u>

There are several further documents required and I list them below including missing searches that will be vital to protect the interests of the proposed lender.

(a) Index map search. The property is not registered but should have been when the seller bought the property. It is therefore necessary to submit a late first registration application but before this goes off, a map index search should be sent to the Land Registry. This search is vital because it will reveal if some or all of the property is already registered or is subject to a pending application for registration. The search result will also show if there is a caution against first registration. A clear result will be required by a prudent lender.

(b) The property is in Selby in Yorkshire. This is an area that to common knowledge is one affected by coal mining. (Even if it were in another area of Yorkshire a coal mining search could still be required and the Law Society's booklet of coal mining areas should always be consulted for counties like Yorkshire.) In these circumstances a coal mining search result is absolutely vital to the lender and indeed the buyer. The search result will show if the property is in an area of active coal mining, proposed coal mining or past coal mining. It will also disclose underground workings that could give rise to subsidence and whether or not there has been compensation paid in respect of past subsidence damage. A clear result will be required by a prudent lender.

(c) A commons registration search will be required as the property seems to be on the edge of town. The search result will reveal if the property is affected by any registrations under the Commons Registration Act 1965 including common land rights and other adverse matters. A clear result will be required by a prudent lender.

(d) Purchase deed. A redraft of this would be sensible given the problems with the title and it should follow the requirements of r. 58 of the Land Registration Rules 2003.

(e) Local search. If necessary another local search result will be required to ensure that there is a result less than six months old at the time of completion.

(f) Enquiries and requisitions. Additional enquiries and requisitions should be raised specific to the property and the title and particularly to the buyer's requirement of the seller to apply for a late first registration application.

(g) There seems to be no final search in the Land Charges Registry. In view of the fact that the property remains unregistered it is vital to carry out such a search as this will certainly be required by the Land Registry on the application for first registration.

3. <u>Steps to be taken to perfect the security</u>

The following steps will be required to ensure that the Society has a valid and enforceable first charge against this freehold property:

(a) First and foremost the seller must be required to make title by submitting a late first registration application. Once this has been completed proper title must be deduced by way of official copy copies of the title and an official copy of the title plan.

(b) The local search must be renewed and the result approved.

(c) A coal mining search must be obtained and the result approved.

(d) A commons registration search must be obtained and the result approved.

(e) A bankruptcy search must be made against the borrower Mr Douglas and the result must be clear. The Society cannot lend to an undischarged bankrupt and would not want to lend to someone involved in pending insolvency proceedings.

(f) A Land Registry search must be made in the name of the Society in connection with their proposed loan and the result must not disclose any adverse entries. A search in the name of the buyer would not confer any priority on the Society and it is for this reason that the search must be in the name of the Society.

(g) A mortgage form must be sent to Mr Douglas for him to sign along with a strong recommendation that he take legal advice on the terms and effect of the mortgage. The mortgage will be in the Society's standard form and as such no amendments by the borrower to the contents of the mortgage will be permitted. His signature should be witnessed by a solicitor or licensed conveyancer.

(h) A report on title should then be submitted to the Society confirming that the property should now be an acceptable security for their loan and the advance monies should be requested.

(i) On receipt of the mortgage advance Mr Douglas should be requested to attend at our offices to complete. In exchange for the deeds the advance monies can be passed to the borrower. Completion must take place within the priority period of the Land Registry search.

(j) Completion should be reported to the Society.

(k) After completion and still within the search priority period the registration application should be submitted to the Land Registry for the registration of the first mortgage in favour of the National Equitable Building Society.

(l) Once the registration application has been completed the title information document should be checked for any errors made by the Land Registry and if it is all correct we should check the Society's requirements about deeds. If they require them then the deeds should be sent to the Society for them to retain until the loan has been repaid.

Question 4

(a) Arthur Black wants to buy Cat Cottage, Deepdale in Northamptonshire from Richard Driver at a price of £45,000. The parties have negotiated the terms of the transaction without using agents. Arthur does not need a mortgage and can proceed quickly because Richard needs to move out expeditiously. To cement the deal, Arthur paid Richard a deposit of £450 in cash and they shook hands and agreed to complete in exactly three weeks' time. A receipt was issued signed by Mr Driver recording the parties, the property and the price. Two days later Arthur called around again to find Richard already packing and so he paid him another £4,050 to make up the full 10%. Two days later Arthur got a note from Richard to say he had another higher offer and was not going to sell to him. Arthur believes he has a deal and wants to enforce the agreement. Can he? (5 Marks)

(b) Diana Spender has agreed to buy the freehold house at 27 High View Milltown in Wiltshire from Charles Quince at a proposed price of £100,000. The property was part let with there being an elderly tenant living in the top floor but the rest of the house on the other three floors are empty. Ms Spender has had a survey that confirmed that the property was in good order and as she is a cash buyer contracts have been exchanged with completion being two months hence. One week after exchange the tenant left unexpectedly to go into a residential care home and Charles Quince wants to re-let to ensure his rental income is maximised and continues up to completion. Can he? (5 Marks)

(c) Tim Harris has exchanged contracts on his purchase of 2 Monument View Maiden Heath Lincolnshire at a price of £155,000 and is due to complete next week. The contract incorporates the Standard Conditions. At the weekend there was a very cold snap and a pipe froze in the house. When the thaw set in on Monday the pipe burst causing damage to the property that will cost a minimum of £16,500 to put right. Tim wants to know if he is liable to pay for the repairs required as a result of the frost damage. Is he? (10 Marks)

Commentary

This three-part question is contained within this chapter as it is a good example of how an examiner will sometimes mix several different topics into a one multi-part question. In this case you have subjects based on topics from areas both before as well as after exchange of contracts. The intention of the examiner is of course to test the breadth of your knowledge. In this particular example you may have the rare opportunity to show your knowledge of case law and to apply that knowledge to the scenarios within the question. Normally questions in LPC assessments will be transactional in nature, i.e. based upon what might be done in the office. However, it is just possible that there may be rare occasions when an essay question may be encountered in a subject assessment. Consequently, this question is an example of just such a problem.

The first part of the question goes to the heart of any conveyance namely the existence or otherwise of a contract. You will be required to show your knowledge of the recent statutory changes in this area. The second part deals with changes to the property or the occupants after exchange and before completion. There is much case law on this and you will need to be able to refer to cases and substantiate your assertions. Finally, the last part touches upon the thorny problem of insurance and who does what when the property is affected by an insurable risk. In this part a good knowledge of the standard conditions will be required.

You will therefore appreciate that this kind of question is perhaps more academic than some others you will have encountered. It is also an atypical LPC question in that it can be answered in an essay format. However, it is also the case that a good answer will require an overall knowledge of the whole process of conveyancing. Finally, you should note the apportionment of the available marks and adjust your time and answer accordingly to ensure that your effort in the third section is greater than in the first two. After all, half of the available marks can be obtained in this part alone.

Suggested answer

(a) Mr Arthur Black ('the buyer') wants to try and force Mr Richard Driver ('the seller') to sell to him Cat Cottage for £45,000. He believes that there is an agreement between them and wants to enforce it. In essence therefore what is needed is to establish whether or not there is a binding agreement between the buyer and the seller that can be enforced if necessary in the courts.

Whether or not the buyer will be able to enforce the agreement depends upon whether or not s. 2 of the Law of Property (Miscellaneous Provisions) Act 1989 has been complied with. This requires that a contract for the sale and purchase of an estate in land must be in writing, must contain all the terms expressly agreed and signed by the all parties. In this case there may have been a document purporting to be a deposit receipt that could be construed as a contract. However, if it was a contract and whilst it was in writing it may not have contained all the express terms and it was certainly not signed by all the parties. If the facts of the purported contract are examined it will be seen that all the terms have not been recorded in the receipt as it did not mention the size of the deposit to be paid or the date for completion. Of greater consequence is the fact that the buyer did not sign the document. Without all the signatures on the receipt there is no possibility of it being construed as a contract. Accordingly in these circumstances it is clear that there can be no enforceable and binding contract between the buyer and the seller as a result of the operation of statute.

Finally, it is of interest to note that had this set of facts occurred before the above Act became effective, (27 September 1989), then these circumstances could well have given rise to an enforceable agreement. This would have arisen from the effects of the now repealed s. 40 of the Law of Property Act 1925 and the obsolete doctrine of part performance. However, on the present facts and current law no contract can exist between Arthur Black and Richard Driver.

(b) Ms Spender has contracted to buy a part possession property from Mr Quince and completion is due shortly. The tenant mentioned in the contract has vacated and Mr Quince wishes to replace the departed tenant with a fresh tenant. The question of whether or not he can do this depends upon his duty to take reasonable care of the property now that contracts have been exchanged.

Once contracts have been exchanged the seller is required to take reasonable care of the property. While the seller remains the legal owner the buyer has an equitable interest as a result of the contract. The case of *Clarke v. Ramuz* [1891] 2 QB 456 established that there is a duty on the seller to maintain the property in the condition it was in at the date of the contract. Does this therefore mean that the logical extension of this duty is to maintain the occupancy of a tenant, albeit a new one? In fact the case of *Abdullah v. Shah* [1959] AC 124 made it clear that it is a breach of the seller's duty to take care if the seller lets the property and thereby creates a protected tenancy. Indeed, if the contract between the parties incorporates the standard conditions then condition 3 applies. Condition 3.2.2(b) requires the seller to inform the buyer without delay if the lease ends and the definition of 'lease' includes a tenancy. The seller is then to act as the buyer reasonably directs although the buyer is to indemnify the seller against all consequent loss and expense.

Accordingly if the standard conditions apply the seller cannot re-let without the buyer approving and even if they do not the seller could be in breach of the duty to take reasonable care.

(c) Tim Harris is the contractual purchaser of 2 Monument View where the contractual completion is due next week. Due to a cold snap the property has been damaged by a burst pipe where the cost of repair could exceed £16,500. Not unnaturally the buyer wants to know if he is liable view of the expense involved. In the absence of any conditions in the contract the insurance risk passes to a buyer on exchange of contracts. This is because the insurable risk runs with the buyer's equitable interest being the beneficial owner behind the trust of the legal estate. (See *Lysaght v. Edwards* [1876] 2 Ch D 499.) However in relation to the purchase by Mr Harris, the buyer's liability will be controlled by the effect of the standard conditions.

Standard condition 5 provides that pending completion the responsibility for the property rests with the seller. Condition 5.1.1 says that the seller will transfer the property in the same physical state as it was at the date of the contract (except for fair wear and tear), which means that the seller retains the risk until completion. Condition 5.1.2 enables the buyer to rescind the contract if the property, at any time before completion, has been damaged so badly that it has become unusable for its purpose. It is not clear from the facts above if this is so, but judging from the amount concerned, £16,500, it is unlikely that the property has become completely unusable. (This is backed up by the fact that the sale price is £155,000 and the repair cost is just a little over 10% of it.) In these circumstances it may well be that the remedy of rescission will not be available to Mr Harris.

Accordingly, it is clear that the standard conditions under which Mr Harris contracted to buy the property ensured that the seller retained the risk until completion unless the special conditions provided otherwise. The facts set out above are silent as to whether or not there are any special conditions. In the absence of special conditions the standard conditions apply and the risk remains with the seller. This being so it should also be noted that standard condition 5.1.3 states that the seller is under no obligation to the buyer to insure the property! This is really a very unsatisfactory state of affairs in that the standard conditions on the one hand require the risk to remain with the seller and yet on the other hand do not require the seller to insure. This undesirable state of affairs might be altered by a special condition requiring the seller to insure but again, from the facts it is not clear if there was such a special condition.

To sum up, the contract would appear to make the seller responsible for the insurance risk for this property and as such Mr Harris must hope that the seller is insured. (In passing it should be noted that a prudent solicitor acting for a buyer under a standard condition contract should always ask if the seller has the property insured and should also change the contract to make sure this insurance continues right up to completion.) As the risk is with the seller and damage has occurred, the seller should deal with the repairs but if the property is unusable the buyer may have a right to rescind. Finally, to complicate matters further there is the difficulty that even if the seller is insured the insurance company could repudiate the claim. Many policies provide that in the case of water damage that if the property has been empty for more than thirty days the cover they offer will not extend to damage occasioned from certain risks including water damage.

13.2.2 **MULTIPLE CHOICE QUESTIONS AND ANSWERS TO MULTIPLE CHOICE QUESTIONS**

We set out below examples of ten multiple choice questions that you might encounter in a subject assessment. Thereafter you will find some typical short answer questions that can also feature in a subject assessment. Answers to both are also set out below. You will see that the spread of topics within these questions is wide. This is deliberate. You will encounter this in Property Law and Practice subject assessments because the whole point of these types of assessment is to test your knowledge as widely as possible. Remember our initial guidance. Never leave multiple choice answers with a blank choice. If there are four possibilities and you are not sure of the answer select the one you think might be right, you have a one in four chance of getting it right! Also look at the instructions on the paper. If it says select the right answer on the paper by circling the correct choice then do just that. Do not make a tick or underline your selection as the strict response would be to fail you even though the selection may be correct.

13.2.2.1 **Multiple choice questions**

Unless otherwise directed, select the right answer by circling it in each question. Should you think that none of the selections apply please explain why not in your answer book.

1. Which of the following does not induce compulsory first registration of title:
   (a) a deed of gift of a freehold farm
   (b) a first mortgage of a leasehold flat with twenty years left to run of the lease term
   (c) grant of a new lease of a house for a term of seven years.
   (d) an assent to the residuary beneficiary of a freehold office block let on a lease of fifteen years with fourteen left to run.

2. Although client affairs are confidential and must never be disclosed to a third party without the client's consent there are exceptions. Which of the following is not an exception and may be kept confidential:
   (a) a client who asks you to hold large sums of cash and who then ask for a cheque from your firm
   (b) a secretive client who will not disclose his or her identity
   (c) a client who makes unusual settlement requests, e.g. paying for a property with large sums of cash
   (d) a secretive client who instructs you to avoid contact with his or her estate agents

3. Except where the seller has a related residential purchase, in an agreement that adopts the standard conditions, it states that the deposit to be paid at exchange of contracts must be held as stakeholder for all transactions.

   Is this statement TRUE/FALSE? Please delete the incorrect choice.

4. You act for a buyer that has instructed you to issue two contracts to two buyers in a contract race for the property she is selling. Which of the following summarises the requirements of Solicitor's Practice Rule 6A:
   (a) provided your client consents, you must immediately inform the practitioners acting for each buyer
   (b) provided your client consents, you must immediately inform the practitioners acting for each buyer and you must also state the rules that will operate for the contract race
   (c) without your client's consent, you must immediately inform the practitioners acting for each buyer and you must also state the rules that will operate for the contract race

(d) without your client's consent, you must immediately inform the practitioners acting for each buyer

5. Your client, Patel Enterprises Limited is buying for cash a registered freehold house in Durham from Mrs Ada Greystone. Which of the following pre-contract searches would you NOT complete on his behalf:

   (a) local authority search

   (b) company search

   (c) water company search

   (d) coal mining search

6. You have clients who have recently changed the use of their premises with a large street level display window from a solicitor's office to a shop selling ladies lingerie. They have not obtained planning consent for this. They now wish to sell with the new use. Your advice is:

   (a) they may proceed as planning consent is not required

   (b) they must first apply for planning consent to sell with the new use

   (c) the local planning authority is out of time for enforcement proceedings

   (d) they only need buildings regulation approval

7. Which of the following would not be acceptable as a good root of title:

   (a) conveyance on sale

   (b) a legal mortgage

   (c) a voluntary conveyance

   (d) a valid will dealing with the whole of the property

8. A recital of fact in a deed at least twelve years old is deemed to be correct unless proved to the contrary (s. 45(6) of the Law of Property Act 1925).

   Is this statement TRUE/FALSE? Please delete the incorrect choice.

9. You act for Chulo Asikra who is buying for £750,000 a registered leasehold flat in Mayfair London from Cavenhamshire Properties Limited. He is buying with the aid of a mortgage from the Megalopolis Bank Plc. Which of the following searches would NOT be required prior to completion:

   (a) Land Registry search

   (b) bankruptcy

   (c) company search

   (d) Land charges search

10. You have completed the purchase for Chulo Asikra. You are now preparing the application for registration. Which of the following will NOT need to accompany the Form AP1:

    (a) signed and dated transfer

    (b) certificate of payment of the Stamp Duty Land Tax

    (c) leasehold land certificate

    (d) mortgage

13.2.2.2 *Answers to multiple choice questions*

1. The correct answer is (c). Section 4 of The Land Registration Act 2002 requires all the others to be submitted for compulsory first registration. Selection of (c) is required because the lease term is only for seven years and therefore not registrable. (Registration being required for leases of more than seven years in duration.)

2. One exception to the confidentiality rule concerns money laundering. The Criminal Justice Act 1993 introduced criminal offences for failing to disclose to the authorities (e.g. the police), knowledge or suspicion of others who are involved in laundering the proceeds of a crime, drug trafficking or terrorism. If you have such knowledge or suspicion, you must disclose it and such disclosure is not treated as a breach of client confidentiality. The Law Society has issued a 'blue card warning' to solicitors alerting them to likely circumstances which could amount to assisting in money laundering. These include all the choices except (d) which is not likely to lead to money laundering and may be kept confidential.

3. This statement is true. The standard conditions provide for the deposit to be held as stakeholder except where the seller before completion agrees to buy another property in England or Wales for his residence (i.e. the seller has a related purchase). In this situation the seller may use all or any part of the sale deposit as a deposit on the related purchase provided it is used only for this purpose (standard condition 2.2.2).

4. The correct answer is (a). Where the seller instructs you to deal with more than one prospective buyer then, provided your client consents, you must immediately inform the practitioners of the instructions you have received from your client to issue more than one contract. If the seller refuses to consent to the disclosure, you must immediately cease to act for the seller. It is a misconception amongst some practitioners that a contract race must have rules (e.g. first buyer to offer a signed contract and deposit cheque wins). This is not so, the only obligation is to tell the other side of your client's decision to deal with more than one buyer.

5. The correct answer is (b). You only need to complete a company search when buying from a company. The fact that your client is a company is irrelevant. If your client was buying with the aid of mortgage finance then the lender may require you to complete a company search for them but you would be unlikely to do so prior to exchange but would complete it with the usual pre-completion searches.

6. The correct answer is (a). General permissions for change across use classes can be authorised by the Town and Country Planning (General Permitted Development) Order 1995. The General Development Order allows as permitted development specific changes between different use classes. One such allows a change from A2, financial and professional services to A1 shop. In this case the subject premises must have a display window at street or ground floor level, which here they do.

7. The correct answer is (d). The best document to use as a root is a conveyance on sale or, failing that, a legal mortgage. These deeds are preferable to gifts of title, such as a voluntary conveyance or an assent, where it is unlikely that any prior title investigation was made before completion of the gift. As a general rule, if there is included within a title a conveyance on sale, the buyer should insist on the conveyance as the root. A will only operates in equity and therefore should never be accepted as a root of a title.

8. The statement is false. A recital of fact in a deed at least twenty years old is deemed to be correct unless proved to the contrary (s. 45(6) of the Law of Property Act 1925).

9. The correct answer is (d). The property being registered a land registry search is appropriate. As the buyer is taking a mortgage a bankruptcy search will be required by the lender. As the seller is a company a company search is required. A land charges search is not appropriate as it is only used for unregistered transactions.

10. The correct answer is (c). Since 13 October 2003 Land and Charge Certificates have been abolished by the effect of the reforms made to the mechanics of land registration by the Land Registration Act 2003.

13.2.3 SHORT ANSWER QUESTIONS WITH ANSWERS

You will have encountered separate and discreet short answer questions elsewhere in this book. They will have been unrelated to each other but will all relate to the chapter topic. In the same way the following three short answer questions all relate to the chapter title but they also relate to each other by sharing the facts of a case and by then tracing steps and raising questions along it. In this way you will encounter short answer questions but with common facts that develop along a single conveyancing transaction. As a result the moral is to read the facts very carefully and to note any changes along the way. Do not assume that facts will remain the same.

1. You act for William Moorcroft the proposed purchaser of a freehold terrace house close to the centre of Sheffield from the seller Paulene Burmantoft at a price of £80,000. Your client is arranging a mortgage of 90% with the National Building Society who intend to insure the property. You have received the contract from the solicitors for the seller that you have seen is straightforward, along with the attached official copy entries of the registered title. (i) Please consider the title details and list any preliminary issues to be referred to the seller for clarification. (ii) Please list the pre-contract searches you should issue.

2. Contracts were exchanged this morning for the sale and purchase of the subject property pursuant to Law Society formula B. Completion is in ten working days time. The contract is based on the 4th Edition of the Standard Conditions save for just two special conditions. First standard condition 5.1 shall not apply and secondly in standard condition 8 the period shall be reduced to five working days. Please list the steps you will take today on behalf of the purchaser William Moorcroft.

3. Completion is due today. You are in funds and all your pre-completion searches are back and there are no issues arising from them. (i) Please list the documents you must have available and also those that you will receive from the sellers at completion. (ii) Please list the main post completion steps you must take to bring the transaction to a successful conclusion.

Suggested answers

1. The following is my list of preliminary issues on the title that I wish to refer to the seller for clarification:

   (a) There is no mention of the title plan and none has been disclosed. I would ask for this as I assume the sellers have overlooked sending it to us.

   (b) The only other title concern is with the caution registered on behalf of what appears to be a money lending company. I assume this entry is to try to protect an unsecured loan made to the seller. Therefore, I must ensure that this is removed forthwith and hopefully before contracts are exchanged. (The sellers might offer a solicitors undertaking to remove this entry but the best course of action would be to ensure the removal of the entry by exchange. However, it may not be possible to deal with the entry until completion when funds may be available to pay of the debt. An undertaking to deal with the entry on this timescale will have to be considered in these circumstances.)

   The following is my list of pre-contract searches that I will issue:

   (a) Local authority search (Local land charges search and enquiries of the local authority).

   (b) Water company search.

   (c) Coal mining search (Sheffield has been associated with such mining for a very long time).

   (d) Environmental search/report.

   (e) Arrange for an inspection/survey of the property.

2. Contracts having been exchanged this morning the following is a list of the steps I will take today on behalf of the purchaser William Moorcroft:

   (a) Because standard condition 5.1 does not apply I must arrange insurance on behalf of the purchaser. The mortgage offer with the National Building Society says they will insure. Therefore I will contact them to make sure cover is available immediately.

(b) Pursuant to the undertaking given when contract were exchanged following the terms of formula B, I will today send the signed contract and a client account cheque for the agreed deposit to the seller's solicitors.

(c) I will ensure that the memorandum or file note recording the formula B exchange is placed on the conveyancing file and I will telephone the client to advise him of exchange and of the agreed completion date.

(d) I will prepare and issue to the seller's solicitors my draft transfer for approval together with the Protocol requisitions on title form.

(e) I will prepare the mortgage form to be signed by the client in readiness for completion.

3. The following is the list of documents that I must have available and also those that I will receive from the sellers at completion:

(a) I must have ready in my file the mortgage deed signed by the buyer and witnessed.

(b) I will receive from the sellers the transfer deed signed by the seller and witnessed.

(c) I will also receive Form DS1 or an undertaking from the seller's solicitors in the Law Society format.

The following is my list of the main post completion steps I must take to bring the transaction to a successful conclusion:

(a) Report to the client and make a transfer from client account to office for my costs.

(b) Complete SDLT1 and arrange for the client to sign it.

(c) On the assumption that the property is not in a Stamp Duty Land Tax exempt deprived area, submit the SDLT1 return to the Inland Revenue with the Stamp Duty Land Tax payment of £800.

(d) On receipt of the certificate of payment submit it with the transfer, form DS1, mortgage copy mortgage and Form AP1 to the Land Registry with the registration fee.

(e) Report completion of the registration process to the lender and to the client.

APPENDIX 13.1
OFFICIAL COPY OF ENTRIES ON THE REGISTER

OFFICIAL COPY

This official copy shows the entries subsisting on the register on **11 June 2004**.

This date **must be quoted as the 'search from date' in any official search** application based on this copy.

Under s. 67 of the Land Registration Act 2002 this copy is admissible in evidence to the same extent as the original.

Issued on 12 October 2003 by HM Land Registry. This title is administered by the **YORK** District Land Registry.

H M LAND REGISTRY

Edition date 18.6.1985 TITLE NUMBER SFD 362638

A. PROPERTY REGISTER

containing the description of the registered land and the estate comprised in the Title

---

COUNTY DISTRICT

SOUTH YORKSHIRE SHEFFIELD

(18 June 1985) The Freehold land shown edged red on the plan of the above title filed at the Registry and being 13 Cutlery Street, Sheffield SF1 2UP

B. PROPRIETORSHIP REGISTER

stating nature of the Title, name, address and description of the proprietor of the land and any entries affecting the right of disposing thereof

TITLE ABSOLUTE

Entry number Proprietor, etc.

---

1. (28 November 1993) Proprietor(s): PAULENE BURMANTOFT of 13 Cutlery Street Blakey Cornshire SF1 2UP

2. (28 October 2002) CAUTION in favour of ORACLE MONEYLENDING Ltd c/o Ulverson & Tonbottom Solicitors, Doncaster, South Yorkshire

---

C. CHARGES REGISTER

containing charges, incumbrances, etc. adversely affecting the land and registered dealings therewith

---

Entry number The date at the beginning of each entry is the date on which the entry was made on this edition of the register

---

1. (28 November 1993) REGISTERED CHARGE dated 19 October 1993 to secure the monies including the further advances therein mentioned

2. (28 November 1993) Proprietor(s): SHEFFIELD BUILDING SOCIETY of 43 Newark Street Sheffield Yorkshire SF2 4PU

INDEX